America, Russia, and the Cold War 1945-1984

AMERICA IN CRISIS 🌿

A series of books on American Diplomatic History

EDITOR: *Robert A. Divine*

America, Russia, and the Cold War 1945-1984

FIFTH EDITION

Walter LaFeber
Cornell University

Alfred A. Knopf
New York

Fifth Edition
987654

Copyright © 1985 by Newbery Award Records, Inc.

Library of Congress Cataloging in Publication Data

LaFeber, Walter.
    America, Russia, and the cold war, 1945–1984.

    (America in crisis)
    Rev. ed. of: America, Russia, and the cold war,
1945–1980. 4th ed. c1980.
    Bibliography: p. 316
    Includes index.
    1. United States — Foreign relations — Soviet Union.
2. Soviet Union — Foreign relations — United States.
3. World politics — 1945-   I. LaFeber, Walter.
America, Russia, and the cold war, 1945–1980. II. Title.
III. Series.
E183.8.S65L34   1985   327.73047   84-15428
ISBN 0-394-34391-3

Cover design: Sharon Glassman.
Cover art: Nuclear Energy by Henry Moore. Courtesy of the
University of Chicago.

For Sandra

FOREWORD

"The United States always wins the war and loses the peace," runs a persistent popular complaint. Neither part of the statement is accurate. The United States barely escaped the War of 1812 with its territory intact, and in Korea in the 1950s the nation was forced to settle for a stalemate on the battlefield. At Paris in 1782, and again in 1898, American negotiators drove hard bargains to win notable diplomatic victories. Yet the myth persists, along with the equally erroneous American belief that we are a peaceful people. Our history is studded with conflict and violence. From the Revolution to the Cold War, Americans have been willing to fight for their interests, their beliefs, and their ambitions. The United States has gone to war for many objectives — for independence in 1775, for honor and trade in 1812, for territory in 1846, for humanity and empire in 1898, for neutral rights in 1917, and for national security in 1941. Since 1945 the nation has been engaged in the continuing Cold War with the Soviet Union.

The purpose of the series is to examine in detail critical periods relating to American involvement in foreign war, from the war with Mexico down through the Cold War. Each author has set out to recount anew the breakdown of diplomacy that led to war and the subsequent quest for peace. The emphasis is on foreign policy, and no effort is made to chronicle the military participation of the United States in these years. Instead the authors focus on the day-by-day conduct of diplomacy to explain why the nation went to war and to show how peace was restored. Each volume is a synthesis combining the research of other historians with new insights to provide a fresh interpretation of a critical period in American diplomatic history. It is hoped that this series will help dispel the illusion of national innocence and give Americans a better appreciation of their country's role in war and peace.

ROBERT A. DIVINE

PREFACE TO THE FIFTH EDITION

For this edition, sections of the material on the origins of the Korean War in Chapter 5 and on the Eisenhower-Dulles-Khrushchev policies in Chapters 6 through 9 have been rewritten. The work of such scholars as Richard Immerman, Robert Divine, Blanche Weissen Cook, Fred Greenstein, Burton Kaufman, and David Alan Rosenberg now allows us to reevaluate the policies of the 1950s. Use has also been made of documents from newly opened collections at the Eisenhower Library in Abilene, Kansas, and the Lyndon B. Johnson Library in Austin, Texas. Jim Leyerzapf of the Eisenhower Library and David Humphrey of the Johnson Library have been especially helpful, and I am deeply in their debt. The final two chapters have been updated and reorganized. The Nixon-Kissinger diplomacy is discussed as a unit in Chapter 11. The post-1977 Carter and Reagan responses to the results of that diplomacy and to what is called a "New Cold War" are analyzed in Chapter 12. The bibliography has also been updated, with special attention paid to works published in the 1980s.

As before, I am greatly indebted to friends who were not reluctant to share materials and even less reluctant to give criticism: Professors Myron Rush, Joel Silbey, Richard Polenberg, and Michael Kammen of Cornell; Lloyd Gardner of Rutgers; David Langbart of the State Department branch of the National Archives; Eric Edelman of the State Department; Max Miller of Congressman Ron Dellums's staff; Stephen Arbogast of Exxon International; Peter Kirstein of Saint Xavier College; and two Cornell graduate students, Virginia Harrington and Richard Mandel. As have many other authors, I have much looked forward to working with the staff at Alfred A. Knopf, particularly David Follmer, Naomi Schneider, and Elaine Romano. As always, Bob Divine of the University of Texas has been a sensitive and helpful editor, and Marie Underhill Noll has been a friend while quietly encouraging research and teaching at Cornell. Most important, I thank the students and faculty who have found this book useful and sometimes, judging from their letters, overly stimulating.

WALTER LAFEBER
MAY 1984

ACKNOWLEDGMENTS
TO THE FIRST EDITION

Robert Divine of the University of Texas, the editor of this series, Gaddis Smith of Yale, Myron Rush of Cornell, and Lloyd Gardner of Rutgers have immeasurably helped this manuscript by reading it in its entirety and making many constructive criticisms. To Lloyd Gardner and to Thomas McCormick of the University of Pittsburgh, William Appleman Williams of the University of Wisconsin, Fred Harvey Harrington, President of the University of Wisconsin, and Robert Bowers of Hanover College, I owe considerably more than mere thanks for professional advice. Knight Biggerstaff of Cornell read many of the sections on Asia and improved them greatly. William Gum of Wiley has been the most helpful and long-suffering editor that an author could wish for. Nancy Unger, also of Wiley, made this a better volume by taking care of the editorial work on the maps.

Tom Rogers, Coordinator of Research at Cornell, Frank Long, Vice President of Research at Cornell, Stuart Brown, Dean of Cornell's College of Arts and Sciences, and Sandy Cheney, Associate Dean of that college, have literally made this book possible by providing the research funds that enabled me to investigate materials in various libraries and to have the manuscript typed. I particularly thank Mrs. Nancy Bressler of the Princeton University Library staff for making the Dulles and Baruch papers so easy to use and also for expediting the clearance of my notes through the Dulles Committee. Phillip Brooks and Phillip Lagerquist were very helpful at the Truman Library. I am, of course, primarily obligated to the fine library staff at Cornell, particularly to Giles Shepherd and Evelyn Greenberg. Herman Phleger, General Nathan Twining, and Sherman Adams graciously consented to allow the use of the quotations from their oral history interviews in the Dulles manuscripts at Princeton. Mrs. Robert Ludgate and Mrs. John Quincy Adams of Ithaca typed the manuscript with great care.

I thank those persons who either supplied me with research

materials or somewhat narrowed the boundaries of my ignorance by talking with me about the Cold War: David Brion Davis, Walter Pintner, Michael Kammen, and Richard Polenberg, all professors at Cornell in the Department of History; Andrew Hacker, Clinton Rossiter, John Lewis, and George Kahin in the Cornell Government Department, Paul Marantz, a graduate student in government at Harvard; David Maisel, an undergraduate at Cornell; Raymond G. O'Connor, professor and chairman of the History Department at Temple University; Professor Barton Bernstein of Stanford; Professor Athan Theoharis of Wayne State University; John Windmuller, professor in the Industrial and Labor Relations School of Cornell; and George Kennan of the Institute for Advanced Study at Princeton. I am particularly indebted to Professor Carl Parrini and the History Department at the University of Northern Illinois for allowing me to try out some of my ideas about the Cold War at their N.D.E.A. Institute in the summer of 1966. The dedication is to a person who has yet to lose a war — either hot or cold — and this has been fortunate for me.

WALTER LAFEBER
APRIL 1967

CONTENTS

MAPS

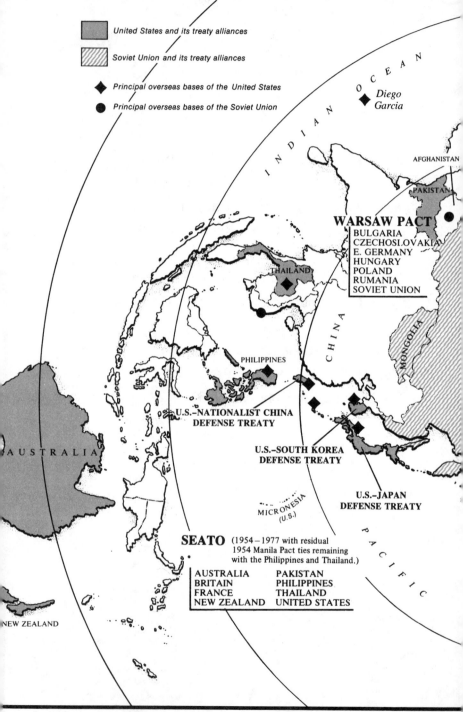

U.S. and U.S.S.R. OVERSEAS COMMITMENTS

United States and its treaty alliances

Soviet Union and its treaty alliances

◆ Principal overseas bases of the United States

● Principal overseas bases of the Soviet Union

INDIAN OCEAN

Diego Garcia

AFGHANISTAN

PAKISTAN

WARSAW PACT
BULGARIA
CZECHOSLOVAKIA
E. GERMANY
HUNGARY
POLAND
RUMANIA
SOVIET UNION

THAILAND

CHINA

MONGOLIA

PHILIPPINES

**U.S.–NATIONALIST CHINA
DEFENSE TREATY**

AUSTRALIA

**U.S.–SOUTH KOREA
DEFENSE TREATY**

**U.S.–JAPAN
DEFENSE TREATY**

MICRONESIA
(U.S.)

PACIFIC

SEATO (1954–1977 with residual
1954 Manila Pact ties remaining
with the Philippines and Thailand.)

AUSTRALIA   PAKISTAN
BRITAIN   PHILIPPINES
FRANCE   THAILAND
NEW ZEALAND   UNITED STATES

NEW ZEALAND

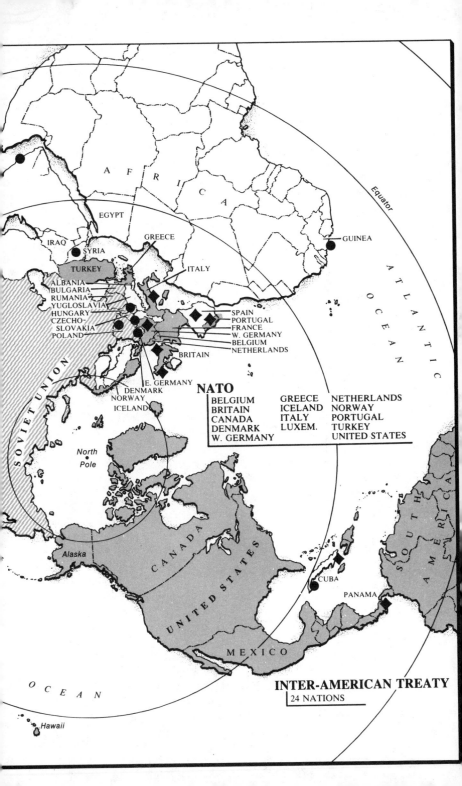

AFRICA

EGYPT

IRAQ
SYRIA
TURKEY

GREECE

ITALY

ALBANIA
BULGARIA
RUMANIA
YUGLOSLAVIA
HUNGARY
CZECHO-
SLOVAKIA
POLAND

SPAIN
PORTUGAL
FRANCE
W. GERMANY
BELGIUM
NETHERLANDS

BRITAIN

E. GERMANY
DENMARK
NORWAY
ICELAND

Equator

GUINEA

ATLANTIC

OCEAN

NATO

BELGIUM	GREECE	NETHERLANDS
BRITAIN	ICELAND	NORWAY
CANADA	ITALY	PORTUGAL
DENMARK	LUXEM.	TURKEY
W. GERMANY		UNITED STATES

SOVIET UNION

North
Pole

Alaska

CANADA

UNITED STATES

CUBA

PANAMA

SOUTH AMERICA

MEXICO

OCEAN

Hawaii

INTER-AMERICAN TREATY
24 NATIONS

Introduction: The Burden of History (to 1941)

The Cold War has dominated American life since 1945. It has cost Americans $2 trillion in defense expenditures, taken the lives of nearly 100,000 of their young men, ruined the careers of many others during the McCarthyite witch hunts, led the nation into the horrors of Southeast Asian conflicts, and in the 1980s triggered the worst economic depression in forty years. It has not been the most triumphant chapter in American diplomatic history.

These tragedies can only be understood—and, it is hoped, some future disasters averted—by understanding the causes of this struggle between the United States and Russia. That conflict did not begin in 1945 or even with the communist victory in Russia during 1917. The two powers did not initially come into conflict because one was communist and the other capitalist. Rather, they first confronted one another on the plains of north China and Manchuria in the late nineteenth century. That meeting climaxed a century in which Americans had expanded westward over half the globe and Russians had moved eastward across Asia.

Until that confrontation the two nations had been good friends. Whenever conflicts arose (as over settlements in California and Alaska), the Russians retreated before the demands of United

States expansionists. Encounters outside the New World, however, could not be settled so easily. Americans swept across a continent while sending out tentacles of trade that quickly seized upon Asia as the great potential market for their magnificently productive farms and factories. By the 1890s Russia, after five centuries of expansion, controlled a grand continental empire containing (like the United States) peoples of many cultures. Americans believed that a "manifest destiny" of supernatural force directed their conquests. The Russians similarly viewed their czar, or emperor, as an instrument of God's will.

But the two nations also differed sharply. The American empire was decentralized, or "federal," with states and outlying territory enjoying considerable freedom. The Russian empire was tightly centralized, with an army of bureaucrats working antlike for the czar (and, later, a small Communist party elite in Moscow). Russian officials agreed that only rigidly enforced order from above could preserve the nation. Such bureaucracies are not renowned for imagination and originality. (In part because of the resulting uncreativity, Russia, both before and after 1917, necessarily borrowed technology and new industrial methods from the West.[1]) The oppressive bureaucracy also was brutal, especially in the post-1880 era when it condemned political dissenters to Siberian prison camps and accelerated pogroms against Russian Jews. Anti-Russian feelings spread across the United States. Congress threatened to cut trade with the czar. Mark Twain caught the mood when he exclaimed that if the regime could be ended only with dynamite, "then thank God for dynamite."

And Americans were also finding another fault with their former friends. The United States honored not bureaucracies, but businessmen who moved across the oceans to profit in open world marketplaces. Russians, however, moved across land, not water. They developed an empire that was more political than commercial. After annexing land in Asia, they tried to control it tightly by closing the markets to foreign businessmen with whom they could not compete. This highlighted the problem between the two countries in the 1890s: the United States believed its prosperity increasingly required an "open door" to trade in China's rich province of

[1]Robert Wesson, "Soviet Russia: A Geopolitical View," *Survey,* XVII (Spring 1971): 1–13.

Manchuria, but the Russians were determined to colonize and close off parts of Manchuria. Two hostile systems confronted one another, much as they would during 1945 in Eastern Europe, and for many of the same reasons.

From the 1890s until 1917 the United States tried to contain Russian expansion, usually by supporting Japan, which, for its own purposes, also wanted an open Manchuria. President Theodore Roosevelt exemplified American sentiments: the Russians "are utterly insincere and treacherous; they have no conception of the truth . . . and no regard for others." As for the czar, he was "a preposterous little creature." More to the point, TR feared Russia was trying to "organize northern China against us."[2]

These views did not change even in 1914 when the czar allied with England and France against Germany. Colonel Edward House, President Woodrow Wilson's closest advisor, starkly outlined the alternatives that would haunt Americans throughout the twentieth century: "If the Allies win, it means the domination of Russia on the continent of Europe; and if Germany wins, it means the unspeakable tyranny of militarism for generations to come."[3] Either way the United States would lose.

The traditional Russian danger grew more threatening in late 1917. Vladimir Lenin's Bolshevik movement used the devastation, chaos, and poverty caused by World War I to overthrow the Russian government and establish a Soviet. The ever-expanding czarist empire now possessed an ideological force, Marxism, that was supposedly driven by historical law and dedicated to world revolution. Between 1918 and 1920 Woodrow Wilson dispatched more than 10,000 American soldiers as he cooperated with Allied attempts to overthrow Lenin by force, and, simultaneously, tried to prevent an invading Japanese army from colonizing and closing off Siberia. The President finally stopped the Japanese, but the Allied intervention was a disaster. In the short run many Russians fled from the foreign troops to support Lenin. In the long run Soviet leaders would not forget that the intervention seemed to confirm their belief that "capitalist encirclement" aimed at strangulating the communist regime.

[2]Quoted in William Henry Harbough, *Power and Responsibility: The Life and Times of Theodore Roosevelt* (New York, 1961), p. 277.

[3]Quoted in Arthur S. Link, *Wilson: The Struggle for Neutrality, 1914–1915* (Princeton, 1960), p. 48.

At the Versailles Peace Conference in 1919, the Allies sought another approach. With the shadow of Lenin darkening every discussion, the Western powers tried to isolate the Soviets by creating such buffer states as Poland, Rumania, Czechoslovakia, and Yugoslavia in Eastern Europe. As a young, embittered American official named Walter Lippmann then phrased it, the Allies created a military *cordon sanitaire*, when peace required a "sanitary Europe," that is, a prosperous, less militarized area that could build a more attractive and equitable society than Lenin could devise.[4] (In 1947, as dean of American journalists, Lippmann would again condemn American postwar policy, and again be rejected by Washington officials.)

Attempting to isolate the Soviets, Woodrow Wilson refused to open diplomatic relations. Sounding like Theodore Roosevelt discussing the czar, Wilson declared that Lenin's government "is based upon the negation of every principle of honor and good faith." But others refused to follow his lead. England began trading with Russia in 1921. A year later the two outcasts, Russia and defeated Germany, signed a treaty of cooperation. Though shocking Americans by condemning religion and private property, the Soviets were apparently here to stay.

The United States by no means ignored the Bolsheviks. An American relief mission distributed over $60 million worth of aid to starving Russians in the 1920s. When Lenin announced in 1921 he would welcome foreign capital for reconstruction projects, Secretary of Commerce Herbert Hoover believed this meant communism was collapsing. Hoping that Americans could control as well as profit from a more capitalist Russia, Hoover encouraged businessmen to look upon Russia as an "economic vacuum" that, like all vacuums, invited invasion. They responded. Ford, General Electric, and Westinghouse were among the many major firms that invested millions of dollars. Young W. Averell Harriman also took the plunge. Heir to a great railway fortune, Harriman began to develop a billion-dollar manganese concession in Russia during 1926. When his venture ran into financial trouble, the Soviets freed him from his contract. (Harriman found them less cooperative when Franklin D. Roosevelt named him Ambassador to Russia during World War II.) Meanwhile, between 1925 and 1930 Soviet-American trade rose to over $100 million, well above the prewar figure.

[4]Walter Lippmann, *New Republic* (March 22, 1919), supplement.

The economic relationship was suddenly transformed after 1928, but not as Hoover had hoped. When Lenin died in 1924, Joseph Stalin used his control of the Soviet party bureaucracy to boost himself to the top. Son of a cobbler, educated at (and expelled from) an Orthodox theological seminary and frequently arrested before 1917 for revolutionary activities, Stalin's brutality had so alienated Lenin that the Soviet leader had nearly broken off personal relations. Lenin's death solved that potential problem; then Stalin brilliantly played faction against faction to defeat his opposition. In 1928 he enhanced his power by announcing five-year plans for rapid economic development. These schemes required a tightly run, self-sufficient society. The communist call for worldwide revolution became less important to Stalin than unchallenged personal power and a rebuilt Russia strong enough to withstand "capitalist encirclement."

American-Russian trade consequently dropped just as the United States entered the worst depression years. Many businessmen pressed the newly elected President, Franklin D. Roosevelt, to recognize Russia formally. He did so in November 1933, but only after overcoming, or ignoring, strong anti-Soviet feeling from his own State Department, as well as from the American Legion, Roman Catholic Church leaders, the Daughters of the American Revolution, and the American labor movement. Justifiably concerned that the Russians might not be warmly welcomed, Roosevelt scheduled the arrival of the Soviet delegation at the same time his countrymen raucously celebrated the end of Prohibition.

Stalin welcomed recognition, but not for economic reasons. He wanted American help against the Japanese army that began rampaging through Manchuria in 1931. Roosevelt refused to respond to the Russian appeal. The State Department even assured the Japanese in 1933 that recognition of Russia should not be taken as a threat against Japan.[5] Until World War II the United States never deviated from this policy. Twice in the next five years, in 1934 and 1937, American officials rejected Soviet requests for joint policies against Japan and Nazi Germany. The administration received strong support from many American liberals, even former commu-

[5] Stanley K. Hornbeck to Secretary of State Cordell Hull, October 28, 1933, and Hornbeck to William Phillips, October 31, 1933, 711.61/333, Archives of the Department of State, Washington, D.C. (Hereafter cited NA, followed by Record Group number.)

nists, who grew disillusioned as Stalin began bloody purges of his political enemies. After the war these liberals would not forget their earlier disenchantment with communism, "the God who failed."

By 1938 Stalin's relations with the Western powers were disintegrating. The climactic blow occurred that year at the Munich conference, when the French and British appeased Hitler by giving Germany part of Czechoslovakia. At the Communist party's Eighteenth Congress in early 1939, Stalin declared that the West hoped to turn Hitler east toward war with the Soviets. This would not happen, he indicated, for although "new economic crises" in the capitalist world made inevitable another "imperialist" war, this time Russia would not pull Western "chestnuts out of the fire."[6] Making much of a terrible situation, Stalin stunned the West in late August 1939 by signing a nonaggression pact with Hitler. The two dictators agreed to divide Poland and the Balkans. A week after the treaty was negotiated, Hitler began World War II.

During the next eighteen months Russian-American relations hit bottom. The Soviet invasion of Finland secured a strategic buffer for Stalin but simply confirmed to Americans that Russia brutalized small neighbors. In early 1941, however, Hitler tired of negotiating with the Russians and decided to take Eastern Europe fully into his own hands. On June 22 Nazi armies swept into the Soviet Union in history's greatest military operation.

The State Department debated for twenty-four hours before issuing an announcement that condemned the Soviet view of religion, declared that "communistic dictatorship" was as intolerable as "Nazi dictatorship," said nothing good about the Russians, but concluded they must be helped since Hitler posed the larger threat. Harry S. Truman, Democratic senator from Missouri, bluntly expressed his and some other congressmen's feelings: "If we see that Germany is winning we should help Russia and if Russia is winning we ought to help Germany and that way let them kill as many as possible, although I don't want to see Hitler victorious under any circumstances."[7]

It was not the best spirit with which to start a new partnership. But such statements only climaxed half a century of Russian-

[6]Myron Rush, ed., *The International Situation and Soviet Foreign Policy: Key Reports by Soviet Leaders from the Revolution to the Present* (Columbus, Ohio, 1970), pp. 85–96.

[7]*The New York Times*, June 24, 1941, p. 7.

American enmity. Possessing drastically different views of how the world should be organized, unable to cooperate during the 1930s against Nazi and Japanese aggression, and nearly full-fledged enemies between 1939 and 1941, the United States and the Soviet Union finally became partners because of a shotgun marriage forced upon them by World War II.

1

Open Doors, Iron Curtains (1941-1945)

A honeymoon never occurred. Despite exchanges of military information and nearly $11 billion of American lend-lease supplies sent to Russia, conflicts quickly erupted over war strategy and plans for the postwar peace.

As the Nazis drove deeper into Russia in 1942, Stalin desperately asked Roosevelt and British Prime Minister Winston Churchill to open a bridgehead in Western Europe. Soviet Foreign Minister V. M. Molotov, according to one observer, knew only four words of English: "yes," "no," and "second front." Twice Roosevelt promised an invasion. Twice he and Churchill reneged. Believing they lacked the power to attack Western Europe, they instead invaded North Africa and Italy. These campaigns stalled the opening of the second front until mid-1944. By then the Russians had themselves driven back the Nazis, although at tremendous cost.

Stalin's suspicions multiplied as he asked Roosevelt and Churchill to agree that postwar Russia should include the Baltic States and parts of Poland, Finland, and Rumania. These areas had belonged to czarist Russia and had been reclaimed by Stalin in 1939 with the Nazi-Soviet pact. Roosevelt gave in on the Baltic States in

1943, but otherwise the President hoped to delay territorial settlements until after the war.

That was a fateful decision. By 1945 the Red Army stood astride Eastern and much of Central Europe. Roosevelt and Churchill, moreover, would have to discuss Stalin's demands in a strikingly different world, for the Allies were destroying Germany and Japan, two nations that historically had blocked Russian expansion into Europe and Asia.

American policy makers soon discovered an even greater problem. Their own policy was contradictory. Neither Roosevelt nor his successor, Harry S. Truman, ever reconciled the contradictions. That failure was a major cause of the Cold War. The contradiction contained an economic and a political factor.

Washington officials believed another terrible economic depression could be averted only if global markets and raw materials were fully open to all peoples on the basis of equal opportunity. American domestic requirements, moreover, dictated such a policy. The world could not be allowed to return to the 1930s, when nations tried to escape depression by creating high tariff walls and regional trading blocs that dammed up the natural flow of trade. If that recurred, Americans could perhaps survive only through massive governmental intervention into their society. If the government dominated the economy, however, it would also regulate individual choice and perhaps severely limit personal freedom.

"In the event of long-continued unemployment," Vice President Henry Wallace warned, "the only question will be as to whether the Prussian or Marxian doctrine will take us over first." Such alternatives could be avoided only if Americans realized, in the words of Assistant Secretary of State Dean Acheson, that "we cannot expect domestic prosperity under our system without a constantly expanding trade with other nations." As one official noted, "The capitalistic system is essentially an international system," and "if it cannot function internationally, it will break down completely." For these reasons the United States required an open world marketplace after the war.[1]

---

[1] Henry Wallace, Herbert Hoover, et al., *Prefaces to Peace* (New York, 1943), p. 413; Lloyd C. Gardner, *Economic Aspects of New Deal Diplomacy* (Madison, Wisconsin, 1964), p. 344; testimony of Secretary of the Treasury Fred Vinson, *The New York Times*, March 6, 1946, p. 8.

In August 1941, at the Atlantic Conference held off Newfoundland with Churchill, Roosevelt moved to implement this policy. In Article III of the Atlantic Charter, the two leaders declared that after the war all peoples should have the right "to choose the form of government under which they will live." Article IV added the economic side to that principle: all states should enjoy "access, on equal terms, to the trade and to the raw materials of the world which are needed for their economic prosperity."[2] That "need" for Americans grew incredibly during the next four years. Their industrial output rose 90 percent. This economic power, developed while other industrial nations were decimated by war, also assured Americans they would be in the most advantageous position to race for "access, on equal terms" in world trade.

The Ghosts of Depression Past and Depression Future thus shaped American postwar objectives. But those objectives were political as well as economic. Closed economic blocs not only hurt trade but easily developed into political blocs. Friction between such blocs caused world wars. That was precisely what had occurred during the 1930s when the British, Germans, Japanese, and Russians had warred on each other economically, then militarily. As State Department economic advisor Will Clayton declared, "Nations which act as enemies in the marketplace cannot long be friends at the council table."[3]

In 1944 the United States tried to ensure that the postwar marketplace would be friendly. An international conference at Bretton Woods, New Hampshire, created a World Bank (the International Bank of Reconstruction and Development) and the International Monetary Fund (IMF). The World Bank would have a treasury of $7.6 billion (and authority to lend twice that amount) to guarantee private loans given for building war-torn Europe and the less industrialized nations. The IMF possessed $7.3 billion to stabilize currencies so trade could be conducted without fear of sudden currency depreciation or wild fluctuations in exchange rates, ailments which had nearly paralyzed the international community in the 1930s. The United States hoped these two agencies would reconstruct, then stabilize and expand world trade. Of course, there was one

---

[2]U.S. Department of State, *Foreign Relations of the United States* [henceforth *FRUS*], *1941*, I (Washington, 1948):366–368.

[3]Quoted in Lloyd Gardner, *Architects of Illusion* (Chicago, 1970), p. 123.

other implication. Voting in the organizations depended on money contributed. Since Americans would have to contribute the most, they would also control the World Bank and IMF.

American policy from the Atlantic Charter through the Bretton Woods conference seemed well thought out. Financier and self-appointed advisor to Presidents and congressmen Bernard Baruch caught the spirit in early 1945: if we can "stop subsidization of labor and sweated competition in the export markets," as well as prevent rebuilding of war machines, "oh boy, oh boy, what long-term prosperity we will have."[4] Like Dorothy, Americans seemed on their way to a happier land of Oz, with their immense economic power serving as ruby slippers. But, like Dorothy, they soon encountered witches — not just one, but wicked witches from both West and East.

In the West the French and British had realized since the 1920s they could no longer compete with the efficient American industrialists in an open marketplace. During the 1930s the British had created their own economic bloc to shut out American goods. Churchill did not believe he could surrender that protection after the war, and he watered down the Atlantic Charter's "free access" clause before agreeing to it. Yet American officials were determined to break open the empire. Combined, British and American trade accounted for more than half the world's exchange of goods. If the British bloc could be split apart, the United States would be well on the way to opening the entire global marketplace.

A devastated England had no choice. Two wars had destroyed its principal industries that paid for the importation of half the nation's food and nearly all its raw materials except coal. The British asked for help. In 1945 the United States agreed to loan $3.8 billion. In return, weary London officials promised to dismantle much of their imperial trading bloc. Will Clayton, who negotiated the agreement, confided to Baruch, "We loaded the British loan negotiations with all the conditions that the traffic would bear."[5]

France received the same treatment. For nearly two centuries French and American interests had clashed in both the Old and New Worlds. During the war French mistrust of the United States

[4]Baruch to E. Coblentz, March 23, 1945, Papers of Bernard Baruch, Princeton University Library, Princeton, New Jersey.

[5]"Memorandum for Mr. Baruch," from Clayton, April 26, 1946, Baruch Papers. For the background, see Warren F. Kimball, "Lend-Lease and the Open Door . . . 1937–1942," Political Science Quarterly, LXXXVI (June 1971):232–259.

was personified by General Charles de Gaulle, president of the French Provisional Government. De Gaulle bitterly fought American officials as he tried to maintain his country's colonies and diplomatic freedom of action. These officials in turn saw de Gaulle as pro-British and a political extremist; one State Department officer even called him "this French Adolf."[6] In 1945 de Gaulle had to swallow his considerable pride to ask Washington for a billion-dollar loan. Most of the request was granted; in return France promised to curtail governmental subsidies and currency manipulation which had given advantages to its exporters in the world market.

The United States was freeing itself to deal with the witch of the East, the Soviet Union.[7] As it did, the contradictions within American policy became stunningly apparent. On the one hand, Washington demanded an open Europe. As a top official later explained, the State Department wanted all Europe "west of the Russian border . . . established as a cooperative continental system economically unified in certain major particulars."[8] On the other hand, Stalin had constantly demanded that Roosevelt and Churchill recognize the Soviet right to control large parts of Eastern Europe. For Stalin the Russian "sphere" would serve as a strategic buffer against the West and could also be exploited economically for the rapid rebuilding of the Soviet economy. Making his intentions clear, Stalin refused to sign the Atlantic Charter until he added provisions that emasculated Articles III and IV.[9]

As early as 1942, therefore, Roosevelt faced the choice: he could either fight for an open postwar world (at least to the Russian

---

[6]H. F. Matthews to Ray Atherton, June 25, 1943, Papers of William Leahy, Box 4, Library of Congress, Washington, D.C.

[7]Unfortunately, the "wicked witch" analogy is not farfetched. Louis Halle, a member of the State Department Policy Planning Staff in the late 1940s, recalled that throughout this era until "almost the end of 1962," the West lived under the terror of "the Moscovite tyranny that was spreading from the East." For those who wished to understand such fears, Halle recommended reading J. R. R. Tolkien's trilogy, *The Lord of the Rings*, which Halle believed "enshrines the mood and emotion of those long years." *The Cold War as History* (New York, 1967), p. 138.

[8]Adolf Berle, "Diplomacy and the New Economics." In E. A. J. Johnson, ed., *Dimensions of Diplomacy* (Baltimore, 1964), pp. 93–95.

[9]Martin F. Herz, *The Beginnings of the Cold War* (Bloomington, Indiana, 1966), pp. vii–viii.

borders) or agree with his ally's demands in Eastern Europe. If he chose the first alternative, Russian-American relations would probably erode until the joint effort against the Axis might collapse. At the least, Americans and Russians would enter the postwar world as enemies. (As it was, a mistrustful Stalin secretly considered a separate peace with Hitler as late as mid-1943.[10]) If Roosevelt chose the second alternative, he would undermine American hopes for the triumph of the Atlantic Charter principles, thus destroying the chances for postwar peace and American prosperity. Not that the United States required Eastern European markets. But a stable, prosperous world did require a healthy Europe, and that meant a united Europe with its eastern sectors providing food and western areas the industrial products. Each depended on the other. As the State Department informed Roosevelt in early 1945, European stability "depends on the maintenance of sound economic conditions and reasonable prosperity in all parts of the Continent."[11] Besides, a dangerous precedent could be set. If Stalin got away with building his own sphere in Europe, Churchill, de Gaulle, and others might try to rebuild their blocs.

Faced with this agonizing dilemma, Roosevelt at first suggested to the Soviets that the postwar world should be stabilized by "four policemen"—the United States, Russia, Great Britain, and China. The Soviets were delighted, for they understood this plan to mean they would be the policeman patrolling Eastern Europe. By late 1943, however, State Department officials were changing Roosevelt's mind. The "four policemen" concept could not be reconciled with a unified, open world. Areas patrolled by one policeman could too easily become closed spheres controlled by one power. Roosevelt began to stall, then to modify the idea. As he delayed, the Red Army started its sweep across Eastern Europe in 1944. Stalin understood what was happening. "This war is not as in the past," he told fellow communists. "Whoever occupies a territory also imposes on it his own social system" as far "as his army can reach."[12]

Churchill also understood. In October 1944 he deserted Roosevelt's policy of delay and flew to Moscow to make a deal. He prom-

[10]Vojtech Mastny, "Stalin and the Prospects of a Separate Peace in World War II," *American Historical Review*, LXXVII (December 1972): 1365–1388.

[11]*FRUS: The Conferences at Malta and Yalta, 1945* (Washington, 1955), pp. 235–236.

[12]Milovan Djilas, *Conversations with Stalin* (New York, 1961), p. 114.

ised to recognize Soviet domination in Rumania and Bulgaria. In return, Stalin agreed that England could control Greece. Thus Churchill protected the Mediterranean lifeline of the British Empire while acknowledging Russia's "first say" in certain Eastern European nations. With accuracy, and sarcasm, Churchill warned Stalin the deal had better be expressed "in diplomatic terms and not . . . use the phrase 'dividing into spheres,' because the Americans might be shocked."[13]

When he learned of the agreement, Roosevelt was shocked anyway, but worse was to come. In February 1945 the Big Three met at the Russian Black Sea resort of Yalta to shape the postwar world. An acrimonious debate erupted over the future of Poland. Throughout 1943–1944 Roosevelt had indicated he understood the need for a Polish government that would (unlike that government in the interwar years) be friendly toward Russia. But he was not prepared for Stalin's moves in early 1945. The Soviets had recognized a communist-dominated regime before the Yalta meetings began. FDR and Churchill demanded that pro-Western Poles be included in the government. The three men finally agreed that the regime must be "reorganized on a broader democratic basis." Admiral William Leahy, Roosevelt's chief military aid, accurately observed the agreement was "so elastic that the Russians can stretch it all the way from Yalta to Washington without technically breaking it." Since the Red Army occupied Poland, however, this was the best FDR could do. He did try to make the agreement less elastic by proposing a "Declaration of Liberated Europe." This provided that each of the three powers would pledge cooperation in applying the self-determination principle to newly liberated nations. The Russians amended the declaration until it was virtually meaningless. Again, FDR had to accept the remains.[14]

Stalin left Yalta doubtless believing his allies had at least acquiesced to his domination over Eastern Europe. That must have been a relief, for throughout much of the war his policy had also been

[13]"Record of Meeting at the Kremlin, Moscow, October 9, 1944," PREM 3, 434/47, Public Record Office, London, England. I am indebted to Professor Lloyd Gardner of Rutgers — New Brunswick and Professor Warren Kimball of Rutgers — Newark for calling my attention to this document. In much the same way, the United States excluded the Soviets from any authority in liberated Italy; see Gabriel Kolko, *The Politics of War, 1943–1945* (New York, 1968), pp. 37–39.

[14]*FRUS: Yalta*, pp. 234–235, 677–678, 668–669, 898.

pulling in two directions. The Soviet dictator insisted on his own sphere but to this point had carefully not explained to his partners what Russian control implied. To have done so might have angered the Allies, slowed American deliveries of war materiel, and perhaps even led to a separate deal between the West and Germany. (After all, why should Stalin have expected capitalist scruples to be more elevated than his own?) With the Red Army so close to total victory, he did not want any last-minute diplomatic bungling. Yalta seemed to remove that danger.

But Stalin miscalculated. Two weeks after the conference adjourned, the Soviets turned the screws on Rumania by demanding that the king appoint a communist-controlled government. Rumanian soldiers, the Soviets recalled, had marched with the Nazis into Russia in 1941. Churchill, moreover, had agreed to turn his back on Rumania in return for Stalin's ignoring Greece. But the United States claimed that Stalin was breaking the Declaration of Liberated Europe. The American case was difficult to argue, and Molotov picked it apart.[15] This was not, however, a mere debate: control of Eastern Europe was at stake.

A crisis developed when Russia refused to allow any more than three pro-Western Poles into the eighteen-member Polish government. For Americans, Poland became the test case of Soviet intentions. As Secretary of State Edward Stettinius observed, Poland, not Rumania, was "*the big apple in the barrel* and we should concentrate on that." The analogy obviously implied that one rotten apple could spoil all the others. On April 1, Roosevelt gravely warned Stalin the Soviet plan could not be accepted. On April 5, Averell Harriman, United States ambassador to Russia, insisted to FDR that Stalin must not be allowed to establish "totalitarianism," for "unless we are prepared to live in a Soviet-dominated world, we must use our economic power to assist countries naturally friendly to us."[16] Writing to Churchill about the crisis the next day, Roosevelt referred to yet another weapon: "Our armies will in a very few days be in a position that will permit us to become 'tougher' than has heretofore appeared advantageous to the war effort."[17]

[15]Daily Staff Summary, March 1, March 19, March 28, 1945, Lot File, NA, RG 59.
[16]"Record," volumes III, IV, 11–17 March 1945. Papers of Edward Stettinius, University of Virginia Library, Charlottesville. Italics in original. "Special Information for the President," from Stettinius, April 5, 1945, Lot File 53 D 444, NA, RG 59.
[17]Roosevelt to Churchill, April 6, 1945. In Francis L. Loewenheim, Harold D. Langley, and Manfred Jonas, eds., *Roosevelt and Churchill* (New York, 1975), p. 705.

Within a week Roosevelt was dead. The new President, Harry S. Truman, inherited a decayed alliance. FDR had not discussed foreign policy (or much else) with him. As Vice President, Truman referred to himself as a "political eunuch." But his affection for Russia had not noticeably increased since 1941. After Roosevelt appeared before Congress to put a good face on the difficulties at Yalta, journalists asked Truman what he thought of the speech. "One of the greatest ever given," he replied — and then joined them in laughter.[18]

Truman entered the White House a highly insecure man. ("I felt like the moon, the stars, and all the planets had fallen on me," he told reporters.) And he held the world's most responsible job in a world that was changing radically. Truman tried to compensate for his insecurity in several ways. First, he was extremely jealous of his presidential powers and deeply suspicious of anyone who challenged those powers. Truman made decisions rapidly not only because that was his character but also because he determined "the buck stopped" at his desk. There would be no more sloppy administration or strong, freewheeling bureaucrats as in FDR's later years.

Second, and more dangerously, Truman was determined that these decisions would not be tagged as "appeasement." He would be as tough as the toughest. After only twenty-four hours in the White House, the new President confidently informed his secretary of state, "We must stand up to the Russians," and he implied "We had been too easy with them."[19] In foreign policy discussions during the next two weeks, Truman interrupted his advisors to assure them he would certainly be "tough."

His determination was reinforced when he listened most closely to such advisors as Harriman, Leahy, and Secretary of the Navy James Forrestal, who urged him to take a hard line. Warning of a "barbarian invasion of Europe," Harriman declared that postwar cooperation with the Soviets, especially economically, must depend on their agreement to open Poland and Eastern Europe. In a decisive meeting on April 23, Secretary of War Henry Stimson argued with Harriman. Stimson declared that peace must never be threatened by an issue such as Poland, for free elections there were impossible, Russia held total control, and Stalin was "not likely to

[18]Margaret Truman, *Harry S. Truman* (New York, 1973), pp. 220–222.
[19]"Private Calendar Notes, 4/13/45," Box 224, Stettinius Papers.

yield . . . in substance."[20] Stimson was not an amateur; he had been a respected Wall Street lawyer and distinguished public servant for forty years, including a term as Herbert Hoover's secretary of state.

But Truman dismissed Stimson's advice, accepted Harriman's, and later that day berated Soviet Foreign Minister Molotov "in words of one syllable" for breaking the Yalta agreements on Poland. Truman demanded the Soviets agree to a "new" (not merely "reorganized") Polish government. An astonished Molotov replied, "I have never been talked to like that in my life." "Carry out your agreements," Truman supposedly retorted, "and you won't get talked to like that."[21]

The next day Stalin rejected Truman's demand, observing that it was contrary to the Yalta agreement. The dictator noted that "Poland borders with the Soviet Union, what [sic] cannot be said of Great Britain and the United States." After all, Stalin continued, the Soviets do not "lay claim to interference" in Belgium and Greece where the Americans and British made decisions without consulting the Russians.[22] In June Truman reluctantly accepted a compromise when Stalin included several more pro-Western Poles in the government. Americans hoped that political recognition of the new regime would allow them to use their economic power to open Poland "to a policy of equal opportunity in trade, investments and access to sources of information."[23] But the Poles refused to open the door to the dollar. Stimson had been correct. Truman's toughness had only stiffened Russian determination to control Poland.

An "iron fence" was falling around Eastern Europe, Churchill blurted out to Stalin in mid-1945. "All fairy-tales," the Soviet leader blandly replied. But it was partly true. The crises over Rumania and Poland only raised higher the fence around those two nations. In other areas, however, the Soviet approach varied. A Russian-sponsored election in Hungary produced a noncommunist govern-

[20]Diary, April 23, 1945. Papers of Henry Stimson, Yale University Library, New Haven, Conn.

[21]Harry S. Truman, *Memoirs, Volume One* (Garden City, N.Y., 1955), p. 82. This precise exchange was possibly created by Truman's imagination. These words are not reported on the official records of the conversation. They doubtless suggest, nevertheless, the tone of what Truman did say.

[22]*FRUS, 1945*, V (Washington, 1967): 263–264.

[23]*FRUS: The Conference of Berlin* (Washington, 1960), I: 262–264; "Memorandum for the President," June 27, 1945, Lot File 53 D 444, NA, RG 59.

ment. In Bulgaria the Soviet-conducted elections satisfied British observers, if not Americans. Stalin agreed to an independent, non-communist regime in Finland if the Finns would follow a foreign policy friendly to Russia. An "iron fence" by no means encircled all of Eastern Europe. There was still room to bargain if each side wished to avoid a confrontation over the remaining areas.

But the bargaining room was limited. Stalin's doctrine and his determination that Russia would not again be invaded from the west greatly narrowed his diplomatic options. So too did the tremendous devastation of the war. Rapid rebuilding required security, access to resources in Eastern and Central Europe, and justified continued tight control over the Russian people. The experience of war was indelible. Russians viewed almost everything in their lives through their "searing experience of World War II," as one psychologist has phrased it.[24] The conflict had destroyed 1700 towns, 70,000 villages, and left 25 million homeless. Twenty million died; 600,000 starved to death at the single siege of Leningrad.

During those terrible years Stalin had shrewdly asked his countrymen not to sacrifice themselves for communism (in whose name, after all, millions had been executed or placed in Siberian prisons during the 1930s), but for "Mother Russia." Little evidence exists, however, that Stalin privately changed his own peculiar brand of Marxist-Leninist doctrine. This was crucial, for all Soviet leaders have cloaked their policies with this doctrine, using it not only in determining foreign policy but also in rationalizing their own power and in silencing internal dissent. To outside observers, therefore, doctrine can act as a weather vane; once officials have decided upon policy they publicly justify it with appropriate doctrine, and the doctrinal changes indicate the policy changes.

Stalin's doctrine during the spring of 1945 differed little from the views he had uttered about Western "imperialists" in 1939. The wartime alliance apparently did not dent his outlook, or if it did the Western attempts to open Eastern Europe rekindled his earlier fears. Consistency of Soviet doctrine also resulted from the remarkably stable membership of the Politburo (the policy-making body of the

[24]Ralph K. White, "Images in the Context of International Conflict." In Herbert C. Kelman, ed., *International Behavior* (New York, 1965), p. 271.

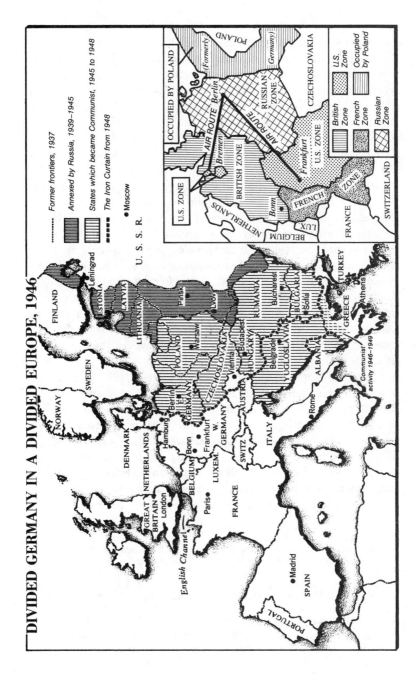

DIVIDED GERMANY IN A DIVIDED EUROPE, 1946

Former frontiers, 1937
Annexed by Russia, 1939–1945
States which became Communist, 1945 to 1948
The Iron Curtain from 1948

Communist party's Central Committee). The Politburo's membership in 1945 almost exactly resembled that of 1939 when the Nazi-
Soviet pact was signed. The leadership's view of Western democracy, capitalist encirclement, the inevitability of further capitalist
wars, the sources of imperialism, and the impossibility of disarmament evidently changed little between 1939 and 1945. In April 1945
Stalin told fellow communists that another war was only a matter
of time. The Germans "will recover, and very quickly," he warned.
"Give them twelve to fifteen years and they'll be on their feet again.
And that is why the unity of the Slavs is important."[25]

During 1945 the triumphs of the Red Army and the growing tension over Eastern Europe led Stalin to tighten his control over
Soviet life. Special schools opened to teach the dictator's doctrine;
"Mother Russia" gave way to "Glorious Stalin." The Red Army
received special attention. It had been exposed to corrupting "bour-
geois" influence in Central Europe and had grown too rapidly for
Stalin to impose rigid political control. He raised his close associate
Lavrenti Beria, chief of the dreaded secret police, to the rank of
marshal of the Red Army and promoted himself to generalissimo.
Army officers, holding the only power capable of challenging
Stalin, slowly disappeared from public view. By the summer of
1945 his authority was unquestioned.[26]

Some scholars have examined Stalin's acts of 1928 to 1945, pronounced them the work of a "paranoid," and concluded that the
United States had no chance to avoid a cold war since it was dealing with a man who was mentally ill. That interpretation neatly
avoids confronting the complex causes of the Cold War but is
wholly insufficient to explain those causes. However Stalin acted
inside Russia, where he had total control, in his foreign policy during 1941 to 1946 he displayed a realism, a careful calculation of
forces, and a diplomatic finesse that undercut any attempt to explain

[25]Djilas, *Conversations with Stalin*, p. 114; John S. Curtiss and Alex Inkeles, "Marx-
ism in the U.S.S.R. —The Recent Revival," *Political Science Quarterly*, XLI (Septem-
ber 1946): 349–364; Frederick C. Barghoorn, "Great Russian Messianism in Postwar
Soviet Ideology," in Ernest J. Simmons, ed., *Continuity and Change in Russian and
Soviet Thought* (Cambridge, Mass., 1955), p. 541. A fine study of this problem is
Paul Marantz, "The Soviet Union and the Western World: A Study in Doctrinal
Change, 1917–1964," unpublished doctoral dissertation, Harvard University, 1971.

[26]Alexander Werth, *Russia at War* (New York, 1964), pp. 943–945; Raymond L. Garthoff, *Soviet Military Policy, A Historical Analysis* (New York, 1966), pp. 42–44.

away his actions as paranoid.[27] If he and other Soviets were suspicious of the West, they were realistic, not paranoid: the West had poured thousands of troops into Russia between 1917 and 1920, refused to cooperate with the Soviets during the 1930s, tried to turn Hitler against Stalin in 1938, reneged on promises about the second front, and in 1945 tried to penetrate areas Stalin deemed crucial to Soviet security.

American diplomats who frequently saw Stalin understood this background. In January 1945 Harriman told the State Department, "The overriding consideration in Soviet foreign policy is the preoccupation with 'security,' as Moscow sees it." The problem was that Americans did not see "security" the same way. They believed their security required an open world, including an open Eastern Europe. No Western diplomat has been found who declared in 1945–1947 that Stalin showed signs of mental illness. Some actually argued that hard-line "boys" within the Politburo forced him to be tougher with the West than he wished.[28] That was inaccurate. Stalin set policy and the policy was consistent. Only timing and tactics varied.

In dealing with foreign Communist parties, Stalin's priority was not world revolution but, once again, Russian security and his own personal power. In 1943 he had made a goodwill gesture by disbanding the Comintern (the organization which directed overseas Communist parties from headquarters in Moscow). It was only a gesture, however, for Stalin determined to control these parties for his own purposes. In 1944–1945 he ordered the powerful French Communist party to cooperate with the Western Allies rather than attempt to seize power. Wanting above all else Anglo-American acquiescence to his acts in Eastern Europe, Stalin restrained the French communists before they became dangerously overambitious.

Similarly, a leading French communist, Jacques Duclos, blasted the American Communist party in the spring of 1945 for moving too close to the New Deal, and ordered it to create a separate identity —but then advised working within the American political system. "Nothing prevents a Communist Party from adapting its electoral

---

[27]Adam B. Ulam, *Stalin* (New York, 1973), pp. 685–686. The most popular expression of Stalin's supposed paranoia is in Arthur Schlesinger's essay, most easily found in Lloyd C. Gardner, Arthur Schlesinger, Jr., and Hans J. Morgenthau, *The Origins of the Cold War* (Waltham, Mass., 1970), pp. 72–73.

[28]*FRUS: Yalta*, pp. 450–451; "Mr. Macmillan to Foreign Office," 21 March 1945, FO 371 N3097/1545/38, Public Record Office, London; *FRUS: Berlin*, I, 13.

tactics to the requirements of a given political situation," observed
Duclos. The State Department, however, informed Truman that
Duclos's advice required the government "to treat the American
Communist movement as a potential fifth column." Traditional
American fear of communist ideology reinforced the administration's dislike of Stalin's actions in Eastern Europe. Such fear was
hardly warranted. Fifty thousand, or half the membership in the
United States Communist party's Political Association, left the
group by 1946.[29] Ironically, Americans began their feverish search
for communists at the same time the Communist party had to begin
its own search for members.

By mid-1945 Stalin's policies were brutally consistent, while
Truman's were confused. The confusion became obvious when the
United States, opposed to a sphere of interest in Europe, strengthened its own sphere in the Western Hemisphere. Unlike its policies
elsewhere, however, the State Department did not use economic
weapons. The economic relationship with Latin America and
Canada could simply be assumed. During the war these two areas
had fed cheap raw materials to United States industry. After the
struggle, and despite promises to the contrary, Washington neglected
its neighbors while sending goods and money to rebuild Europe.

But Latin America was not neglected politically. A young assistant secretary of state for Latin American affairs, Nelson Rockefeller, and Senator Arthur Vandenburg (Republican from Michigan) devised the political means to keep the Americas solidly within
Washington's sphere. Their instrument was Article 51 of the United
Nations Charter. This provision was largely formulated by Rockefeller and Vandenberg at the San Francisco conference that founded
the United Nations in the spring of 1945. The article allowed for
collective self-defense through special regional organizations to be
created outside the United Nations but within the principles of the
charter. In this way, regional organizations would escape Russian
vetoes in the Security Council. The United States could control its
own sphere without Soviet interference.

[29] *Daily Worker,* May 24, 1945, pp. 7–9; *FRUS: Berlin,* I: 267–282; Joseph R. Staro-
bin, *American Communism in Crisis, 1943–1957* (Cambridge, Mass., 1972), pp.
74–120.

Intimately acquainted with Latin America because of his family's investments (especially in Venezuelan oil), Rockefeller wanted Russia excluded so that North and South America could be economically integrated and developed without outside interference. He also understood that unless the United States "operated with a solid group in this hemisphere" it "could not do what we wanted to do on the world front."[30] Vandenberg had other reasons. Although he was known as a 1930s "isolationist" who became an "internationalist" in 1945, it is questionable how far he actually turned.

The portly, white-haired senator exemplified the truism that Americans tend to become political "isolationists" when they cannot dominate international affairs and "internationalists" politically when they can. (They have been economic and cultural "internationalists" since the seventeenth century.) Rarely have Americans been prepared to bargain or to compromise their freedom of action. They have joined such organizations as the United Nations when they could control them. Throughout the war Vandenberg gradually left his earlier political "isolationism" because he believed the United States would have the power to internationalize the Atlantic Charter freedoms. These principles, he proclaimed in early 1945, "sail with our fleets. They fly with our eagles. They sleep with our martyred dead." And they must be had by all, including Eastern Europeans. But the Yalta agreements shocked him. Terming the Polish settlement "awful," he doubted that the United Nations, burdened with the Soviet veto in the Security Council, could enforce the Atlantic Charter. The Western Hemisphere could nevertheless be protected. When he and Rockefeller finished with Article 51, they thought they had obtained the best of both worlds: exclusive American power in the New and the right to exert American power in the Old.

The obvious confusion in that approach was pinpointed by Secretary of War Stimson when he condemned Americans who were "anxious to hang on to exaggerated views of the Monroe Doctrine and at the same time butt into every question that comes up in Central Europe." Almost alone, Stimson argued for an alternative policy. Through bilateral U.S.-U.S.S.R. negotiations (and not negotiations within the United Nations, where the Russians would be defensive and disagreeable because the Americans controlled a

---

[30]David Green, *The Containment of Latin America* (Chicago, 1971), p. 234.

majority), Stimson hoped each side could agree that the other should have its own security spheres. But as he had lost the argument over Poland, so Stimson lost this argument. Truman was prepared to bargain very little. He might not get 100 percent, the President told advisors, but he would get 85 percent. Even in Rumania, where the Russians were particularly sensitive, the State Department secretly determined in August 1945, "It is our intention to attain a position of equality with the Russians." When, however, the Americans pressed, the Soviets only tightened their control of Rumania.[31]

Not even Stimson, however, could suggest a solution for Germany, the biggest problem of all. Throughout 1943–1945 Roosevelt had wavered between virtually destroying the nation (he even once mentioned mass castration) and allowing Germany to reindustrialize under tight controls. Stimson and Secretary of State Cordell Hull fought for the latter policy. They believed world recovery depended on a strong, industrialized Europe. That required at its heart, as it had for a century, a rebuilt Germany. Roosevelt — typically — never made a clear choice.

For his part, Stalin agreed when Roosevelt suggested dismemberment, but the Russian cared more about taking reparations (in the form of industrial machines and goods) out of Germany. In this way he could rebuild Russian industry while killing off any possibility that Germany could again threaten Russia in the foreseeable future. Stalin also insisted upon territorial changes. He wanted the Poles to have part of eastern Germany as compensation for the land they were being forced to give Russia in eastern Poland. At first Churchill and Roosevelt had not objected to this demand, but by 1945 they opposed the new German-Polish boundary. They rightly feared this simply masked communist control of eastern Germany.

At the Potsdam conference, held outside captured Berlin in July 1945, Truman and Secretary of State James Byrnes offered Stalin a deal. The West would de facto recognize the new Polish-German boundary. The Russians could also take reparations out of their own occupation zone of eastern Germany, an area primarily agricultural. But in the three Western occupation zones (controlled by the Americans, British, and French) the Soviets could have only 25 percent of the reparations; about half of those would have to be

[31]"Memorandum for the Secretary," August 20, 1945, Lot File, Staff Officers' Summary, NA, RG 59.

paid for with foodstuffs from the Russian zone. With considerable grumbling, Stalin accepted the deal. The United States had finally made the choice: it would not rush to dismember Germany but would hold tightly to the nation's western industrial heartland and methodically rebuild the shattered German economy. Of course there was one other implication. An economic division of Germany could lead to a political division. The deal laid the basis for an eastern and a western Germany.

Although Truman did not obtain his "85 percent" at Potsdam, en route home he received the news that a weapon of unimaginable power, the atomic bomb, had obliterated Hiroshima, Japan, on August 6. Eighty thousand had died. This was some 20,000 fewer than had been killed by a massive American fire bombing of Tokyo earlier in the year, but it was the newly opened secret of nature embodied in a single bomb that was overwhelming. Since Roosevelt had initiated the atomic project in 1941, American policy makers had never doubted they would use the weapon if it could be rapidly developed. Roosevelt, moreover, had decided at least by late 1944 not to share information about the bomb with the Soviets, even though he knew Stalin had learned about the project. By the summer of 1945 this approach, and the growing Soviet-American confrontation in Eastern Europe, led Truman and Byrnes to discuss securing "further *quid pro quos*" in Rumania, Poland, and Asia from Stalin before the Russians could share the secret of atomic energy.[32]

Militarily, the Americans dropped the first bomb to end the war as quickly as possible and before perhaps a million casualties resulted from an invasion of Japan. A diplomatic objective was also apparent. Stalin had promised to invade Japanese strongholds in Manchuria approximately three months after the war with Germany ended, or sometime in August. In early 1945 American officials were greatly relieved that the Russians would help in the bloody fighting around the Japanese home islands. By midsummer, however, Truman and Byrnes were no longer certain they wanted Russia that close to Japan. On August 8 the Soviets attacked Manchuria. The next day a second atomic bomb destroyed Nagasaki. On August 10 Japan began negotiations to surrender.

[32]Martin J. Sherwin, "The Atomic Bomb and the Origins of the Cold War . . . ," *American Historical Review*, LXXVIII (October 1973): 945–968.

The bomb "is the greatest thing in history," Truman boasted. Nor was he sorry he had used it. Noting the "unwarranted attack on Pearl Harbor," the President explained to a journalist, "When you deal with a beast you have to treat him as a beast."[33] On August 19 Admiral Leahy announced over national radio that the United States possessed a more powerful navy than any other two fleets in existence, the best-equipped ground force in the world, the "largest and most efficient air force," and "with our British allies, the secret of the world's most fearsome weapon." Clearly, Americans held most of the high cards as World War II ended. That same month Secretary of State Byrnes publicly announced the stakes for which the game would be played.

"Our international policies and our domestic policies are insepa-rable," he began. "Our foreign relations inevitably affect employ-ment in the United States. Prosperity and depression in the United States just as inevitably affect our relations with the other nations of the world." Byrnes expressed his "clear conviction that a durable peace cannot be built on an economic foundation of exclusive blocs . . . and economic warfare." Specifically he warned: "In many countries . . . our political and economic creed is in conflict with ideologies which reject both of these principles." Byrnes con-cluded: "To the extent that we are able to manage our domestic affairs successfully, we shall win converts to our creed in every land."[34] John Winthrop had not expressed it more clearly 300 years earlier at Massachusetts Bay. Only now the City Upon a Hill, as Winthrop called it, was industrialized, internationalized — and held the atomic bomb.

But the Soviets refused to budge. Byrnes and Molotov agreed on little at a Foreign Ministers conference in the autumn of 1945. In-side Russia the threat of "capitalist encirclement" was trumpeted. Ominous rumors spread that Stalin would respond by further regi-menting the Soviets with more five-year plans. Stimson, about to retire from the War Department, made one final attempt to stop an East-West confrontation. In a September 11 memorandum to Tru-man, Stimson prophesied "that it would not be possible to use our possession of the atomic bomb as a direct lever to produce the change" desired inside Eastern Europe. If Soviet-American negotia-

[33]Quoted in Lisle A. Rose, *Dubious Victory: The United States and the End of World War II* (Kent State, 1973), p. 363.

[34]Raymond Dennet and Robert K. Turner, eds., *Documents on American Foreign Relations*, VIII (1945–1946) (Princeton, 1948): 601–602.

tions continue with "this weapon rather ostentatiously on our hip, their suspicions and their distrust of our purposes and motives will increase." He again urged direct, bilateral talks with Stalin to formulate control of the bomb and to write a general peace settlement.[35] Stimson's advice was especially notable because several months before he himself had hoped to use the bomb to pry the Soviets out of Eastern Europe. Now he had changed his mind.

Truman again turned Stimson's advice aside. A month later the President delivered a speech larded with references to America's monopoly of atomic power, then attacked Russia's grip on Eastern Europe. Molotov quickly replied that peace could not be reconciled with an armaments race advocated by "zealous partisans of the imperialist policy." In this connection, he added, "We should mention the discovery of . . . the atomic bomb."[36]

With every utterance and every act, the wartime alliance further disintegrated. Stalin understood and regimented the Russian people for the struggle. Americans did not yet understand. Public and congressional opinion followed, not shaped, presidential and State Department policy. Harriman and other officials had defined the issues and called for a tough policy before Congress or its constituents knew about an "iron fence." In this, as in most foreign-policy issues, the executive branch could create a public opinion for policies it believed in the national interest.[37] American interest was not threatened by a possible Soviet invasion of Western Europe. As the State Department informed Truman in June 1945, the Russians "are not too greatly concerned about developments in Western Europe so long as the Western European countries do not show signs of ganging up on them."[38]

A U.S. intelligence report spelled out Stalin's military problems in a stunning analysis of November 1945. The report listed Soviet military weaknesses and "the time required to remedy" them so the U.S.S.R. would be "willing to risk a major armed conflict:"[39]

[35] See Henry Stimson and McGeorge Bundy, *On Active Service in Peace and War* (New York, 1948), pp 638–650.

[36] *Department of State Bulletin*, XIII (October 28, 1945): 653–656; V. Molotov, *U.S.S.R. Foreign Policy* (Shanghai, 1946), pp. 7–8.

[37] For the best analysis of this general problem, see Bernard Cohen, *The Public's Impact on Foreign Policy* (New York, 1973), especially pp. 155–156 on Acheson.

[38] *FRUS: Berlin*, I: 264.

[39] A superb analysis is in Matthew A. Evangelista, "Stalin's Postwar Army Reappraised," *International Security*, VII (Winter 1982–1983): 121–122.

1. War losses in manpower and industry (15 years)
2. Lack of technicians (5–10 years)
3. Lack of a Strategic Air Force (5–10 years)
4. Lack of a modern navy (15–20 years for a war involving major naval operations)
5. Poor condition of railway and military transportation systems and equipment (10 years)
6. Vulnerability of Soviet oil, rail, and vital industrial centers to long-range bombers
7. Lack of atomic bomb (5–10 years, possibly less)
8. Resistance in occupied countries (5 years or less)
9. Quantitative military weakness in the Far East — especially naval (15–20 years)

The report concluded that Russia would be unlikely to chance a major war for at least fifteen years. Since half the transport of the standing Soviet army was horse-drawn (and would remain so until 1950), fifteen years seemed a safe estimate.

Thus at the outset of the Cold War, Truman's problem was certainly not the threat of Soviet invasion of Asia or Europe. Nor was it American public opinion. The problem lay in Eastern Europe, where Stalin militarily roped off the region — and thus directly challenged the Atlantic Charter principles and the growing belief in Washington that the American system could only work globally. The division of Germany was set. Poland and Eastern Europe sank behind an "iron fence." The question now became: How would the world's most powerful nation respond to these frustrations of its dreams for the postwar world?

2

Only Two Declarations of Cold War (1946)

In late 1945, General George Patton, as heroic a figure to some Americans in the 1980s as in the 1940s, addressed eight-year-olds in a Sunday School class. "You are the soldiers and nurses of the next war. There will be another war," Patton assured the children. "There has always been."[1]

During 1946 war became more imminent than even Patton had expected. In Manchuria, Iran, Turkey, and Europe, the American and Russian military forces confronted one another. Several times they approached flashpoint. The crisis did not develop quite so far in China, but that situation was nevertheless critical, for the United States was losing a position in the western Pacific won during the war with American blood.

Harry Truman determined to maintain that position. "The future foreign interests of the United States will be in the Western Hemisphere and in the Pacific," he told an advisor in September 1945. The President believed Asian interests depended upon strengthening the Nationalist Chinese regime of Chiang Kai-shek. Chiang was to replace Japan as the stabilizing force in the area.

[1]Quoted in L. Wittner, *Rebels Against War . . . 1941–1960* (New York, 1969), p. 98.

And then there would also be economic benefits. By working through Chiang, Washington officials believed they could develop not only the great China market but other Asian countries as well. For more than a century Yankee tradesmen had pursued the mirage of that market. It now finally seemed real. A billion Asian customers would be of considerable help in avoiding another economic depression. John Carter Vincent, the State Department's expert on China, encouraged restoration of postwar trade "with all the speed we can generate. We are endeavoring to get businessmen back into China for their sake and for China's sake."[2] Whether a China could be created that would be both strong and friendly to Western interests was a question the West had avoided facing for a century.

This ambitious policy banged immediately into a major obstacle. Chiang's control was being chipped away by communist forces led by Mao Tse-tung. Although outnumbered five to one in 1945, Mao's army had increased dramatically since 1935 when Chiang had isolated it in northern China. At the end of World War II, the communists controlled one-fifth of China and more than 105 million people. Chiang's regime, meanwhile, was shot through with corruption, squandered more than a billion dollars of American aid, and drove the peasants (who comprised four-fifths of the population) into Mao's hands. Of special importance, the Nationalists could not control a roaring inflation that shot prices up some 2000 percent between 1937 and 1945, nearly wiping out the middle classes.

Intent on preventing a Communist China, Roosevelt, then Truman, developed a policy that first aimed at separating Mao from the Soviets. In 1945 FDR obtained Stalin's promise to deal with Chiang, not Mao. In return for this pledge and his promise to enter the war against Japan, Stalin received substantial territorial concessions: the lease of Port Arthur as a Soviet naval base, internationalization of the port of Darien, joint Sino-Soviet operation of the Chinese-Eastern and South Manchurian railroads, possession of southern Sakhalin and the Kurile Islands (then held by Japan), and a plebiscite to be held in Outer Mongolia (which in October 1945 voted under Soviet supervision to become independent of China and move closer to Russia by the amazing score of 483,291 to 0).

[2]"Seymour to Foreign Office," 24 November 1945, FO 371 F11517/36/10, Public Record Office, London.

Chiang and Stalin agreed to most of these terms in a Treaty of Friendship and Alliance. The State Department and such periodicals as Henry Luce's *Time-Life* publications, which kept close watch over American interests in Asia, cheered the treaty.

Only Mao was bitter. He later recalled that "Stalin tried to prevent the Chinese Revolution by saying . . . we must collaborate with Chiang." Soviet policy was clear. Stalin preferred a chaotic, divided China that would not threaten Russia rather than a united China under either Chiang or Mao. As head of a giant nation, Mao could particularly challenge Stalin within the communist world.[3]

With Mao's regime apparently isolated, the State Department moved to the next goal: ending the civil war by forcing Mao and Chiang into a coalition that Chiang could control. But Chiang refused to be locked into the same room with the communists. He had more direct methods. When asked about the danger of Russian-Chinese communist cooperation, Chiang replied "there is nothing to worry about" because he "was going to liquidate Communists."[4] Knowing that approach would not work, Truman pressured Chiang to accept the coalition idea.

Chiang-Mao talks broke down over whose army would control Manchuria, a key industrial area occupied by Japan since 1931. In the autumn of 1945, the problem became more complicated and ominous when Russian armies moved into Manchuria to disarm the Japanese, then remained to carry out what officials on the scene termed "scientific looting" of industrial machinery for the rebuilding of Russian industry.[5] Mao and Chiang raced to control Manchuria. Mao won, despite Truman's attempt to help Chiang by keeping Japanese soldiers in place against the communists until Chiang's troops could move into position. The President even dispatched 50,000 American soldiers to help Chiang push northward. Soon 100,000 Americans were in China.

With Chiang's position eroding, Truman sent General of the Army George Marshall on his famous mission to reconcile Chiang and Mao in order, in the general's words, to avert "the tragic consequences of a divided China and of a probable Russian reassumption

[3] Seymour Topping, *Journey Between Two Chinas* (New York, 1972), p. 54.

[4] Daily Staff Summary, February 26, 1945, Lot File, NA, RG 59.

[5] "Memorandum for the President," 17 September 1945, OSS Memoranda for the President, Donovan Chronological File, Box 15, Truman Library.

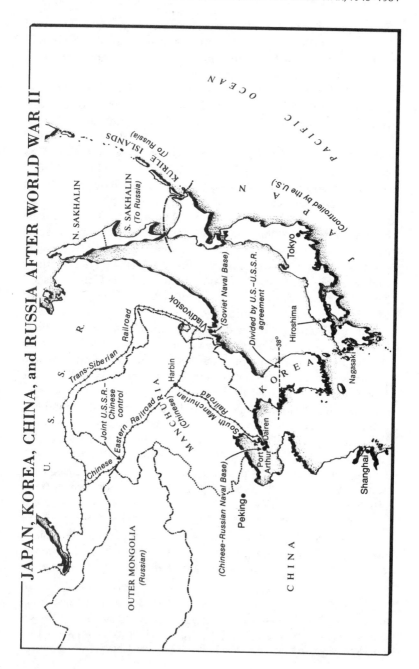

JAPAN, KOREA, CHINA, and RUSSIA AFTER WORLD WAR II

PACIFIC OCEAN

KURILE ISLANDS
(To Russia)

N. SAKHALIN

S. SAKHALIN
(To Russia)

J A P A N
(Controlled by the U.S.)

Tokyo

(Soviet Naval Base)

Divided by U.S.–U.S.S.R. agreement

Hiroshima

38°

Nagasaki

Vladivostok

R.

Trans-Siberian Railroad

S.

S.

U.

Joint U.S.S.R.–Chinese control

Chinese Eastern Railroad

Harbin

M A N C H U R I A

South Manchurian Railroad

K O R E A

(Chinese) Railroad

Dairen

Port Arthur

(Chinese-Russian Naval Base)

OUTER MONGOLIA
(Russian)

Peking

C H I N A

Shanghai

of power in Manchuria, the combined effect of this resulting in the defeat or loss of the major purpose of our war in the Pacific."[6] Few Americans dissented from Marshall's analyses of the potential Russian danger.

By late February 1946 Marshall had worked out an agreement, including a cease-fire. This was the closest the United States or the Chinese themselves would come to a peaceful settlement. By mid-April the arrangement had collapsed. Marshall later placed much blame on Chiang for this disaster, since the latter insisted on taking Manchuria by force. The American, however, also noted that toward the end of the negotiations the communists were unwilling "to make a fair compromise," particularly on the disposition of their army.[7]

Believing he could defeat the communists militarily and that the United States had no alternative but to provide him with all the arms he required, Chiang refused Marshall's suggestions for further compromise. The Chinese leader sadly miscalculated. As the State Department had feared, Mao's armies obtained a treasure when, in March and April 1946, Soviet occupation troops in Manchuria suddenly withdrew, leaving behind vast stores of Japanese arms and equipment for the communist forces. Chiang launched a major military offensive into Manchuria. At first he was successful, then his army overstretched its supply lines. By late 1946 Mao was successfully counterattacking.

As the military tide began to turn, even worse lay in wait for Americans. They would suffer for their involvement with Chiang. American officials warned that "widespread resentment" by the Chinese people "which cannot be openly expressed is being turned almost entirely against the U.S." Even the American troops were being pressured to leave. It was a terrible dilemma. If the United States remained, it would be "an immediately available target . . . for . . . Chinese xenophobia." On the other hand, Chiang required American aid. "If we break" with him, a top White House advisor observed, "the result will be that we will have no friends in either of the Chinese factions and no friends in China."[8]

[6]Quoted in Tang Tsou, *America's Failure in China, 1941–1950* (Chicago, 1963), pp. 355–356.

[7]For Marshall's later assessment and hope for a liberal middle way for China, see Department of State, *U.S. Relations with China* (Washington, 1949), pp. 686–689.

[8]Daily Staff Summary, January 8, 1947, Lot File, NA RG 59.

Marshall cut through to the core of the problem. If Americans tried to save Chiang they would "virtually [have] to take over the Chinese government. . . . It would involve the [United States] in a continuing commitment from which it would practically be impossible to withdraw" and could make China "an arena of international conflict."[9] Neither Truman nor Marshall would get sucked into that kind of war. The President tried to cover his retreat after late 1946 with a small aid program for Chiang, but Truman was pulling out of China. He and Marshall could only hope that the revolution would not be completed "for a long time."

Stalin shared that hope. Indeed, Truman could downgrade China precisely because the Russians had withdrawn from Manchuria and were behaving throughout Asia. On the other hand, viewing international events in the context of the American-Soviet confrontation forced Washington officials to give top priority to European and Middle Eastern affairs. As China dropped down the American priority list in 1946, these two elements—Washington's determination to counter all Soviet threats, and total commitment to keeping Western Europe within the American camp—fused and exploded into a dramatic crisis in the Middle East.

For nearly a century the Middle East had formed the lifeline of the British and French empires. More recently it provided the Western world with oil. American companies had moved into a dominating position in the petroleum industry. In order to protect this vital area, the British, Russians, and Americans had agreed in 1942 to occupy Iran jointly. They further agreed to withdraw six months after the conflict ended. Several times during the war Churchill and Roosevelt assured Stalin that Russia, which bordered Iran, would have its interests protected in the postwar settlement. By 1944, however, the State Department was developing a tough policy to fight Soviet claims.[10]

By early 1946 most of the British and American forces had withdrawn, but the Russians stalled. They demanded oil concessions

[9]Daily Staff Summary, January 8, 1947, Lot File, NA, RG 59; Leahy diaries, Box 5, August 12, 1946, Leahy Papers; Akira Iriye, *The Cold War in Asia* (Englewood Cliffs, New Jersey, 1974), p. 166.

[10]The best analysis is Mark Lytle, "American-Iranian Relations 1941–1947 and the Redefinition of National Security," unpublished doctoral dissertation, Yale University, 1973, especially chapters III–VI.

approximating those obtained by the British. The Soviets then supported a revolt of the Azerbaijanian population in northern Iran. The State Department panicked. The Russians seemed on the move everywhere, a top official warned, not only in the east and west but through this "third barrier" in the south. They threatened to "sweep unimpeded across Turkey . . . into the Mediterranean and across Iran . . . into the Indian Ocean."[11]

Washington officials decided on a two-pronged policy. First they took the Iranian case to the United Nations. The opening session of the new Security Council was thus poisoned by a bitter exchange between the Soviets and Americans. Second, when Russian tanks rumbled toward the Iranian border in early March, Secretary of State James F. Byrnes smacked one fist into his other hand and declared, "Now we'll give it to them with both barrels." Byrnes sent a message to the Soviets that they must withdraw from the country. In late March, Iran and Russia announced that the Red Army would leave and a joint Iranian-Soviet oil company would be formed subject to ratification of the Iranian Parliament (the Majlis). The Iranian army then put down the Azerbaijan revolt. Several months later the Majlis rejected the oil company. Russia had suffered a major diplomatic defeat.

Another setback quickly followed in Turkey. This crisis had grown from historic Russian-Turkish antipathy, Soviet determination to gain joint control of the strategic Dardanelles Straits (the key link between the Mediterranean and Soviet ports on the Black Sea), and Stalin's inherited Georgian trait of hating everything Turkish except tobacco. In early 1945 he revived an ancient Russian demand for partnership with the Turks to control the straits. Again, during the war FDR and Churchill had assured Stalin that Russia was "justified" in having access to the Mediterranean, particularly since Turkey had collaborated with Hitler.[12] And again, as in Iran, by 1945 the British and Americans had changed their minds. They were determined to keep the Soviets away from the Mediterranean.

Quiet diplomatic probing by both sides followed until August 1946, when Stalin sent a note to Turkey which Under Secretary of

[11] *FRUS, 1946, Near East,* pp. 1–5.

[12] Adam Ulam, *Expansion and Coexistence* (New York, 1968), pp. 430–431; "Record of Meeting at the Kremlin," October 9, 1944, PREM 3, 434/7, Public Record Office, London.

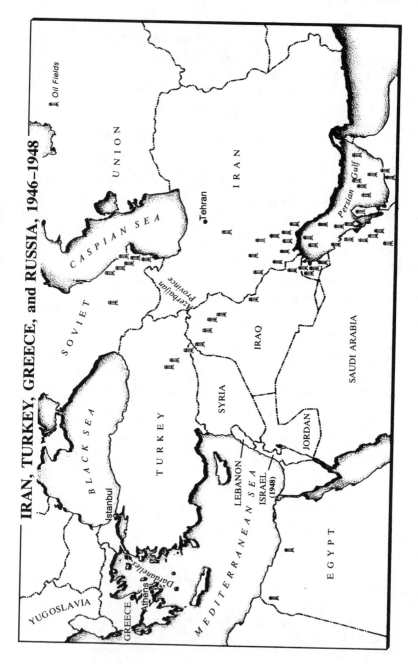

IRAN, TURKEY, GREECE, and RUSSIA, 1946–1948

State Dean Acheson interpreted as a Soviet attempt to dominate Turkey, threaten Greece, and intimidate the remainder of the Middle East. Acheson advised a showdown with the Russians before the fall of Turkey led to the collapse of "the whole Near and Middle East," then even "India and China." Here, as in the Iranian crisis, American officials justified their policy on the basis of what would later be termed the "domino theory." This theory rested on the assumption that Stalin, like Hitler, was intent on unlimited conquest. That assumption was another vivid demonstration that using a false historical analogy is one of the most dangerous forms of argument. Soviet policy in 1946 and Hitler's ambitions of 1938 were not comparable. But few officials (or historians) wished to point that out at the start of the Cold War.

Harry Truman saw nothing wrong with Acheson's view. "We might as well find out whether the Russians were bent on world conquest now as in five or ten years," the President asserted.[13] So he informed the Soviets that Turkey would continue to be "primarily responsible" for the straits. The State Department then reinforced an American naval unit (including marines) which had been sailing in the Mediterranean since early spring. The *Franklin D. Roosevelt*, the most powerful American aircraft carrier, moved into the area. By the autumn of 1946, Soviet pressure on Turkey had eased. A tough Washington response had kept the dominoes upright.

Stalin probably believed that, because of its wartime sacrifices and geographic location, Russia had as much right to Iranian oil and control of the Dardanelles as any other power. Thwarted in these areas, in February 1946, Stalin brought charges in the Security Council against the British repression of the Greek rebellion and British and Dutch attempts to suppress revolution in Indonesia. The bitterest outburst occurred three months later at the Paris Foreign Ministers conference. Molotov gave the Soviet view of what was occurring:

> Nineteenth century imperialism may be dead in England, but there are new twentieth century tendencies. When Mr. Churchill calls for a new war and makes militant speeches on two continents, he represents the worst of 20th century imperialism. . . . Britain has troops in Greece, Palestine, Iraq, Indo-China and elsewhere. Russia

[13]James Forrestal, *The Forrestal Diaries*, Walter Millis, ed. (New York, 1951), p. 192; Thomas Paterson, *Soviet-American Confrontation* (Baltimore, 1973), pp. 192–193.

has no troops outside of security zones and their lines of communication. This is different. We have troops only where provided by treaties. Thus we are in Poland, for example, as our Allies are in Belgium, France and Holland. I also recall that Egypt is a member of UNO [the United Nations]. She demands that British troops be withdrawn. Britain declines. . . . What shall we say of UNO when one member imposes its authority upon another? How long can such things go on?[14]

During early 1946 Stalin and Churchill issued their declarations of Cold War. In an election speech of February 9, the Soviet dictator announced that Marxist-Leninist dogma remained valid, for "the unevenness of development of the capitalist countries" could lead to "violent disturbance" and the consequent splitting of the "capitalist world into two hostile camps and war between them." War was inevitable as long as capitalism existed. The Soviet people must prepare themselves for a replay of the 1930s by developing basic industry instead of consumer goods and, in all, making enormous sacrifices demanded in "three more Five-Year Plans, I should think, if not more."[15] There would be no peace, internally or externally. These words profoundly affected Washington. Supreme Court Justice William Douglas, one of the reigning American liberals, believed that Stalin's speech meant "The Declaration of World War III."[16]

Winston Churchill delivered his reply at Fulton, Missouri, on March 5. The former prime minister exalted American power with the plea that his listeners recognize that "God has willed" the United States, not "some Communist or neo-Fascist state" to have atomic bombs. To utilize the "breathing space" provided by these weapons, Churchill asked for "a fraternal association of the English-speaking peoples" operating under the principles of the United Nations, but not inside that organization, to reorder the world. This unilateral policy must be undertaken because "From Stettin in the Baltic to Trieste in the Adriatic, an iron curtain has descended across the Continent" allowing "police government" to rule Eastern Europe.

---

[14] Arthur Vandenberg, Jr., ed., *The Private Papers of Senator Vandenberg* (Boston, 1952), pp. 277–278.

[15] J. V. Stalin, *Speech Delivered by J. V. Stalin at a Meeting of Voters of the Stalin Electoral Area of Moscow, February 9, 1946* (Washington, Embassy of the U.S.S.R., March 1946).

[16] *Forrestal Diaries*, pp. 134–135.

The Soviets, he emphasized, did not want war: "What they desire is the fruits of war and the indefinite expansion of their power and doctrines."[17]

The "iron curtain" phrase made the speech famous, but, as Churchill himself observed, the "crux" of the message lay in the proposal that the Anglo-Americans, outside the United Nations and with the support of atomic weaponry (the title of the address was "The Sinews of Peace"), create "a unity in Europe from which no nation should be permanently outcast." The Soviets perceived this as a direct challenge to their power in Eastern Europe. Within a week Stalin attacked Churchill and his "friends" in America, whom he claimed resembled Hitler by holding a "racial theory" that those who spoke the English language "should rule over the remaining nations of the world." This, Stalin warned, is "a set-up for war, a call to war with the Soviet Union."[18]

Within a short period after the Churchill speech, Stalin launched a series of policies which, in retrospect, marks the spring and summer of 1946 as a milestone in the Cold War. During these weeks the Soviets finally rejected the terms of a $1 billion American loan after having worked for such a loan during the previous fifteen months. They also refused to become a member of the World Bank and the International Monetary Fund. These rejections ended the American attempt to use the lure of the dollar to make the Soviets retreat in Eastern Europe and join the capitalist-controlled bank and IMF. Actually there had never been reason to hope. Control of their border areas was worth more to the Russians than $1 billion, or even $10 billion. Moreover, as early as September 1944 an American intelligence report had indirectly warned against trying to use financial pressure. It observed that with internal sacrifices Russia "could carry through this reconstruction with its domestic resources, without foreign loans or reparations."[19] The State Department either did not read or believe such reports. By 1946, however, the attempt to buy off the Soviets had worked no better than Washington's vague hope that the atomic bomb might somehow make them more "manageable."

[17] Text in *The New York Times*, March 6, 1946, p. 4.

[18] Interview in *Pravda*, reprinted in *The New York Times*, March 14, 1946.

[19] "Memorandum for Baruch from Sam Lubell," March 1945, Papers of Bernard Baruch, Princeton University Library, Princeton, New Jersey.

At home Stalin announced a new five-year plan, then initiated an intense ideologic effort to eliminate Western influences, purify and propagate Stalinist dogma, and deify the dictator himself. The name of Andrei Zhdanov soon became synonymous with this campaign. One close observer described this supposed "intellectual" of the Politburo as "short, with a brownish clipped mustache, high forehead, pointed nose, and sickly red face," who had "some knowledge of everything," but did not know a single field thoroughly, "a typical intellectual who became acquainted with and picked up knowledge of other fields through Marxist literature." Zhdanov prophesied that Marxism-Leninism had a messianic destiny, "the right to teach others a new general human morality."[20]

The Stalinist and Churchillian declarations of Cold War appeared by the summer of 1946 to have a dramatic effect on those two touchstones of world politics, Germany and the control of atomic weapons. In Germany reparations were the central issue. Secretary of State Byrnes attempted to meet Russian fears of a remilitarized Germany by proposing that the Big Four powers sign a treaty unifying the country and guaranteeing its demilitarization. Molotov rejected this because of a key Russian policy change on reparations. Sometime during the spring the Soviets stopped removing machinery from eastern Germany and determined instead to produce goods in their zone, where labor and resources were more readily available, then ship the products to Russia. While Molotov was rejecting Byrnes's overture, General Lucius Clay informed Russian commanders in Germany in May that no more reparations would be removed from the Western zones. These areas, Clay feared, were becoming bankrupt. Unless reparations were stopped and the zones rebuilt, he was convinced the population had little chance for survival. Molotov's and Clay's moves were decisive moments in the Cold War, for they terminated any real hope of useful negotiations on Germany. Each power had now set out to develop its own zone.

[20]Milovan Djilas, *Conversations with Stalin* (New York, 1961), pp. 149–150; Frederick C. Barghoorn, "Great Russian Messianism in Postwar Soviet Ideology." In Ernest J. Simmons, ed., *Continuity and Change in Russian and Soviet Thought* (Cambridge, Mass., 1955), pp. 545–546.

Byrnes analyzed this growing rigidity in a highly publicized speech at Stuttgart, Germany, on September 6. The secretary of state announced that Germany must develop exports in order to be "self-sustaining," refused to recognize the Oder-Neisse boundary for eastern Germany, specified that Germans should be given primary responsibility for running their own affairs (this was particularly frightening to the Russians and the French), and emphasized that the American presence in Central Europe would not be withdrawn. This was the first time a high American official had said such things publicly. The speech, however, was historical, not prophetic; it only summarized events of the previous eighteen months.

A second occurrence in the summer of 1946 intensified the Cold War. Since Hiroshima, the horror of atomic energy had overhung every diplomatic exchange. In March 1946 the United States released a plan for the control of the atom, the so-called Acheson-Lilienthal proposal. This report suggested a series of stages through which the world could pass to international control of atomic weapons. Throughout the transition period the United States, possessing the only atomic bombs, would remain in a favored position while other nations agreed to be inspected by international agencies. A month later Truman named Bernard Baruch as the first American delegate to a new United Nations Atomic Energy Commission. American policy soon began to change. Deeply suspicious by nature, Baruch distrusted the Acheson–Lilienthal report, partly because he had not sat on the committee and partly because it said nothing about the Russian veto in the Security Council.

Baruch determined to eliminate any Soviet power to veto inspections or sanctions. The Acheson-Lilienthal report, on the other hand, planned to obtain Russian agreement to general principles and then discuss the veto problem. Baruch became increasingly bitter about Under Secretary of State Acheson (whom he mistakenly accused of recording their telephone conversations) and those "One Worlders" like columnist Walter Lippmann "whom I can't understand any more." All the "One Worlders" criticized Baruch's belief that he could force the Soviets to surrender their veto power.[21] But he finally triumphed by convincing Truman that it was better to be tough with Russia sooner rather than later. After recalling the dis-

[21] Acheson file, Atomic Energy, Baruch Papers, especially telephone conversation between Baruch and Acheson, November 26, 1946.

mantling of the American Navy in the 1920s, the President agreed: "We should not under any circumstances throw away our gun until we are sure the rest of the world can't arm against us."[22] Military and political advisors bolstered this view by avowing that Russia could not build atom bombs for at least five to fifteen years. Only a few scientists warned that the period might be considerably shorter.

In a dramatic speech at the United Nations in June, Baruch presented his plan: atomic energy would be controlled through international management of the necessary raw materials and inspection by international agencies, no vetoes of these controls and inspections would be allowed, and majority vote would rule. In the realm of peaceful uses of atomic energy, an Atomic Development Authority, again free of the veto, would establish atomic plants not according to need (as in underdeveloped areas or in large stretches of Russia) but according to strategic and geographic criteria. By controlling a majority within the authority, the United States could thus control the development of the industrial uses of nuclear energy *within* the Soviet Union.

This was totally unacceptable to the Russians. They countered by demanding destruction of all atomic bombs, the cessation of their production, agreement of all powers not to use these weapons, and then a discussion of controls. When they offered to bargain, Baruch retorted they must accept the entire American plan or there would be no plan. So there was no plan. Instead, Congress established a United States Atomic Energy Commission under the Atomic Energy Act of 1946. Under strong military pressure, the act prohibited an exchange of information on the use of atomic energy with any nation until Congress should decide by joint resolution that "effective" international controls were in force. That, obviously, would be a long time off.

So, a year after Japan's surrender, the Pandora's box of atomic power remained open, Byrnes's speech illustrated the deadlock over Germany, and Russian-American loan discussions had collapsed. Stalin and Churchill had issued world-shaking statements. But — significantly — Harry Truman had not. He and other Americans even reacted coldly to Churchill's suggestion of an Anglo-American partnership that would tie the United States to a declining, nearly

---

[22]"BMB [Bernard M. Baruch] Memorandum of Meeting on June 7, 1946, with the President and J.F. Byrnes," Truman file, Atomic Energy, Baruch Papers.

bankrupt England. The President publicly offered no alternative to Churchill's. Throughout 1946, even during the Iranian and Turkish crises, Truman never publicly condemned Soviet policy.

No one doubted that the Western world would be shaped by Truman's decisions. On the train ride to Fulton, Missouri, Churchill delighted his hosts when he recited by memory long portions of John Greenleaf Whittier's poetry. Truman meanwhile walked up to the engine. While the Britisher quoted American authors, the President drove the train. It was all appropriate. Throughout 1945–1946 Truman had confronted the Russians, but he had not formulated a coherent policy or a consensus at home to support such a comprehensive policy. The question was in which direction, and how rapidly, Truman would drive the train of the Western nations.

By the autumn the President's task was, oddly, made more difficult as the Soviets became quiet. Truman's problem was no longer centered on the threat of immediate Russian expansion, as in Iran or Turkey. It rapidly became the infinitely more complex chore of rebuilding war-devastated Western Europe as it entered perhaps the harshest winter in living memory. Great Britain was so deeply discouraged that a radical swing to the left seemed politically possible. Parts of Central Europe faced starvation. France was chaotic. Truman had so feared a French Communist party seizure of power from within that in May he secretly ordered the United States Army in Germany to prepare for a march into France.[23] The West was threatened not by the Red Army, but by internal collapse. Truman's closest advisors urged him to use massive economic and military aid "to build up a world of our own" before the Soviets won by default.[24]

But for the President this advice seemed only a pipe dream. Congress and the American people would respond to a Soviet attack; spending billions of the taxpayers' dollars in Europe, however, was different. Americans recalled with bitterness how ungrateful Europeans appeared for help given during World War I. Nor would it be popular to enrich England and France, whose trade practices and imperial policies had long angered the United States. Moreover, Americans had sacrificed during the war. Now they wanted to spend on themselves. This was not easy, for a rush of

[23] FRUS, 1946, Europe, V: 435–438.

[24] The best discussion of this approach is Richard M. Freeland, The Truman Doctrine and McCarthyism (New York, 1972), pp. 56–57; see also John Lewis Gaddis, The United States and the Origins of the Cold War (New York, 1972), pp. 321–322.

inflation, labor strikes, and meat shortages in late 1946 wounded both the economy and Truman's popularity. Many Americans believed that if the President wanted to help someone he should help them by cutting taxes. Truman's difficulties came into the open during the autumn of 1946, when he was attacked by liberals for being too militaristic and by conservatives for his economic policies.

The liberal attack was led by Henry Agard Wallace, a great secretary of agriculture during the early New Deal, Vice President from 1941 to 1945, maneuvered out of the vice-presidential nomination in 1944 so Harry Truman could be FDR's running mate, and finally secretary of commerce in 1945. Here he devoted himself to the cause of what he liked to call the "Common Man," by extending increased loans to small businessmen and, above all, enlarging the economic pie by increasing foreign trade. Wallace soon discovered that Truman threatened to clog the trade channels to Russia, Eastern Europe, perhaps even China, with his militant attitude toward the Soviets.

At a political rally in New York on September 12, 1946, Wallace delivered a speech, cleared personally, and too rapidly, by Truman. The address focused on the necessity of a political understanding with Russia. This, Wallace declared, would require guaranteeing Soviet security in Eastern Europe. He hoped the capitalist and communist systems could compete "on a friendly basis" and "gradually become more alike." Wallace, however, added one proviso for his happy ending: in this competition "we must insist on an open door for trade throughout the world. . . . We cannot permit the door to be closed against our trade in Eastern Europe any more than we can in China."[25] At that moment Byrnes and Vandenberg were in Paris, painfully and unsuccessfully trying to negotiate peace treaties with Molotov. They immediately demanded Wallace's resignation. On September 20, Truman complied.

The vigor of their reaction to Wallace's speech measured the distance American policy had moved since the close of World War II. Wallace was essentially pleading for a renewal of the administration's invitation of 1945 to the war-decimated Soviet economy to join a friendly game of economic competition with the American industrial mammoth and to play the game according to American

[25] Henry Wallace, "The Way to Peace," *Vital Speeches*, October 1, 1946, pp. 738–741.

rules.[26] By mid-1946 Truman and Byrnes had moved far beyond this. They now assumed that Stalin would not accept such rules but would cooperate only when directly faced with the threat of superior force. Given this background and the ringing declaration of a worldwide open door, little wonder that the Communist party newspaper *Daily Worker* in New York at first attacked Wallace's speech as a cover for "American imperialism." Only after Byrnes and Truman had landed on Wallace did the *Worker* discover virtue in his ideas.

Wallace nevertheless voiced the concerns of many New Dealers. In late September a group of labor leaders met with Harold Ickes and Henry Morgenthau, Jr., two stalwarts of the Roosevelt years, to proclaim support for Wallace's views and to issue a plea to end tests of atomic bombs. Truman was meanwhile convinced that Wallace was a "pacifist," more dangerous than the pro-Nazi groups in the country during World War II, and part of "a sabotage front for Uncle Joe Stalin."[27]

This splitting of the New Deal coalition badly wounded Truman's political fortunes, but worse lay ahead. The President had become so unpopular that only 32 percent of those polled thought he provided adequate leadership. His fellow Democrats did not even ask him for support in the 1946 congressional campaign. They preferred to broadcast recordings of Roosevelt's speeches. The election was a disaster for the administration. Republicans gained solid control of both Senate and House for the first time since 1928. The Republican "Class of 1946," moreover, included such notable conservatives as Joseph McCarthy of Wisconsin, John Bricker of Ohio, George Malone of Nevada, and William Knowland of California. The new legislators had stressed their anticommunism during the campaign, but had also called for deep tax cuts. There seemed little chance they would support any large-scale economic and military program to help Europe, particularly if Stalin remained quiet.[28] Several leading Americans, including Senator J. William Fulbright (Democrat of Arkansas) and columnist Walter Lippmann, suggested that Truman could best serve his country by resigning.

[26]Ronald Radosh, "The Economic and Political Thought of Henry Wallace," unpublished masters thesis, State University of Iowa, 1960, pp. 46–50, 130–134.

[27]Margaret Truman, *Harry S. Truman* (New York, 1973), pp. 346–347.

[28]Susan M. Hartmann, *Truman and the 80th Congress* (New York, 1971), p. 49.

During the last days of 1946 the counterattack began. A group of liberals prepared to meet in Washington to form the Americans for Democratic Action. This organization, in contrast to Wallace's, pledged to continue working within the Democratic party and to fight communism both at home and abroad. Chairing the founding session was Reinhold Niebuhr, theologian, philosopher, historian, and perhaps the most important contemporary influence on American thought. Not since Jonathan Edwards's day of the 1740s had an American theologian so affected his society. Like Edwards, Niebuhr emphasized the importance of sin and sinful power in that society. He disavowed the "sentimental optimism" that had shaped American thought during the 1900 to 1930 era and which again was appearing in the post-1945 world under the guise of "positive thinking."

In a remarkable series of books and lectures, Niebuhr developed his central theme that, because of avarice, finiteness, and inability to realize the limits of their own power, humans were overwhelmed with anxieties and unable to use freedom constructively. This anxiety led to a will-to-power and this, in turn, to conflict. Given such "egoistic corruption in all human virtue,"[29] Niebuhr warned that reason, and particularly faith in science, could not be wholly trusted, for both reason and science often refused to use the religious and historic insights required to solve secular problems.

As the Cold War heightened, Niebuhr stood ready with an explanation and a solution. Communism was at once the worst and most aggressive of societies because its faithful believed they could find a perfect union among the sinful simply by changing economic relationships. Private property, he warned, "is not the cause but the instrument of human egotism."[30] Niebuhr charged that communists overlooked what was more important and ineradicable, the will-to-power. Worse, communism historically had sought to achieve the better society by centralizing power in one or several leaders rather than working out a balance of power within that society. By employing science and so-called scientific rationales, moreover, communism had proven once again to Niebuhr that science is highly serviceable to and easily maneuvered by a totalitarian society.

---

[29]Reinhold Niebuhr, "The Foreign Policy of American Conservatism and Liberalism." In *Christian Realism and Political Problems* (New York, 1953), p. 66.

[30]*The Nation,* March 6, 1948, p. 268.

Since "all life is an expression of power," he believed that the West could only preserve its freedoms by creating the best possible balance-of-power situations. Inside the United States he thought New Deal capitalism offered the most promise. Abroad, no trust could be placed in world government. He supported instead the Baruch Plan for atomic energy (Russia must accept it or "embark upon an isolationist course," Niebuhr wrote, thus giving an interesting liberal view of the supposed alternatives[31]), and wrote article after article in 1946 and 1947 pleading for a revitalized Europe to offset the communist threat.

After a visit to Europe in 1946, Niebuhr fixed upon the German problem. Here again he became an important symbol, and strong influence, in American foreign policy. Niebuhr was one of the earliest to spell out in detail the spiritual, political, and economic unity of the Atlantic community and the pivotal role that Germany must play if Europe was to be saved from communism. "Russian truculence cannot be mitigated by further concessions," he wrote in October 1946. "Russia hopes to conquer the whole of Europe strategically or ideologically." Then came a thrust at Wallace: "It has been the unfortunate weakness of both liberalism and liberal Christianity that they have easily degenerated into sentimentality by refusing to contemplate the tragic aspects of human existence honestly."[32] In applauding the rapid development of the German steel industry in 1947, Niebuhr accepted the "explicit division between East and West which has taken place. . . . Only God can bring order out of this kind of mixture of good and evil. We must, meanwhile, keep our powder dry."[33]

Niebuhr's work thus provided points of departure for criticizing Wallace, condemning communism, formulating a Europe-first policy, and rebuilding Germany. Most important, he provided a historical basis and rationale for the tone, the outlook, the unsaid, and often unconscious assumptions of these years.

But transforming Niebuhr's views into policy would require time. Given the slide of Western Europe and the Republican hold on Congress, Harry Truman did not appear to have enough time or support. Knowledgeable Americans who were usually calm began

[31]*Christianity and Crisis*, July 8, 1946, p. 2.

[32]*Life*, October 21, 1946, pp. 65–72.

[33]*Christianity and Crisis*, August 4, 1947, p. 2.

to sound shrill and desperate. For example, exactly one year after Henry Stimson had advised reasoning with the Soviets, Secretary of the Navy James Forrestal counseled with the retired statesman. "He said," Forrestal recorded in his diary that night, "the way things had now developed he thought we should not delay in going forward with the manufacture of all the atomic missiles we could make."[34] Others agreed with Stimson's suggestion, but it would not prevent the economic collapse of Europe no matter how many missiles were built.

Truman, unlike Churchill and Stalin, had not yet publicly joined the Cold War. The direction and speed of the Western train remained to be determined. Meanwhile the President's winter promised to be nearly as bleak as Europe's.

[34] *Forrestal Diaries*, p. 200.

3

~~~

Two Halves of the Same Walnut (1947-1948)

On March 12, 1947, President Truman finally issued his own declaration of Cold War. Dramatically presenting the Truman Doctrine to Congress, he asked Americans to join in a global commitment against communism. The nation responded. A quarter of a century later, Senator J. William Fulbright declared, "More by far than any other factor the anti-communism of the Truman Doctrine has been the guiding spirit of American foreign policy since World War II."[1]

An odd circumstance, however, must be explained if the Truman Doctrine is to be understood. The Soviet Union had been less aggressive in the months before the President's pronouncement than at any time in the postwar period. Stalin consolidated his hold over Rumania and Poland through manipulated elections, and at home Soviet propagandists encouraged Western socialists and other "proletarians" to undertake revolutionary action. But throughout the winter of 1946–1947, the Soviets acted cautiously. State Department officials privately believed that "the USSR is undergoing serious economic difficulties" which have led to "the less aggressive international attitude taken by Soviet authorities in

[1]J. William Fulbright, *The Crippled Giant* (New York, 1972), pp. 6–24.

recent weeks." This policy was only "a temporary retreat." Nonetheless, the problems seemed so great that the Russians gave military discharges to "hundreds of thousands of young men [who] will now become available for labor force in industry, agriculture and construction."[2] Stalin reduced his 12 million military men of 1945 to between 3 and 4 million in 1947. (American forces dropped from 10 million to 1.4 million, but Americans enjoyed a monopoly of atomic weapons.) Russian military levels would go no lower, for the Red Army was Stalin's counter to Truman's atomic bomb. Poised in Eastern Europe, the troops threatened to take the continent hostage in case of atomic attack on Russia. Stalin had no navy capable of long-range offensive strikes. The fleet depended on 300 submarines geared for defensive purposes.[3]

Truman's immediate problem was not the threat of a Russian invasion. As Dean Acheson privately remarked, the Russians would not make war with the United States "unless they are absolutely out of their minds." The greater danger was that Stalin might be proven correct when he indicated the communists could bide their time since a "general crisis" was becoming so "acute" in the West that it would sweep away "atom-dollar" diplomacy. Communist party power rose steeply in Europe, particularly in France where the first cabinet of the new Fourth Republic contained four communists, including the minister of defense. Chaotic conditions in former colonial areas also opened exceptional opportunities to revolutionaries. The two gems of the British Crown, India and Egypt, shattered the empire with drives for independence. They were soon joined by Pakistan, Burma, Ceylon, and Nepal. France began a long, futile, eight-year war to regain Indochina. The Dutch faced full-scale revolution in Indonesia. The Middle East was in turmoil over the determination of a half-dozen countries to be totally independent, as well as over the influx of 100,000 Jews who hoped to establish a homeland in Palestine.

In late 1946 and early 1947, American officials gave increasing attention to these newly emerging areas. Europe could not be fully stabilized until England, France, and the Netherlands settled their colonial problems. The State Department also assumed that the

[2]Daily Staff Summary, January 3, 1947, January 15, 1947, February 24, 1947, February 10, 1947, Lot File, NA, RG 59.

[3]Thomas Wolfe, *Soviet Power and Europe, 1945–1970* (Baltimore, 1970), pp. 10–11, 33, 45–46.

American economy, as well as the economy of the Western community, which depended upon American prosperity, demanded a proper settlement of these conflicts. In a speech in November 1946, Will Clayton explained that the expansion in the domestic economy and the "depletion of our natural resources" would make the United States much more dependent on the importation of raw materials and minerals. Many of these came from the newly emerging areas. "No nation in modern times," the assistant secretary of state warned, "can long expect to enjoy a rising standard of living without increased foreign trade." Adolf Berle, economist, advisor to Roosevelt and Truman, and State Department official, declared in late 1946 that the Soviets and the United States had begun a battle for the allegiance of the less industrialized nations. "Within four years the world [will] be faced with an apparent surplus in production beyond any previously known," Berle explained. If American surpluses were used to "take the lead in material reconstruction" of the newly emerging countries, the United States could level off those "cycles of 'boom and bust' which disfigured our prewar economy."[4]

"Boom and bust" already threatened. The American economy sagged, and unemployment rose in early 1946 before some expansion began. State Department experts worried that the improvement was temporary, for it rested on a $15 billion American export trade, nearly four times the level of the 1930s. Most of these exports were rebuilding Western Europe, but the Europeans were rapidly running out of dollars to pay for the goods. When its remaining dollars and gold were spent, Europe would stagnate, then perhaps grasp at socialism to save itself. Americans would face the loss of their most vital market and probably the return of the 1930s with all the attendant political consequences. Truman understood this by early 1947, but a tax-cutting Republican Congress and his own low popularity seemed to block any action.

The turn came on Saturday morning, February 21, 1947, when a British embassy official drove to the near-deserted State Department building. He informed Acheson that because of its own economic crisis (more than half its industry was quiet), England could not provide the $250 million of military and economic support needed by Greece and Turkey. As Secretary of State George Marshall

[4]*Documents on American Foreign Relations*, VIII, R. Dennett, ed. (Princeton, 1951): 607–608.

later observed, "It was tantamount to British abdication from the Middle East with obvious implications as to their successor."[5]

American officials were not taken by surprise. From 1944 until early 1947 they had closely watched the British attempt to regain control of Greece become bogged down in a Greek civil war. On one side was a conservative-monarchical group supported by London. On the other was the National Liberation Front (NLF), with communist leadership, which had gained popularity and power by leading resistance efforts against the Nazis. By 1947 the NLF received support from Yugoslav communist leader Josep Broz (Marshal Tito). The Yugoslav was not motivated by affection for his fellow communists in Greece. Rather, he hoped to annex parts of Greece to a large Yugoslav federation. Stalin was not directly involved and indeed developed a strong dislike for Tito's ambitions.

But as NLF strength grew, the United States did become involved. Throughout 1946 it sent special missions, poured in $260 million of aid, and sided with the British. Drawing on this experience, the State Department was able to work out a detailed proposal for assistance within a week after Acheson received the British message. After only nineteen days, Truman could appear before Congress with a complete program. Clearly, the President's request on March 12 for $400 million in Greek and Turkish aid (the Truman Doctrine speech) was not a sudden, drastic departure in American foreign policy.

But the reasoning in Truman's speech was radically new. That reasoning was worked out by American officials who had long been waiting for this opportunity. As they developed the speech, "they found release from the professional frustrations of years," as one later declared. "It seemed to those present that a new chapter in world history had opened and they were the most privileged of men."[6] Those words help explain why the officials made certain choices. For example, they could have determined simply that Greece was in a civil war and therefore the United States had no business intervening. Or they could quietly have asked Congress to continue aid to Greece and Turkey while transferring to those nations weapons left from the war. The administration, however, rejected those alternatives, choosing instead to appear dramatically

[5]James Forrestal, *The Forrestal Diaries*, Walter Millis, ed. (New York, 1951), p. 245.
[6]Joseph M. Jones, *The Fifteen Weeks* (New York, 1955), pp. 146–147.

before Congress to request support for a global battle against communism. A White House advisor remarked that the message would be "the opening gun in a campaign to bring people up to [the] realization that the war isn't over by any means."

As State Department officials prepared drafts of the speech, Truman, Secretary of State Marshall, and Acheson met with congressional leaders. It was not a warm audience. The Republicans were busily cutting taxes 20 percent and chopping $6 billion from Truman's already tight budget. The legislators remained unmoved until Acheson swung into the argument that the threat was not a Greek civil war but Russian communism; its aim was the control of the Middle East, South Asia, and Africa; and this control was part of a communist plan to encircle and capture the ultimate objective, Germany and Europe. It was a struggle between liberty and dictatorship. By defending Greece and Turkey, therefore, Americans were defending their own freedoms. "The Soviet Union was playing one of the greatest gambles in history at minimal cost," Acheson concluded. "We and we alone are in a position to break up the play."[7]

The congressmen were stunned. Silence followed until Arthur Vandenberg (now chairman of the Senate Foreign Relations Committee) told Truman that the message must include Acheson's explanation. As the senator advised, the President "scared hell" out of the American people. Insofar as public opinion was concerned, this tactic worked well for Truman (at least until three years later when Senator Joseph McCarthy and others turned the argument around and accused the administration of too gently handling such a horrible danger). The President also won over Congress with assurances that the United States would not only control every penny of America's aid to Greece but run the Greek economy by controlling foreign exchange, budget, taxes, currency, and credit.

Inside the State Department, however, Acheson ran into opposition. George Kennan, the top expert on Soviet affairs, objected bitterly to sending military assistance to nations such as Turkey that had no internal communist problems and bordered the Soviet Union. Unlike economic help, military aid could be provocative. Acheson rejected the argument. The opportunity to build Turkey's military strength was too good to miss. Thus in the words of one official, "Turkey was slipped into the oven with Greece because that

---

[7]Dean Acheson, *Present at the Creation* (New York, 1969), pp. 292–293.

seemed the surest way to cook a tough bird." Kennan also protested against the harsh ideological tone and open-ended American commitment in the speech drafts. He was joined by Secretary of State Marshall and Charles Bohlen, another expert on Russia, who told Acheson that "there was a little too much flamboyant anticommunism in the speech." Acheson stood his ground. Marshall was informed that Truman believed the Senate would not approve the doctrine "without the emphasis on the Communist danger."[8]

Acheson, however, carefully kept the central economic factors out of the speech. He and Truman wanted a simple ideological call to action that all could understand, not a message that might trigger arguments over American oil holdings in the Middle East. The economic interests were nevertheless crucial. As State Department official Joseph Jones noted, if Greece and similar key areas "spiral downwards into economic anarchy, then at best they will drop out of the United States orbit and try an independent nationalistic policy; at worst they will swing into the Russian orbit," and the result would be a depression worse than that of the 1930s.[9]

Jones's insight was incorporated into a major speech made by Truman at Baylor University on March 6. The address provided the economic dimension to the Truman Doctrine pronounced six days later. The President frankly declared that if the expansion of state-controlled economies (such as the communists') was not stopped, and an open world marketplace restored for private businessmen, depression would occur and the government would have to intervene massively in the society. Americans could then bid farewell to both their traditional economic and personal freedoms. "Freedom of worship—freedom of speech—freedom of enterprise," Truman observed. "It must be true that the first two of these freedoms are related to the third." For "Peace, freedom and world trade are indivisible." He concluded, "We must not go through the thirties again."[10] The President had given the economic reasons for pronouncing the Truman Doctrine. The Baylor speech (written by Acheson and Will Clayton) explained why Americans, if they hoped to

---

[8]George Kennan, *Memoirs, 1925–1950* (Boston, 1967), pp. 315–322; Charles E. Bohlen, *Witness to History, 1929–1969* (New York, 1973), p. 261.

[9]Barton J. Bernstein, ed., *Politics and Policies of the Truman Administration* (Chicago, 1970), p. 57.

[10]*Public Papers of the Presidents . . . Truman . . . 1947* (Washington, 1963), pp. 167–172.

preserve their personal freedom, had to rebuild the areas west of the Iron Curtain before these lands collapsed into anarchy, radical governments, or even communism.

The Truman Doctrine speech itself laid out the ideological and political reasons for the commitment. The President requested $400 million for military and economic aid, but he also asked for something else. Truman warned Congress that the world must now "choose between alternative ways of life." He urged Americans to commit themselves to helping "free peoples" and to opposing "totalitarian regimes." This request, plus Truman's failure to place any geographical limits on where Americans must commit themselves (Africa as well as Germany? Southeast Asia as well as Western Europe?), raised criticism.

Robert Taft of Ohio, the Senate's Republican leader, accused Truman of dividing the world into communist and anticommunist zones, then said flatly, "I do not want war with Russia." On the left, Henry Wallace, traveling in Europe, accused Truman of "reckless adventury" that would cost the world "a century of fear." Senator Vandenberg rushed to the President's defense by calling Wallace an "itinerant saboteur." But such fear was not only on Taft's and Wallace's minds. Shortly before the speech, Acheson told J. Robert Oppenheimer, a leading scientist in the atomic weapons field, "We are entering an adversary relationship with the Soviet," and "we should bear that in mind" while making atomic plans.[11]

Congress wriggled uncomfortably. As Senator Vandenberg began closed-door hearings on what he called "the most fundamental thing that has been presented to Congress in my time," Acheson hedged on whether the Truman Doctrine had any limitations. "If there are situations where we can do something effective, then I think we must certainly do it." But he was clear on one issue: "I think it is a mistake to believe that you can, at any time, sit down with the Russians and solve questions." Only when the West built insuperable bastions of strength would Stalin listen to American terms. Acheson assumed Russia was primarily responsible for the Greek revolution. After all, said Lincoln MacVeagh, United States ambassador to Greece, "Any empire that bases itself on revolution always has expansionist tendencies." (The ambassador was alluding

---

[11]Jones, *Fifteen Weeks*, pp. 175–178; Lloyd Gardner, *Architects of Illusion* (Chicago, 1970), p. 201.

to the revolution of 1917, not 1776.) This view of Soviet involvement was wrong. The Greek problem was caused by internal forces and fueled by Tito for his own purposes. But this point made little difference. The administration asked for a commitment against communism anywhere, not just against the Soviets.

That caused a special problem in Greece, for as MacVeagh admitted, "the best men" in Greece "are the heads of the Communist movement. . . . That is the sad part of it." But Americans had to keep on "trying to make bricks without straw . . . or you are going to lose the country." The Greek government became so brutal that the State Department privately warned it must stop torturing its political prisoners or "the President's program" would be damaged. When criticized for helping the Greek and Turkish right-wing parties, however, Truman could simply ask Americans whether they preferred "totalitarianism" or "imperfect democracies." This settled that question.[12]

The President and Acheson mousetrapped those in Congress who wanted to be both anticommunist and penny pinchers. As a leading Democrat chuckled privately, of course the Republicans "didn't want to be smoked out. . . . They don't like Communism but still they don't want to do anything to stop it. But they are all put on the spot now and they all have to come clean." The President, moreover, had moved so quickly that Congress had no choice but to give him increased powers. "Here we sit," mourned Vandenberg, "not as free agents," but dealing with something "almost like a Presidential request for a declaration of war." "There is precious little we can do," the senator concluded, "except say 'yes.'"[13] Vandenberg was correct. Congress's acceptance of Truman's definition of the crisis marked the point in the Cold War when power in foreign policy formulation began shifting rapidly from Capitol Hill to the White House.

Nine days after his speech, Truman helped ensure his victory by announcing a loyalty program to ferret out security risks in govern-

[12]Material in the preceding two paragraphs is from U.S. Senate, Committee on Foreign Relations, 80th Cong., 1st Sess., *Legislative Origins of the Truman Doctrine: Hearings . . .* (Washington, 1973), pp. 5, 17, 95, 46, 45; *FRUS, 1947,* V: 142–143.

[13]Phone conversation between Carl Vinson and Forrestal, Speech to Congress on Greece file, 13 March 1947, Box 28, Papers of Clark Clifford, Truman Library; Senate, *Legislative Origins,* p. 128.

ment. The first such peace-time program in American history, it was so vaguely defined that political ideas and long-past associations were suddenly made suspect. Most ominously, the accused would not have the right to confront the accuser.[14] Truman thus strikingly dramatized the communist issue, exerting new pressure on Congress to support his doctrine. By mid-May Congress had passed his request by large margins.

The Truman Doctrine was a milestone in American history for at least four reasons. First, it marked the point at which Truman used the American fear of communism both at home and abroad to convince Americans they must embark upon a Cold War foreign policy. This consensus would not break apart for a quarter of a century. Second, as Vandenberg knew, Congress was giving the President great powers to wage this Cold War as he saw fit. Truman's personal popularity began spiraling upward after his speech. Third, for the first time in the postwar era, Americans massively intervened in another nation's civil war. Intervention was justified on the basis of anticommunism. In the future, Americans would intervene in similar wars for supposedly the same reason and with less happy results. Even Greek affairs went badly at first, so badly that in late 1947 Washington officials discussed sending as many as two divisions of Americans to save the situation. That proved unnecessary, for when Yugoslavia left the communist bloc in early 1948, Tito turned inward and stopped aiding the rebels. Deprived of aid, the Greek left wing quickly lost ground. But it had been close, and Americans were nearly involved massively in a civil war two decades before their Vietnam involvement. As it was, the success in Greece seemed to prove that Americans could, if they wished, control such conflicts by defining the problem as "communist" and helping conservatives remain in power.[15]

Finally, and perhaps most important, Truman used the doctrine to justify a gigantic aid program to prevent a collapse of the European and American economies. Later such programs were expanded globally. The President's arguments about anticommunism were

[14]Richard Freeland, *The Truman Doctrine and the Origins of McCarthyism* (New York, 1972), pp. 208–211.

[15]*FRUS, 1947, V:* 466–469; Thomas Paterson, *Soviet-American Confrontation* (Baltimore, 1973), p. 205. An interesting State Department view on how American opinion was changed is in H. Schuyler Foster, "American Public Opinion and U.S. Foreign Policy," *Department of State Bulletin,* XLI (November 30, 1959).

confusing, for the Western economies would have been in grave difficulties whether or not communism existed. The complicated problems of reconstruction and the United States dependence on world
trade were not well understood by Americans, but they easily comprehended anticommunism. So Americans embarked upon the Cold
War for the good reasons given in the Truman Doctrine, which they
understood, and for real reasons, which they did not understand.
Thus, as Truman and Acheson intended, the doctrine became an
ideological shield behind which the United States marched to rebuild
the Western political-economic system and counter the radical left.
From 1947 on, therefore, any threats to that Western system could be
easily explained as communist inspired, not as problems which arose
from difficulties within the system itself. That was the most lasting
and tragic result of the Truman Doctrine.

The President's program evolved naturally into the Marshall
Plan. Although the speech did not limit American effort, Secretary of
State Marshall did by concentrating the administration's attention on
Europe. Returning badly shaken from a Foreign Ministers conference
in Moscow, the secretary of state insisted in a nationwide broadcast
that Western Europe required immediate help. "The patient is sinking," he declared, "while the doctors deliberate." Personal conversations with Stalin had convinced Marshall that the Russians believed
Europe would collapse. Assuming that the United States must lead in
restoring Europe, Marshall appointed a policy planning staff under
the direction of George Kennan to draw up policies.
    Kennan later explained the basic assumption that underlay the
Marshall Plan and, indeed, the entire range of America's postwar
policies between 1947 and the mid-1950s. Excluding the United
States, Kennan observed,

> . . . there are only four aggregations which are major ones from
> the standpoint of strategic realities [that is, military and industrial
> potential] in the world. Two of those lie off the shores of the Eura-
> sian land mass. Those are Japan and England, and two of them lie
> on the Eurasian land mass. One is the Soviet Union and the other is
> that of central Europe. . . .
> Viewed in absolute terms, I think the greatest danger that could
> confront the United States security would be a combination and
> working together for purposes hostile to us of the central European

and the Russian military-industrial potentials. They would really
create an entity . . . which could overshadow in a strategic sense
even our own power. It is not anything, I think, which would be as
easy of achievement as people often portray it as being here. I am
not sure the Russians have the genius for holding all that together
. . . . Still, they have the tendency of political thought, of Communist political expansion.[16]

Building on this premise, round-the-clock conferences in May
1947 began to fashion the main features of the Marshall Plan. Kennan insisted that any aid, particularly military supplies, be limited
and not given to just any area where communists seemed to be enjoying some success. The all-important question then became how to
handle the Russians. Ostensibly, Marshall accepted Kennan's advice
to "play it straight" by inviting the Soviet bloc. In reality, the State
Department made Russian acceptance improbable by demanding
that economic records of each nation be open for scrutiny. For good
measure Kennan also suggested that the Soviets' devastated economy, weakened by war and at that moment suffering from drought
and famine, participate in the plan by shipping Soviet goods to
Europe. Apparently no one in the State Department wanted the
Soviets included. Russian participation would vastly multiply the
costs of the program and eliminate any hope of its acceptance by a
purse-watching Republican Congress, now increasingly convinced
by Truman that communists had to be fought, not fed.

Acheson's speech at Cleveland, Mississippi, in early May and
Marshall's address at Harvard on June 5 revealed the motives and
substance of the plan. In preparing for the earlier speech, Acheson's
advisors concluded that American exports were rapidly approaching the $16 billion mark. Imports, however, amounted to only half
that amount, and Europe did not have sufficient dollars to pay the
difference. Either the United States would have to give credits to
Europeans or they would be unable to buy American goods. The
President's Council of Economic Advisors predicted a slight business recession, and if, in addition, exports dropped in any substantial amount, "the effect in the United States," as one official wrote,

[16]U.S. Senate, Subcommittee to Investigate the Administration of the International
Security Act . . . of the Committee on the Judiciary, 82nd Cong., 1st Sess., *The In-
stitute of Pacific Relations* (Washington, 1951), pp. 1557–1558. (Hereafter cited as
I.P.R. Hearings.)

"might be most serious."[17] Acheson underlined these facts in his Mississippi speech.

At Harvard, Marshall urged Europeans to create a long-term program that would "provide a cure rather than a mere palliative." On June 13 British Foreign Minister Ernest Bevin accepted Marshall's suggestion that Europeans take the initiative. Bevin traveled to Paris to talk with French Foreign Minister Georges Bidault. The question of Russian participation became uppermost in their discussions. *Pravda* had labeled Marshall's speech as a Truman Doctrine with dollars, a useless attempt to save the American economy by dominating European markets. Bidault ignored this; pressured by the powerful French Communist party and fearful that Russia's absence might compel France to join the Anglo-Saxons in a divided Europe dominated by a resurrected Germany,[18] he decided to invite Molotov. The Russian line immediately moderated.

On June 26 Molotov arrived in Paris with eighty-nine economic experts and clerks, then spent much of the next three days conferring over the telephone with Moscow officials. The Russians were giving the plan serious consideration. Molotov finally proposed that each nation individually establish its own recovery program. The French and British proposed instead that Europe as a whole create the proposal for American consideration. Molotov angrily quit the conference, warning that the plan would undermine national sovereignty, revive Germany, allow Americans to control Europe, and, most ominously, divide "Europe into two groups of states . . . creating new difficulties in the relations between them."[19] Within a week after his return to Moscow, the Soviets set their own "Molotov Plan" in motion. The Poles and the Czechs, who had expressed interest in Marshall's proposal, now informed the Paris conference that they could not attend because it "might be construed as an action against the Soviet Union."

As the remaining sixteen European nations hammered out a program for Marshall to consider, the United States moved on another front: it determined to revive Germany quickly. In late 1946 the Americans and British had overridden French opposition to merge economically the United States and British zones in Ger-

---

[17]Jones, *Fifteen Weeks*, p. 207.
[18]For example, *The New York Times*, June 19, 1947, p. 1.
[19]Text in *The New York Times*, July 3, 1947, p. 3

many. Administrative duties were given to Germans. By mid-July 1947 Washington officials so rapidly rebuilt German industry that Bidault finally pleaded with Marshall to slow down or else the French government would never survive to carry through the economic recovery program. The United States nevertheless continued to rebuild German nonmilitary industry to the point where the country would be both self-sufficient and able to aid the remainder of Western Europe. On September 22, the Paris meeting completed its work, pledging increased production, tariff reductions, and currency convertibility in return for American aid. The State Department could view its successes in Germany during the summer as icing on the cake.

The European request for a four-year program of $17 billion of American aid now had to run the gauntlet of a Republican Congress, which was dividing its attention between slashing the budget and attacking Truman, both in anticipation of the presidential election only a year away. In committee hearings in late 1947 and early 1948, the executive presented its case. Only large amounts of government money which could restore basic facilities, provide convertibility of local currency into dollars, and end the dollar shortage would stimulate private investors to rebuild Europe, administration witnesses argued. Then a rejuvenated Europe could offer many advantages to the United States: eradicate the threat of continued nationalization and socialism by releasing and stimulating the investment of private capital; maintain demand for American exports; encourage Europeans to produce strategic goods, which the United States could buy and stockpile; preserve European and American control over Middle Eastern oil supplies from militant nationalism, which might endanger the weakened European holdings; and free Europeans from economic problems so they could help the United States militarily. It would all be like magic.

George Kennan summarized the central problem in a note to Acheson. "Communist activities" were not "the root of the difficulties of Western Europe" but rather "the disruptive effects of the war on the economic, political, and social structure of Europe." So in the final plan Italy, with Europe's largest Communist party, received less aid than other, more economically important nations. In this sense the plan revolved around a rebuilt and autonomous Germany. As Secretary of State Marshall told Congress, "The restoration of Europe involved the restoration of Germany. Without a revival of German production there can be no revival of Europe's economy. But we must be very careful to see that a revived Germany can not again threaten the European community." The Marshall Plan offered a way to circumvent Allied restrictions on German development, for it tied the Germans to a general European program and then offered vast sums to such nations as France which might otherwise be reluctant to support reconstructing Germany.[20]

The Marshall Plan served as an all-purpose weapon for Truman's foreign policy. It charmed those who feared a slump in American exports and who believed, communist threat or no communist threat, that American and world prosperity rested on a vigorous export trade. A spokesman for the National Association of Manufacturers, for example, appeared considerably more moderate toward communism than some government officials when he argued that Europe suffered not from "this so-called communistic surge," but from a "production problem" which only the Marshall Plan could solve.[21] Appropriately, Truman named as administrator of the plan Paul Hoffman, a proven entrepreneur who, as Acheson once observed, preached a "doctrine of salvation by exports with all the passion of an economic Savonarola."[22] The plan also attracted a group, including Reinhold Niebuhr, which placed more emphasis upon the containment of communism. The plan offered all things to all people. Or almost all, for Henry Wallace decided to oppose it in late 1947 on the grounds that only by channeling aid through the United Nations could calamitous relations between the United States and the Soviet Union be avoided.

The Marshall Plan now appears not the beginning but the end of an era. It marked the last phase in the administration's use of economic tactics as the primary means of tying together the Western world. The plan's approach, that peaceful and positive approach which Niebuhr applauded, soon evolved into military alliances. Truman proved to be correct in saying that the Truman Doctrine and the Marshall Plan "are two halves of the same

[20]*FRUS, 1947, III:* 225–229; U.S. House of Representatives, Foreign Affairs Committee, 80th Cong., 1st and 2nd Sess., *United States Foreign Policy for a Post-War Recovery Program . . .* (Washington, 1948), I: 354–359.

[21]U.S. House of Representatives, *U.S. Foreign Policy for a Post-War Recovery Program,* I: 680–681.

[22]Dean Acheson, *Sketches from Life of Men I Have Known* (New York, 1959), p. 19.

walnut." Americans willingly acquiesced as the military aspects of the doctrine developed into quite the larger part.

Why such programs could so easily be transformed into military commitments was explained by George Kennan in a well-timed article appearing in July 1947 under the mysterious pseudonym "Mr. X." Washington's most respected expert on Soviet affairs, Kennan (who once called Niebuhr "the father of us all") had warned throughout the early 1940s against any hope of close postwar cooperation with Stalin. In early 1946 he sent a long dispatch to Washington from Moscow suggesting that at the "bottom of the Kremlin's neurotic view of world affairs is the traditional and instinctive Russian sense of insecurity." In post-1917 Russia, this became highly explosive when mixed with communist ideology and "Oriental secretiveness and conspiracy."[23] This despatch brought Kennan to the attention of Secretary of the Navy James Forrestal, who helped bring the diplomat back to Washington and then strongly influenced Kennan's decision to publish the "Mr. X" article.

The article gave the administration's view of what made the Russians act like communists. The analysis began not by emphasizing "the traditional Russian sense of insecurity" but by assuming that Stalin's policy was shaped by a combination of Marxist-Leninist ideology, which advocated revolution to defeat the capitalist forces in the outside world, and the dictator's determination to use "capitalist encirclement" as a rationale to regiment the Soviet masses so that he could consolidate his own political power. Kennan belittled such supposed "encirclement," although he recognized Nazi-Japanese hatred of the Soviets during the 1930s. (He omitted mentioning specifically the American and Japanese intervention in Russia between 1918 and 1920 and the United States attempt to isolate the Soviets politically through the 1920s.) "Mr. X" believed Stalin would not moderate communist determination to overthrow the Western governments. Any softening of the Russian line would be a diversionary tactic designed to lull the West. For in the final analysis Soviet diplomacy "moves along the prescribed path, like a persistent toy automobile wound up and headed in a given direction,

[23]Barton J. Bernstein and Allen J. Matusow, *The Truman Administration: A Documentary History* (New York, 1966), pp. 198–212; *Forrestal Diaries*, pp. 135–140.

stopping only when it meets some unanswerable force." Endemic Soviet aggression could thus be "contained by the adroit and vigilant application of counterforce at a series of constantly shifting geographical and political points." The United States would have to undertake this containment alone and unilaterally, but if it could do so without weakening its prosperity and political stability, the Soviet party structure would undergo a period of immense strain climaxing in "either the break-up or the gradual mellowing of Soviet power."[24]

The publication of this article triggered one of the more interesting debates of the Cold War. Walter Lippmann was the dean of American journalists and one of those who did not accept the "two halves of the same walnut" argument. He condemned the military aspects of the Truman Doctrine while applauding the Marshall Plan because he disagreed with Kennan's assessment of Soviet motivation. And that, of course, was a crucial point in any argument over American policy. In a series of newspaper articles later collected in a book entitled *The Cold War*,[25] Lippmann argued that Soviet policy was molded more by traditional Russian expansion than by communist ideology. "Stalin is not only the heir of Marx and of Lenin but of Peter the Great, and the Czars of all the Russias." Because of the victorious sweep of the Red Army into Central Europe in 1945, Stalin could accomplish what the czars for centuries had only hoped to obtain. This approach enabled Lippmann to view the Soviet advance as a traditional quest for national security and, in turn, allowed him to argue that Russia would be amenable to an offer of withdrawal of both Russian and American power from Central Europe. The fuses would thus be pulled from that explosive area.

Lippmann outlined the grave consequences of the alternative, the "Mr. X"–Truman Doctrine policy: "unending intervention in all the countries that are supposed to 'contain' the Soviet Union"; futile and costly efforts to make "Jeffersonian democrats" out of Eastern European peasants and Middle Eastern and Asian warlords; either

[24]"The Sources of Soviet Conduct," *Foreign Affairs*, XXV (July 1947): 566–582. Kennan much later believed the essay had been misinterpreted; see George Kennan, *Memoirs, 1925–1950* (Boston, 1967), pp. 364–367. But also see Gardner, *Architects of Illusion*, pp. 270–300.

[25]Walter Lippmann, *The Cold War: A Study in U.S. Foreign Policy* (New York, 1947).

the destruction of the United Nations or its transformation into a useless anti-Soviet coalition; and such a tremendous strain on the American people that their economy would have to be increasingly regimented and their men sent to fight on the perimeter of the Soviet bloc. The columnist warned that if "Mr. X" succeeded in applying counterforce to the "constantly shifting geographical and political points," the Soviets would perforce be allowed to take the initiative in the Cold War by choosing the grounds and weapons for combat. Finally, Lippmann, like the administration, emphasized Germany's importance, but he differed by observing that Russia, which controlled eastern Germany, could, at its leisure, outmaneuver the West and repeat the 1939 Nazi-Soviet pact of offering the ultimate reward of reunification for German cooperation. "The idea that we can foster the sentiment of German unity, and make a truncated Germany economically strong," Lippmann wrote, "can keep her disarmed, and can use her in the anti-Soviet coalition is like trying to square the circle."

Lippmann was profound, but he had no chance of being persuasive. By the end of August 1947, the State Department rejected Lippmann's proposals for disengagement in Germany. American officials instead assumed that the "one world" of the United Nations was "no longer valid and that we are in political fact facing a division into two worlds."[26] The "Mr. X" article also indicated the administration was operating on another assumption: economic development could not occur until "security" was established. This increasing concern with things military became evident in late 1947 when Kennan suggested that the United States change its longstanding hostility to Franco's government in Spain in order to cast proper military security over the Mediterranean area. A year earlier the United States had joined with Britain and France in asking the Spanish people to overthrow Franco by political means because his government was pro-Nazi and totalitarian. Kennan's suggestion marked the turn in Spanish-American relations, which ended in close military cooperation after 1950.[27]

The quest for military security also transformed American pol-

[26] *Forrestal Diaries*, p. 307.
[27] *Forrestal Diaries*, p. 328.

icy in Asia. With Chiang Kai-shek's decline, the State Department searched for a new partner who could help stabilize the Far East. The obvious candidate was Japan, which from the 1890s until 1931 had worked closely with Washington. It was also the potential industrial powerhouse of the area, the Germany of the Orient. Since 1945 the United States had single-handedly controlled Japan. The Soviets had been carefully excluded. Even Australia was allowed to send occupation forces only after promising not to interfere with the authority of General Douglas MacArthur, head of the American government in Japan. MacArthur instituted a new constitution (in which Japan renounced war for all time), then conducted elections which allowed him to claim that the Japanese had overwhelmingly repudiated communism. To the general, as to Washington officials, this was fundamental. In 1946 MacArthur privately compared America in its fight against communism to the agony of Christ at Gethsemane, for "Christ, even though crucified, nevertheless prevailed."[28]

He added that Japan was becoming "the western [sic] outpost of our defenses." In 1947–1948 Japan received the "two halves of the same walnut" treatment. The State Department decided to rebuild Japanese industry and develop a sound export economy. At the same time, American bases on the islands were to be expanded and maintained until, in one official's words, "the at present disarmed soldiers of Japan are provided with arms and training to qualify them to preserve the peace."[29] As in Europe, economic development and security moved hand in hand as Americans buttressed the Pacific portion of their system.

The new security policy underwent a trial run in that long-time laboratory of United States policies, Latin America. After several postponements, the American nations convened at Rio de Janeiro in late summer of 1947. The United States delegation candidly laid out the rules for the conference. There would be no discussion of economic aid, Secretary Marshall explained, because European recovery took precedence over Latin American development. The conference must instead initiate steps toward a collective security arrangement. In doing so, the United States expected each nation to

[28] *Forrestal Diaries*, pp. 177–178.
[29] Leahy Diaries, Box 6, September 22, 1948, Leahy Papers.

take some action against future aggressors, whether that action be military or otherwise. No nation, the American delegation argued, could remain truly neutral.

On September 2 the delegates signed the Rio Treaty providing for collective self-defense for the hemisphere, the first such treaty formulated under Articles 51 and 52 of the United Nations Charter. The treaty provided that an attack against one American nation would be considered as an attack upon all, and that when two-thirds of the hemispheric nations agreed to resist such an attack, all states must cooperate by contributing either troops or supplies.[30] Nine months earlier Vandenberg had lamented that a "Communistic upsurge" in Latin America was dividing the hemisphere, although he provided no evidence of this "upsurge."[31] After the signing of the Rio Treaty, Vandenberg rested more easily: "This is sunlight in a dark world," he informed his Senate colleagues.

The following March the Ninth Inter-American Conference convened at Bogotá, Colombia, to provide yet more sunlight for depressed Washington officials. Again, the United States refused to make any economic commitments. At the most, Marshall hoped that he could use the occasion to create the proper atmosphere so that Latin American laws, particularly those relating to oil resources, might be made more attractive to United States investors. Out of this approach came the Charter of the Organization of American States, which established administrative machinery for hemispheric consultation and an Advisory Defense Committee for military strategy. This much the United States welcomed. The Latin Americans, however, stubbornly insisted on adding a statement of the principles and standards that would govern hemispheric relations. Over American objections, the move carried. Articles 15 and 16 were incorporated in the charter. The first stated: "No State or group of States has the right to intervene, directly or indirectly, for any reason whatever, in the internal or external affairs of any other State." Article 16 was more specific: "No State may use or encourage the use of coercive measures of an economic or political character in order to force the sovereign will of another State and ob-

---

[30]Raymond Dennet and Robert K. Turner, eds., *Documents on American Foreign Relations,* IX (1947) (Princeton, N.J., 1948), 531–543.

[31]Arthur H. Vandenberg, ed., *The Private Papers of Senator Vandenberg* (Boston, 1952), p. 335.

tain from it advantages of any kind.[32] The United States Senate ratified the charter, but this was the last major inter-American conference held during Truman's presidency. The administration had obtained the desired military arrangements and, perhaps, too many
political obligations.

Of special importance to Truman's "security" effort, the President transformed what he termed "the antiquated defense setup of
the United States" by passing the National Security Act through
Congress in July 1947. This bill provided for a single Department of
Defense to replace the three independently run services, statutory
establishment of the Joint Chiefs of Staff, a National Security Council to advise the President, and a Central Intelligence Agency to
correlate and evaluate intelligence activities. James Forrestal, the
stepfather of "Mr. X" and the leading advocate among presidential
advisors of a tough military approach to Cold War problems,
became the first secretary of defense. Forrestal remained until he
resigned in early spring 1949. Two months later on the night of May
22, Forrestal, suffering from mental and physical illness, jumped or
accidentally fell to his death from the twelfth floor of the Bethesda
Naval Hospital.

The military and personal costs of the Truman Doctrine–"Mr.
X" policy would be higher than expected. And the cost became
more apparent as Truman and J. Edgar Hoover (director of the
Federal Bureau of Investigation) carried out the President's Security
Loyalty program. Their search for subversives accelerated after
Canadians uncovered a Soviet spy ring. During hearings in the
Senate on the appointment of David E. Lilienthal as chairman of
the Atomic Energy Commission, the first major charges of "soft on
communism" were hurled by Robert Taft because of Lilienthal's
New Deal background and his opposition to the Baruch position on
the veto in 1946. (See page 41.)

Taft's action sickened Vandenberg, who compared it to "the
'Lynch law,'" but such charges were just beginning. The House Un-
American Activities Committee began to intimate that Truman was
certainly correct in his assessment of communism's evil nature but
lax in destroying it. In March 1948 the committee demanded the
loyalty records gathered by the FBI. Truman handled the situation

---

[32]Raymond Dennet and Robert K. Turner, eds., *Documents on American Foreign
Relations,* X (1948) (Princeton, N.J., 1950): 484–502.

badly. Unable to exploit the committee's distorted view of the internal communist threat, he accused it of trying to cover up the bad record of the Republican Congress. He refused to surrender the records, ostensibly because they were in the exclusive domain of the executive, more probably because of his fear that if the Republicans saw the FBI reports, which accused some federal employees of disloyalty on the basis of hearsay, unproved allegations, and personal vendettas, November might be an unfortunate month for Truman's political aspirations.[33] Not able to discredit the loyalty program he had set in motion, trapped by his own indiscriminating anticommunist rhetoric designed to "scare hell" out of the country, Truman stood paralyzed as the ground was carefully plowed around him for the weeds of McCarthyism.

Since the Iranian and Turkish crises of 1946, the Soviets had not been active in world affairs. But Molotov's departure from the Marshall Plan conference in Paris during July 1947 marked the turn. Russian attention was riveted on Germany. The Politburo interpreted the Marshall Plan to mean the American "intention to restore the economy of Germany and Japan on the old basis [of pre-1941] provided it is subordinated to interests of American capital."[34] Rebuilding Europe through the plan and tying it closer to American economic power threatened Stalin's hope of influencing Western European policies. Incomparably worse, however, was linking that Europe to a restored western Germany. This not only undercut Soviet determination to keep this ancient enemy weak, as well as divided, but vastly increased the potential of that enemy, tied it to the forces of "capitalist encirclement," and revived the memories of two world wars.

Molotov quickly initiated a series of moves to tighten Soviet control of the bloc. A program of bilateral trade agreements, the so-called Molotov Plan, began to link the bloc countries and Russia in July 1947. The final step came in January 1949, when the Council for Mutual Economic Assistance (COMECON) provided the Soviet answer to the Marshall Plan by creating a centralized agency for

[33] A useful analysis is Athan Theoharis, *Seeds of Repression: Harry S. Truman and the Origins of McCarthyism* (New York, 1971).

[34] Quoted in telegram from Moscow Embassy to Secretary of State Marshall, May 26, 1947, Papers of Joseph Jones, Truman Library.

stimulating and controlling bloc development. As a result of these moves, Soviet trade with the East European bloc, which had declined in 1947 to $380 million, doubled in 1948, quadrupled by 1950, and exceeded $2.5 billion in 1952. Seventy percent of East European trade was carried on with either the Soviet Union or elsewhere within the bloc.[35]

Four days after his return from Paris, Molotov announced the establishment of the Communist Information Bureau (Cominform). Including communists from Russia, Yugoslavia, France, Italy, Poland, Bulgaria, Czechoslovakia, Hungary, and Rumania, the Cominform provided another instrument for increasing Stalin's control. This was his answer to the Czech and Polish interest in joining the Marshall Plan. In late August, a month before the first Cominform meeting, Soviet actions in Hungary indicated the line that would be followed. After a purge of left-wing anticommunist political leaders, the Soviets directly intervened by rigging elections. All anticommunist opposition disappeared. Three weeks later at the Cominform meeting in Warsaw, Zhdanov formally announced new Soviet policies in a speech that ranks next to Stalin's February 9, 1946, address as a Russian call to Cold War.

Zhdanov's analysis of recent international developments climaxed with the announcement that American economic power, fattened by the war, was organizing Western Europe and "countries politically and economically dependent on the United States, such as the Near-Eastern and South-American countries and China" into an anticommunist bloc. The Russians and the "new democracies" in Eastern Europe, Finland, Indonesia, and Vietnam meanwhile formed another bloc which "has the sympathy of India, Egypt and Syria." In this way, Zhdanov again announced the rebirth of the "two-camp" view of the world, an attitude that had dominated Russian policy between 1927 and 1934 when Stalin bitterly attacked the West, and a central theme in the dictator's speech of February 1946. In some respects Zhdanov's announcement resembled the "two-world" attitude in the United States. The mirror image was especially striking when Zhdanov admonished the socialist camp not to lower its guard. "Just as in the past the Munich policy united the hands of the Nazi aggressors, so today concessions to the new

---

[35]Stanley J. Zyzniewski, "Soviet Foreign Economic Policy," *Political Science Quarterly*, LXXIII (June 1958): 216–219.

course of the United States and the imperialist camp may encourage its inspirers to be even more insolent and aggressive."[36]

Following Zhdanov's call to action, the Cominform delegates sharply criticized French and Italian communists, who seemed to want a more pacific approach, and, once again following the disastrous practices of the 1927–1934 era, ordered all members to foment the necessary strikes and internal disorder for the elimination of independent socialist, labor, and peasant parties in their countries. The meeting was the high-water mark of the tough Zhdanov line in Soviet foreign policy. Its effect was soon felt not only in bloc and Western European countries but inside Russia as well. Stalin cleansed Soviet economic thinking by discrediting and removing from public view Eugene Varga, a leading Russian economist who had angered the Politburo by warning that Marxists were wrong in thinking that the Western economies would soon collapse.

American officials fully understood why the Soviets were trying these new policies. As Secretary of State Marshall told Truman's cabinet in November 1947, "The advance of Communism has been stemmed and the Russians have been compelled to make a re-evaluation of their position."[37] America was winning its eight-month Cold War. But the Soviets' difficulties provided an excuse for Congress, which was not anxious to send billions of dollars of Marshall Plan aid to Europe if the Russians posed no threat. Congress dawdled as the plan came under increased criticism. Taft urged that good money not be poured into a "European TVA." On the other side of the political spectrum, Henry Wallace labeled it a "Martial Plan." In speeches around the country, Marshall tried to sell the program for its long-term economic and political benefits. His arguments fell on deaf ears. The American economy seemed to be doing well. Just weeks before the 1948 presidential campaign was to begin, Truman faced a major political and diplomatic defeat.

And then came the fall of Czechoslovakia. The Czechs had uneasily coexisted with Russia by trying not to offend the Soviets while keeping doors open to the West. This policy had started in late 1943, when Czech leaders signed a treaty with Stalin that, in the view of most observers, obligated Czechoslovakia to become a part

---

[36] Andrei Zhdanov, "The International Situation," reprinted in *The Strategy and Tactics of World Communism*, Supplement I (Washington, 1948), pp. 212–230.

[37] *Forrestal Diaries*, pp. 340–341.

of the Russian bloc. President Eduard Beneš and Foreign Minister Jan Masaryk, one of the foremost diplomatic figures in Europe, had nevertheless successfully resisted complete communist control. Nor had Stalin moved to consolidate his power in 1946 after the Czech Communist party emerged from the parliamentary elections with 38 percent of the vote, the largest total of any party. By late 1947 the lure of Western aid and internal political changes began to pull the Czech government away from the Soviets. At this point Stalin, who like Truman recalled the pivotal role of Czechoslovakia in 1938, decided to put the 1943 treaty into effect. Klement Gottwald, the Czech Communist party leader, demanded the elimination of independent parties. In mid-February 1948 Soviet armies camped on the border as Gottwald ordered the formation of a wholly new government. A Soviet mission of top officials flew to Prague to demand Beneš's surrender. The communists assumed full control on February 25. Two weeks later Masaryk either committed suicide, or, as Truman believed, was the victim of "foul play."

Truman correctly observed that the coup "sent a shock throughout the civilized world." He privately believed "We are faced with exactly the same situation with which Britain and France was faced in 1938-9 with Hitler."[38] In late 1947 Hungary had been the victim of a similar if less dramatic squeeze. Within two months, new opportunities would beckon to the Cominform when the Italian election was held. On March 5 a telegram arrived from General Clay in Germany. Although "I have felt and held that war was unlikely for at least ten years," Clay began, "within the last few weeks, I have felt a subtle change in Soviet attitude which . . . gives me a feeling that it may come with dramatic suddenness." For ten days, government intelligence worked furiously investigating Clay's warnings and on March 16 gave Truman the grim assurance that war was not probable within sixty days.[39] Two days before, on March 14, the Senate had endorsed the Marshall Plan by a vote of 69 to 17. As it went to the House for consideration, Truman, fearing the "grave events in Europe [which] were moving so swiftly," decided to appear before Congress.

---

[38]Margaret Truman, *Harry S. Truman* (New York, 1973), p. 392; for the Czech–U.S.S.R. background, see Vojtech Mastny, *Russia's Road to the Cold War* (New York, 1979), pp. 133–142, 281–282.

[39]*Forrestal Diaries*, pp. 387, 395.

In a speech remarkable for its repeated emphasis on the "increasing threat" to the very "survival of freedom," the President proclaimed the Marshall Plan "not enough." Europe must have "some measure of protection against internal and external aggression." He asked for Universal Military Training, the resumption of Selective Service (which he had allowed to lapse a year earlier), and speedy passage of the Marshall Plan.[40] Within twelve days the House approved authorization of the plan's money.

With perfect timing and somber rhetoric, Truman's March 17 speech not only galvanized passage of the plan but accelerated a change in American foreign policy that had been heralded the previous summer. Congress stamped its approval on this new military emphasis by passing a Selective Service bill. Although Universal Military Training, one of Forrestal's pet projects, found little favor, a supposedly penny-proud Congress replaced it with funds to begin a seventy-group Air Force, 25 percent larger than even Forrestal had requested.

Perhaps the most crucial effect of the new policy, however, appeared in the administration's determination to create great systems that would not only encourage military development but would also compel the Western world to accept political realignments as well. The first of these efforts had been the Rio Pact and the new policies toward Japan. The next, somewhat different, and vastly more important effort would be the North Atlantic Treaty Organization (NATO).

[40]*Documents on American Foreign Relations*, X (1948): 5–9.

4

~~~

The "Different World" of NSC-68 (1948-1950)

During the spring of 1948 a united administration, enjoying strong support on foreign policy from a Republican Congress, set off with exemplary single-mindedness to destroy the communist threat that loomed over Europe. Within two years this threat had been scotched, but the officials who created the policy had split, the Congress that ratified the policy had turned against the executive, the administration had fought off charges that it had been infiltrated by communists, and the United States found itself fighting a bloody war not in Europe but in Asia. These embarrassments did not suddenly emerge in 1950 but developed gradually from the policies of 1948-1949.

During March 1948, as Congress approved the Marshall Plan, the British, French, and the Benelux signed the Brussels Treaty. In this defense arrangement each signatory promised to aid the other parties in the event of attack with all military and other aid "in their power." Truman applauded the treaty, and soon Senator Vandenberg and Robert Lovett, Acheson's successor as under secretary of state, were spending long evenings in Vandenberg's Wardman Park Hotel suite drawing up a congressional resolution to pave the way for American entry into the new European association. Presented to the Senate on May 19, the Vandenberg Resolution genuflected briefly before the United Nations Charter, then passed on to the more vital business of requesting a regional arrangement, under Vandenberg's pet Article 51, in which the United States would participate militarily. This breezed through the Senate on June 11 by a 64 to 4 vote, and Lovett began a three-month long series of conferences with European leaders to draft a final treaty. These discussions had barely begun when they were shaken by two events. In Europe the Berlin blockade severely tested Western unity. In the United States a foreign policy debate erupted during the presidential campaign.

The Berlin blockade had its beginnings in those moments of 1945 and 1946 when the breakdown of the Four Power Allied Control Council made impossible the reunification of Germany. The Soviets continued to hope they could create a unified but demilitarized Germany under their own aegis, or, as Molotov told Byrnes in 1946, a united Germany which could be neutralized after Russia received adequate industrial reparations. As Americans stressed, however, the prosperity of Western Europe depended on German industrial recovery. If it could not reunify Germany, the West could develop the western, industrial portions controlled by France, Great Britain, and the United States and integrate the areas into a new European community. These three powers plus the Benelux reached agreement on this approach during intermittent meetings in London from February into June. As outlined in a communiqué of March 6, 1948, the London Conference determined to bring Germany within the "economic reconstruction of western Europe." The basis for an independent Germany with a "federal form of government" would also be shaped through a fusion of the three Western zones. The Ruhr's great resources were to be brought under joint control of the Western powers.[1] By late June the conference began a currency reform to repair the inflation and widespread black market activities caused in Germany and West Berlin by the weak Reichsmark.

For the Soviets the crisis was at hand. The Western moves were obviously designed to accept and exploit the status quo in Germany. The Soviets, however, predicated their European policy on a weakened non-Western Central Europe, and with the passage of the Marshall Plan and the rebuilding of West Germany they now faced

---

[1] U.S. Senate, Committee on Foreign Relations, 87th Cong., 1st Sess., *Documents on Germany, 1944–1961* (Washington, 1961), pp. 87–88.

the imminent defeat of that policy. Worse, Stalin confronted the prospect of a revitalized West Berlin deep inside the Soviet zone. Then, suddenly, the dictator's authority was challenged from within the bloc itself.

Tito was quite unlike Stalin's other followers in Eastern Europe. As a guerrilla leader he had successfully resisted the Nazis, and in doing so had created a mass basis of support at a time when Stalin and other communist leaders increasingly rested their power on elite groups. His country, unlike Czechoslovakia, did not border on the Soviet Union and enjoyed access to the Mediterranean area. Tito's belief in communism had never been in question. He was the only bloc leader who fully supported Stalin's and Zhdanov's creation of the Cominform. Tito's nationalism, however, had never been questioned either. When Stalin began to demand full Yugoslav adherence to the new economic and mutual assistance pacts, Tito balked. Enraged, Stalin claimed, "I will shake my little finger – and there will be no more Tito."[2]

The Yugoslav's secret police, however, proved superior to Stalin's, and after the Soviet dictator tried in vain to overthrow Tito with an internal coup, Stalin called a special Cominform meeting in June 1948 to expel Yugoslavia from the bloc for "taking the route of nationalism." Tito not only successfully challenged Stalin's power but disproved Stalin's key assumption that the world was divided into "two camps," with any so-called third force only a cover for capitalism. Having shaken both Stalin's power and theory, Tito's example threatened Soviet control throughout Eastern Europe. At that moment in mid-June when Stalin was preparing to bring Tito's many sins into the open, the Allies challenged Soviet policies in Germany. Stalin's first reaction was the ordering of bloody purges in Eastern Europe to exterminate nascent Titos. During the next two years, probably one out of every four communist members in the bloc fell from grace.

He next attempted to sever the West from the 2.4 million West Berliners. On June 24 the Soviets stopped all surface traffic between Berlin and the Western zones. The Western powers had never negotiated a pact guaranteeing these rights. The Soviets now rejected arguments that occupation rights in Berlin and the use of the routes

[2]Nikita S. Khrushchev, *The Crimes of the Stalin Era. Special Report to the 20th Congress of the Communist Party of the Soviet Union*, annotated by Boris I. Nicolaevsky (New York, 1956), p. 48. This copy from *The New Leader* is well annotated.

during the previous three years had given the West legal claim to unrestricted use of the highways and railroads. On June 28 came the American response. Without consulting anyone but a few cabinet members, Truman decided, as Forrestal recalled the President's words, "We [are] going to stay period." Secretary of State Marshall later placed this decision within a context that bore an eerie resemblance to Stalin's policy framework: "We had the alternative of following a firm policy in Berlin or accepting the consequences of failure of the rest of our European policy."[3] The domino theory could work, apparently, on both sides of the Iron Curtain, and Germany had become the first domino.

The United States began a massive airlift, ultimately lasting 324 days, which soon delivered 13,000 tons of supplies a day. Stalin was playing for high stakes, but so was Truman. In July he transferred to England two groups of B-29 bombers, the planes designated to carry atomic bombs. Truman's action indicated how the monopoly of these bombs allowed the administration to balance the budget and cut back conventional army forces, yet not diminish its capacity or willingness to brandish military force. The President assured Forrestal and Marshall that, although he prayed the bomb would not have to be used, "if it became necessary, no one need have a misgiving but what he would do so." The evening after Truman made this remark, a meeting of leading newspaper publishers agreed that if war occurred over Berlin, the American people would expect the bomb to be dropped. Taking these words at face value, the Pentagon requested that control of the bomb be transferred from the President to the military so preparations could be made for its use. Here Truman drew the line: he did not intend "to have some dashing lieutenant colonel decide when would be the proper time to drop one." This decision became more significant when Lovett brought word back to Washington that General Clay, the American commander in Berlin, "was now drawn as tight as a steel spring."[4]

In mid-May 1948 Truman gave further evidence of his presidential power, although this occurred less in the context of possible atomic war against the Soviets than inevitable political war against Republicans. Shortly after 6:00 P.M. on May 14, the President rec-

---

[3] James Forrestal, *The Forrestal Diaries*, Walter Millis, ed. (New York, 1951), pp. 454–455.

[4] *Forrestal Diaries*, pp. 487–489, 460–461, 480–481.

ognized the state of Israel just minutes after the Israelis had proclaimed the existence of their new nation. Truman did this after
rejecting the advice of both his military and diplomatic advisors.
For months Forrestal had warned that recognizing the Israelis, who
were fighting a bloody war against the Arabs for possession of
Palestine, would lead to the loss of vital Middle Eastern oil
resources in the Arab states. Truman, however, had supported
large-scale Jewish immigration into Palestine. In 1947 he hoped
Palestine could be partitioned so a separate Jewish state could be
created. Not illogically, therefore, he agreed with his political
rather than his diplomatic advisors. The Jewish vote could be decisive in such key states as Ohio, New York, and California.
Although the President sincerely sympathized with the Israeli effort
in Palestine, British Prime Minister Clement Attlee was also correct
when he observed that Truman overrode his diplomatic advisors
because "There's no Arab vote in America but there's a very heavy
Jewish vote and the Americans are always having elections."[5]

In the decisions on Berlin and Israel, Truman enjoyed such strong
congressional support (although Congress had not been formally
consulted in either instance) that foreign policy never became a major issue between Truman and the Republican nominee, Thomas E.
Dewey of New York, during the 1948 presidential campaign.
Reinhold Niebuhr summarized the basic viewpoint of most Republicans and Democrats when he wrote in *Life* magazine in September
1948, "For peace we must risk war." The Soviets were weaker and
would not fight, Niebuhr declared. "We cannot afford any more
compromises. We will have to stand at every point in our far-flung
lines."[6] These views underlay the foreign policy planks of both parties, although the platforms did not agree in every particular. In contrast to the Democrats, the Republicans emphasized the need to save
China, lauded bipartisanship, placed heavier emphasis on building
the military, and accused the President of not comprehending the
real nature of the Russian peril. The Democrats answered the last
charge by inserting a plank (which had no counterpart in the
Republican platform) condemning communism "overseas and at
home," and pledging strong enforcement of antisubversive laws.

[5]Clement Attlee, *Twilight of Empire* (New York, 1961), p. 181.
[6]Reinhold Niebuhr, "For Peace We Must Risk War," *Life*, XXV (September 20, 1948):
38–39.

The Cold War entered the campaign, but the clash occurred between the Democrats and Henry Wallace's Progressive party. As the Progressives cried that the "old parties" did not want a settlement with Russia, Wallace, along with many of his noncommunist supporters, became fair game to those Americans committed to fighting the Cold War with no holds barred. Apparently because of his political views, one Wallace supporter was stabbed to death in Charleston, South Carolina. At Evansville College, Bradley University, Northwestern, the University of Georgia, the University of Miami, and the University of New Hampshire, Progressive party adherents were either fired or made to suffer in other ways for their political convictions. The Americans for Democratic Action, afraid that Wallace might split the liberal vote and hand the victory to Dewey, tried to use guilt-by-association tactics by printing in major urban newspapers the names of the Progressive party's principal contributors and then listing the organizations on the attorney general's list of subversive groups to which these contributors belonged — or had belonged long before.[7]

The growing tension over Berlin and Truman's shift to the left on domestic issues killed off any hopes the Progressives nursed of determining the election. Clark Clifford, Truman's closest political advisor, was prophetic, for a year before he had told the President: "There is considerable political advantage to the Administration in its battle with the Kremlin. . . . The worse matters get, up to a fairly certain point — real danger of imminent war — the more there is a sense of crisis. In times of crisis the American citizen tends to back up his President."[8] Wallace received only 1,157,326 votes; half came from New York. Overcoming handicaps imposed by defections to the Wallacite left and the Dixiecrat right, and by public opinion polls which showed him trailing Dewey, Truman lustily enjoyed scoring the greatest upset in twentieth-century American politics. The Progressive party rapidly declined, Wallace finally quitting in 1950 when he supported Truman's actions in Korea. In Europe negotiations resumed on the NATO treaty.

These negotiations for a military alliance moved to the front of

[7]Karl M. Schmidt, *Henry A. Wallace: Quixotic Crusade, 1948* (Syracuse, 1960), pp. 86–88, 159, 252.

[8]Allan Yarnell, *Democrats and Progressives* (Berkeley, 1974), chapter III, especially p. 37.

American diplomatic activity. In his Inaugural Address of January 20, 1949, Truman made a slight effort to restore some balance when, in outlining the four major points of his foreign policy, he suggested as the so-called Point Four "a bold new program" to spread scientific and industrial knowledge to the newly emerging areas. The President and Congress moved slowly in implementing this glamorous concept. The business community, on which Truman depended for the passage and implementation of any large aid program, attacked the probability of more governmental interference in the less industrialized countries, asking instead that Truman negotiate with these nations treaties assuring fair and equitable treatment of private investment and personnel. For a year and a half Truman could obtain no Point Four legislation. In the summer of 1950, Congress finally passed a token appropriation of $27 million to begin a technical aid program in conjunction with the United Nations. Even the method was attacked by Senator Tom Connally, Democratic chairman of the Foreign Relations Committee: "I don't see why in the world we need to turn this over and let . . . the United Nations run it and . . . mess it all up."[9] Senator Connally's feeling ran somewhat contrary to Point One of Truman's Inaugural Address — full support of the United Nations.

The other two points of the address — the encouragement of European recovery and the pledging of aid to help nations defend themselves — were more plausible. Here Truman dealt with the familiar cultures and policies of Europe. He also worked with a new secretary of state who knew Europe intimately. The most important American policy maker in the post–World War II era, Dean Acheson founded his foreign policy on those Atlantic ties which statesmen in Europe traditionally considered the last hope of Western civilization. As a young, brilliant lawyer whom Roosevelt had plucked out of Washington's most august law firm, Acheson had resigned from the early New Deal because he considered Roosevelt's monetary policies rather weird. The approach of war, however, drew Acheson back into government, and between 1941 and 1947 he devoted himself to the European policies which climaxed with the Marshall Plan.

As a good conservative, Acheson's allegiance to the Western partnership, in which he correctly viewed the United States to be senior

[9]Quoted in Richard P. Stebbins, *United States in World Affairs, 1950* (New York, 1951), p. 98.

partner, overcame his few qualms about the later New or Fair Deals. His fear of the Soviet menace satisfied even Vandenberg: Acheson "is so totally anti-Soviet and is going to be so *completely tough*," the Michigan senator wrote from a Foreign Ministers conference in May 1949, "that I really doubt whether there is any *chance at all*" for an agreement.[10]

Nor did Acheson allow the wishes of the multitude to disturb his outlook. The growing popularity of public opinion polls, he remarked in 1946, signifies that "we have become of a somewhat hypochondriac type, and ascertain our state of health by this mass temperature taking. Fortunately this was not one of the hardships of Valley Forge." As for the United Nations, "in the Arab proverb, the ass that went to Mecca remained an ass, and a policy has little added to it by its place of utterance." Congress did not escape his wrath. Its function in foreign policy, he later observed, "is the function of people who don't know and don't care and are obstructive, and they are just generally raising hell around." As for individuals, "the question of sincerity of a United States Senator is beyond me. . . . He is an honest man, he is an intense fellow, he gets all worked up, the blood rushes to his head, he takes on kind of a wild, stary look at you, and I just do not think his mind works in a normal way when he gets excited."[11]

Acheson preferred to place his confidence in power manipulated by an elite. In certain respects he sounded much like Niebuhr. After World War II, Acheson declared, Americans "learned how wrong the prophets of the Enlightenment had been about what moved peoples. These prophets overestimated the influence of wisdom, virtue, and understanding of experience, and underestimated prejudice, passion and dogma." And there was power: "Power politics had no place in our Celestial City; but a substantial place in the twentieth century." So there they were, sin and power. His war against communism, his trust in power (especially military power) to contain sin, and the veneration he had for traditional Europe admirably suited Acheson for the new era to be opened by the NATO pact.[12]

[10]Arthur H. Vandenberg, Jr., *The Private Papers of Senator Vandenberg* (Boston, 1952), p. 485.

[11]Princeton Seminar, October 10–11, July 22–23, 1953, Acheson Papers, Truman Library.

[12]Dean Acheson, *Pattern of Responsibility; Edited by McGeorge Bundy from the Record of Secretary of State Dean Acheson* (Boston, 1952), pp. 17, 21; Dean Acheson, "The Truman Years," *Foreign Service Journal*, XLII (August 1965): 23.

The world in which NATO was to be born was undergoing rapid change. Nowhere was this more evident than in the Soviet Union. The Allied response to the Berlin blockade and Tito's defiance of the Cominform forced Stalin to question Zhdanov's fanaticism. By the end of July 1948, Zhdanov was dead, perhaps poisoned, more likely the victim of a heart attack after violent arguments with Stalin. Zhdanov's supporters disappeared in a mass purge, and Georgi Malenkov and Nikita Khrushchev, both of whom wanted Stalin to devote more attention to internal economic problems, moved up the rungs of power.

During April 1949 the Soviets began lifting the Berlin blockade. In Western Europe, which NATO was to undergird, Italian and French communists lost considerable ground. Despite a recession caused by an American economic downturn, overall production in Western Europe exceeded the 1938 level by 15 percent. As Truman's chief diplomatic troubleshooter W. Averell Harriman testified, fear in Europe "no longer exists as it existed 18 months ago."[13]

In this changing, quieter international environment, the Senate opened hearings on the NATO pact. Twelve nations had signed it: the United States, Canada, Denmark, France, Iceland, Italy, Portugal, Norway, Great Britain, and the Benelux. They pledged to use force only in self-defense and to develop "free institutions," particularly through the encouragement of "economic collaboration between any or all" of the parties. Article 5 was central:

> The Parties agree that an armed attack against one or more of them in Europe or North America shall be considered an attack against them all; and consequently they agree that, if such an armed attack occurs, each of them . . . will assist the Party or Parties so attacked by taking forthwith, individually and in concert with the other Parties, such action as it deems necessary, including the use of armed force.

Article 11 modified this commitment by adding that the pact's provisions shall be carried out in accordance with each nation's "constitutional processes." Vandenberg and Connally had inserted this clause in an attempt to curb executive powers. Article 9 established a council to implement defense policies. Articles 12 and 13 provided

[13]U.S. Senate, Committee on Foreign Relations, 81st Cong., 1st Sess., *Hearings . . . on . . . The North Atlantic Treaty* (Washington, 1949), p. 203.

for a review in ten years; after twenty years any member could quit after giving one-year notice.

At first the hearings went well. Acheson calmed some fears by emphasizing that no one "at the present time" contemplated following NATO with "a Mediterranean pact, and then a Pacific pact, and so forth." Everyone present agreed that European defense could not be entrusted to the United Nations. A consensus formed on the proposition that NATO "is to create not merely a balance of power, but a preponderance of power." This fitted into Truman's and Acheson's policies of dealing with the Russians from "positions of strength." The West, however, already enjoyed such a "preponderance" because of its possession of the atomic bomb. NATO promised to add little more. This led to questions which soon revealed that even administration spokesmen had difficulty discovering the pact's military importance.

At the time, the West's dozen, underequipped divisions faced twenty-five fully armed Russian divisions in Central Europe. When asked whether the administration planned to send "substantial" numbers of United States troops to shore up the European defenses, Acheson and General Omar Bradley, Chairman of the Joint Chiefs of Staff, assured the Senate, in Acheson's words, "The answer to that question, Senator, is a clear and absolute 'no.'" Continuing their search for the manpower that would fill NATO, Acheson was asked whether he contemplated putting Germans back into uniform. "We are very clear," he replied, "that the disarmament and de-militarization of Germany must be complete and absolute."[14]

The questioning necessarily took another line. Perhaps NATO was then aimed at preventing internal subversion in Western Europe? Acheson called the possibility of successful subversion "remote" and thought the American reaction to a coup would be the less-than-drastic response of allowing the victim to leave the NATO alliance. Another dimension of the problem was noted by Senator Arthur Watkins, a strong opponent of the treaty. Because of the "constitutional processes" clause, Watkins observed, an opponent could strike and take much of Europe before "we could ever get the Congress together to declare war."[15] Clearly the treaty's military significance was not overwhelming.

[14]Committee on Foreign Relations, *Hearings on* [NATO], pp. 54, 57, 47, 183, 144.
[15]Committee on Foreign Relations, *Hearings on* [NATO], pp. 25, 310, 317.

The key to the American view of the treaty emerged when Harriman remarked that if NATO was not carried through "there would be a reorientation" in Europe climaxing in "a restrengthening of those that believe in appeasement and neutrality." In a similar vein, Acheson commented a year later, "Unity in Europe requires the continuing association and support of the United States. Without it free Europe would split apart." Now that the Marshall Plan was reviving Europe economically, the United States, in the full splendor of its postwar power, was attempting to strengthen its political ties with, and influence over, Europe through the creation of common military institutions. Senator Connally succinctly phrased this in the Senate debate: "The Atlantic Pact is but the logical extension of the principle of the Monroe Doctrine."[16]

The Senate ratified the treaty 82 to 13. On the day he added his signature in mid-July 1949, Truman sent Congress a one-year Mutual Defense Assistance (MDA) bill providing for $1.5 billion for European military aid. This was the immediate financial price for the NATO commitment. A memorandum circulating through the executive outlined the purpose of MDA: "to build up our own military industry," to "create a common defense frontier in Western Europe" by having the Allies pool "their industrial and manpower resources," and particularly, to subordinate "nationalistic tendencies."[17] In the House, however, the bill encountered tough opposition from budget-cutting congressmen. On September 22 President Truman announced that Russia had exploded an atomic bomb. Within six days the NATO appropriations raced through the House and went to the President for approval.

Although publicly playing down the significance of the Russian test, the administration painfully realized that, in Vandenberg's words, "This is now a different world." Few American officials had

[16]Committee on Foreign Relations, *Hearings on* [NATO], p. 231; Acheson, *Pattern of Responsibility*, p. 55; Tom Connally, *My Name Is Tom Connally* (New York, 1954), p. 231. This political (rather than military) importance of NATO is also emphasized in U.S. Senate, Committee on Foreign Relations, 81st Cong., 1st and 2nd Sess., *Review of the World Situation, 1949–1950* [Executive hearings of 1949–1950 made public in 1974] (Washington, 1974), pp. 6, 12–13.

[17]"Effect of the MAP on U.S. Security," draft from Foreign Assistance Coordinating Committee, June 22, 1949, Papers of David D. Lloyd, Truman Library.

expected the Soviet test this early. Because it was simultaneous with the fall of China, the American diplomatic attitude further stiffened. As Leo Szilard, one of the foremost scientists in the development of the American bomb, explained, "The Russians can affect the political attitude of Western Europeans just by threatening to bomb them."[18] For American policy makers, the struggle for Europe had reopened. Truman took a first step in the new battle by ordering that development of the hydrogen bomb be accelerated. The second step occurred when American military authorities determined to build a large conventional European army which would include German military units. In August the first elections in West Germany for a national parliament had given Konrad Adenauer's Christian Democratic Union a plurality of 31 percent of the votes. A vigorous seventy-three years of age, Adenauer had spent his early political life in Cologne city government and then, from 1933 to 1945, in Nazi prisons. His rise to power in 1949 resulted more from ruthless political infighting than from charisma. He personally enjoyed little national support, but he had a clear vision: a restored, independent Germany could develop only through close cooperation with the United States. Adenauer dedicated the last two decades of his life to realizing this vision.

American officials appreciated Adenauer's obvious statesmanship but disagreed over tactics. A United States Army planning unit outlined a program for German rearmament and launched a campaign to procure NATO's acceptance. The State Department, however, demurred, arguing that building a German army could create political reaction at home, unpleasant responses from Poland and Russia, and strong hostility in France.[19] The French probably knew little about this Washington infighting, but they fully comprehended the threat that overpowering American influence in NATO, and a possibly rearmed Germany, posed to their own independence. As it had in the past and would in the future, France retaliated by trying to increase its power on the continent at the expense of the Americans.

French Foreign Minister Robert Schuman proposed in early 1950 that "Little Europe" (France, Germany, Italy, and the Benelux)

[18]Leo Szilard, "A Personal History of the Bomb." In "The Atlantic Community Faces the Bomb," *University of Chicago Roundtable*, September 25, 1949, p. 4.

[19]Laurence W. Martin, "The American Decision to Rearm Germany." In Harold Stein, ed., *American Civil-Military Decisions: A Book of Case Studies* (Birmingham, Alabama, 1963), pp. 646–651.

combine their heavy iron, coal, and steel industry. Like the American military's plans for German rearmament, the "Schuman Plan" would have political repercussions. Germany's basic industry would be integrated into Western Europe; the Ruhr would essentially be internationalized, thus (the French hoped) destroying Germany's military capacity while giving France entry to the area's rich coal deposits; the combining of basic industries would shortly force transport and agriculture to follow in a movement of spectacular European integration. Last, but not least, exclusion of England and the United States from the plan would increase the ability of France to influence all of Western Europe.

The French hoped to tie down Germany and shape Western Europe through economic means. Americans planned to influence Germany and Western Europe through NATO. These two approaches, in full view by early 1950, would pose the alternatives for European development through the next quarter century. They would also make understandable the growing competition and bitterness between the United States and France. In 1949-1950 George Kennan offered a third alternative. He concluded that Russia could be contained, yet Cold War tensions eased, through some kind of neutralization plan for Central Europe. Kennan considered NATO an obstacle to such neutralization, since the new alliance permanently divided and threatened to rearm Germany.[20]

When Kennan made such arguments within the State Department, he encountered vigorous opposition from Acheson.[21] The secretary of state preferred the old to the new "Mr. X." But the Russian atomic bomb explosion deepened Kennan's convictions. In early 1950 he announced he was leaving the State Department for a year of study at Princeton. So ended another "disengagement" debate within the State Department.

Kennan's departure did not free Acheson from criticism. As a Europe-first advocate, and as secretary of state during the months when Chiang Kai-shek finally gave up China, Acheson became the target for a growing body of Chiang's supporters known as the China Lobby. The lobby had begun in the Chinese embassy during

---

[20]George Kennan, *Memoirs, 1925-1950* (Boston, 1967), pp. 446-449.
[21]*U.S. News and World Report*, XLIV (January 17, 1958): 63.

World War II, coordinating pro-Chiang propaganda in the United States and paying its expenses by illegally smuggling narcotics into the country. Until 1948 the China Lobby was not significant but then became transformed into a highly effective pressure group. First, it gained the adherence of wealthy, conservative Americans who believed Truman was selling out China and the free enterprise system to communists. Second, many Americans could not understand why the greatest power in the world stood helplessly by while Mao conquered China. Such frustration and their incredible ignorance of China (and of the limits of American power) led to the easy conclusion that communist sympathizers hidden in the bowels of the State Department must be doing the dirty work. The wealth, the political attractiveness of these reasons for China's fall, and, in some cases, their own personal experience in Asia, attracted political support from key congressmen. These included Walter Judd, William Knowland (later Senate majority leader for the Republicans), Joseph Martin (who would be Speaker of the House in the early 1950s), and Senator Kenneth Wherry (who had uttered, "With God's help we will lift Shanghai up and up, ever up, until it is just like Kansas City."[22]).

When the China enthusiasts argued that more American aid could save Chiang, Acheson correctly responded that lack of supplies was not causing the Nationalists' headlong retreat. The chief of the American advisory group in China reported in late 1948 that these "military debacles in my opinion can all be attributed to the world's worst leadership and many other morale destroying factors that lead to a complete loss of will to fight."[23] By February 1949 the Nationalists had lost nearly half their troops, mostly by defection. Eighty percent of the American equipment given Chiang had fallen into communist hands. In April, as Mao's troops successfully crossed the Yangtze and began to sweep across southern China, Truman finally moved to terminate aid. This aroused the full fury of the China bloc, but the critics could only attack the administration, for they had no useful alternatives to offer. As Knowland candidly remarked, no responsible opponent of the Truman policy had ever proposed sending an American army to fight in China.

---

[22]Quoted in Eric Goldman, *The Crucial Decade and After, 1945–1961* (New York, 1960), p. 116; Ross Koen, *The China Lobby* (New York, 1960).

[23]Tang Tsou, *America's Failure in China* (Chicago, 1963), pp. 482–483.

In August 1949 Acheson tried for the knockout blow by releasing the so-called White Paper, a 1054-page compilation of documents to support the administration's thesis that, as Acheson wrote in a long introduction, "The unfortunate but inescapable fact is that the ominous result of the civil war in China was beyond the control of the government of the United States. . . . It was the product of internal Chinese forces, forces which this country tried to influence but could not." The only alternative policy would have been a "full-scale intervention" of American troops, which "would have been resented by the mass of the Chinese people, would have diametrically reversed our historic policy, and would have been condemned by the American people." He looked forward to the time when the Chinese would throw off the "foreign yoke" of communism, but Acheson warned that if China lent "itself to the aims of Soviet Russian imperialism," the United States would consider this a violation of the United Nations Charter and, he implied, move to stop any aggression. The China Lobby retaliated by terming the White Paper a "whitewash of a wishful, do-nothing policy which has succeeded only in placing Asia in danger of Soviet conquest."[24]

Despite the China Lobby, Truman and Acheson almost took a historic step during midsummer 1949: they nearly gave their approval when the American ambassador to China, J. Leighton Stuart, asked if he could talk with Mao. The initiative had come from the communists, who clearly hoped to have some kind of diplomatic relationship with the United States. State Department officials urged that Stuart be sent to the new government. After hurried meetings at the White House, however, Acheson told Stuart that a decision "at the highest level" forbade him from talking with Mao. It was a turning point of history, but Truman and Acheson refused to turn. They believed that Mao had already pledged himself to follow Stalin. Acheson made the decision final by announcing October 12 that the new Chinese regime could not be recognized by the United States. Americans were particularly angered when Mao's government seized American consular property and later jailed American Consul Angus Ward.

Chiang Kai-shek fled to Formosa (now Taiwan) to establish a rival Chinese government. This presented another set of problems

[24]Dean Acheson, "Letter of Transmittal, July 30." In *United States Relations with China . . . 1944–1949* (Washington, 1949), pp. xiv–xvii. Quoted in H.B Westerfield, *Foreign Policies and Party Politics: Pearl Harbor to Korea* (New Haven, 1955), p. 356.

to Washington. In late December the Joint Chiefs and Acheson agreed that since Mao would probably conquer Formosa sometime in 1950, the United States should not give military aid to the Nationalists.[25] Chiang's supporters again organized for battle in Congress, forcing the administration to compromise when they threatened to cut off aid to Korea if some assistance was not immediately sent to Formosa. The battle was bitter, and Vandenberg, seriously ill in Michigan, could not heal the wounds suffered by bipartisanship. This fight, waged just five months before the outbreak of the Korean War, left bipartisanship a shattered ideal and no longer a practice.

Truman and Acheson determined to move slowly in the revolutionary Asian situation. American experts were not certain whether a common allegiance to Marxism-Leninism would suffice to link China and Russia in a friendly partnership. Stalin remembered the debacle of his China policies during the 1920s. The Chinese communists recalled how Stalin had cooperated with Roosevelt in recognizing Chiang's government and had kept a Soviet ambassador with the Nationalists in 1949 after most Western governments had deserted Chiang. Perhaps common ideology would blot out such unhappy memories. The more fundamental question soon arose, however, of who would define that ideology. In a widely publicized interview in 1946, Liu Shao-ch'i, Mao's chief theoretician, announced that Mao had given Marxism "a new development. He has created a Chinese or Asiatic form of Marxism. . . . There are similar conditions in other lands of southeast Asia. The courses chosen by China will influence them all." In November 1949, just days before Mao left for Moscow to negotiate with Stalin, the Chinese revived Liu's 1946 interview.[26] Within the Politburo itself, Stalin's policies were also being questioned.

A debate evidently erupted among top Soviet officials over whether the possession of the atomic bomb and the victory of the Chinese communists had so weakened the threat of "capitalist encir-

[25]U.S. Senate, Committee on Armed Services and Committee on Foreign Relations, 82nd Cong., 1st Sess., *Hearings to Conduct an Inquiry into the Military Situation in the Far East . . .* (Washington, 1951), pp. 1770–1771; cited hereafter as *Military Situation in the Far East.*

[26]Quoted in Donald S. Zagoria, *The Sino-Soviet Conflict, 1956–1961* (Princeton, 1962), pp. 14–15.

clement" that internal discipline could be eased and domestic consumer production increased. On November 6 Georgi Malenkov,
one of Stalin's closest associates since the early 1930s, delivered a
speech which subtly advanced the thesis that "capitalist encirclement" was crumbling. He stressed the unity of the Russian peoples
and the security of Soviet borders. Boasting that the five-year plan
was ahead of schedule, Malenkov challenged the West to "peaceful
competition with socialism." Within this general context, he made
two significant points. First, he admonished the Soviets to prepare
for this competition by removing further "difficulties and obstacles"
that hindered production. Second, he argued that the economic
recession in the West bore the "signs of an approaching crisis" for
which the Soviets had long been waiting. This line of argument implied that Stalin no longer had to apply pressure, for the West was
collapsing of its own inherent contradictions.[27]

Old-line Stalinists lashed back in a speech made to the Cominform in late November. Mikhail A. Suslov, chief of the Department
of Agitation and Propaganda, took Malenkov's premises and neatly
turned them around to the opposite conclusion: the rising successes
of Soviet power increased the immediate danger of armed conflict.
Suslov argued that because the Soviets had scored such great economic and political victories, the United States had created NATO
and begun work on the hydrogen bomb. Such "war-mongering" attempts to change the balance of power, now tipping slowly in favor
of the Soviets, could, Suslov warned, lead to Western attacks on
Eastern Europe, Communist China, and North Korea.[28]

Stalin himself reacted more indirectly. Five days before the
Korean War began, he countered growing arguments that Russia
was now prepared (as Malenkov indicated) for a sudden, explosive
break that would force the withering away of the socialistic, that is,
Stalinist, state and give birth to the long-promised utopia of communism. Explaining in an article on linguistics that language
develops gradually, not through "explosions," Stalin suddenly turned
on "comrades who are engrossed in explosion," informing them that
neither was the theory of sudden transition "always applicable to
other social phenomena."[29] Textbooks were to be rewritten to con-

[27] *Current Digest of the Soviet Press,* I (November 22, 1949): 3–10.

[28] Marshall D. Shulman, *Stalin's Foreign Policy Reappraised* (Cambridge, Mass.,
1963), pp. 118–119.

[29] Robert C. Tucker, *The Soviet Political Mind: Studies in Stalinism and Post-Stalin
Change* (New York, 1963), pp. 24–25, 100–114.

struct a state-controlled educational system which would mold the New Soviet Man and, more important, keep him under control. For Stalin wanted control, not revolution. Although brandishing the vocabulary of Marx and Lenin, he had become not only conservative, but reactionary, in an attempt to secure himself against the challenges of Malenkov and Mao.

The challenge from the East became apparent in discussions between Chinese and Russian leaders which began in December. More than two months of hard bargaining ensued. Stalin gained economic advantages in Sinkiang and restricted credit arrangements to China for the purchase of Soviet exports to the value of $300 million spread over five years. The Soviets later cut the value of the loan about one-fifth by devaluating the ruble. China did succeed in making the treaty one of "mutual assistance"; Russia would consult with China in the event that Japan "or any other state that should unite" with Japan threatened aggression against China. Perhaps of most importance to Mao, the Soviets promised to surrender their special rights in Manchurian ports and the Manchurian railway system. While these points were argued, Stalin moved unsuccessfully back of the scene to loosen the allegiances of Manchuria and Inner Mongolia to Peking. The "fraternal alliance" was enduring an uncommon amount of horse trading and attempted backstabbing.

George Kennan privately explained the State Department's view of the talks. He believed the Soviets "will be extremely cautious" in spreading Marxism around Asia "because they are very, very well aware of the fact that if you cannot overshadow a country militarily, ideology is in itself an untrustworthy means with which to hold them." He recalled "Stalin one time snorting rather contemptuously and vigorously because one of our people asked them what they were going to give to China when [the war] was over and [Stalin] said in effect, 'What the hell do you think we can give to China.' He said, 'We have a hundred cities of our own to build in the Soviet Far East. If anybody is going to give anything to the Far East, I think it's you.' And I think," Kennan concluded, "he was speaking quite sincerely."[30]

On January 12, 1950, as the Mao-Stalin talks edged along, Acheson developed Kennan's basic points before the National Press Club in Washington. He viewed the Soviet attempt to control Outer

[30] *I.P.R. Hearings*, pp. 1558–1563.

and Inner Mongolia, Manchuria, and Sinkiang as "the single most significant, most important fact" in Asia. Such attempts would prove to Mao that the Soviets wished not to help but to dominate. Acheson stressed that nationalism, not communism, had become the dominant fact in postwar Asia and that consequently the United States, not Russia, would prove to be the best friend of those Chinese who want "their own national independence." In this context Acheson issued his famous declaration that the Pacific "defensive perimeter" of the United States ran from the Aleutians to Japan, the Ryukyus, and down to the Philippines. (This was not a newly announced policy. In March 1949 General MacArthur defined the perimeter as encompassing exactly the same area.[31]) Acheson doubted that the Far East was threatened as much by military aggression as by "subversion and penetration." The secretary of state, however, carefully made two exceptions to these general policies: first, in both Japan and Korea, the United States had special economic responsibilities; second, if attack occurred west of the defense perimeter (for example, in Korea), the "entire civilized world under the Charter of the United Nations" would aid "people who are determined to protect their independence."[32]

Acheson had issued a fascinating document, acute in its view of Asian nationalism, accurate in its pinpointing of a Sino-Soviet split, precise in its sorting out of Japan and Korea as of paramount importance to American policy, but wrong in its assumption that military aggression in the area was not imminent. He had left many options open for policy maneuvers. Within a month these options were severely cut. On January 13 Yakov Malik, the Soviet delegate to the Security Council, walked out of the United Nations after his proposal to unseat Chiang's regime in favor of Mao's lost 6 to 3. The next day the Chinese communists raided American consulate grounds in Peking. The United States view toughened. A month later the Sino-Soviet treaty became public. Acheson interpreted the agreement as Mao selling out the Chinese people to Stalin. Extending his sympathy to the Chinese, Acheson warned them against being "led by their new rulers into aggressive or subversive adventures beyond their borders."[33]

[31] The New York Times, March 2, 1949, p. 22.

[32] Dean Acheson, "Crisis in Asia," Department of State Bulletin, XXII (January 23, 1950): 111–117.

[33] Dean Acheson, "United States Policy Toward Asia," Department of State Bulletin, XXII (March 27, 1950): 4–8.

The Sino-Soviet pact, the explosion of the Russian bomb, the divisive arguments over NATO, the whimpering end of bipartisanship added up to an unpleasant winter for the Truman administration. Peace would not be found soon. Indeed, it was not to be found at all. Americans, who, like other peoples, prefer their wars short and triumphant, wondered why.

One answer had already been suggested on July 30, 1948, as the nation felt the reverberations of the Czech coup and the Berlin blockade. Elizabeth Bentley and Whittaker Chambers, a self-confessed former Communist party member, claimed before the House Un-American Activities Committee that communists had infiltrated the State Department a decade before. Chambers specifically accused Alger Hiss of being a party agent. Hiss had worked in several executive departments after 1933, including the State Department, where in 1944 he helped lay the groundwork for the United Nations. His friends included Dean Acheson and John Foster Dulles. Hiss replied to Chambers with a $75,000 libel suit. Chambers then took federal agents to his Maryland farm and picked from a hollowed-out pumpkin microfilms of State Department documents which Chambers claimed Hiss had passed to him in 1938. The typing irregularities on the microfilms, so the FBI claimed, seemed to match those of one of Hiss's old typewriters. Acheson supported the former Harvard Law School graduate in the strongest terms. But a newly arrived congressman from California, Richard Nixon, determined to pursue the case until Chambers was vindicated. After one hung jury, Hiss was finally convicted of perjury on January 21, 1950. Many Americans now believed they understood why the Cold War was not ending quickly and happily.

Hiss's fall carried with it much of the reputation of the Eastern liberal-intellectual group which had become identified with the reforms of the New Deal. Wallace's defection and resounding defeat, Truman's failure to pass much of his Fair Deal domestic program, and Hiss's conviction illustrated how Roosevelt's remark during World War II that "Dr. Win-the-War" had replaced "Dr. New Deal" remained relevant far into the Cold War era. The American mood by 1949 was not founded on reform but conservativism and consensus.

Perhaps nowhere was this more noticeable and explicit than in the writing of American history. In 1948 Charles Beard, the greatest of those historians who between 1910 and 1940 had emphasized and applauded reform and class and political divisions in American history, published *President Roosevelt and the Coming of the War.* Charging that FDR had knowingly broken the constitutional boundaries imposed on the executive branch so he could take the nation into war, Beard warned that this tragedy could be repeated in any new campaign undertaken by Americans to bring peace to "the whole world." Such a campaign would undermine the Constitution, Beard argued, for the President would possess "limitless authority publicly to misrepresent and secretly to control foreign policy, foreign affairs, and the war power." As he had throughout his life, Beard used James Madison and *The Federalist* as his primary references.

Such dissent from waging the Cold War was not the fashion in 1948 and 1949, and most American historians wanted to be fashionable. Samuel Eliot Morison, Boston Brahmin, rear admiral (appointed by Roosevelt), and president of the American Historical Association, attacked Beard's legacy in an article subtitled, "History Through a Beard." The year after Morison's article appeared, Arthur Schlesinger, Jr., whose intellectual debt to Niebuhr was great, published a primer for the new liberals, which viewed their role not to the left, where Beard had wanted it, but in *The Vital Center.* Schlesinger attacked American businessmen ("capitalists") who, since they were "incapable of physical combat," developed "a legal system which penalized the use of force and an ethic which glorifies pacifism." War had been useful, particularly when it closed domestic "rifts" between Americans, as in 1917 and 1941.[34] Like the historians, President Truman took pride in his ability to search the past for present policies, but he looked elsewhere as well. "We are on the right track, and we will win," he announced in early 1950, "because God is with us in that enterprise."[35]

The Antichrist nevertheless seemed to be everywhere, even in an age that venerated consensus. On January 14 the Chinese communists attacked the American consulate offices, a week later Hiss was convicted, and on January 31 the White House announced orders to make a hydrogen bomb. "Annihilation of any life on earth has been brought within the range of technical possibilities," Albert

[34]Samuel Eliot Morison, "Did Roosevelt Start the War: History Through a Beard," *Atlantic Monthly,* CXLII (August 1948): 91–97; Arthur Schlesinger, Jr., *The Vital Center* (Boston, 1949, 1962), especially pp. 13–14, 173.

[35]U.S. Government, *Public Papers of the Presidents of the United States, Harry Truman . . . 1950.* (Washington, 1965), p. 344.

Einstein reported over national television. On February 3 London announced that a British spy ring headed by German-born, British-naturalized Klaus Fuchs had been discovered relaying atomic secrets to Soviet agents. Six days later at Wheeling, West Virginia, the junior senator from Wisconsin, Joseph McCarthy (Republican), announced that he held in his hand proof that the Department of State was riddled with communists. The paper he waved could prove nothing even faintly related to his charges, but no matter. The timing was perfect.

The senator had not previously been known for such ideological zeal, but for an uncommon amount of political savvy. In 1946 he overcame a reputation as one of the worst circuit court judges in Wisconsin history to win the Senate seat from the popular Robert M. La Follette, Jr. McCarthy accomplished this in part by running on the slogan, "Congress needs a tail-gunner," which he had never been, and by apparently destroying the legal records that reflected unfavorably on his judiciary abilities. In early 1950, with another election fight in Wisconsin only two years away, he searched for an issue. During a conversation with advisors, McCarthy first dismissed the St. Lawrence Seaway project as a possibility; then, with the Hiss case in the headlines, he eagerly seized on the communist issue. After the Wheeling speech, he became the center of some of the wildest scenes in Senate history. As his fellow legislators tried to pinpoint what he had charged, McCarthy's figures whirled from the 205 communists, at Wheeling, to 57 the following night, 81 on February 20, and when brought before a special Senate committee headed by the highly respected Millard Tydings, Democrat of Maryland, his figures changed again to 10, then to 116, and finally to 1. The one was Owen Lattimore, a specialist on Far Eastern studies at John Hopkins University. On Lattimore's conviction, McCarthy said, he would "stand or fall." When pressed for evidence, the senator responded in part by reverting to Truman's refusal to allow Congress to examine the loyalty files. The executive, McCarthy claimed, was keeping the evidence locked up. The Tydings committee dismissed McCarthy as a fraud and exonerated Lattimore, but the Wisconsin senator had only begun.[36]

[36]Richard N. Rovere, *Senator Joe McCarthy* (New York, 1959), pp. 6, 54, 39–100, 120–122, 130, 140–160.

Mao, Malenkov, the China Lobby, McCarthy. Stalin and Truman had learned that forming consensus on the Cold War was not free of complications. A grim President, pressed by domestic critics and the new Soviet bomb, demanded a wide-ranging reevaluation of American Cold War policies. In early 1950 the National Security Council began work on a highly secret document (declassified only a quarter of a century later, and then through an accident) that would soon be known as NSC-68. Truman examined the study in April, and it was ready for implementation when Korea burst into war.

NSC-68 proved to be the American blueprint for waging the Cold War during the next twenty years. It began with two assumptions that governed the rest of the document. First, the global balance of power had been "fundamentally altered" since the nineteenth century so that the Americans and Russians now dominated the world: "What is new, what makes the continuing crisis, is the polarization of power which inescapably confronts the slave society with the free." It was us against them. Second, "the Soviet Union, unlike previous aspirants to hegemony, is animated by a new fanatic faith, antithetical to our own, and seeks to impose its absolute authority," initially in "the Soviet Union and second in the areas now under [its] control." Then the crucial sentence: "In the minds of the Soviet leaders, however, achievement of this design requires the dynamic extension of their authority and the ultimate elimination of any effective opposition to their authority. . . . To that end Soviet efforts are now directed toward the domination of the Eurasian land mass."[37]

The two top State Department experts on Russia, George Kennan and Charles Bohlen, fought against using these phrases. They believed that Stalin had no grand design for world conquest, that his attention was focused almost entirely within the Soviet bloc, and that as a conservative he actually feared overextending Russian power. Kennan went further, arguing that NSC-68 should not be drawn up at all, for it could make American policies too rigid, simple, and militaristic. Acheson overruled Kennan and Bohlen.[38] The secretary of state determined to launch a global offensive to reclaim

[37]"NSC-68. A Report to the National Security Council by the Executive Secretary on United States Objectives and Programs for National Security, April 14, 1950, Washington," pp. 4, 8, 6, 34. (Hereafter cited "NSC-68.")

[38]Paul Y. Hammond, "NSC-68: Prologue to Rearmament." In Warner P. Schilling et al., *Strategy, Politics and Defense Budgets* (New York, 1962), pp. 308–311.

the initiative in the Cold War and to shut up critics at home. To do this he needed a justification. The justification would be his own view of the Soviet menace. That view undergirded NSC-68.

Given Acheson's outlook, the document moved to the inevitable conclusion: the United States "must lead in building a successfully functioning political and economic system in the free world," for "the absence of order among nations is becoming less and less tolerable." To impose "order" around the globe was a rather large task, but the United States was up to it. The key would be military power that could deter "an attack upon us" while Americans went about arranging the world so "our free society can flourish." But the administration's confidence in the use of military power went beyond mere deterrence: limited wars could be fought "to compel the acceptance of terms consistent with our objectives." To wage this kind of war the country had to mobilize its own and its allies' economies for a vast military effort. ("Foreign economic policy is a major instrument in the conduct of United States foreign relations" and "peculiarly appropriate to the Cold War.") This military rebuilding was immediately required, particularly since the Western economies were going to decline "within a period of a few years at most . . . unless more positive governmental programs are developed." The crisis was at hand.

In conclusion, therefore, NSC-68 recommended (1) against negotiations with Russia since conditions were not yet sufficient to force the Kremlin to "change its policies drastically"; (2) development of hydrogen bombs to offset possible Soviet possession of an effective atomic arsenal by 1954; (3) rapid building of conventional military forces to preserve American interests without having to wage atomic war; (4) a large increase in taxes to pay for this new, highly expensive military establishment; (5) mobilization of American society, including a government-created "consensus" on the necessity of "sacrifice" and "unity" by Americans; (6) a strong alliance system directed by the United States; (7) and — as the topper — undermining the "Soviet totalitariat" from within by making "the Russian people our allies in this enterprise." How this was to be done was necessarily vague. But no matter. The assumptions and recommendations of NSC-68 were not overburdened with modesty. Truman and Acheson were no longer satisfied with containment. They wanted Soviet withdrawal and an absolute victory.[39]

[39]"NSC-68," pp. 9, 12, 25–26, 28, 31, 45, 57, 23, 65, 24, 10.

But, as in early 1947 before Truman "scared hell" out of them, the American people were by no means prepared to pay such costs for victory. Republicans and many Democrats demanded lower taxes. Even Secretary of Defense Louis Johnson fought against NSC-68, arguing that Acheson's policies could bankrupt the country. The secretary of state finally brought the military around to accept the civilian call for larger defense budgets. The Soviet Union meanwhile appeared quiet and contained. The political circumstances threatened to destroy Acheson's hopes that NSC-68 could be used to build global "positions of strength." Only he, the President, and a few others seemed to have a clear idea of what had to be done. NSC-68 was a policy in search of an opportunity. That opportunity arrived on June 25, 1950, when, as Acheson and his aides later agreed, "Korea came along and saved us."[40]

---

[40] Princeton Seminar, July 8–9, 1953, Acheson Papers, Truman Library.

5

Korea: The War for Both Asia and Europe (1950-1951)

In June 1950 Korea was a Cold War–wracked country which lacked nearly everything except authoritarian rulers, illiteracy, cholera epidemics, and poverty. For nearly a century, it had been a pawn in Far Eastern power plays. In 1905 Japan, after using force to stop a Russian thrust, had established a protectorate over Korea and in 1910 annexed that country. In 1945 Japanese armies, according to Soviet-American agreement, were disarmed north of the 38th parallel by Russia and south of the line by the United States. Lengthy conferences failed to unify the nation, for neither the Soviets nor the Americans wanted to chance the possibility that a unified Korea would move into the opposing camp.

Both superpowers, however, found themselves trapped in a bloody civil conflict, Korean killing Korean, which astonishingly claimed 100,000 lives after 1946 and *before* the formal beginning in June 1950 of what Americans call the "Korean War." New scholarship reveals that the main struggle was not the United States versus the Soviet Union but left-wing Koreans (including both communists and noncommunists) against right-wing Koreans.[1] The United States worked desperately to keep the rightist groups in power. These groups were led by the venerable Syngman Rhee, who had spent long years of exile in the United States. Meanwhile middle-of-the-road factions moved increasingly to the left, for the leftists espoused an ardent nationalism aimed at uniting the divided nation, while Rhee appeared to be dependent on the United States for survival and was willing to accept elections only in South Korea. Vicious guerrilla war erupted between left and right in 1946. As it continued over the next two years, several crack South Korean military units defected to leftist forces.

Harry Truman never wavered in his determination to keep South Korea in the West's camp, but the growing bloodshed and Rhee's authoritarian methods (including press censorship and mass arrests of political opponents) embarrassed Truman. In 1948 he moved to pull out the remaining United States troops and turn the headache of pacifying the area over to the United Nations. Soviet troops also retreated from the North, but they left behind the communist regime of Kim Il-Sung and Red Army advisors to whip the North's army into shape. By 1949, with North and South Korea independent nations, the fighting escalated into conventional battles. Many of these were launched by Rhee to show that he was serious about reuniting the country by force. In early 1950 the fighting died down, but the pause lasted only until Kim believed he had amassed the forces to overthrow Rhee and unite Korea under his own control.

When, therefore, Harry Truman decided in late June to commit U.S. men and machines to war, he was involving Americans not in a conflict against Stalin but in a Korean civil war that had long been waged between Rhee and Kim. Three causes probably triggered the invasion from the North on June 24, 1950. The first was Kim's belief that Rhee was highly vulnerable. The State Department had even issued public protests against Rhee's crackdown on his own people. In a May 1950 election the South Korean leader lost control of his legislature, despite arrests of leading political opponents before the balloting. As he grew less secure at home, Rhee became more belligerent toward the North. Kim might well have struck not only

[1] The best accounts are Bruce Cumings's prize-winning *The Origins of the Korean War . . . 1945–1947* (Princeton, 1981); and the essays by Cumings, Mark Paul, Stephen Pelz, John Merrill, and James I. Matray in *Child of Conflict; The Korean-American Relationship, 1943–1953*, Bruce Cumings, ed. (Seattle, 1983).

because Rhee was wobbling, but before the South Korean president could launch his own invasion of the North.

Second, since 1946 Kim had been closely tied to Mao's Chinese communists, indeed too closely for a Korean who was a nationalist as well as a communist. He had gained a measure of independence by moving closer to the Soviet military in 1949. In early 1950 Kim traveled to Moscow to ask Stalin for help in conquering the South. The Russian dictator gave the green light and promises of supplies, but he made clear that neither Soviet forces nor prestige would be involved. If Kim's grand plans collapsed, the cautious Stalin was going to be standing clear of the debris. If Kim succeeded, however, he would break free of Mao and unite Korea under Korean control. It was worth the risk.

Third, Kim's plans fitted with a general strategy which Stalin was designing to counter two threats. In mid-May Truman announced that discussions on a Japanese peace treaty would receive high priority. The negotiations would particularly consider Japanese independence and the establishment of American military bases on Japan's soil under long-term agreements. The talks, American officials said, were not to be burdened with Russian representation. For Stalin this announcement opened the unhappy prospect of unity between the two greatest industrial nations in the Pacific, perhaps even the extension of a NATO-like organization to the Asian periphery of the Soviet Union. The Sino-Soviet pact in February had singled out Japan as a potential threat to Asian communism, and this had been followed by the Soviet press accusing Truman of attempting to "draw the Asiatic and Pacific countries into aggressive military blocs, to entangle those countries in the chains of some 'little' Marshall Plan for Asia."[2] If North Korea could unify the country, peacefully or otherwise, the threat of a militarized, Western-oriented Japan would be blunted, perhaps neutralized.

Another threat might well have caused Stalin even more concern. Mao's success had not created but probably encouraged revolutions throughout Asia, particularly in Indochina, the Philippines, and Indonesia. The possibility that some of these revolutions might triumph, perhaps following the pattern set by Mao, could weaken Stalin's two-camp premise and loosen his direction over the world

[2]*Current Digest of the Soviet Press,* II (April 22, 1950): p. 19; Nikita Khrushchev, *Khrushchev Remembers,* Strobe Talbott, trans. and ed. (Boston, 1970), pp. 367–370.

communist bloc. Stalin's view of world matters had become so rigid that he could not accept the nationalist content of these revolts without wrecking his own doctrines and tempering his grip on Soviet and satellite affairs. Malenkov had added to these troubles with his November speech, but by the spring of 1950 (that is, after the Chinese had shown their obstinacy in the Sino-Soviet negotiations and the revolutionary situation had intensified in Asia), Malenkov came back into line. Stalin had confined the domestic debate. A short and successful war by a Russian-controlled North Korea could intimidate Japan and check the expansive aims and reputation of Mao.

Attending to family business in Independence, Missouri, when the attack occurred, Truman immediately returned to Washington. He and Acheson assumed the invasion was Russian directed, perhaps the beginning of an extensive Sino-Soviet thrust. Their initial reaction, however, was carefully measured. They ordered MacArthur in Tokyo to dispatch supplies to the South Korean troops. Then, moving to contain the action, Truman ordered the American Seventh Fleet to sail between China and Formosa, and sent additional assistance to counterrevolutionary forces in the Philippines and Indochina. In a hurriedly called session of the United Nations Security Council, an American resolution branding the North Koreans as aggressors, demanding a cessation of hostilities, and requesting a withdrawal behind the 38th parallel, passed 9 to 0, with Yugoslavia abstaining. The Soviet Union was not represented, for Yakov Malik continued his boycott to protest the exclusion of Red China. Two days later, as the military situation worsened, Truman ordered American air and naval units into action. That same day, June 27, the United Nations passed a resolution recommending that its members aid South Korea in restoring peace. This passed 7 to 1, with Yugoslavia opposing and Egypt and India abstaining. Malik still had not appeared; the rapidity and extent of Truman's reaction had taken the Soviets by surprise.

The day after American units had been committed, the President conferred with congressional leaders for the first time to inform them of his action. The only strong objection was voiced by Senator Taft, who approved of Truman's action but disliked the sending of Americans to war without consulting Congress. Neither then nor later did the President discuss Taft's objection with the full Congress. On June 30 Truman made the final commitment. The

South Korean army of 65,000 men had suffered heavy losses in the first week of fighting. The President decided that only American ground units could stop the southward flood. In sending these troops Truman emphasized that the United States aimed only "to restore peace there and . . . restore the border." Supporting air attacks were similarly to be limited to the area around the 38th parallel.

Throughout the first week of the war the President carefully refrained from publicly linking the Russians to the attack. He hoped thereby to enable them to stop the aggression without loss of public face. On June 27 Truman dispatched a note to Moscow assuring Stalin that American objectives were limited; the President expressed the hope that the Soviets would help in quickly restoring the *status quo ante bellum.*[3] The Soviets initially responded to Truman's overtures by accusing South Korean forces of invading North Korea. Within ten days this view underwent considerable change. The war was a "civil war among the Koreans," Deputy Minister of Foreign Affairs Andrei Gromyko claimed on July 4. Under these circumstances, Gromyko concluded, the Soviet Union could take no action.[4]

Privately in June and publicly during the late summer, the Truman administration became less restrained in defining the Soviet role. "In Korea the Russians presented a check which was drawn on the bank account of collective security," Acheson claimed. "The Russians thought the check would bounce. . . . But to their great surprise, the teller paid it."[5] The terms "collective security" and "UN action" became the catchwords which supposedly explained and justified Truman's decision in late June. Both terms were misleading. The United States had no collective security pact in the Pacific in 1950. As Acheson used the term "collective security," it meant the United States would both define the extent of the "collective" and unilaterally, if necessary, furnish the "security." Nor is there any indication that the President consulted his European or Asian allies before committing American air and naval units on June 27.[6] This was not the first nor would it be the last time the

---

[3] Harry S. Truman, *Memoirs,* II (Garden City, N.Y., 1955–1956): 341, 346.

[4] Max Beloff, *Soviet Policy in the Far East, 1944–1951* (London, 1953), p. 186.

[5] Dean Acheson, *Pattern of Responsibility,* McGeorge Bundy, ed. (Boston, 1952), p. 254.

[6] For example, Truman, *Memoirs,* II: 330–340.

United States would take unilateral action in an explosive situation without consulting its Western European partners.

As for the sudden American concern to bolster the United Nations, this had not been apparent when the United States acted unilaterally or with some Western powers to establish the Truman Doctrine, the Rio Pact, the Marshall Plan, and NATO. American actions in Korea were consistent with this history, for the United States used the resolution of June 27 to establish a military command in Korea that took orders not from the United Nations but from Washington. "The entire control of my command and everything I did came from our own Chiefs of Staff," MacArthur later recalled. "Even the reports which were normally made by me to the United Nations were subject to censorship by our State and Defense Departments. I had no direct connection with the United Nations whatsoever."[7] Sixteen nations finally contributed to "United Nations" forces, but the United States provided 50 percent of the ground forces (with South Korea providing most of the remainder), 86 percent of the naval power, and 93 percent of the air power. In October, during the Truman-MacArthur conference at Wake Island, a dozen American officials prepared plans for the reconstruction of *all* Korea without consulting anyone, not even the United Nations or Syngman Rhee. The United States suffered 142,000 casualties in Korea not for the sake of "collective security" or the United Nations, but because the executive branch of the government decided that the invasion signaled a direct threat to American interests in both Asia and Europe.

Indeed, although the war was limited to Korea, Truman and Acheson used the war as the opportunity to develop new American policies around the globe. Because of these American initiatives, the six months between June and December 1950 rank among the most important of the Cold War era.

Truman and Acheson moved to the offensive globally for two particular reasons: the Korean War gave them an opportunity to shut up their critics at home and to take advantage of new openings abroad. Within the United States Acheson was in trouble because

---

[7]U.S. Senate, Committee on Foreign Relations and Committee on Armed Services, *Hearings: Military Situation in the Far East* (Washington, 1951), p. 10.

he had happened to be in office when China fell to Mao. He compounded this problem by courageously reaffirming his faith in Alger Hiss while Hiss was convicted for perjury. Of perhaps equal importance, Acheson's impeccable mustache and attire, his sarcastic and brilliant arguments, his Ivy League background, did not endear him to people who disliked so-called eggheads who made the world seem more complicated than did down-home folks like Joseph McCarthy. In his memoirs he termed the onslaught "The Attack of the Primitives," and he viewed some critics as "animals."[8] But his January remarks implying that Korea was outside the primary area of American military responsibility left him open for those who had been waiting for just such a mistake. Never again would he make that error. Instead of defining defense perimeters, he would take the offensive and undercut the "primitives."

The offensive would also allow the administration to put plans into motion that had been on drawing boards up to a year or more. These included the NSC-68 blueprint and the revitalization of American military alliances around the world. So began the spectacular summer of 1950 in which Truman and Acheson transformed the United Nations, committed the United States to Formosa and Indochina, began rearming Germany, nearly tripled American defense spending and — in the climactic act — invaded North Korea in order to show opponents at home and abroad that the United States was no longer content with mere "containment" but now aimed for liberation.

The secretary of state first went to the United Nations, which had given its support to the American commitment in Korea. It had done so, however, only because the absence of the Soviet delegation had prevented a Russian veto of the United Nations resolution. The United States could not trust to such luck in the next crisis. During the autumn Acheson pushed through the General Assembly a "Uniting for Peace" proposal giving the assembly the right to make recommendations to members for collective security measures, including the use of force, if the use of the veto stopped the Security Council from acting. This resolution transfigured the United Nations. It no longer rested on agreements among the great powers, without which neither the United Nations nor the world peace could be viable. Instead power was thrown into the General

[8]Dean Acheson, *Present at the Creation* (New York, 1969), chapter 39.

Assembly, where Costa Rica had voting power equal to that of the United States or the Soviet Union. Weakening the Russian veto, the United States also weakened its own. Assuming, however, that it could control the General Assembly, the administration had taken a calculated risk. It had, to paraphrase Acheson, issued a blank check on the future. After a decade of increased neutralist feelings among the multiplying nations in Africa and Asia, that check would appear increasingly rubberized by the 1980s.

A second part of the diplomatic offensive involved Formosa. During early 1950 Truman and his military advisors expected Communist China to conquer the island. When North Korea attacked, however, the President placed the American Seventh Fleet between the mainland and Formosa to stop any possible conflict in the area. The next step occurred in August when MacArthur's recommendations that American advisors and assistance be sent to Chiang were accepted by Truman. The early 1950 policy had been reversed. The United States had bedded down with Chiang Kai-shek and had placed itself on his side in the intra-Chinese dispute over Formosa.

A similar revolution occurred in American policy toward Indochina. The French had been the dominant colonial power in Southeast Asia since the late nineteenth century. The area's riches made it a formidable prize: Burma, Thailand, and Indochina provided rice for much of Asia. Southeast Asia produced nearly 90 percent of the world's natural rubber, 60 percent of the world's tin, and the bulk of Asia's oil. During World War II, Franklin D. Roosevelt became convinced the French could not control this strategic area (particularly after the Japanese had humiliated the white colonial rulers in warfare during 1940–1941) and tried to ease the French out so Indochina could become a United Nations trusteeship, with actual control in Chinese and American hands. In the weeks before his death, however, Roosevelt changed his mind. Chiang could no longer be trusted, and the United States had major problems elsewhere. His alternatives were clear: either allow the French to reenter, or part of the area would be controlled by the revolutionary nationalism of the Vietnamese communist leader Ho Chi Minh. Ho's forces made overtures to the United States throughout 1945, but neither Roosevelt nor Truman was in any mood to allow Ho to control such a vital area. First FDR and then Truman encouraged the French to reclaim their colonies. By late 1946 France and Ho's forces were locked in war, a war that would not end for Vietnam until nearly thirty years later.

The Soviets also refused to recognize Ho's Republic of Vietnam. By 1948 Ho was turning to Communist China for aid. He had not easily reached this decision, for the Indochinese had feared and fought against their giant neighbor for a thousand years. (In 1946, when he tried to negotiate with the French, Ho quieted his Vietnamese critics by declaring, "It is better to sniff the French dung for a while than eat China's all our lives."[9]) In January 1950 China recognized Ho's government. The Soviets followed within two weeks. After an intensive policy review, the United States fully committed itself to the French cause in early February, four and one-half months before the Korean War began. Financial aid began to flow from Washington to the French in May. But not until after the Korean War began did American personnel become involved. On July 27, in the same announcement giving American support to South Korea, Truman revealed he was dispatching a military mission to Vietnam.

The commitment had been made, as a State Department pamphlet noted in 1951, because the United States had such vital interests as the "much-needed rice, rubber, and tin," in Southeast Asia. The pamphlet added, "perhaps even more important would be the psychological effect of the fall of Indochina. It would be taken by many as a sign that the force of communism is irresistible and would lead to an attitude of defeatism." Without American aid, "it is doubtful whether [the French] could hold their ground against the Communists."[10] John Foster Dulles was more specific at a private dinner of Asian experts in October. Japan, Dulles warned, could move in only one of two directions if it hoped to become prosperous and stable: either toward its traditional markets in China, now communist, and thus deal with Mao's government, or else find markets in Southeast Asia.[11] Because Japan was the key to the entire American position in the Pacific, Southeast Asia had to remain open for Japanese exploitation.

At the same time new American commitments were forged in Asia, Acheson concentrated on Europe, the area he and Truman considered of most importance. The secretary of state moved quickly

[9] Jean Lacouture, *Ho Chi Minh* (New York, 1968), p. 119.

[10] U.S. Department of State, *Indochina: The War in Southeast Asia* (Washington, 1951), pp. 1–7; Dean Rusk, *The Underlying Principles of Far Eastern Policy* (Washington, 1951), p. 8222.

[11] Council of Foreign Relations Study Group Reports, October 23, 1950, Conference Dossiers, Draft of Japanese Peace Treaty, Dulles Papers, Princeton.

to tighten the American military alliance with Western Europe, but he did not do so solely for military objectives. Acheson never believed that the military, political, or economic aspects of a problem could, in his words, "be separated in the intellectual equivalent of a cream separator."[12] Acheson knew that intelligence reports interpreted the Korean invasion as a "local affair" which did not apparently foreshadow a communist attack in Europe.[13] He nevertheless believed that future European political problems, particularly those which threatened American interests, could be solved through the use of military alliances. It was in this context, not in that of an imminent Russian invasion which few expected, that Acheson proposed to horrified British and French officials that Germany be rearmed.

The Joint Chiefs had approved a German rearmament plan as early as April 1950. After the Korean outbreak, State Department officials restudied the problem. During long and bitter discussions, the State and Defense Departments worked out a package deal in September. Germany would be rearmed and Western European qualms quieted with three devices: more American money to aid Europe with its financial problems, four to six divisions of American troops to assure Europe of American aid in case of future Russian — or German — aggression, and an integrated military command headed by an American general. Agreement was reached just before Bevin and French Foreign Minister Robert Schuman sailed from Europe to meet Acheson at the Waldorf-Astoria Hotel in New York City for the September NATO Council meetings.[14]

On September 12 Acheson dropped, as one official called it, "the bomb at the Waldorf." To the unbelieving British and French he proposed the creation of ten German divisions. Bevin finally went along, believing that the French would never accept the plan anyway.

In December the NATO foreign ministers discussed a compromise: German troops at the regimental level would be incorporated into the NATO establishment but not constitute more than 20 percent of its strength. Despite strong, last-minute Soviet protests,

[12]Dean Acheson, *Sketches from Life of Men I Have Known* (New York, 1961), p. 103.

[13]Richard J. Barnet and Marcus Raskin, *After 20 Years* (New York, 1965), p. 29.

[14]Lawrence W. Martin, "American Decision to Rearm Germany." In Harold Stein, ed., *American Civil-Military Decisions: A Book of Case Studies* (Birmingham, Alabama, 1963), pp. 653–659.

which some officials believed threatened war if Germany were rearmed, the foreign ministers finally accepted in principle German participation, but they could not agree on details. The ministers did approve an integrated force under a supreme commander. President Truman appointed General Dwight D. Eisenhower to this post on December 19.

Truman and Acheson next sent four divisions of American soldiers to Europe in September. This immersed the administration in deep political trouble. During congressional hearings in April 1949, Acheson had assured touchy senators that he expected no large numbers of American troops would be sent to the NATO command. In early 1950, however, NSC-68 had proposed rapid and costly rebuilding of Western defenses. The Korean conflict provided the opportunity to move ahead. Congress cooperated with Truman's request in July for an additional $4 billion of defense funds and a rapid buildup of the army. The President announced on September 9 that this buildup would be followed by "substantial increases" in the number of American troops in Europe. To have the administration that had "lost" China send troops to Europe while war was raging in Asia was too much for Republican and some Democratic politicians.

On January 5, 1951, Taft accused Acheson of misleading the American people with his April 1949 statement. Taft's timing was excellent; Chinese intervention had turned Korea into a nightmare for American officials, and just the month before, the French and British had proven most obstinate in cooperating with the United States plans for NATO. Truman hurriedly told the rebellious congressmen that the serious European situation demanded four divisions but no more. After hearings in which Acheson described the troops as serving political as well as military objectives, the Senate on April 4 approved by a 69 to 21 vote a resolution that endorsed the administration's proposals for NATO, including the integrated command; urged the military utilization of Germany, Italy, and Spain in order to protect Europe; and approved the sending of the four divisions but asked the President to send no more without consulting Congress. The administration had successfully used the Korean War to create the framework within which European and general East-West problems would be discussed during the next decade.

This debate over the commitment to NATO did not occur in an atmosphere of congenial executive-legislative relations. The junior senator from Wisconsin had just launched a new onslaught against "communists," especially those in the State Department. As Cold War passions rise, rational public debate correspondingly sinks, and as the Korean War intensified, McCarthyism received a second life. "Today American boys lie dead in the mud of Korean valleys. Some have their hands tied behind their back, their faces shot away by Communist machine guns," the senator wrote the President in mid-July 1950. These horrors occurred, McCarthy charged, because the congressional program for Korea "was sabotaged."[15] He was not clear on the substance of that program, but during the following months he did not hesitate in condemning the man he believed to be the chief saboteur. George Catlett Marshall, former army chief of staff, architect of military victory over Germany and Japan, secretary of state, now secretary of defense, was, McCarthy claimed, part of a "conspiracy so immense and an infamy so black as to dwarf any previous such venture in the history of man." Because Henry Stimson, a man with impeccable credentials as an anticommunist and a conservative, had ranked Marshall only with George Washington, McCarthy felt compelled to have his aides document his accusations with a book on Marshall. The senator himself probably never read the book through; if he did, he found no evidence to substantiate his charges.

Truman also considered Marshall one of the greatest Americans who ever lived, and the President began replying to McCarthy's charges by calling the senator, among other things, the Kremlin's greatest asset. In the ensuing war of slanderous personal abuse, Truman did not stand a chance. McCarthy's use of the "multiple lie" (an accusation so long and containing so many untruths that no one could ever pin down all the lies at one time), and his repeated emphasis on so-called "facts" and "documents" in a society which easily accepts the superficial appearance of truth for the truth itself, made McCarthy invulnerable to Truman's retaliation.[16] Nor had Truman helped his cause by advancing his own conspiratorial view of Soviet activity and creating a noxious loyalty program. In 1949 and 1950 Attorney General J. Howard McGrath crossed the country

---

[15]Joseph R. McCarthy to President Truman, July 12, 1950, Office File 20, Truman Papers, Truman Library.

[16]Richard Rovere, *Senator Joe McCarthy* (Cleveland, 1959), pp. 110, 167–170. The book on Marshall is *America's Retreat From Victory: The Story of George Catlett Marshall* [n.p.], 1952.

protesting against professors of dubious political beliefs who infected student minds, pressed the need to bring increased numbers of anticommunist speakers and literature to campuses, and warned that the "many Communists in America" were "everywhere — in factories, offices, butcher stores, on street corners." With such tactics, the President and the attorney general played into the hands of the spreading McCarthyism.

Soon few were free of suspicion. A McCarthyite line properly applied could end any controversy. "It seems that the only argument some persons can present is to holler about Alger Hiss and then refer to Yalta," Senator Tom Connally complained. "Every time something comes up, they get out a Communist and chase him around."[17] In too many cases this sufficed. Even the Americans for Democratic Action, that staunch defender against the Progressives in 1948, fell under suspicion because its 1950 convention urged the abolition of the House Un-American Activities Committee and suggested ties "sooner or later" with "the Chinese people." As soon as the Korean War erupted, the Americans for Democratic Action dropped all references to the House committee and continued to do so until 1959; it also modified its enthusiasm for the Chinese.[18]

Congress demonstrated its patriotism in September by passing the McCarran Internal Security bill. A measure so confused that its supporters could not explain parts of it, the act required communist organizations and their members to register with the attorney general. It did not call such membership a crime, but this was covered by the Smith Act of 1940, which prohibited membership in any group advocating violent overthrow of the government. If the Supreme Court declared the Communist party to be such a group, those registering under the McCarran Act would automatically incriminate themselves. With such conditions, skeptics doubted that registrars would be overwhelmed by people insisting on labeling themselves criminals. The bill also allowed the deportation of aliens who had been communists, no matter when, and in time of war allowed detention of persons whether they were communist or not. This legislation passed the House 354 to 20 and the Senate 70 to 7. Many congressmen who hated it in private voted for it in

[17]Tom Connally, *My Name is Tom Connally* (New York, 1954), pp. 351–352.

[18]Clifton Brock, *Americans for Democratic Action* (Washington, 1962), pp. 143–144.

public. Their political lives were at stake. Truman gave the bill a ringing veto on September 20, arguing that the act could not work properly and so would result in an even more repressive act in the future. The House took one hour to pass the act over the President's veto. The Senate did so after a handful of liberals led by Hubert Humphrey and Paul Douglas engaged in a twenty-two-hour fili-buster. The political facts were plain for all to see, and the doubters were soon convinced by the results of the November congressional election. The Republicans picked up twenty-eight seats in the House. In the Senate they won five more seats, and in three of those contests (John Marshall Butler's victory over McCarthy nemesis Millard Tydings in Maryland, Everett Dirksen's defeat of Senate Majority Leader Scott Lucas in Illinois, and Richard Nixon's triumph over Helen Gahagan Douglas in California), McCarthy happily accepted credit for helping the winners.

The election occurred when American forces were advancing to greater victories in Korea. What uplifting effects some battle losses would have on Republican power and McCarthyism, Democrats did not wish to contemplate. Truman and Acheson, however, believed they had removed that danger — indeed, had cut the ground out from under the "primitives" — by deciding to cross the 38th parallel and liberate North Korea. This decision can only be fully understood when placed with the administration's initiatives in Korea, the United Nations, Formosa, Indochina, and Germany. Together these commitments provided Acheson with new and exceptionally strong "situations of strength" from which he could deal with communists and domestic critics.

The origins of the decision to cross the 38th apparently date from mid-July. MacArthur had finally halted the North Korean advance. Rumors circulated in the State Department that plans were being made to advance beyond the 38th. George Kennan considered such a move highly dangerous. He did not want MacArthur to go to "the gates of Vladivostok [the giant Soviet naval base bordering North Korea]. The Russians would never under any circumstances agree to this." Kennan had intense arguments with Dulles and Assistant Secretary of State for the Far East Dean Rusk, both of whom apparently supported Acheson's hope that the United States could forcefully unite the Koreas.

The decision was finally based upon an evaluation of possible Soviet reaction. By August Stalin had defined Russia out of Korea's "civil war." Moreover, Secretary of Defense Louis Johnson privately told the Senate Foreign Relations Committee that the Soviets would not attack in either Asia or Europe "because Russia was probably aware of the fact that at the present time we had a greater supply of atomic bombs than she had."[19] China was of less concern, partly because Acheson believed Stalin controlled Chinese movements and also because Mao's army, after the long civil war, did not seem capable of effectively fighting the United States.

On September 1 the directive allowing MacArthur to drive beyond the 38th was completed by the National Security Council. Truman signed it on September 11. Four days later MacArthur made a brilliant landing at Inchon, back of North Korean lines, cut off large numbers of enemy troops, and began a rapid northward drive. With the general's triumph, Truman instructed him on September 27 to move through North Korea if he did not encounter Chinese or Russian resistance and if he was certain of success in the field. Given MacArthur's self-confidence, if not arrogance, that was an invitation for him to drive to the Yalu. On October 7 the United Nations followed along obediently, endorsing Truman's order by a lopsided vote.

All eyes now turned to China. In late August American officials had asked for the open door "within all parts of Korea." At that point Foreign Minister Chou En-lai reminded the world that "Korea is China's neighbor" and asked for negotiations so the affair could be settled "peacefully." In late September Peking warned India, which had become China's main link with the Western world, that it would not "sit back with folded hands and let the Americans come to the border." Chou formally told India in a dramatic midnight meeting that China would attack if United Nations troops moved into North Korea. The United States discounted the threat,

[19]Kennan's views are in George Kennan, *Memoirs, 1925–1950* (Boston, 1967), p. 488; Johnson's in "Memorandum of Executive Meeting of the Foreign Relations Committee," August 23, 1950, Foreign Relations, 1950, Secretary Louis Johnson, Box 101, Papers of H. Alexander Smith, Princeton. The decision to cross the 38th is discussed at length, and with more extensive bibliographical references, in W. LaFeber, "The Cold War in Microcosm." In Ronald Pruessen and Lynn Miller, eds., *Reflections on the Cold War* (Philadelphia, 1974). See also William Stueck, "The March to the Yalu." In *Child of Conflict*, Bruce Cumings, ed. (Seattle, 1983), pp. 195–238.

and MacArthur responded by issuing an ultimatum for North Korea's total surrender. On October 16 a few Chinese "volunteers" crossed the Yalu from Manchuria into North Korea.[20]

American officials made no changes. On September 10 Acheson commented on national television, "I should think it would be sheer madness for the Chinese to intervene." On October 9 the danger reached a new high when two American F-80 jets strafed a Soviet airfield only a few miles from Vladivostok. After the Soviets protested, the United States apologized. Vexed that the crisis arose, and angered that he had to back down before the Soviets just a month before national elections, Truman canceled a trip to Independence and flew to Wake Island to check on MacArthur. In the heavily censored text of the meeting the general assured the President, "We are no longer fearful of [Chinese] intervention. We no longer stand hat in hand." China might move 60,000 men across the Yalu, but if these troops tried to move farther south without air cover (and the Chinese had no air force), "there would be the greatest slaughter."[21]

On October 26 the first Chinese prisoner was captured, "so that you began to know, at that point," Acheson later commented, "that something was happening." MacArthur nevertheless continued his drive toward the Yalu. On November 21 advance elements of American troops peered at Chinese sentries stationed across the river. Three days later MacArthur grandly announced the launching of the end-the-war offensive. On November 26 the Chinese moved across the Yalu in mass, trapping and destroying large numbers of United Nations troops, including 20,000 Americans and Koreans at the Chosin Reservoir. Three weeks later the retreating United Nations forces again fought below the 38th, and now it was Chou En-lai who proclaimed his nation's intention of reunifying Korea. "They really fooled us when it comes right down to it, didn't they?" a senator once asked Acheson. "Yes, sir," the secretary of state replied.[22]

On November 15 Acheson, usually so debonair in his public appearances, became nearly incoherent in explaining why the Chinese

[20]This account follows in most respects that of Allen Whiting, *China Crosses the Yalu* (New York, 1960).

[21]U.S. Senate, Committee on Armed Services and Committee on Foreign Relations, *Substance of Statements Made at Wake Island Conference on October 15, 1950,* compiled by General of the Army Omar N. Bradley (Washington, 1951), p. 5.

[22]*Military Situation in the Far East,* pp. 1832–1835.

should not fear American forces on the Yalu. "Everything in the world" was being done to reassure the Chinese their interests were not jeopardized, he declared, "and I should suppose that there is no country in the world which has been more outstanding in developing the theory of brotherly development of border waters than the United States."[23] Such an American "brotherly development" of the Yalu, of course, was precisely what the Chinese were determined to prevent. From a position on the Yalu the United States could exert pressure on both Mao's internal and external policies. China's intense hatred for the West, reaching a peak after a century of Western exploitation of the country, and Mao's determination to restore Chinese supremacy in Asia made impossible the acceptance of such an American presence.

The decision to cross the 38th proved exceptionally costly to the United States. Four-fifths of all American casualties in the war occurred after United Nations forces crossed the parallel. The war froze the United States into a Cold War posture for the next two decades, paralyzing particularly American-Chinese relations. As one observer noted, "700 million potential customers had turned into the apparition of 700 million dangerous adversaries."[24] The United States began to look upon ferocious Chinese armies as a new and more dangerous form of the "yellow peril" that had long haunted Americans. The "peril" became more dangerous in the 1950s and 1960s precisely because so few Americans knew anything about it.

Washington officials were frightened. Truman reiterated that the United States had no "aggressive intentions toward China." He believed the Chinese people opposed this sending of troops by their leaders. This belief was in line with Truman's general theory that communism anywhere never had popular support. The aggression must be crushed, the President continued, or "we can expect it to spread throughout Asia and Europe to this hemisphere."[25] Truman's response, however, was measured. He countermanded MacArthur's order to bomb Chinese troops and supplies in Manchuria. In a news conference of November 30 he showed signs of losing this restraint. The President intimated the United States would use all

[23]*Department of State Bulletin*, XXIII (November 27, 1950): 855.

[24]A. T. Steele, *The American People and China* (New York, 1966), p. 60.

[25]U.S. Government, *Public Papers of the Presidents of the United States. Harry S. Truman . . . 1950* (Washington, 1965), pp. 724–727.

its power to contain the Chinese. He explicitly did not exclude using atomic bombs. This remark brought British Prime Minister Attlee flying to the United States on December 4.

Attlee was not without responsibility for the crisis; his government had participated in the decision to send United Nations troops to the Yalu. He now worried that in the newly expanded war Truman would not be able to control the military and particularly wondered at the spectacle of Truman flying 5000 miles to Wake Island to meet MacArthur, who had flown 1900. ("I thought it a curious relationship between a Government and a general," Attlee commented later.) The prime minister received Truman's assurances that the United States was not planning to use the bomb. The two men then undertook a full, candid, and most revealing evaluation of the Asian tinderbox.

Both agreed that a general war must be averted and that the United Nations forces should not evacuate Korea unless forced out militarily. Then basic differences emerged. Attlee argued that China's admission to the United Nations could bring it into regular consultations leading to a cease-fire. Acheson doubted that in their present advantageous military position the Chinese would want a cease-fire; if they did and negotiations resulted, Mao would next demand a United Nations seat and concessions on Formosa. The United States had refused to discuss these two items before the intervention, and Acheson now was in no mood to reward aggressors. Attlee countered that a cease-fire would make explicit the divisions between China and Russia: "I want them [the Chinese] to become a counterpoise to Russia in the Far East," Attlee argued. If "we just treat the Chinese as Soviet satellites, we are playing the Russian game."

Truman now hardened his earlier view of the Chinese. They were "Russian satellites," and if they succeeded in Korea "it would be Indo-China, then Hong Kong, then Malaya." Acheson interposed that he did not think it mattered whether China was a satellite or not, for it would act like Russia anyway. He believed the invasion into Korea "had design," and, like Truman, he adopted the domino theory to warn that any compromise with the Chinese would have a "serious" effect on the Japanese and Philippine Islands. Acheson recalled a "saying among State Department officials that with communistic regimes you could not bank good will; they balanced their books every night." Therefore, he argued, the West must develop great military power to stop "this sort of thing from happening in the future." Acheson and Truman also reminded Attlee that the United States could not be "internationalist" in Europe and "isolationist" in Asia; domestic political pressures made that impossible.

At that point Attlee questioned the basic American premise, the fundamental belief that underlay United States policy in Europe as well as Asia. He emphasized that the United Nations must be kept together even if this meant alienating important segments of American public opinion. Whatever the United States and Great Britain did would have to be done through the United Nations, Attlee argued, and this could not be accomplished by the efforts and votes of only the United States and the United Kingdom, "important as we are."[26] Truman and Acheson disagreed; they believed the two nations were "important" enough. By controlling the United Nations forces and now, apparently, the United Nations itself through the "Uniting for Peace" resolution, American officials believed they could keep the American people united, prevent a bigger war in Asia, follow an "internationalist" policy in both Europe and Asia, punish China for moving into Korea by excluding it from the United Nations and Formosa, build up great military power throughout the world, and through it all keep the other United Nations members in agreement with American policies. It was a tall order, so demanding and inflexible that it fixed Washington's position on China for the next twenty years.

American intelligence estimates reinforced Truman's and Acheson's views. A December 13 report stated that the Soviet Union hoped to use the war to move American power away from Korea and Formosa, establish China as the dominant power in the Far East and seat it in the United Nations, eliminate American power in Japan, and prevent German rearmament.[27] The administration expected little help from the United Nations in thwarting these Soviet drives. The most the United Nations could do was brand the Chinese as aggressors, which it did on February 1, 1951, by a vote of 44 to 7 with 9 abstentions.

Although the military situation steadily eroded, not even the other nations in the Western Hemisphere would offer much assistance. The Latin Americans dutifully voted with the United States

[26] Truman, *Memoirs*, II: 396–411.
[27] Truman, *Memoirs*, II: 420–421.

on resolutions in the United Nations and the Organization of American States, but in the early spring of 1951, when Truman personally appealed to Latin American foreign ministers to "establish the principle of sharing our burdens fairly," only Colombia responded with troops. Several other nations sent materiel, but Latin America as a whole failed to see the relevance of Korea to its own economic deprivation and political instability. Later in 1951 a shocked administration attempted to woo its southern neighbors by extending to them the Mutual Security Program of military aid. Eight nations took the money in 1952 to protect themselves against communist aggression; this both giver and receiver interpreted to mean preservation of the domestic status quo. No other Latin American nation, however, sent men to Korea.

The United States would have to depend primarily upon its on resources in defending what Niebuhr had called "our farflung lines." In December and January the President requested emergency powers to expedite war mobilization. Closely following the guidelines suggested in NSC-68, he submitted a $50 billion defense budget; this contrasted with the $13.5 billion budget of six months before. The administration doubled the number of air groups to ninety-five and obtained new bases in Morocco, Libya, and Saudi Arabia. Army personnel increased 50 percent to 3.5 million men.

In Asia the administration focused on tightening American military ties with Japan through a new peace treaty. John Foster Dulles assumed control of the negotiations and almost single-handedly drove the treaty through to a successful conclusion in September 1951. It was a bravura performance. The pact restored Japanese sovereignty over the home islands but not over the Ryukyus (which included the large American base at Okinawa). In an accompanying security agreement Japan allowed the stationing of American troops and planes on its soil but not those of any third power. Dulles simply excluded Russia from the early, decisive negotiations. When the Soviets were allowed to participate, Dulles interpreted their proposal as an attempt to dominate the area around Japan. As one participant recalled, Dulles demonstrated the effect of the Soviet plan on a map, "took this map dramatically and held it up like this . . . and then threw it on the floor with the utmost contempt. And that made a tremendous impression."[28]

[28]Interview with C. Stanton Babcock, in Dulles Oral History Project, Dulles Papers, Princeton.

Dulles also ran roughshod over demands from American allies and neutrals in Asia, who demanded reparations from Japan for its occupation during World War II. He warned that the United States would brook no "Carthaginian peace" which would "lead to bitter animosity and in the end drive Japan into the orbit of Russia." Some American allies wanted reparations to weaken Japanese potential for producing weapons. Dulles solved this problem by negotiating a series of mutual defense treaties to ensure the Philippines, Australia, and New Zealand against both reemerging Asian giants, Japan and China. Thirty months before, Acheson had assured the Senate that other than NATO the administration contemplated no further regional pacts. On September 1, 1951, the United States signed with Australia and New Zealand the so-called ANZUS Treaty, pledging the security of those two nations.

Because Australia and New Zealand belonged to the British Commonwealth, Great Britain was conspicuous by its absence from ANZUS. As early as March 1914, Winston Churchill, then First Lord of the Admiralty, predicted that with British resources increasingly devoted to Europe, the "white men" in the Pacific would soon have to seek American protection. Thirty-seven years later the British were not so understanding. When Great Britain protested that the United States had not adequately consulted it on the Japanese or ANZUS pacts, Dulles granted the point, but countered that if Britain came in the French and Dutch would also and thereby transform ANZUS in the eyes of suspicious Asians into a colonial alliance. This argument effectively reduced British influence in the Pacific. "All roads in the Commonwealth lead to Washington," a Canadian official observed.[29] The United States was single-handedly preparing Asia for the containment of China.

These negotiations determined the geographical extent of the American commitment in the Pacific. During the spring of 1951, with drama and flourishes seldom seen in American history, the military extent of that commitment was decided. In late January, United Nations forces opened a successful drive back to the 38th parallel. As the battle stalemated along the former boundary line,

[29]Interview with General Matthew Ridgway, in Dulles Oral History Project, Dulles Papers, Princeton; Churchill and the Canadian official are quoted in Geoffrey Barraclough, *An Introduction to Contemporary History* (New York, 1964), p. 67.

State Department and Pentagon officials cautiously explored the possibility of negotiations with the Chinese on March 20. Three days later General MacArthur issued a personal statement urging that the Red military commanders "confer in the field" with him on surrender; if he could attack China's "coastal areas and interior bases," the general insisted, that nation would be "doomed" to military collapse. MacArthur had again undercut his superiors in Washington.

As early as July 1950 he had shown reluctance to accept Truman's decision that Chiang Kai-shek should be contained on Formosa rather than unleashed on the mainland or allowed to ship troops to Korea. A month later MacArthur sent a message to the annual convention of the Veterans of Foreign Wars, which the President viewed as an attack upon his policy toward Chiang. Truman angrily demanded that this message be recalled, and MacArthur complied although it had already been published. The Wake Island conference muted these differences, but the published minutes are embarrassing in their revelation of MacArthur's incredible condescension and Truman's tittering insecurity. Once the President was back in Washington, this insecurity disappeared. After MacArthur again recommended a naval blockade of China, air attacks to level Chinese military and industrial installations, and the use of 30,000 Formosan troops in Korea, Truman patiently explained on January 13 "the political factors" involved in the "world-wide threat" of the Soviet Union which made containment of the Korean War necessary.[30] When MacArthur issued his ultimatum of March 23, Truman's patience, never inexhaustible, evaporated.

Only the method and timing of relieving the general remained to be decided. On April 5 Joe Martin, the leading Republican in the House, read a letter from MacArthur which charged that "here we fight Europe's war with arms while the diplomats there still fight it with words." "We must win," the letter emphasized. "There is no substitute for victory." The Joint Chiefs of Staff agreed with Truman that MacArthur would have to be relieved immediately; reports from the field indicated that the general was losing the confidence of his men and had already lost confidence in himself.[31] On April 11 the President recalled MacArthur.

[30]*Military Situation in the Far East*, pp. 503–504.
[31]Cabell Philipps, *The Truman Presidency* (New York, 1966), pp. 337–347.

Truman knew the political dynamite in the decision. Less than two weeks earlier he had agreed with top advisors that an all-out speaking campaign would have to be undertaken by cabinet-level officers because the administration's "'story' was not reaching the American public."[32] The American people preferred quick victory to containment. This preference was dramatically demonstrated when the general returned to the greatest popular reception in American history. Senator McCarthy expressed the feelings toward Truman of not a few Americans when, with characteristic restraint, he told a press conference, "The son of a bitch ought to be impeached." Congress warmly received MacArthur's speech before a joint session, then in April and May settled down to investigate the case of the President versus the general.

In a battle of MacArthur versus Truman, the long-range issues tended to be overshadowed by the personalities involved. In MacArthur's case this was not an advantage. Having last set foot in the United States fourteen years before, the general seemed unable or unwilling to grasp the political and social as well as the diplomatic views of his country. Although he had repeatedly advocated policies which contained the most somber worldwide ramifications, he now admitted having only a "superficial knowledge" of NATO and European affairs.

His basic message was curiously close to Truman's and Niebuhr's in 1948: because communism posed a threat to all civilization, "you have got to hold every place." Or again, "What I advocate is that we defend every place, and I say that we have the capacity to do it. If you say that we haven't you admit defeat." Like Acheson, he insisted on not putting military power and politics into the intellectual equivalent of a cream separator. In time of war, however, MacArthur demanded the reversal of Acheson's priority: once involved in war, the general argued, the military commander must be supreme over all military and political affairs in his theater, "or otherwise you will have the system that the Soviet once employed of the political commissar, who would run the military as well as the politics of the country." Such a remark cut across the grain of traditional American policies of subordinating military to civilian officials even if the nation was involved in total war. When

---

[32]"Memorandum for the President," from Joseph Short, Secretary to the President, April 2, 1951, Office file 386, Truman Papers, Truman Library.

the embattled general heard the suggestion of Assistant Secretary of State Dean Rusk that war in Korea must not become a "general conflagration," MacArthur branded it "the concept of appeasement, the concept that when you use force, you can limit the force."

The general believed that by controlling the sea and air no one could "successfully launch an effort against us," but the United States could "largely neutralize China's capability to wage aggressive war and thus save Asia from the engulfment otherwise facing it." He expressed contempt for the Chinese communists. "Never, in our day, will atomic weapons be turned out of China. They cannot turn out the ordinary weapons." Nor was there a threat of Soviet intervention. Time, however, was short. If, as MacArthur once remarked, Europe was a "dying system," and the Pacific would "determine the course of history in the next ten thousand years," victory must be won immediately. The "dreadful slaughter" had to end, MacArthur pleaded; American blood as well as dust is settling in Korea, and the "blood, to some extent" rests "on me." But now, he concluded emotionally, "There is no policy — there is nothing, I tell you, no plan, or anything."[33]

The administration had a plan, and Acheson outlined it in his testimony after MacArthur finished. Korea must be viewed as part of a "collective security system," Acheson argued. When so viewed, two things readily became apparent. First, all-out war in Korea would suck in Russian force to aid Stalin's "largest and most important satellite." "I cannot accept the assumption that the Soviet Union will go its way regardless of what we do," the secretary of state declared. If Russia did intervene, there could be "explosive possibilities not only for the Far East, but for the rest of the world as well." Unlike MacArthur, Acheson insisted on keeping the European picture uppermost in dealing with Korea. (Truman once added a variant on this: expansion of the war would "destroy the unity of the free nations," the President declared. "We cannot go it alone in Asia and go it with company in Europe.") Second, if Europe and the prevention of Russian entry in force did comprise the main objectives, American forces were not engaged in a "dreadful slaughter" or, as Acheson remarked, "a pointless and inconclusive struggle," but had "scored a powerful victory" by dealing "Communist impe-

[33] *Military Situation in the Far East*, pp. 39, 45, 54, 66–68, 78, 81, 83, 86–87.

rialist aims in Asia a severe setback" in preventing the armed conquest of all Korea.[34]

MacArthur lost the argument. He lost it so decisively, moreover, that, while negotiations to conclude a stalemated war fitfully began in Korea during the summer of 1951, Acheson accelerated the military buildup of Europe.

[34]*Military Situation in the Far East*, pp. 924–926.

6

New Issues, New Faces (1951-1953)

The MacArthur hearings epitomized a wide-ranging debate over American foreign policies during the twenty-four months before the 1952 presidential election. From the vantage point of twenty years later, the importance of this debate is not limited to those particular months, but has grown with time until historians can discover at that early point the turn of American thinking that led the nation into the involvements, particularly in Asia, of the next decade. One can also observe the beginnings of the dissent which would later divide American liberals and split intellectuals from policy makers. If the period is extended to 1953, it is equally important for Soviet policy, but with one difference: the internal debates arising out of the Party Congress of late 1952 and Stalin's death five months later marked an end to an epoch in Russian history.

By the time the de facto armistice was agreed upon in July 1953, the Korean War had made as much impact upon American aid to Europe as to Asia. The agreement in principle on German rearmament and the sending of additional American troops to Europe were major steps in this direction. American strategy in NATO during 1951 and 1952 rested first upon the "tripwire" theory that any Soviet attack upon a NATO command containing American troops would automatically trip a nuclear attack from the United States. One European official stated this theory in elementary terms; when asked how many American soldiers must be stationed in Europe to protect the West, he replied one would be enough if that one was shot during the first wave of an attack. To further its nuclear capability, the United States conducted its first successful thermonuclear test at Eniwetok Island in the Pacific during March 1951. In mid-June 1952 the keel went down for the USS *Nautilus*, the first submarine to be powered by atomic energy. Truman proposed a $60 billion defense budget for 1952, 20 percent above that of 1951. If the wire was tripped, the United States was preparing to respond massively.

NATO strategy also rested upon the hope that the war could be contained east of the Elbe. For this, a large conventional force would be needed; Eisenhower wanted thirty-five to forty ready divisions and ninety-six more which could be brought up within a month. The present 300 aircraft would have to multiply ten times. These grandiose plans, Truman observed, "tripped over one hard, tough fact. This fact was the poverty of western Europe."[1] Three years after the launching of the Marshall Plan, the recipient nations were sinking back into an economic morass. Only Germany gained ground; it used the new concern over military power to rearm and end the Allied occupation of its territory.[2] The other Europeans discovered that jamming their meager resources into defense spending produced scanty results. They owned more conventional arms in a nuclear era and lost resources that they had hoped to invest in their own overseas empires.

Some nations attempted to bolster their economies with increased exports to the communist bloc. These shipments included goods that, many Americans feared, would greatly aid the Sino-Russian war machines. Congress retaliated by passing the Kem Amendment and the Battle Act, which in certain circumstances cut American aid going to those nations that exported strategic goods to communists. Another response was more positive. In 1951 Congress passed the Mutual Security Act (MSA), which coalesced the economic, military, and technical assistance programs. This allowed an injection of a stronger military emphasis than ever before. As

[1]Harry S. Truman, *Memoirs*, II (Garden City, New York, 1955–1956): 258.
[2]Charles Wolf, Jr., *Foreign Aid: Theory and Practice in Southern Asia* (Princeton, 1960), pp. 115–116.

Acheson remarked, the "whole impact" of MSA would be "to carry out the rearmament program," for, he somehow concluded, the Marshall Plan's "original task has been accomplished."[3]

NATO strategy, as well as Cold War politics, rested also on a third approach: that the basis of the alliance be expanded as far as possible. In May 1951 the United States proposed adding Greece and Turkey to the military pact in order to prevent those two nations from entertaining ideas of becoming neutral politically. Yugoslavia, although not wishing to enter NATO, began requesting military assistance in addition to the economic aid that it had already obtained from the West. In September 1951 the Western Foreign Ministers agreed to release Italy from restrictions imposed in 1945 upon its military. Most notable was the rapidly evolving American attitude toward Franco's Spain.

Kennan had observed in 1947 that the Truman Doctrine implied a new view of Franco. By 1949 a congressional–Defense Department axis had formed to force the issue. Senators Pat McCarran, Owen Brewster, and Robert Taft urged the administration, in Taft's words, to "shake loose from its communist-front philosophy" by working with Franco. One congressman, among the many who junketed to Madrid in 1949 and 1950, publicly called the Spanish dictator a "very, very lovely and loveable character." Lower-echelon naval and air force officers heartily cooperated; they wanted bases as widely dispersed, as close to the Soviet bloc, and as independent of British bases as possible. In several secret meetings in McCarran's Senate office, these Pentagon officers and congressmen charted political strategy. In March 1950 McCarran succeeded in securing a $62.5 million loan for Franco. For ideological reasons, Truman despised this and every other pro-Spanish move, but after June 1950 the logic of his own military policy forced him to recognize the Franco government late that year. The following summer the administration began negotiations to obtain Spanish military bases. On August 25, 1953, the Spanish ambassador to the United States pinned the special medal of the Grand Cross on McCarran for the senator's exceptional devotion to Spain. A month and one day later the base treaty was completed. Franco had driven a hard bargain. The United States granted economic assistance and

[3]Wolf, *Foreign Aid*, pp. 114–116.

a quarter-billion dollars of military aid in return for the right to construct and use military bases which would remain under Spanish sovereignty.[4]

The Spanish base treaty augmented American military power in Europe but contributed less to Acheson's political objectives; most of Western Europe too vividly remembered Franco's cooperation with Hitler. The political aims rested instead on the success of the Pleven Plan and German rearmament. To the accompaniment of shrill Soviet protests, the Western Foreign Ministers worked on these issues throughout 1951, then gathered at Lisbon in February 1952 to hammer out final ground rules for the new Western alliance. Agreement did not come easily. The big four split down the middle on the form of German rearmament as well as on other problems. "More often than not, I found myself agreeing with . . . Adenauer," Acheson recalled, "and Eden [agreed] with Schuman."[5]

The French and British split, however, on the critical issue. The Pleven Plan had been transformed in earlier negotiations into a European Defense Community (EDC) comprised of France, Germany, and the Benelux. The EDC would operate under separate European control but be linked with NATO so Germany could directly participate in NATO defenses. Schuman and the Netherlands officials now insisted that Great Britain formally join the EDC. They did not want to be in the EDC virtually alone with German power and refused to consider American and British presence in NATO sufficient to control the possibility of German domination of the new grouping. The newly elected government of Winston Churchill refused to commit itself so solidly to European affairs. Too many Anglo-American ties would be severed. Any British integration into European affairs would have to come "in doses rather than at a gulp," Eden later remarked.[6] Acheson could not settle this dispute by quieting the French fear. Several months after the Lisbon conference, President Vincent Auriol of France told the secretary of state "with considerable passion," as Acheson later recalled, "that our policy toward Germany was a great mistake. He knew Germany; he reviewed German history since Bismarck. We were

[4]Theodore J. Lowi, "Bases in Spain." In Harold Stein, ed., *American Civil-Military Decisions: A Book of Case Studies* (Birmingham, Alabama, 1963), pp. 667–697.

[5]Dean Acheson, *Sketches from Life of Men I Have Known* (New York, 1961), p. 47.

[6]Anthony Eden, *Full Circle: The Memoirs of Anthony Eden* (New York, 1960), p. 34.

wrong in thinking that the greater danger came from Russia. It came from Germany."[7]

Acheson finally obtained Schuman's consent to allow 500,000 Germans in twelve divisions to enter the EDC, but the French exacted a price. Adenauer agreed to allow Western forces to remain in Germany for internal security as well as military purposes, swore to deal with Russia only through the Allies, and allowed the West to continue governing Berlin. Acheson opened wide the American and German pocketbooks, promising to help France meet its defense expenditures in Vietnam and Europe. For this, Acheson even won an agreement to double NATO manpower to fifty divisions (including twelve French) by the end of 1952.

There would never be fifty NATO divisions; there would never be an EDC. In the long run, the Lisbon conference produced much ill will. Acheson's troubles began immediately after the conference adjourned. On March 10 the Soviets proposed to the three Western powers that discussions be held on a peace treaty which would declare Germany united and independent. Russia further suggested allowing Germany to have a national army with ties to neither the East nor West, withdrawing all foreign troops, and admitting Germany to the United Nations. This breathtaking proposal came out of cold Russian fear of a rearmed, Western-oriented Germany. It might have been a propaganda ploy, a mere delaying tactic. Or it might have been an opportunity to neutralize Germany and drastically reduce the Cold War tensions infecting the Central European hothouse which had germinated so many hot wars in the past.

No one will ever know what the Soviets meant. Acheson refused to follow up on the proposal. At this point, his diplomacy stood revealed not as the building of "positions of strength" to facilitate negotiations for the easing of East-West conflict but the building of strength so that such negotiations might be avoided. The West had to be kept together. This meant Germany had to be rearmed under Western guidance. The "peace offensive" out of Moscow was a "'golden apple' tactic," Acheson announced in April. The Soviets resembled the Goddess of Discord who, angered that she had not been invited to a wedding party, threw a golden apple over the fence "hoping to cause a ruckus among the guests and break up the party."[8] The wall would be built higher to make such apple throwing

[7] Acheson, *Sketches from Life*, p. 53.

[8] Dean Acheson, "Progress Toward International Peace and Unity," *Department of State Bulletin*, XXVI (April 28, 1952): 648.

more difficult, and so on May 26 and 27 Acheson, Eden, and Schuman signed the agreement ending the occupation of Germany. They then initialed the EDC treaty. Now the EDC had only to pass the various parliaments before coming into effect.

Even as Acheson threaded his way through the EDC negotiations of 1951 and 1952, Americans vigorously debated new policies which, by the middle-1950s, would set their foreign policies on new paths. In short, the debates of 1951–1952 thrashed out the premises which governed American foreign policy for at least the next decade and a half. At the simplest level, the arguments pivoted on the question of whether Asia should enjoy equal priority with Europe in American policy. Overall, the debate was far more complex. It became a prime example of how oversimplified (often unquestioned) premises of one historical era could, almost inevitably, develop into apparently unrelated but far-reaching policies affecting life and death in a later era. Chiang's defeat on mainland China, American involvement in Korea, and the sending of additional United States soldiers to Europe initiated the debate. The MacArthur hearings greatly intensified it. Then the arguments were systematically reformulated and can now be found in Senator Robert Taft's *A Foreign Policy for Americans,* Hans Morgenthau's *In Defense of the National Interest,* Reinhold Niebuhr's *The Irony of American History,* and, finally, the 1952 election campaign.[9]

Taft's and Morgenthau's books chalked in the boundaries of the debate. Like the vast majority of Americans, both men agreed on the need to contain Russia. They substantially differed on the means to accomplish this, and it was on the issue of these means that the argument was waged. Morgenthau was a distinguished professor of international relations at the University of Chicago and Taft was running for the 1952 Republican presidential nomination, but despite their different vantage points, the two men surprisingly agreed on a number of issues. Both considered the United Nations, particularly after the passage of the "Uniting for Peace" resolution, to be a fifth wheel in world diplomacy; both badly oversimplified their argument by tracing the origins of the Cold War

[9]Robert A. Taft, *A Foreign Policy for Americans* (New York, 1951); Hans J. Morgenthau, *In Defense of the National Interest* (New York, 1951); Reinhold Niebuhr, *The Irony of American History* (New York, 1952).

back only to the 1945 Yalta and Potsdam conferences. More fundamentally, both feared that Truman and Acheson used insufficient restraint in employing American power. Morgenthau attacked Acheson for harping about "positions of strength" when "the supreme test of statesmanship," to Morgenthau's mind, was not building power blocs but discovering areas in which tensions could be reduced through negotiations. Morgenthau did not believe Acheson could stand up to that test.

On four basic points, however, the senator and the professor profoundly differed. Taft tended to see the Cold War as a crusade against the Antichrist, and he bolstered this view by emphasizing the purity of American intentions. Morgenthau realized the unique virtues of American democracy, but he held no brief for the spotlessness of American morality or ideology. After all, he was not running for office. Nor in this particular did he share Taft's view of history, for Morgenthau believed that the new technological and political problems which appeared in 1945 marked "the definite and radical end of the . . . conditions under which the Western world lived for centuries." The professor drily observed that Russia's use of the "religious order" of communism to remake the world in its image was not unlike those Americans who "heed the noble words of Jefferson, Wilson, and Franklin D. Roosevelt, and . . . set out on a crusade to make the world safe for true democracy."

Taft would not entirely discard military power. He advocated the development of air and naval units but not the infantry. He believed that this policy would save manpower, cut military expenditures, and, in all, be politically attractive. Taft could also in this way slash the executive power to involve the United States in European problems through the commitment of American troops. Morgenthau would have none of this. He deplored the common tendency of both Taft and the Truman Doctrine to lay out "a world-embracing moral principle" that committed American power, of whatever nature, to such broad, undefined, and dangerous limits. The United States must realize, Morgenthau admonished, that military threats to its interests in Europe called for different solutions than did dangers posed by "genuine revolutions" in Asia. American policy makers must follow not the dictates of "moral principle" but the classic formula of spheres of interest. The United States could no longer wish for an open world. It would have to accommodate itself to the realities of power, and anyone who refused to believe in balances of power, Morgenthau added, resembled "a scientist not believing in the law of gravity."

The professor considered the spheres-of-interest approach feasible because the Soviet threat was fueled not by communist ideology but by traditional Russian national power. Unlike the religious passion of communism, Russian national power could effect compromises because it was subject to the same restraints and limitations as American power. Taft, on the other hand, viewed communist ideology as the principal threat. He cared little whether it was attached to Soviet national power, except that by being so attached, its power became immeasurably increased. The senator, therefore, refused to settle for the spheres-of-interest approach, for this would not neutralize communist ideology; instead, he advocated fighting communism everywhere, including inside the labyrinthine bureaucracy of the State Department. Here Morgenthau sharply scored Taft. Many "anticommunists," the professor observed, talk about protecting American security when they really mean protecting the "security of the status quo" at home and abroad.

These differences on the roles of morality, the place of power, and the nature of the Soviet threat inevitably led Taft and Morgenthau to opposite conclusions on the climactic question of Asia. The senator deplored past American policy which treated Western Europe like one big happy family while allowing Asia to go communist almost by default. Running close to the MacArthur line, Taft sought "only . . . the same policy in the Far East as in Europe." That is, he wanted the use of air and naval power as a deterrent in both Europe and Asia. In case of a conflict, his policy lessened the chances for limiting the war short of nuclear exchange, but he could reply that, by making no further commitments in Europe and by allowing European nations to solve their own problems, that area would remain stable, while in Asia no power would be able to challenge American naval and air power. He left unanswered the question of how this naval and air power could deflect the considerably more subtle threat of communist ideology.

Morgenthau necessarily reversed Taft's priorities. Europe, particularly Germany, he argued, comprised such a technological, industrial, and cultural powerhouse that "he who controls all of Europe is well on his way toward controlling the whole world." Europe could not be left to chance, possibly to communism. A further point necessarily shaped American policy: the United States could understand and cooperate with Europe because of common backgrounds and values. Asia, however, was immeasurably different. Unlike the "phoney" revolutions in Eastern Europe, those in Asia were "genuine." This meant that Russian imperialism and "genuine" revolution were by no means the same thing. To confuse the two could lead to an American involvement in Asia which would be calamitous. Asian revolutions, Morgenthau observed, were generated not by communism but, ironically, by the political, technological, and moral revolutions which the West transferred to the Orient. Once Asia mastered this technology, a "shift in the distribution of power" would result which, "in its importance for the history of the world, transcends all other factors. It might well mean the end of the bipolarity centered in Washington and Moscow." Given their different race and culture, Americans could not hope to control this momentous change, but only adjust to it. The United States had no real means of dealing with "genuine revolutions" in non-Western lands, according to Morgenthau.

In 1951 and 1952 Niebuhr neatly combined Taft's emphasis on ideology with Morgenthau's conclusions. Partly because of such feats, one observer called Niebuhr's views "part of the canon of a new generation of American liberals and the spiritual guide of those who are now revisiting conservatism."[10] More significant than his appeal to various shades of the political spectrum was Niebuhr's change of tone. Something had happened to the earlier advocate of a quickly revitalized Germany; now he acknowledged that the rearming of Germany "was too precipitate and too indifferent" to European feelings. The loud cry of 1948 to guard the far-flung battle lines became a quiet listing of the reasons why American policy makers must not become overly committed to battle lines in the newly emerging world, especially Asia. Niebuhr now lectured the wielders of the titanic American power that they too were subject to the sins of all mankind.

The Irony of American History argued that because of pride, presumed innocence, and lack of restraint, American power was walking the rim of the abyss. American idealism, which had been instrumental in developing immense national power, now ironically blinded the United States to the dangers of overusing that power. "American power in the service of American idealism," Nie-

[10]Morton White in *New Republic*, May 5, 1952, pp. 18–19.

buhr approvingly quoted a European official as saying, "could create a situation in which we would be too impotent to correct you when you are wrong and you would be too idealistic to correct yourself." In addition, not even extensive use of this power could solve fundamental American dilemmas. This provided a second irony: a century or two before, when their power was much less, Americans could solve their problems more easily.

To Niebuhr, communism remained as evil as it had been in 1947 and 1948, but the United States had become the victim of many of the same inconsistencies and delusions about human nature and the so-called virtues of science that had corrupted communism. In the past, Americans had been protected from themselves by the Constitution, whose authors knew more about human nature and the limitations of science than their twentieth-century descendents. They had been protected also by the good fortune that, in having blown hot and cold in their dedication to remake the world, Americans had been saved by their own historical inconsistencies. Niebuhr cited John Adams: "Power always thinks it has a great soul and vast views beyond the comprehension of the weak; and that it is doing God's service when it is violating all His Laws." Niebuhr extended Adams's observation by adding that Americans believed they could solve problems simply "by the expansion of our economy." The frontier, Niebuhr intimated, had closed; expanding production "has created moral illusions about the ease with which the adjustment of interest to interest can be made in human society."

In the penultimate section of *Irony*, Niebuhr applied his views to the Asian situation. The United States, he echoed Morgenthau, had little in common with the Orient. Any attempt to use the present American Cold War weaponry to save Asia from communism would be, as he had mentioned earlier in the book, like the "spears of the knights when gunpowder challenged their reign." In phrases not untinged with condescension, Niebuhr warned that Asia wanted Western technology, but refused to accept the West's view of man, society, or history. He advised working with Japan and the Philippines to contain Asian communism by means of a militarized Pacific "island littoral." So contained, communism would repeat the history of Islam during the Middle Ages and be destroyed "not so much by its foes as by its own inner corruptions." But if it hoped to witness that collapse, the United States would have to remedy its own "inner corruptions" first.

Niebuhr's fear of extending the Cold War to the mainland of Asia partly explained the changed tone in his writings. No doubt the explosion of the Russian atomic bomb, the growth of McCarthyism, and the Truman administration's fervent dedication to remolding Europe also gave the theologian pause. Above all, Niebuhr feared that the new Republican administration of Dwight D. Eisenhower could commit the ultimate transgressions in foreign policy. A year earlier, in 1951, Niebuhr had looked with much concern on the rising influence of businessmen and Republicans on foreign policy formulation. Eisenhower's victory transformed this influence into domination: "His victory was significantly engineered by eminent proconsuls of the budding American imperium, partly drawn from the Army and partly from business." Niebuhr feared the effect of this victory upon Washington's Asian policies, for "American conservatives" viewed communist gains in that area as resulting from State Department perfidy

> and as capable of rectification by rigorous military action on our part. This "illusion of American omnipotence," . . . is a natural mistake of a commercial community which knows that American hegemony is based upon our technical-economic power but does not understand the vast complexities of ethnic loyalties, of social forces in a decaying agrarian world, of the resentments which a mere display of military power creates among those who are not committed to us.[11]

Niebuhr's abhorrence of "the budding American imperium" did not noticeably brake the Eisenhower steamroller in 1952. The general won on a platform that committed the party to save Asia and with a campaign in which he refused to repudiate McCarthysim. Adlai Stevenson ran a more literate and less successful campaign for the Democrats, but significantly patterned his appeal after Eisenhower's in two respects: Stevenson refused to embrace the record of the Truman administration with any enthusiasm (at one point asking privately that Acheson publicly announce his intention to resign after the election), and he once went further than Eisenhower in a specific commitment to save Asia.

[11]Reinhold Niebuhr, "The Foreign Policy of American Conservatism and Liberalism." In *Christian Realism and Political Problems* (New York, 1953), pp. 58, 64.

On October 24 the Democratic nominee warned that to with-draw American troops from Korea and allow "Asians to fight Asians," as the general wanted, "we would risk a Munich in the Far East, with the probability of a third world war not far behind." Un-like Eisenhower, Stevenson did see indigenous nationalism, not in-ternational communism, at the root of the Asian upheavals but, as the campaign progressed, Stevenson's dedication to Asia and his determination to apply military strength in the area seemed to in-crease as Eisenhower's declined. On September 4 the Republican candidate explained how the United States must protect "the far corners of the earth" which provided the nation with "materials es-sential to our industry and our defense." Yet on October 24, when he dramatically pledged, "I shall go to Korea," he advocated as a military backstop only the building up of the South Korean forces and shaping "our psychological warfare program into a weapon ca-pable of cracking the Communist front." This was a less militant course than Stevenson was advocating in a speech that same day.[12]

Beneath the Eisenhower moderation, however, was the less-restrained Republican platform. It contrasted "Russia's 'Asia first' policy" with "the 'Asia last' policy" of the Truman administration. "We have no intention to sacrifice the East to gain time for the West," the platform echoed MacArthur. It went further. "Contain-ment is defensive," one plank read, "negative, futile and immoral [in abandoning] countless human beings to a despotism and God-less terrorism." John Foster Dulles, who was largely responsible for these sections of the platform, later announced in a campaign speech at Buffalo, New York, that the new Republican administration would, if elected, use "all means to secure the liberation of Eastern Europe." When Eisenhower heard this, he immediately phoned Dulles to inform him that the phrase should have read "all peaceful means." "Yes," Dulles promptly replied, "it's just a complete over-sight."[13] It was a strange oversight for a renowned international lawyer who had spent forty years honing words to great precision.

Behind Eisenhower also loomed the figure of Joseph McCarthy. We will "eliminate" from the federal government, the platform pledged, those "who share responsibility for the needless predica-ments and perils in which we find ourselves." This was a rather loose

[12]*The New York Times,* October 25, 1952, pp. 1, 8.

[13]Interview with Dwight Eisenhower, Dulles Oral History Project, Papers of John Foster Dulles, Princeton.

definition of malfeasance, but the Republicans were not to be denied the profit of hammering the point at the voters. "There are no Communists in the Republican Party," began one long party plank.[14]

Eisenhower's speeches were not that blunt. He also refused to invite General Douglas MacArthur to participate in the campaign, although this would have appeased a large number of conservative Republicans. Eisenhower, however, never publicly repudiated McCarthy's activities. That would not have been sound politics. Sitting on the same stage with McCarthy in Milwaukee, Eisenhower held a speech paying loving tribute to General George Marshall, who had been a sponsor of Eisenhower's rise in the military but termed a traitor by McCarthy. At the last minute, Eisenhower bowed to McCarthy's brand of Americanism and deleted the tribute.

Stevenson and many other Democrats seemed particularly open to the charge that, as one McCarthyite journal phrased it, "Chinese coolies and Harvard professors are the people . . . most susceptible to Red propaganda." At Wheeling, West Virginia, in 1950, McCarthy had declared that it was "not the less fortunate" Americans who "have been selling this nation out, but rather those who have had all the benefits." Those "bright young men" in the State Department who were "born with silver spoons in their mouths are the ones who have been worse." Such attacks on the "Eastern intellectual establishment" paid dividends, especially when voters were reminded that Acheson and Stevenson had rushed to the defense of Alger Hiss. Many of the "less fortunate" supported McCarthy and the Republicans, and thus one more group left the New Deal coalition. Polls revealed that the most earnest supporters of the Wisconsin senator were the small businessmen, who felt squeezed between the big unions and big corporations, and manual laborers. Other support came from the new wealth groups (such as oil wildcatters and real estate manipulators), ethnic groups such as Irish and Germans determined to prove their "Americanism," and, paradoxically, some Eastern intellectuals who had prayed to the communist "God Who Failed" in the 1930s and now attempted to gain redemption by embracing either McCarthy's causes or effects, or both.[15] These groups

[14]Clarence W. Baier and Richard P. Stebbins, eds., *Documents of American Foreign Relations, 1952* (New York, 1953), pp. 80–85.

[15]Seymour Lipset, *Political Man: The Social Bases of Politics* (New York, 1960), pp. 171–172; Daniel Bell, *The End of Ideology: On the Exhaustion of Political Ideas in the Fifties* (Glencoe, Illinois, 1960), pp. 110–112; Richard Rovere, *Senator Joe McCarthy* (Cleveland, Ohio, 1959), p. 13.

endorsed the senator's definition of McCarthyism as "Americanism with its sleeves rolled." No Republican politician without quixotic tendencies tried to buck that slogan in 1952.

Having won on issues that Republican Senator Karl Mundt neatly formulated as K_1C_2 — Korea, Communism, and Corruption — the Eisenhower administration's foreign policy could not be impervious to McCarthy or the Cold War mentality which had spawned McCarthyism. Unlike 1948, foreign policy played a central role in the 1952 campaign,[16] and the campaign in turn left its mark on the foreign policy of the following months. In early 1953 the new chief counsel for McCarthy's committee, Roy M. Cohn, and a friend, David Schine, junketed throughout Europe upbraiding American diplomats supposedly soft on communism, attacking United States Information Service libraries for exhibiting the work of such "radicals" as Mark Twain and Theodore Dreiser, and provoking the wrath of the European press. Secretary of State Dulles did nothing to stop Cohn and Schine. On the contrary, Dulles accepted the appointment of a McCarthy adherent, Scott McLeod, as the State Department's personnel and security officer.

The test came when Dulles, without consulting either McCarthy or McLeod, suggested Soviet expert Charles Bohlen as ambassador to Russia. The senator immediately unleashed an attack that centered on Bohlen's role as Roosevelt's interpreter at Yalta. Bohlen correctly assured Dulles that there was nothing injurious in his past record. The secretary of state was glad to hear this, since, as he sighed, "I couldn't stand another Alger Hiss." Dulles, however, did little to aid Bohlen, refusing even to have pictures taken of them together. The appointment finally went through the Senate only after Eisenhower and Taft worked out a deal whereby Taft and Senator John Sparkman, Democrat of Alabama, closely examined Bohlen's record in confidential State Department files, and the President promised not to make any more major appointments to which McCarthy might object.

Within four months after taking office, the administration bragged that it had fired 1456 federal employees under its "security program." The program had not, however, uncovered one proven communist. So challenged, the Democrats replied that they had effectively fired

[16]Angus Campbell, Gerald Gurin, and Warren E. Miller, *The Voter Decides* (Evanston, Illinois, 1954), pp. 46, 67, 119.

even more "risks" under Truman's loyalty program.[17] In the midst of this frenzy, one distinguished American Foreign Service officer who had never been tainted by any McCarthyite accusation commented, "If I had a son, I would do everything in my power to suppress any desire he might have to enter the Foreign Service of the United States."[18] The McLeod-McCarthy group countered with the slogan, "An ounce of loyalty is worth a pound of brains." The price, however, would soon be paid for such slogans. As the McCarthyites threw many of the ablest people out of the State Department (and Dulles and Eisenhower uttered too little protest), experts, particularly in the areas of China and South Asia, left government. A decade later they would not be on hand to inform Presidents about the realities of China and Vietnam. The 1960s' generation paid in blood and treasure for the excesses of the early 1950s.

Dulles contented himself with his favorite biblical quotation: "All things work together for good to them that love God, to them who are called according to His purpose."[19] Like Truman, the new secretary of state was confident about whom the Creator was calling. Dulles nevertheless left little to chance. He built his power base within the administration with care. No cabinet officer in American history had a closer working relationship with a President than did Dulles. When competing power centers began to appear in the White House in the person of Harold Stassen or Nelson Rockefeller, the secretary of state moved ruthlessly. "He cut off Nelson at the ankles," was the way one official described the encounter. "We will make the most successful team in history," Dulles supposedly told Eisenhower.[20]

Few could challenge Dulles's grasp of world events. He had learned much about Europe as a young law student in Paris. As a senior partner in the powerful law firm of Sullivan and Cromwell of New York City, he operated regularly during the 1920s and 1930s out of the firm's Paris and Berlin offices. He had undertaken his first important diplomatic mission in 1919–1921 with his uncle, Robert Lansing, who was Woodrow Wilson's secretary of state. In cabinet

---

[17]Rovere, *McCarthy,* pp. 17–18, 32–33.

[18]Emmet John Hughes, *The Ordeal of Power: A Political Memoir of the Eisenhower Years* (New York, 1963), p. 91.

[19]Dulles to John Nagel, January 21, 1952, Correspondence, Papers of John Foster Dulles, Princeton.

[20]Sherman Adams, *First-Hand Report* (New York, 1961), p. 89.

meetings few took issue with him. "After all," one Eisenhower assistant remarked, "how are you going to argue with a man who has lived with a problem—for instance, in respect to Iran—for longer than most of us knew there was such a country?"[21]

But one person did have greater knowledge about, and experience with, world issues and leaders than Dulles—Eisenhower. The general from Abilene, Kansas, had not only commanded the greatest invasion force in history during World War II, but he had almost daily dealt successfully with some of the most complex giants of the twentieth century, including Roosevelt, Churchill, and French leader Charles de Gaulle. After he became President, Eisenhower seemed to do little but flash his famous grin and play many rounds of golf. The joke circulated that an Eisenhower doll was one that could be wound up and then do nothing for eight years. Fresh research and the opening of new documents from the 1950s, however, now reveal that Eisenhower's calm exterior hid a strong hand, which he wielded to control policy behind the scenes.[22] Nor was the exterior always calm. Privately he could explode and become what one friend called "a human Bessemer furnace." His Vice President, Richard Nixon, later observed that the avuncular Ike was "a far more complex and devious man than most people realized." Eisenhower had early learned how to control those around him. "He's a great poker player," a chief military aid remarked, "and [an] extremely good bridge player. . . . He's a tremendous man for analyzing the other fellow's mind, what options are open to the other fellow, and what line he [Eisenhower] can best take to capitalize or exploit the possibilities." Truman, with his penchant for desk pounding, liked the phrase, "The buck stops here." On his desk Eisenhower had a plaque with a Latin phrase that translated, "Gently in manner, strong in deed." Part of the manner was delegating authority and allowing his subordinates, such as Dulles, to act as lightning rods for both public praise and criticism. Eisenhower once told his press secretary to take a certain action. The secretary objected that if he did that he "would get hell." Eisenhower patted him on the back and said, "My boy, better you than me."

[21]Interview with Sherman Adams, Dulles Oral History Project, Princeton.

[22]Much of the following is based on the pioneering work of Fred I. Greenstein, *The Hidden-Hand Presidency: Eisenhower as Leader* (New York, 1982), especially pp. 9, 26, 57, 69, 91–92; and Richard Immerman, "Eisenhower and Dulles: Who Made the Decisions?" *Political Psychology*, I (Autumn 1979): 3–19.

A major reason why he had run for the presidency was his fear that the Republican party might fall into the hands of the Asia-first, "isolationist" faction that rallied around Senator Robert Taft. Eisenhower agreed with Taft on the need for smaller military budgets and on drastically slicing government spending, but he determined to make the party accept its global, not merely Asian, responsibilities. He once told a friend that Senator William Knowland (Republican of California), a leader of the pro–Chiang Kai-shek group, had "no foreign policy except to develop high blood pressure whenever he mentions the words 'Red China.'" With such views, Eisenhower became the transition figure that transformed the Republican party of Taft into the party of Ronald Reagan. While agreeing with Taft on spending cuts, Eisenhower anticipated Reagan (and before him, Senator Barry Goldwater's conservative campaign of 1964) by creating a strong presidency that was especially active in foreign policy; by showing a determination to exercise United States power globally; and by holding fast to the belief that the overriding threat to world stability was communism, not starvation, inequality, or other wants that led the have-nots to rebel against the haves. Eisenhower understood the demands of the have-nots and could eloquently articulate the policy problems they presented, but he believed they could be handled in the long run by private investment, while communism posed an immediate threat and had to be destroyed by various forms of military power. Eisenhower changed the more limited commitments of Taft Republicanism into the virtually unlimited commitments of Reagan Republicanism. And he did this by shaping a consensus at home that has been unmatched by any other President after 1945. In a Gallup Poll of 1955 nearly two-thirds of those calling themselves liberals saw Eisenhower as liberal, and almost the same percentage considering themselves conservatives saw him as conservative.

Similar dramatic changes occurred in the Soviet Union. In August 1952 Stalin surprised the world by calling the Nineteenth Party Congress to convene on October 5. Eighteen years had passed since the eighteenth session of 1939. The Soviet dictator obviously had a task for the obedient members to perform.

Western officials doubted that Stalin aimed to ease tensions. Throughout 1951 and 1952 he had taken a tougher foreign policy line than before and nearly doubled the Soviet Army to 4.9 million men while increasing defense expenditures by 50 percent. On October 2 Stalin published his *Economic Problems of Socialism*, a text enunciating the main line of Soviet domestic and foreign policies. This set the tone for the congress. The Soviet dictator announced not only that primary emphasis would continue to be placed on heavy industry but that state ownership must be extended over portions of the agricultural economy that had long remained in the hands of agricultural collectives.

Stalin then assaulted those who challenged his foreign policies. The West, he predicted, would soon be overwhelmed by economic catastrophe. Communist successes since 1945 had contracted the capitalists' market. This contraction had so aggravated the Western economic system that the capitalists would soon begin a death struggle among themselves. Because the United States had placed Western Europe, Germany, and Japan on a "dole," Stalin observed sarcastically, "some comrades" see only "the external appearances which glitter on the surface." "To think that these countries will not attempt to rise to their feet again, smash the U.S. 'regime' and break away on a path of independent development is to believe in miracles." (Malenkov dutifully repeated this section in his keynote address.) This development, Stalin concluded in a brief speech at the congress, indicated two courses for communists: the tightening of party control to prepare fully for the protection of the bloc against capitalist warfare, and cooperative efforts with nationalists everywhere, but especially those in Germany, Japan, and France, in order to accelerate the revolt against American control.[23]

The theme of the congress was a renewed emphasis on the inevitability of war. This was only partly tempered by Stalin's and Malenkov's remarks upon the desirability of international peace movements, united fronts, and a German treaty. The strategy toughened while the means softened. A second, more implicit theme also became apparent. The congress emphasized through

[23]J. V. Stalin, "Economic Problems of Socialism in the U.S.S.R." in *Current Soviet Policies: The Documentary Record of the 19th Communist Party Congress and the Reorganization After Stalin's Death*, edited and with an introduction by Leo Gruliow (New York, 1953), pp. 1–10, 235–236. This is an exceptionally useful compendium of primary documents which emerged from those events between October 1952 and April 1953.

omission the Soviet domination of the communist world. Although Chinese officials attended and spoke, only insignificant references to China occurred in the hundreds of thousands of published words uttered by Russians at the congress.

Another outcome of the congress was the most significant. In an apparent attempt to cement his control over both the Malenkov and Khrushchev factions, Stalin announced at the congress the creation of a new Politburo, to be named the Party Presidium, consisting of twenty-five instead of eleven members. The new additions would be fervent young Stalinists. This stroke cut the present and potential power of both Malenkov and Khrushchev while giving Stalin even greater authority. In January 1953 Stalin's power received further impetus from an important article which appeared in the party's leading theoretical journal, *Kommunist*. After elaborately developing the "capitalist encirclement" doctrine, the analysis concluded that, because of the growth of the Western economic crisis and the success of the international communist movement, not détente but "a fierce struggle against the enemy" must now be pursued.[24]

On January 13, 1953, concrete evidence dramatically appeared to support the "capitalist encirclement" thesis. A group of Kremlin doctors was suddenly arrested by Soviet security police for the killing of Andrei Zhdanov in 1948 and was accused of being in the hire of American and British espionage agents. Some observers believed the episode indicated Stalin's firm belief that an East-West détente of any kind, including possible armistice in Korea, was impossible. Closer to the ruling circles of the Kremlin, the "Doctors Plot" had another meaning. As the plot unfolded, Stalin evidently made indirect threats to the lives of Central Committee members, including some as close to him as Molotov and Anastas Mikoyan. These threats, apparently, were the breaking point. On February 17, the chief of security in the Kremlin who had protected Stalin for thirty years suddenly was announced by the Soviet press to be dead. Within three weeks Stalin fell victim to what was officially termed "hemorrhage of the brain."

The truth, as usual, was more complex and interesting. Stalin's policies were failing abroad (especially in the key area of West Ger-

[24] *Current Soviet Policies*, p. 105, has Malenkov's speech; the *Kommunist* article is analyzed in Robert C. Tucker, *The Soviet Political Mind* (New York, 1963), pp. 30–31.

man rearmament) and becoming yet more terrifying at home. He had seemed determined to eliminate even those closest to him in the Kremlin. Harrison E. Salisbury, correspondent of *The New York Times* in Moscow during those extraordinary days of 1953, later concluded that the cause of Stalin's death was suspect. On the night of Saturday, February 28, Georgi Malenkov, Lavrenti Beria, Nikolai Bulganin, and Nikita Khrushchev—the four leading contenders for Stalin's throne—had an all-night drinking bout with the dictator at his villa outside of Moscow. The next day Stalin was found asleep on the floor. He reportedly had suffered a stroke. The four contenders were summoned for advice. But they did nothing for twenty-four hours. Salisbury surmised that the four men decided that "if they let him go a few more hours they might be rid of him for all time." A visitor to Stalin's home on the day of his death, March 5, believed that he "was speeded to his grave."[25]

Malenkov quickly took over Stalin's top jobs. He immediately cut back Politburo membership to throw out the ardent young Stalinists whom the old dictator had just appointed. Malenkov also announced that new policies would arise from a "collective" rather than from the whims of one man. He issued amnesties for many political prisoners, including those locked up by Stalin for the alleged "Doctors Plot." The doctors' confessions, the Soviet press suddenly discovered, had been obtained "through the use of impermissible means of investigation which are strictly forbidden under Soviet law."[26]

This final twist to the "Doctors Plot" indicated changes in Soviet foreign policies. Malenkov confirmed the changes in a speech before the Supreme Soviet: "At the present time there is no disputed or unresolved question that cannot be settled peacefully by mutual agreement of the interested countries," he announced. "This applies to our relations with all states, including the United States of America."[27] Soon the new Russian leaders allowed Soviet citizens married to foreigners to leave the country; reestablished diplomatic relations with Greece, Israel, and later Yugoslavia; renounced Soviet claims to Turkish territory; and, most important, agreed to an end to the Korean War.

---

[25]Harrison E. Salisbury, "The Days of Stalin's Death," *The New York Times Magazine*, April 17, 1983, pp. 38–48.

[26]*Current Soviet Policies*, pp. 249–251.

[27]*Current Soviet Policies*, pp. 256–260.

Eisenhower and Dulles suddenly found themselves dealing with a new set of Soviet policies. A fresh set of issues, a different kind of Soviet challenge had dramatically appeared. The question became whether the new American leaders could become flexible enough to deal with the new faces in Moscow, particularly in the aftermath of the terrible war in Korea and amidst the plague of McCarthyism.

7

A Different
Cold War
(1953-1955)

Former Secretary of the Treasury George Humphrey recalled his impressions of Washington when the Eisenhower administration moved into power. "We were under war controls," Humphrey remembered, "and we were in war."[1] Entering office as the struggle continued in Korea, the President pledged that he would more efficiently and successfully wage the Cold War against Stalinist Russia. "Let's face it," one Republican advisor had remarked in early 1952. "The only excuse for Ike's candidacy is that he's the man best qualified to deal with Stalin."[2]

In early March 1953, Stalin died. The Cold War that began to confront Eisenhower and Dulles during their first months in power assumed new and puzzling traits. Georgi Malenkov assumed Stalin's place in the Soviet government, but he did not appropriate the departed leader's foreign policies. Malenkov instead began urging friendly negotiation in Europe and peace in Korea. Rapid changes in other parts of the world also began to confuse Ameri-

---

[1] Interview with George Humphrey and Herbert Hoover, Jr., Dulles Oral History Project, Princeton.

[2] Norman A. Graebner, *The New Isolationism* (New York, 1956), p. 98.

146

cans. The Republicans had won with a platform promising more military firepower and a firming up of the containment policy, but new international crises increasingly revolved around rampaging nationalisms in the Middle East, Latin America, and Southeast Asia rather than around military problems in Europe or Korea. As Morgenthau and Niebuhr had foreseen, the Eisenhower administration was soon engaged in a new kind of Cold War.

Immediately after Stalin's death, American intelligence informed the President that the new Soviet premier would have to consolidate his internal control and consequently would not undertake new departures in foreign affairs.[3] Many Americans believed that Stalin's death would create a chaos which might permanently damage Soviet power, or at least force a long, painful, and unproductive transition period upon new leadership. This did not happen. The possibility of one-man rule by Malenkov apparently disappeared after a severe internal party struggle. He maintained his premiership but surrendered the key post of first party secretary to Nikita Khrushchev.

A precarious collective leadership emerged as Malenkov, with his power based on the technicians and government bureaucracy, and Khrushchev, with his strong support from the party, began a struggle for supreme power. The first important casualty in the battle was Lavrenti Beria. When Beria moved too fast and overtly in making the secret police his own political tool, the new rulers arrested and executed him in July. In stark contrast to Stalin's methods, however, Beria was probably the only victim of execution within the high party hierarchy. While conveniently blaming Beria for many of the excesses of previous years, Malenkov cautiously moved to liberalize the functioning of the party and demanded a reduction of investment in heavy industry so that Russians could enjoy more consumer goods.

This policy of relaxation soon stretched to foreign affairs. If the Western alliance was unable to agree upon such ventures as the European Defense Community in the present "tense international situation," Malenkov observed to the Supreme Soviet on August 8, 1953, "a lessening of this tension might lead to [the] disintegration" of that alliance. The premier, however, hedged his bet. In the same

---

[3] Dwight D. Eisenhower, *The White House Years: Mandate for Change, 1953–1956* (Garden City, New York, 1963), pp. 148–149.

speech he announced that the Soviets had successfully tested a thermonuclear, or hydrogen, bomb. With the American thermonuclear monopoly broken, the Soviets stood ready to negotiate on European problems. To strengthen their position further, they dropped their emphasis on revolution by an international proletariat and attempted to influence Western policies by playing upon the peace hopes of the European middle classes.[4]

The American response to these Soviet changes was slow and unsure. The Washington bureaucracy was fearful and confused, partly because of its terror of the ubiquitous McCarthyism, partly because of the usual problems found in changing governments. Underneath this confusion lay a deeper problem. Soviet communism, Dulles told the Senate Foreign Relations Committee in January, "believes that human beings are nothing more than somewhat superior animals . . . and that the best kind of a world is that world which is organized as a well-managed farm is organized, where certain animals are taken out to pasture, and they are fed and brought back and milked, and they are given a barn as shelter over their heads." Apparently the secretary of state had read George Orwell literally. "I do not see how, as long as Soviet communism holds those views," Dulles concluded, ". . . there can be any permanent reconciliation. . . . This is an irreconcilable conflict."[5] By defining the conflict as so intensely ideological, Dulles severely limited the possibility of easing tensions through a flexible diplomacy.

On April 16, 1953, Eisenhower made the first formal response to Malenkov's new tactics. If the Soviets sincerely desired détente, the President remarked, there must be "free elections in a united Korea," the end of communist revolts in Malaya and Indochina, "United Nations control and inspection" of disarmament, "a free and united Germany, with a government based upon free and secret elections," the "free choice" of governments in Eastern Europe, and a treaty restoring Austria's independence.[6] The day following this address, Dulles appeared before the Senate Foreign Relations Committee; his testimony was headlined by *The New York Times* as "Dulles Bids Soviet Cooperate or Face Vast West Arming."

[4]*Current Digest of the Soviet Press,* V (September 5, 1953): 3–12, 26.

[5]U.S. Senate, Committee on Foreign Relations, 83rd Cong., 1st Sess., *Nomination of John Foster Dulles . . . , January 15, 1953* (Washington, 1953), pp. 10–11.

[6]Department of State, *American Foreign Policy, 1950–1955, Basic Documents,* 2 vols. (Washington, 1957), I: 65–71.

Within a month, however, the American approach was questioned by the most eminent statesman within that alliance. Without previously informing either Eisenhower or his own Foreign Office, Winston Churchill announced on May 11 that the time had arrived for world leaders to confer "on the highest level" to see which problems might be solved. The prime minister indirectly attacked Eisenhower's demand that a multitude of questions would have to be settled at once. This was obviously impossible and, moreover, might unfortunately "impede any spontaneous and healthy evolution which may be taking place inside Russia." Churchill instead recommended a piecemeal approach, tackling solvable problems but assuming all the while that Russian security must be assured. Another theme also appeared in the speech. Great Britain would defend its own interests, Churchill warned, particularly in the Middle East where nationalism threatened Suez; this would be accomplished without help from "the United States or anyone else." The prime minister was trying to bring the United States into an East-West détente while, at the same time, cutting back his ties with Americans as he dealt with the whirling problems of nationalism in the newly emerging nations.[7]

Senate Majority Leader William Knowland responded by accusing Churchill of "urging a Far Eastern Munich." The official Washington response was characterized as "cool." Eisenhower explained why to a news conference: "The world happened to be round and it had no end and he didn't see how you could discuss the problem, the great basic problems of today, which were so largely philosophical in character, without thinking in global terms," or so reported the official text of the conference.[8]

The President was arguing that, because the Soviet menace was basically ideological, or "philosophical," it was also indivisible and thus posed a threat everywhere in the world. One implication followed: problems in Europe and those in Asia were linked and could be approached with similar strategies. A second implication was that the ideology posed a worldwide threat regardless of whether the Soviets possessed the military, economic, and political power to support that ideology globally. In a sense, this seemed an accurate appraisal, for communism could become disruptive in areas closed to Soviet arms. But Eisenhower's approach quickly led to confusion.

[7] *The New York Times*, May 12, 1953, pp. 8–9.
[8] *The New York Times*, May 15, 1953, p. 6.

In May 1952 and again in January 1953, Dulles had condemned "containment" as a "policy which is bound to fail because a purely defensive policy never wins against an aggressive policy." He advocated instead "liberation of these captive peoples" in Eastern Europe through such "processes short of war" as "political warfare, psychological warfare and propaganda." In late May 1953 the Soviets loosened political controls in East Germany but also demanded more production from workers for the same wages. Laborers protested with a march down East Berlin's Stalinallee on June 16. The next day began with a general strike and demonstrations which climaxed with the tearing down of communist flags and demands for free elections. The American radio in West Berlin broadcast encouragement to the workers and lauded the spreading of the strikes throughout East Germany. Then suddenly Soviet tanks appeared in Berlin, Dresden, Leipzig, Magdeburg, and Jena. As the armor smashed the demonstrations, Dulles made no move. "Liberation" had failed its first test and had done so in Germany, the European prize of the East-West struggle.

Facing the problem of captive peoples in North Korea shortly after, the administration came up with a more satisfactory, if not exactly happy, solution by recognizing the limits of its military and political power. Eisenhower's trip in Korea in December 1952 buttressed his belief that the United States should not be entrapped in a conventional war on the Asian mainland. For his own reasons, Secretary of the Treasury Humphrey supported this view. One-third of the budget had to be cut to eliminate deficit spending, Humphrey told the President, and that means "you have to get Korea out of the way."

To get Korea "out of the way," the administration first employed what would later be called "brinksmanship." Returning from Korea on December 14, Eisenhower warned that, unless the war ended quickly, the United States might retaliate "under circumstances of our choosing." Six weeks later in his first State of the Union message, the President announced that the American Seventh Fleet would "no longer be employed to shield Communist China." He hurriedly added that this meant no intended aggression "on our part," but this so-called unleashing of Chiang Kai-shek so frightened England and France that Dulles flew to Europe to reassure the Allies. As tension mounted, Stalin conveniently died. The new Soviet leaders hinted their willingness to sponsor negotiations. On the crucial question of prisoner exchange (the United Nations forces reported that many North Korean and Chinese prisoners did not want to return home and should not be compelled to do so), the Chinese suggested on March 30 that prisoner repatriation be placed in the hands of international authorities. On April 23 armistice talks recommenced, but Dulles soon concluded that the Chinese were raising unnecessary barriers to a peace. On May 22 he hinted to Peking through Indian diplomats that if peace were not forthcoming the United States would bring in atomic weapons. The next day the State Department issued more moderate instructions on the prisoner exchange problem.

Within eleven days the communists accepted the plan with minor changes. They held to the agreement even after President Syngman Rhee of South Korea tried to sabotage the negotiations by releasing 27,000 Chinese and North Korean prisoners on June 18. The seventy-eight-year-old Rhee was outraged that the American acceptance of a division roughly along the 38th parallel would prevent him from ever ruling a unified Korea. The final armistice was signed on July 27. Talks in 1953 and 1954 on reunification failed, and the United States proceeded to pour $6 billion of aid into South Korea over the next decade. Industrial production tripled, exports increased eight times to nearly $250 million, and the economy became increasingly self-sufficient. Rhee was not as fortunate politically. He fell from power after students rioted against his autocratic regime in April 1960 and was replaced by a military-controlled government. The North Korean government also endured political upheavals, although on lower levels, and rebuilt its air force with hundreds of modern Soviet fighter planes. The United States installed tactical guided missiles with atomic warheads pointing northward. Outside Panmunjom, where negotiators still gather to insult one another, grandstands and loudspeakers accommodated tourists who liked to witness the spectacle of international diplomacy and peer out over the desolate, bare hills where thousands of men died in a "limited" war.[9]

Many lessons were to be learned from the Korean involvement. Dulles chose to apply most of them to both Europe and the rest of Asia. In his European policies, Dulles made Germany the pivot. As a lawyer in Germany between the wars, he had come to admire the German people; he prized Germany's location, industrial power, and

[9]David Rees, *Korea, The Limited War* (New York, 1964), pp. 450–452.

military potential as a bulwark against Soviet expansion; and, by means of a steadily developing friendship, he enjoyed a similarity of views with Konrad Adenauer that he had with no other world leader.

In July 1953 Dulles made these views clear to everyone. Following the Churchill speech in May, Russia had proposed a coalition of East and West Germans to prepare a peace treaty which would neutralize Germany; then, and only then, Germany could have free elections. In July Dulles rejected this procedure. He proposed instead that free elections first be held throughout Germany and then a peace treaty be drawn. The Russians would have none of this, particularly after Dulles also insisted that the EDC could not be involved in the discussions; if a reunited Germany wanted to rearm and tie itself to the West through the EDC, Dulles thought it should be able to do so. He continued these strategies inherited from Acheson in the belief that any immediate détente was impossible, for, as he had told a distinguished assemblage of European statesmen, "The Soviet leaders are to a very large extent the prisoners of their own doctrine which is intensively held by their followers, who are fanatics."[10]

Accepting the status quo in Europe, or at least the status quo once the French formally endorsed the EDC, Dulles turned to ponder the problems of the newly emerging areas. These now required more and more attention. He hoped to build into those areas many of the same military and political institutions which had established the status quo in Europe. This policy moved from the assumption that disturbances anywhere outside the Iron Curtain usually worked against American interests sooner or later. Such a view had deep roots in U.S. history.

From the Declaration of Independence until the Civil War, Americans generally sympathized with revolutions abroad. In several respects, however, they dispensed their sympathy with care. They disliked revolutions that went beyond the political, social, and economic boundaries of their own. Americans also believed their own revolution superior to revolutions on the "right" (as John Quincy Adams viewed the Latin American upheavals) or on the

---

[10]"Statement of Secretary Dulles at April 23 Session of North Atlantic Council Ministers' Meeting," Conference Dossiers, Dulles Papers, Princeton.

"left." They best liked revolts on the North American continent, such as those in Florida, Texas, California, and Canada, which opened up possible areas for annexation to the expanding Union.

In the middle of the nineteenth century, two events began to reshape American views toward revolutions: the continental conquest was completed, and Americans began emphasizing the commercial aspects of their foreign policy instead of landed expansion. These overseas commercial interests became especially important, for stability, peace, and confidence in the sanctity of contract were essential to any great trading venture. By 1900 the United States had burgeoned into a power which combined the interesting characteristics of being conservative ideologically and expansive economically. Such a combination would not be encouraging to revolution. Interventions against rebellions in Cuba and the Philippines were followed by Theodore Roosevelt's pronouncement that the United States would act as a policeman to prevent upheavals in the Caribbean area. A decade later Woodrow Wilson rationalized the use of economic and military force against Mexico with an ideological justification that employed the traditional American liberal rhetoric. The threat of revolution reached a crisis when, in 1917, Lenin joined the use of force to a doctrine worldwide in its ambitions and repugnant to most Americans.

The Eisenhower administration inherited this significant historical legacy. It became an heir to opposing revolutions at the point European colonial rule and conservative monarchies crumbled before nationalist uprisings in the Middle East, Africa, Asia, and Latin America. The new spirit was captured by the highly corrupt and overweight King Farouk of Egypt. As nationalist army officers threw him out of Egypt, Farouk predicted that in a decade there would only "be five kings left: Hearts, Clubs, Diamonds, Spades, and England." He was not far wrong.

Eisenhower and Dulles understood and sympathized with much of the new nationalism. Their own people, after all, had won the first modern anticolonial struggle in 1776. Both men realized, moreover, that the worn-out British and French empires were breathing their last. They wanted the colonials quickly out of the way. When colonials remained, revolutionaries tended to move leftward in order to continue the struggle. Eisenhower preferred to attack that problem at the root by pushing out the Europeans. But Americans seldom seemed able to move fast enough. Revolutionaries in Iran,

Indochina, and Guatemala gained ground. The President determined to stop them with force if necessary.

The problem thus became what kind of force Americans should use to control revolutions abroad. Eisenhower and Dulles, and indeed all later Americans, found themselves in a terrible bind. They did not want to fight conventional ground wars in Asia and Africa. Korea had vividly proven the dangers of such involvements. Using covert weapons employed by the Central Intelligence Agency could work in certain instances (and Eisenhower proved to be exceedingly skillful in employing the CIA), but in other cases the revolutionaries had gathered too much strength to be beaten by James Bond–like operations. Sometimes they even enjoyed direct Soviet or Chinese assistance.

Eisenhower devised a package of tactics for dealing with unwanted revolutionaries. First, he turned loose the CIA in such places as Iran and Guatemala, which were not yet out of control. Second, he sent United States military advisors to train native troops, as in Vietnam, where Eisenhower began the so-called Vietnamization of the war against the communists a generation before "Vietnamization" became a catchword of Richard Nixon's policy in the early 1970s. Third, Eisenhower and Dulles engineered a series of military alliances to tie friends together in a common fight against the Soviets outside, and left-wing revolutionaries inside, various regions. The Baghdad Pact in the Middle East and the Southeast Asia Treaty Organization (SEATO) became two of the more famous examples of "pactomania," as Dulles's critics labeled the policy. Fourth, Eisenhower based his overall military policy on the use of huge hydrogen bombs as well as small tactical atomic weapons that planners believed could be deployed with almost surgical precision on battlefields. He especially threatened to use these weapons if Soviet or Chinese forces launched a direct invasion or became heavily involved with the revolutionaries (as, indeed, he had already threatened in Korea in mid-1953).

The President's growing reliance on nuclear bombs also grew out of his determination to cut back government spending. No President in the post-1945 years has been as fanatic in this regard as this famous military commander who dedicated himself to slashing military budgets. He preached repeatedly that the key to American power was its economic system and marvelous productivity, not its weapons. He feared that military spending on the level of Truman's

$50 billion annually would set off a terrible inflation and ruin the economy. "We must not go broke," he reiterated. To Eisenhower, "broke" meant either a deficit in the federal budget, or an economy growing dependent on a "military-industrial complex," as he later termed it. "To Eisenhower," a close observer later remarked, "the United States economy was like the source of a mother's milk — tender and soft and not to be abused."[11]

At the same time, however, the President set out to stop left-wing revolutions and continue Truman's "containment" policy. These conclusions had been hammered out in a series of discussions during 1953 in "Operation Solarium" (named after the White House sun room in which they were held). If Eisenhower hoped to carry out Truman's policies without Truman's budget, his only solution was to rely on nuclear weapons that were cheaper than maintaining men in arms in a conventional force. In two years Eisenhower reduced Truman's military budget by nearly one-third to about $34 billion. His reliance on nuclear armaments to accomplish this reduction soon became evident as he allowed the development of the B41 bomb of over 20 megatons, or the equivalent of 400 Hiroshima-type bombs. (The B41 proved less usable than originally anticipated after tests revealed that if it were dropped close to Soviet coastlines, the radiation would pose greater dangers to United States forces and ships at sea than it would to large parts of Russia itself.) The size of the nation's nuclear stockpile doubled between 1953 and 1955, while new, huge B-52 bombers rolled off assembly lines to deliver the weapons. Eisenhower became the first President to consider atomic and nuclear bombs "conventional" weapons — to "be used exactly as you would use a bullet or anything else," as he remarked publicly in 1955. Eisenhower refused repeatedly to accept a nuclear test ban that would have stopped the deadly radioactive fallout from weapons tests that began to infect the world's food supplies. His refusal was based in part on the Soviets' refusal to agree to what he considered adequate inspections, in part on the belief that the development of his main weapons systems depended on such tests. Thus, Eisenhower was prepared to consider starting a nuclear war if necessary — not only if the Soviets invaded Europe but also if Cold War costs became so

[11]Douglas Kinnard, *The Secretary of Defense* (Lexington, Kentucky, 1980), pp. 44–45.

high that they were forcing "us to war — or into some form of dictatorial government."[12]

His strategy became known as "the new look," or "more bang
for a buck." Dulles used the phrase "massive retaliation," by which
he meant being "willing and able to respond vigorously at places
and with means of [our] own choosing."[13] Eisenhower had a clear
sense of when he might launch "massive retaliation," as noted
above. But he also had an idea of the destruction that could result. In
certain situations, no matter how tempting, war had to be avoided.
For example, he made a remarkable response to Syngman Rhee in
mid-1954 when the South Korean leader tried to shame him into
supporting a war to unify Korea. Eisenhower interrupted to say
that he "regretted very much" the division of Korea, Germany, Austria, and Vietnam, "but . . . no one in this world will get America
to go to war over these problems. . . . We cannot undertake any
engagement that involves [the] deliberate intention of going to war
with Iron Curtain countries."[14]

Eisenhower thereby defined the two extremes in which he would
or would not go to war. But the extremes turned out not to be the
problems. His dilemma involved the "gray areas" — as a young Harvard professor, Henry Kissinger, called them in 1955 — the newly
emerging areas where kings and colonials were giving way to nationalist revolutionary movements. In these areas Eisenhower faced
the great challenge that has confronted all of his successors: finding a
way of successfully using United States power and — most important
— understanding these movements. His first challenges arose in
Iran, Guatemala, and Vietnam. The nation's response to these challenges was historic for it demonstrated the irrelevance of "massive
retaliation" and unfortunately locked into place American beliefs
about handling revolutionaries for the next twenty years.

[12]"Memorandum for the Secretary of State," September 8, 1953, Dulles Papers,
Princeton. The discussion in this paragraph is also from Lawrence Freedman, *The
Evolution of Nuclear Strategy* (New York, 1983), pp. 77–78, 81–83; David Alan
Rosenberg, "'A Smoking Radiating Ruin at the End of Two House,'" *International
Security*, VI (Winter 1981–1982): 3–38; Robert A. Divine, *Blowing on the Wind: The
Nuclear Test Ban Debate, 1954–1960* (New York, 1978), especially chapters 2, 3, 7;
Samuel F. Wells, Jr., "The Origins of Massive Retaliation," *Political Science Quarterly*,
XCVI (Spring 1981): 31–52; and *Washington Post*, December 27, 1983, p. A9.

[13]A standard version of Dulles's theory is his "Policy for Security and Peace,"
Foreign Affairs, XXXII (April 1954): especially 357–358.

[14]"Korean-American Talks, July 27, 1954," Dwight D. Eisenhower Diary Series, Box
4, Dwight D. Eisenhower Library, Abilene, Kansas.

In 1951 an Iranian nationalist movement headed by Mohammed Mossadegh had undercut the power of the shah and proceeded to nationalize the Anglo-Iranian Oil Company. The British government had received more taxes from the company than the Iranian government had received for its own natural resource. The company consequently provided a convenient target in an impoverished land where 500 babies died out of every 1000 births. The British demanded payment for the confiscated holdings, a demand that the Iranians could not meet without binding themselves to foreign lenders. With oil exports at a standstill, the Iranian economy began to sink, since income from oil provided 30 percent of its total income and 60 percent of its foreign exchange. When Eisenhower entered office, the United States, in spite of extensive efforts by Acheson, had not been successful in acting as a mediator.

After a three-week trip through the Middle East in May 1953, Dulles reached some disturbing conclusions. Western power had "deteriorated" in the area, he believed, and unless drastic action was taken, the Arab nations would become "outright" neutrals in "the East-West struggle." Israel and intra-Arab squabbles accounted for some of the problems, but Dulles also wondered about the British. "They interpret our policy as one which in fact hastens their loss of prestige in the area. To some extent," the secretary admitted, ". . . this may be true," but Great Britain's loss of power was also due to "altered world power relationships." Dulles decided that he would have to convince the Middle East that the United States had little to do with British and French colonialism.[15]

The opportunity came within the next two months when the State Department concluded that Mossadegh was moving into the Soviet orbit. Rumors of a Soviet loan to Iran began to circulate, and in August, Mossadegh received 99.4 percent of the votes in a plebiscite, a percentage which Eisenhower later used as proof of increased communist influence.[16] Having earlier refused to help Mossadegh rebuild the Iranian economy, the United States now cut off all aid.

In August the shah staged a successful coup to regain power. The United States provided guns, trucks, armored cars, and radio

[15]"Conclusions on Trip," May 9 to May 29, 1953, Conference Dossiers, Dulles Papers, Princeton.
[16]Eisenhower, *The White House Years*, pp. 160–166.

communications for the shah's forces.[17] The new government quickly undertook discussions with representatives of the oil company, but the representatives were not those of the year before. Since the turn of the century, the United States had been trying to get into the Iranian oil fields only to be constantly repulsed by the British. Now the breakthrough occurred by the grace of the shah and under the guidance of State Department official Herbert Hoover, Jr., who had gained wide experience in the complexities of the international oil problem as a private businessman. A new international consortium was established giving the British 40 percent, five American firms (Gulf, Socony-Vacuum, Standard Oil of California, Standard Oil of New Jersey, and Texaco) 40 percent, and Dutch Shell and French Petroleum the remaining 20 percent of Iranian oil production. Profits would be divided equally between the consortium and Iran.[18] Iranian oil once more freely flowed into international markets, the shah's government was securely within the Western camp, and the British monopoly on the oil fields had been broken. For Dulles and Eisenhower, it was one revolution with a happy ending. More accurately, it was not a revolution at all.

Seven years before, American diplomats had hoped that similar problems would be avoided in Latin America by the formation of the Rio Pact and the Organization of American States (OAS). Dulles found to his frustration that Latin American governments too often moved outside the United States interpretation of these agreements. Dulles had phrased the problem dramatically in February 1953. Latin American conditions, he stressed, "are somewhat comparable to conditions as they were in China in the mid-thirties when the Communist movement was getting started. . . . Well, if we don't look out, we will wake up some morning and read in the newspapers that there happened in South America the same kind of thing that happened in China in 1949."[19] Despite this awareness, Dulles never attempted to work out a comprehensive policy for encouraging Latin America to follow a path different from that which China trod in the 1930s. He instead approached the problem piecemeal. The first test for this approach came in Guatemala during the spring of 1954.

[17]Robert Engler, *The Politics of Oil* (New York, 1961), p. 206; Kermit Roosevelt, *Countercoup: The Struggle for the Control of Iran* (New York, 1979).

[18]Engler, *The Politics of Oil*, p. 207.

[19]U.S. Senate, *Nomination of Dulles*, p. 31.

That country's population is mainly comprised of diverse groups of Indians who are poor, illiterate, and isolated. In an area roughly the size of Tennessee, only 10 percent of the land is tillable, yet 74 percent of the population is agrarian. Two percent of the landowners own 60 percent of the usable land. Until 1944 a succession of strong men prevented any radical change in this society, but in that year student riots and unrest among professional classes brought in a new government, led by Juan José Arévelo, which supported land and labor reform. In 1951, Colonel Jacobo Arbenz Guzmán replaced Arévelo through proper constitutional procedures. Guatemalan politics polarized; the communists, who supported Arbenz, insisted, against strong conservative opposition, that further reforms were requisite. Arbenz's main objective became the United Fruit Company. For more than a half century that company had employed as many as 40,000 Guatemalans; monopolized shipping, communications, and railroads; and had helped shape the country's politics.

In 1953 Arbenz confiscated 178,000 acres of company property. The State Department demanded proper payment, a demand Arbenz could not meet partly on nationalist grounds but also because it would require his country to tie itself economically to obligations which would prevent the financing of desperately needed internal reforms. When Arbenz refused to take the dispute to the Court of Arbitration at The Hague, Dulles moved to isolate Guatemala at the Tenth Inter-American Conference meeting at Caracas, Venezuela, in March 1954. He pushed through by a 17 to 1 vote a declaration that because "international communism . . . is incompatible with the concept of American freedom," the American states would "adopt within their respective territories the measures necessary to eradicate and prevent subversive activities."[20] Guatemala voted against, Mexico and Argentina refused to vote, and Costa Rica did not attend the meeting. Dulles interpreted the resolution as an application of the historic Monroe Doctrine. As Monroe's original message had been aimed at the political system of the Holy Alliance, now the doctrine sent similar warning to international communism, a political threat "more dangerous than the open physical aggression."[21]

[20]Department of State, *American Foreign Policy, 1950-1955, Basic Documents,* I, pp. 1300-1302.

[21]U.S. Senate, Committee on Foreign Relations, 83rd Cong., 2nd Sess., *Statements of Secretary John Foster Dulles and Admiral Arthur Radford . . .* , March 9 and April 14, 1954 (Washington, 1954), p. 18.

On May 15 Guatemala unloaded 1900 tons of arms from Czechoslovakia. The United States responded by airlifting arms to Nicaragua and Honduras, where the CIA trained Guatemalan exiles for an invasion of their homeland. The Eisenhower administration also secretly planned to erect a blockade around Guatemala and stop any "suspicious foreign-flag vessels" possibly carrying arms.[22] That decision could have led to a direct confrontation with Soviet ships. On June 18 Colonel Carlos Castillo Armas and his American-trained force of 150 men moved across the Honduran border into Guatemala. Armas did not distinguish himself in battle, but at the decisive moment several small planes, piloted by CIA operatives, bombed Guatemala City and key towns. United States aid was crucial, but equally significant, Arbenz lost support from his army and the supposedly communist-controlled labor unions. By late June 1954 Castillo Armas ruled Guatemala.

Eisenhower's overthrow of Arbenz marks a turning point in United States foreign policy for at least four reasons. First, Americans misunderstood the Guatemalan situation. Arbenz had been constitutionally elected and headed a reform — not communist — movement. A handful of communists sat in the national legislature and influenced the labor movement, but no one ever argued that they in any way shaped the country's most important institutions: the presidency, the army, and the Roman Catholic Church. Americans too easily confused nationalism with communism. Second, despite the confusion, the administration pulled off such a successful and covert operation that Dulles could deny that his brother Allen (director of the CIA) was involved with Arbenz's removal. The administration announced that the Guatemalan people themselves had deposed their president. Americans too quickly and mistakenly concluded that such an operation could easily be repeated elsewhere. Third, Arbenz finally fell when his military deserted. Future Latin American revolutionaries drew the appropriate lesson. Fidel Castro of Cuba and, in the 1980s, the Sandinista government of Nicaragua would make the army and the government parts of a single unit. Overthrowing such regimes would require a war, not simply a covert CIA operation. Finally, the United States won the battle but lost the longer war. In Guatemala (and later elsewhere),

[22]"Memo for President for Leaders' Meeting, May 24/53," May 22, 1954, Meetings with the President, 1954 (3), White House Memoranda Series, Dulles Papers, Eisenhower Library, Abilene, Kansas.

Americans failed to replace the deposed regime with an effective liberal reformer. Castillo Armas carried out large-scale executions that killed more Guatemalans after the invasion than had died during the conflict. Reactionary and ineffective, he was assassinated by members of his own regime three years later. The United States poured more aid into Guatemala between 1954 and 1965 than into any other Latin American nation, but the only results by the mid-1960s were a brutal military government and the growth of a revolutionary guerrilla movement more radical than any group in the country before 1954.

During the same hours that the Dulles brothers acted in Guatemala, Eisenhower made an equally fateful decision on the crisis in Southeast Asia. The United States was deeply involved in the conflict between the French colonial forces and the army of the nationalist communist leader, Ho Chi Minh. Between 1950 and 1954 Washington sent $1.2 billion for the French effort, and by 1954 it had paid for over 70 percent of the French military budget. Several hundred American military technicians were also helping. In early 1954 Eisenhower viewed the implications of such aid with some concern. "I cannot conceive of a greater tragedy for America," he told a press conference in February, "than to get heavily involved now in an all-out war in any of those regions, particularly with large units."[23] Then came Dien Bien Phu.

Ground down by the guerrilla tactics of Ho and the political instability in Paris, the dispirited French army decided to make its major stand at Dien Bien Phu. It was an odd choice. The town was located away from the coast, close to the Laotian and Chinese borders, and lay at the bottom of a valley easily commanded by the Viet Minh forces controlling the mountain tops. Wheeling up large artillery pieces, a feat the French refused to believe Ho's forces could accomplish, the Viet Minh lobbed a murderous bombardment upon the French garrison. On March 20 General Paul Ely, the French chief of staff, flew to Washington to request United States intervention. This set off a tumultuous six-week debate within Washington and among the Western Allies. Dulles and the chairman of the Joint Chiefs, Admiral Arthur W. Radford, urged an American air strike to save the French. Air Force Chief of Staff Nathan Twin-

[23]*Public Papers of the Presidents . . . , Eisenhower, 1954* (Washington, 1960), pp. 247–253.

ing agreed and later outlined his thoughts on how the crisis might have been handled:

> I still think it would have been a good idea [to have taken] three small tactical A-bombs — it's a fairly isolated area, Dien Bien Phu — no great town around there, only Communists and their supplies. You could take all day to drop a bomb, make sure you put it in the right place. No opposition. And clean those Commies out of there and the band could play the Marseillaise and the French would come marching out of Dien Bien Phu in fine shape. And those Commies would say, "Well, those guys might do this again to us. We'd better be careful." And we might not have had this problem we're facing in Vietnam now had we dropped those small "A" weapons.[24]

Dulles and Eisenhower disagreed with Twining on the use of atomic bombs, but the President began to waver on the question of American intervention in any form. On April 3 Dulles intimated to congressional leaders that the administration would appreciate a resolution allowing the commitment of United States forces. The congressmen and senators refused after questioning revealed that the joint chiefs were split on the problem (Army Chief Matthew Ridgway especially opposed any massive intervention) and that the Western Allies had not been consulted. The next day Eisenhower wrote Churchill that the threat in Vietnam compared with the dangers of "Hirohito, Mussolini and Hitler" and asked that the United States and Great Britain form a coalition to prevent a catastrophe.[25]

Three days later, the President outlined what was at stake by presenting his "domino theory" to a news conference. The struggle was crucial, Eisenhower observed, because the area contained tin, tungsten, and rubber; if, moreover, France lost, "many human beings [would] pass under a dictatorship. . . . Finally you have . . . what you would call the 'falling domino' principle. You have a row of dominoes set up, you knock over the first one, and what will happen to the last one is the certainty that it will go over very quickly. So you could have a beginning of a disintegration that would have the most profound influences." He especially worried

---

[24] Interview with General Nathan Twining, Dulles Oral History Project, Princeton.
[25] Eisenhower, *The White House Years*, pp. 346–347.

about the economic and political effects upon Japan, the key to the containment of Russia and China in the Far East.[26]

The administration next intensified the pressure on the British. At the height of the crisis, April 20–24, Dulles flew to London to ask for the go-ahead from Churchill so the President could send Congress the intervention resolution. The prime minister never flashed the green light. He refused to commit his government to the lost French effort, particularly during the forty-eight hours before the interested powers were to meet in Geneva on April 26 to negotiate the Indochinese problem. Without British cooperation, Senate and House leaders refused to support an intervention resolution. Within the White House, General Ridgway was persuading Eisenhower not to follow any line that might lead to the landing of American conventional forces. Logistics, politics, and the memories of Korea, Ridgway argued, worked against such a commitment. On May 7 the decimated French garrison surrendered.

Despite the debacle at Dien Bien Phu, the diplomats made little progress in their negotiations at Geneva. Then in mid-June the government fell in Paris and was replaced by a Gaullist-radical coalition led by Pierre Mendès-France. The new premier promised either a peace in Indochina or his resignation by July 20. In the two pacts concluded on July 20–21, the Geneva Accords (or Final Declaration) and the Geneva Armistice Agreement, the parties agreed: first, that a truce would occur between Ho's forces and the French (not, it is important to note, any southern Vietnamese government); second, on a temporary partition at the 17th parallel with French troops withdrawing from north of that line; third, that North and South Vietnam would neither join military alliances nor allow foreign military bases on their territories; fourth, that national elections, supervised by a joint commission of India, Canada, and Poland, would be held within two years to unify the country, and—the parties understood—France would remain in the south to carry out those elections; fifth, that regrouping of procommunist Pathet Lao forces would be allowed in Laos, and in that country and Cambodia general elections would be held (see map, p. 222).

Ho's armies controlled two-thirds of Vietnam, but by accepting these agreements he pulled his troops into the northern half of the nation. He so compromised because he apparently preferred to deal

[26]*Public Papers of the Presidents . . . , Eisenhower, 1954,* pp. 382–383.

with Mendès-France rather than with another premier who might come in after the July 20 deadline, and because Ho further believed that the French would hold to their promise of conducting elections in 1956. In such an election the North Vietnamese leader would certainly win, for he was the best-known and most powerful nationalist in all Vietnam. (Eisenhower later estimated that Ho would have received possibly 80 percent of the vote if the elections had been held at that time.) The triumphant Vietnamese also needed time to solve their political and economic chaos in the north; this they set about accomplishing with important aid from the Soviets. In his careful analysis of the situation, Ho had overlooked just one possibility: the United States might replace the French in South Vietnam. If this occurred, the Geneva agreements would become devalued.

The American delegation had not been a party to the negotiations on the armistice and had refused to agree formally to the accords. Affixing an American signature to an agreement with communists that turned over half of Vietnam to Ho would not have enhanced the administration's popularity at home. The United States only announced that it would support "free elections supervised by the United Nations" and look on with "grave concern and as seriously threatening international peace and security" any renewal of "aggression in violation of the aforesaid agreements."[27]

Within a year the United States replaced France as the Western power in South Vietnam. The process began at least as early as September–October 1954, when Dulles announced that henceforth American aid would go directly to the South Vietnamese and not through the French. As the secretary explained, this change would destroy the French "protected preferential market" and allow good friends like the Japanese to sell goods directly to the Vietnamese. Dulles denied any "desire" to "displace" French influence, but "a certain displacement is, I think, inevitable."[28] Military advisors under General J. Lawton Collins began training a South Vietnamese Army; they hoped it could defend its homeland without the aid of American troops. The effect of Korea upon American thinking was immense. Collins had been chief of staff during the Korean War and was a charter member of the "Never-Again Club," a group of Ameri-

---

[27]Department of State, *American Foreign Policy, 1950–1955, Basic Documents*, I (Washington, 1957): 750–788.

[28]Press conference in Manila, March 2, 1955, Conference Dossiers, Dulles Papers, Princeton.

can Army officers, including Matthew Ridgway, who swore they
would never again commit American troops to Asia without having an ironclad promise from Washington that the troops would be
supported by the bombing of such enemy cities and supply lines as
sanctuaries in Manchuria and China. The Vietnamese Army now
learned from its American advisors how to move in large units with
heavy weapons from fortified points. The Vietnamese were being
prepared to fight the Korean War all over again.[29]

This American aid carried political implications. For example,
the revitalized Vietnamese Army soon was plotting against the government. That government had been placed in the hands of Ngo
Dinh Diem over strenuous French objections. The United States had
brought in Diem from his self-imposed exile at Maryknoll Seminary
in Ossining, New York. Eisenhower pledged in a letter of October
1954 that the United States would support the Vietnamese government in the south with economic aid in order to enable Diem to resist
subversion or aggression. The President made no offer of open-
ended military aid, further hedging his pledge by asking Diem for
economic and social reforms so that the aid could be beneficially used.

By July 1955 most of the French had evacuated Vietnam. Diem
announced that the elections agreed to in the Geneva Accords
would not be held. Dulles fully supported the announcement with
the argument that Diem's government had not signed the accords
which promised the elections. More to the point, Dulles and Diem
knew that the latter would have grave difficulties defeating Ho in a
fair election, and American officials did not believe that the northern government had any intention of running a fair election. The
secretary of state had set the stage for this announcement in May
1955, when he gave reporters a lesson in comparative history. The
United States, he warned, would recognize an anti-Diem government in the south only if "it seems to be expressive of the real will of
the people and if it is truly representative." The American Revolution, Dulles observed, deferred to what "is called a decent respect
for the opinions of mankind," and, he continued, all "changes"
should be undertaken soberly and "with a decent respect for the
opinions of mankind."[30]

---

[29]Joseph Kraft, *Profiles in Power* (New York, 1966), pp. 139–143.

[30]Off the Record News Conference, May 7, 1955, in Paris, Conference Dossiers,
Dulles Papers, Princeton.

Despite such remarks, Dulles no doubt realized that Asian revolutions bore a closer relationship to the ideas of Mao Tse-tung than to those of Thomas Jefferson. At least he acted upon such an assumption shortly after the Geneva Conference, when he led the drive to establish the Southeast Asia Treaty Organization. Such a military pact had long been discussed. Dulles brought the idea into reality in a treaty signed at Manila on September 8, 1954, by the United States, France, Great Britain, Australia, New Zealand, Thailand, Pakistan, and the Philippines. These nations agreed that any armed attack upon them "or against any State or territory which the Parties by unanimous agreement may hereafter designate" (which would include, through a separate protocol, Cambodia, Laos, and Vietnam) would endanger the "peace and safety" of each of the signatories.[31]

This agreement hid crucial differences among the signatories. Dulles realized that the treaty would have to run the gamut of the United States Senate, so he carefully provided for sending American forces only when "communist aggression" was evident, and only then after due "constitutional processes" were observed by Congress. He further assured the Senate that any immediate American response would be with bombs and not infantry. Pakistan, however, did not like the "communist aggression" clause because it wanted help against possible trouble with India. (India refused to join because Prime Minister Pandit Nehru feared association with the Western colonial powers.) After an intense debate, the defensive zone of SEATO was not extended to either Taiwan or Hong Kong but did include Cambodia, Laos, and South Vietnam. This left the treaty open to the charge that it was violating the Geneva Accords by implicitly bringing the former French colonies into an alliance system. Despite such potentially explosive issues, the treaty sailed through the Senate by a vote of 82 to 1.

The Senate ratification is of major significance in American diplomatic history. As Republican Senator Alexander Wiley of Wisconsin observed, SEATO differed from NATO because the United States was now committed not only "to resist armed attack, but also to prevent and counter subversive activities directed from

---

[31]U.S. Senate, Committee on Foreign Relations, 83rd Cong., 2nd Sess., *Hearing . . . on the Southeast Asia Collective Defense Treaty . . .* (Washington, 1954), Part I, pp. 4–5, 28.

without."[32] Dulles acknowledged this and had earlier warned the cabinet of the inherent dangers in such an agreement: "If we take a position against a Communist faction within a foreign country, we have to act alone," he lamented. "We are confronted by an unfortunate fact — most of the countries of the world do not share our view that Communist control of any government anywhere is in itself a danger and a threat."[33] Dulles was nevertheless willing to commit the United States to such a view.

This carried another historic implication. The traditional "open-door" policy would no longer be followed in Asia. Instead of a policy of "fair field and no favor" to anyone, as Secretary of State John Hay had asked for at the turn of the century, Dulles announced that the Monroe Doctrine was being extended to Asia. As the doctrine had warned the Holy Alliance to keep "hands-off" Latin America in the nineteenth century, now the United States, in Dulles's words, "declared that an intrusion [in the Far East] would be dangerous to our peace and security."[34] Whether the United States could unilaterally enforce that doctrine in Asia remained to be seen.

A first challenge was successfully blunted in 1954 and 1955 when the Chinese communists threatened the offshore islands of Quemoy, Matsu, and the Tachens, which lay between the mainland and Taiwan. As the communists shelled the islands and then announced the imminent "liberation" of Taiwan, Eisenhower warned that such liberation forces would have to run over the American Seventh Fleet stationed in the Formosa Straits. Dulles flew to Taiwan in December and signed a mutual defense pact with Chiang Kai-shek, pledging the United States to defend Chiang in return for his promise not to try to invade the mainland without American approval. Nothing was said in the pact about the offshore islands. On January 18, 1955, the communists took the small, northernmost island of the Tachen group. Eisenhower declared that, because this island had no relationship to the defense of Taiwan, the attack required no counteraction. Within five days, however, he asked Congress for authority to "assure the security of Formosa and the Pescadores [Matsu and the rest of the Tachen group]" and, if necessary,

[32]U.S. Senate, *Hearing . . . on the Southeast Asia Collective Defense Treaty,* Part 1, p. 10.

[33]Sherman Adams, *First-Hand Report* (New York, 1961), p. 124.

[34]U.S. Senate, *Hearing . . . on the Southeast Asia Collective Defense Treaty,* Part 1, p. 21.

"closely related localities." Congress whipped through the resolution by a vote of 409 to 3 in the House and 85 to 3 in the Senate.

Some questioned the means involved. Perhaps the resolution was a dangerous precedent for less responsible Presidents who would demand open-ended authorizations from Congress to use force against communism. Herman Phleger, the legal advisor of the Department of State who helped Dulles draft the resolution, called it a "monumental" step, for "never before in our history had anything been done like that." The method, Phleger later observed, solved for future Presidents the problem that had brought down severe criticism upon Truman when he did not obtain congressional assent for the Korean intervention.[35] Anthony Eden, on the other hand, told Dulles of his concern about the objective of the resolution. Dulles vigorously defended protecting Chiang in this way, since, the secretary of state warned, the Chinese communists "have become more intemperate."[36]

Eden's questioning was a symptom of the strains working upon the Western alliance between 1953 and 1956. Many of the disputed points became clear when Dulles struggled to obtain French ratification of the EDC. The secretary of state had tried to force the hand of the French government in mid-December 1953, when he warned that France must ratify or face an "agonizing reappraisal" by Washington of American commitments to Europe. This implied a retreat to a "Fortress America" concept, which would leave Great Britain and France alone to face once again a revitalized Germany. Dulles was playing a risky game, but he was deadly serious. Realizing that any French government which forced the passage of the EDC could well be committing political suicide, Dulles was willing to have one French coalition do this, for without the EDC Adenauer might well lose interest in his links with the West. The French also seemed expendable because Dulles wondered if they could ever again become a great power.[37]

[35] Interview with Herman Phleger, Dulles Oral History Project, Princeton.

[36] "Copy of paper used in conversation with Eden," February 24, 1955, Conference Dossiers, Dulles Papers, Princeton.

[37] Anthony Eden, *Full Circle: The Memoirs of Anthony Eden* (Boston, 1960), pp. 64, 108.

The French had become the pawns in a climactic power struggle. They tried to stall the fateful vote by following a policy best described as *de conserver le cadavre dans le placard* ("keeping the corpse in the closet"). Three governments refused to bring the agreements to a vote. With the delay, French hostility grew. France, opponents argued, had an army that could lose its nationality in such a community; but West Germany had nothing to lose for it had no army. Anyway, why create a German army? France would also have to divide its armies between Europe and overseas possessions; any German military force could concentrate on Europe. And why do such things when Malenkov was attempting to ease tensions? If France must take the step, why could not Eden also commit British troops so that France would not be the only major power locked in military embrace with the Germans? Eden answered the last question by announcing that neither Britain's ties with the Commonwealth nor its links with the United States would permit such a venture. Dulles answered the other points by declaring that German power was essential to the European alliance; that because Soviet ideology precluded any meaningful détente, the arming of Germany must receive priority; and that only through the EDC could the revival of German militarism be adequately controlled.

In a dramatic last-minute meeting in August 1954, Mendès-France told Western diplomats he would finally take the corpse from the closet, but only after conditions were attached to the EDC. But not even these modifications were enough. After a bitter debate on August 30 in which Mendès-France significantly refused to stake his government's life upon the outcome, the Assembly defeated the EDC 314 to 264 with 43 abstentions.

France had miscalculated. Not fully realizing how they were being acted upon rather than acting in the unfolding diplomacy, the French believed the defeat of the EDC had scotched, perhaps killed, German rearmament. Instead they had simply exchanged the EDC, which provided for controls upon that rearmament, for perhaps NATO, which had no such controls and would allow the development of a national German army. For Dulles insisted that West Germany must be rearmed. United States policy rested upon that imperative. As Dulles defined the aftermath of the French vote as "a crisis of almost terrifying proportions," Anthony Eden worked out a solution.

The British foreign secretary advocated enlarging the Western European Union (WEU) of 1948 (which originally had been an anti-

German tool) by including West Germany. The WEU would not allow complete supranational control, but it would give France what it had begged for during the EDC struggle, the commitment of four British divisions to mainland Europe. The French were doubly assured when Dulles pledged that American troops would remain in Europe if France accepted the WEU idea. Adenauer cooperated by promising that Germany would not manufacture long-range missiles, or atomic, bacteriological, or chemical weapons without the approval of the NATO commander and a two-thirds majority of the WEU Council. The other signatories pledged that West Germany would not "have recourse to force to achieve the reunification of Germany or the modification of the present boundaries" of Germany. These promises were written into the Paris Agreements of October 1954.[38] On Christmas Eve, Mendès-France drove the pact through the French Assembly but only after overcoming strong opposition. West German armies entered NATO in 1955.

In Indochina and Europe, Paris officials had learned lessons in Cold War power politics which would reorient their foreign policies and make them less amenable to American pressure. By no means coincidentally, Mendès-France secretly initiated the independent development of a French atomic and nuclear power project in the midst of these crises. Dulles, on the other hand, believed that the Paris Agreements created a situation which was in the best interests of both Europe and the United States. With that status quo apparently assured, the Eisenhower administration returned its attention to the newly emerging nations.

[38]Department of State, *American Foreign Policy 1950–1955, Basic Documents*, I: 1476–1496.

8

East and West
of Suez
(1954-1957)

The mass of the newly emerging peoples had little interest in the
ideological struggle between the Soviet Union and the United
States. They wanted only political independence and release from
grinding poverty. To obtain these, they were willing to borrow
from both systems, and if Soviets and Americans would compete
for their allegiance and resources, so much the better. That was indeed a compelling argument not to become too firmly aligned with
either side but to remain in a "Third World." Neither Russians nor
Americans, however, appreciated such views. When in April 1953
Dulles accused the Russians of looking "upon anybody who is not
for them as against them," he was unfortunately also characterizing
American attitudes. The secretary of state knew that, as he once
phrased it, "to oppose nationalism is counter-productive," but as
late as June 1956, his views of communism and an apparent confusion over the meaning of nationalism enabled Dulles to say that
neutrality had "increasingly become an obsolete conception and,
except under very exceptional circumstances, it is an immoral and
short-sighted conception."

By the mid-1950s each superpower believed that the future vital-
ity of its ideological, economic, and strategic systems depended

upon "winning" the Third World. Each would have believed this even if the other superpower had not existed. The United States and Russia were expansive forces and had been so in many areas (as, for example, in Asia) since at least the nineteenth century. The Cold War sharpened these drives, allowing each side to intensify its dynamic, historic expansion with the defensive terms "anticommunism" or "anti-imperialism." As the nature of the Cold War changed between 1953 and 1956, pulling the attention of the United States and Russia away from Europe and toward long-time interests in the less developed world, this different Cold War required important adjustments in the Soviet and American societies.

In the Soviet Union a bitter internal party struggle obscured the meaning and extent of the Russian adjustment. Throughout 1953 and 1954 Malenkov attempted to brace his position by weakening the Communist party apparatus controlled by Khrushchev, strengthening the governmental-bureaucratic powers which he ruled, and bringing into the decision-making process the industrial managers and technicians who agreed with his emphasis on investment in consumer goods instead of in military and heavy industry sectors. Khrushchev began undercutting Malenkov by appealing to the military and stressing the need for investment in heavy industry. Khrushchev was following many of Stalin's tactics of the 1920s as he mobilized his power within the party. The question became whether the party would control the bureaucracy, or vice versa.

On New Year's Day 1955, Malenkov announced that the Russian possession of hydrogen bombs made peaceful coexistence "necessary and possible." Khrushchev immediately accused the premier of attempting to intimidate the proletariat revolution with atomic weapons.[1] This line of attack won the support of such military leaders as Defense Minister Nikolai Bulganin and World War II hero Georgi Zhukov, and brought old-time Stalinists like Molotov to Khrushchev's side. On February 8 Khrushchev demanded and obtained Malenkov's resignation. Bulganin became premier, but Khrushchev held the real power as first party secretary. With the simultaneous fall from power of some of Malenkov's more liberal associates in Russia and throughout the bloc (such as Imre Nagy as

---

[1]Myron Rush, *Political Succession in the U.S.S.R.* (New York, 1965), pp. 48, 60; Arnold L. Horelick and Myron Rush, *Strategic Power and Soviet Foreign Policy* (Chicago, 1966), pp. 17–30.

prime minister in Hungary), Russia appeared to be sinking back into Stalinist political, economic, and foreign policies.

Such appearances deceived. By the middle of 1955 Khrushchev turned against Molotov's policies and worked out a rapprochement with Yugoslavia and a peace treaty for Austria. Having used the questions of economic investments and foreign policy to oust Malenkov, Khrushchev now shrewdly adopted the former premier's policies. As early as 1949 Malenkov had realized that Stalin's two-camp policy paralyzed Soviet attempts to influence the newly emerging nations. Khrushchev used this insight to work out a more subtle foreign policy, which attempted through the brandishing of military prowess, ideology, and economic aid to conciliate nationalist leaders.

Khrushchev structured this approach carefully. He safeguarded Soviet security both ideologically and militarily by developing the Warsaw Pact—a bloc military alliance, patterned after NATO, which could allow Soviet military control of Eastern Europe after the political controls were relaxed. On Aviation Day 1955 the Soviets flexed awesome military muscles by flying unit after unit of new jet planes over Moscow. (Only later did American intelligence learn that Khrushchev simply had a relatively few planes fly around in circles.) He also tried to deal with the challenges posed to Soviet authority by independently minded Yugoslavia and China. Khrushchev first announced that Russia was further along the road to communism than any other nation. This supposedly assured the Soviets of acting as the chief ideologist within the communist world. In 1954 he had magnanimously traveled to China and had personally returned to Mao the former Chinese possessions of Port Arthur and the Chinese Eastern Railway, long controlled by Russia. He also sought to bring China within the Soviet economic orbit by signing a new agreement to deliver large amounts of capital goods. A similar line was followed in Yugoslavia, despite Molotov's warning that easing relations with Tito would weaken Soviet control over the satellites. Khrushchev nevertheless went to Belgrade, blamed past Soviet-Yugoslav troubles on Stalin, and negotiated improved diplomatic and economic ties.

With the communist world supposedly reconsolidated, Khrushchev launched an aid program for the newly emerging nations which, as he candidly told a group of junketing American congressmen in 1955, he valued "least for economic reasons and most for political purposes." By the end of 1956 fourteen economic and military assistance agreements had been signed with nations in Asia and the Middle East. Khrushchev was highly selective in compiling the list. North Vietnam and Indonesia were favored in Southeast Asia. In the Middle East, Iran, Afghanistan, Turkey, and Egypt were targets of the Soviet economic offensive.[2]

The Chinese provided the proper ideological accompaniment for this drive by attending the Bandung conference of nonaligned states in April 1955 and reaffirming the Five Principles of Peaceful Coexistence, which had been agreed upon between India and China the year before. These promised mutual respect for sovereignty and territorial integrity, noninterference in one another's domestic affairs, and peaceful coexistence. Soviet ideologists supported the Chinese proclamation by emphasizing that Stalin's old two-camp approach had been replaced with a confidence that communists and nationalists could work against Western imperialism and enter the promised land of socialism hand in hand. Never had the reputation of Communist China and Russia been higher among the newly emerging nations. Like the Eisenhower administration, Khrushchev was also thinking in global terms.

Dulles fully appreciated what communism was accomplishing. The secretary of state analyzed in detail the new world situation for the NATO Foreign Ministers during the May meetings of 1955 and 1956. Communism was on the move in Asia, Dulles warned. The Chinese brand posed a greater threat than the Russian, since it controlled a greater population mass and possessed a cultural prestige in Asia not enjoyed by Russia in either Europe or Asia. The secretary noted the major Chinese colonies which existed in many free Asian nations and feared that Mao could follow a rule of divide and conquer because the noncommunist countries were scattered geographically and divided politically, culturally, and economically. The West, Dulles declared, must never surrender those nations: "The stakes are too high." Japanese industrial power could not be allowed to combine with China; Indonesia and Malaya contain vast amounts of oil, rubber, tin, iron ore, as well as hold stra-

[2]Russell H. Fifield, *Southeast Asia in United States Policy* (New York, 1963), pp. 252–253.

tegic positions. The Philippines "represent a symbol of how the West can create independence in Asia." There were 1.6 billion people in the underdeveloped areas now exposed to communist economic tactics. If those tactics prevailed, "the world ratio as between communist dominated peoples and free peoples would change from a ratio of two-to-one in favor of freedom to a ratio of one-to-three against freedom. "That," Dulles emphasized, "would be an almost intolerable ratio given the industrialized nature of the Atlantic Community and its dependence upon broad markets and access to raw materials."[3]

In understanding the differences between the Chinese and Russian expansion, as well as defining the economic-strategic importance of the Far East, Dulles was ahead of most Americans, particularly those within the Eisenhower cabinet. None of the President's advisors could contrive a coherent program that would appeal to the newly emerging nations while at the same time preserving American interests as Dulles defined them. Militarily, for example, the administration held fast to its determination to base security upon massive retaliation. Neither the Soviet development of a hydrogen bomb nor the evidence in Iran, Egypt, Guatemala, and Indochina that the threats to American interests did not come in open aggression by Red armies significantly changed that policy after it was adopted officially in 1954.

During the Dien Bien Phu crisis in Vietnam one slight swing in American strategic thinking had begun to appear. Because NATO did not have manpower to match the communists, the secretary argued that the West should "use atomic weapons as conventional weapons against the military assets of the enemy whenever and wherever it would be of advantage to do so, taking account of all relevant factors."[4] When this tactic was employed in NATO war games in Europe, the results demonstrated that the type of limited war Dulles urged would incinerate most of Central Europe.

The only alternative seemed to be the development of American forces to fight wars which would stop short of nuclear exchanges. Scholars such as Bernard Brodie and Henry Kissinger began to advance this argument in late 1954. Within a year, Army Chief of Staff

[3]"Far East Presentation," May 10, 1955, and "NATO Meeting, Etc." Paris, May 1–7, 1956, Conference Dossiers, Dulles Papers, Princeton.

[4]"Proposed 'Talking Paper,'" April 23, 1954, Conference Dossiers, Dulles Papers, Princeton.

General Maxwell D. Taylor split the Joint Chiefs by unsuccessfully demanding, against Admiral Arthur Radford's opposition, that the military response become more flexible. Taylor left the administration, as did Generals Matthew Ridgway and James M. Gavin. The new trend, which would become fully apparent in 1961, had set in and had done so as experts realized that massive retaliation was too inflexible for the demands of the changing Cold War. Whether, on the other hand, limited conventional war protected American interests in the less developed areas remained to be seen. Limited wars did not automatically exclude massive retaliation; what could not be limited might have to be destroyed. The problem would always be less a proper choice of military means than a wise understanding of the objectives. In postwar American foreign policy, the debate over the nature of the communist threat usually lagged behind the debate over which weapons to use against that threat.

Similar problems confronted the administration in the economic realm. Here Dulles recognized the importance of aid for the newly emerging nations but was powerless to do much about it, in part because of his own intellectual and political inhibitions. With the end of the demand generated by the Korean War, raw material prices slumped; economic depression struck underdeveloped areas that relied upon the export of such materials. No one in the administration had a solution. Eisenhower placed strong faith in productivity, "because it relieves pressures in the world that are favorable to Communism." He defined China as one huge claw reaching out for anyone who had five cents. Dulles's comment was dry and to the point: "In India today, the great peril of Communism comes from intellectual centers."[5] In his concern with productivity, Eisenhower had overlooked the demand of the newly emerging peoples for a rapidly developing productivity regardless of the social and political costs.

Innovation was also wanting in the field of foreign aid. Eisenhower responded to the Soviet economic offensive by reorganizing the foreign aid administration, but this did not touch the real problem. In the newly emerging areas, development had to occur literally from the ground up. This required internal stability and huge amounts of outside capital and technical aid. The Marshall Plan had worked because the Europeans had the technical know-how and

[5]Robert J. Donovan, *Eisenhower:The Inside Story* (New York, 1956), pp. 3, 9.

capital resources to turn every dollar of American aid into six dollars of capital formation. This would obviously not be the case in Asia, Africa, or Latin America. Secretary of the Treasury George Humphrey warmly endorsed placing the burden on private capital, while allowing the World Bank (which depended upon the private money market) to make necessary long-term capital loans. The Export-Import Bank (operated by the government on money appropriated by Congress) would make only short-term loans to move American exports. Dulles attempted to show Humphrey that this approach would be insufficient, arguing that, because of the growing importance of the newly emerging nations, an agency must be formed "to make political loans and 'soft' loans [that is, loans with low interest rates and payable in terms of local currencies] on a long term basis."

Dulles then proceeded to give Humphrey a lesson in political economy. In former days private capital could provide soft, long-term loans because private persons ran the banks of issue and the governmental policies. "This," Dulles observed, "is all now changed." Governments everywhere make rules "for reasons quite unrelated to their effect upon investment." Private lenders consequently were no longer willing to make investments in unstable areas. Only governmental funds could promote such development in a meaningful way. Unless something was done quickly, Dulles warned, South America, for example, "might be lost" under Humphrey's policy: "It might be good banking to put South America through the wringer, but it will come out red."[6]

Dulles knew his history, but Humphrey essentially won the argument. Primary reliance was placed upon private capital. Humphrey then reduced the lending powers of the Export-Import Bank until outraged American exporters and congressmen forced him to issue more credit for American businessmen to use in their overseas trade. Despite such protests, Humphrey cut back so drastically that from fiscal 1955 to fiscal 1957 total loans repaid to the bank actually exceeded disbursements by $58 million. Only after Humphrey's departure from the cabinet was the bank allowed to become a "soft loan" agency in 1958.[7] Meanwhile private capital did not assume the

---

[6]"Memorandum Re NAC Meeting," September 30, 1953, in file on NATO Meeting, December 8–15, 1956, Conference Dossiers, Dulles Papers, Princeton.

[7]Robert Reuben Dince, Jr., "The Lending Policy of the Export-Import Bank: A Study in Public Policy," unpublished doctoral dissertation, Cornell University, 1960.

task, for it favored more stable areas; between 1953 and 1956, for example, United States investments in Latin America increased $1.4 billion or 19.2 percent, while they climbed in Western Europe and Canada $3.4 billion, or over 30 percent.[8]

Over all of these debates hung the pall of McCarthyism. Wisconsin's junior senator, according to a public opinion poll, was regarded favorably by over half of those polled in early 1954. His popularity had jumped 16 points in six months, the same months he was encouraging the burning of supposedly "left-wing" books and accusing the President of the United States of allowing the American allies to carry on a "blood trade" with China. One ramification of this feeling occurred early in 1954 when Senator John Bricker of Ohio proposed an amendment to the Constitution which aimed to eliminate the possibility of any more one-man "sell-outs" similar, as some claimed, to that which Roosevelt accomplished at Yalta through executive agreements made between himself and Stalin or Churchill. The Bricker amendment, like McCarthyism, grew out of sentiment both anti-Democrat and antipresidential. "Since 1948," Bricker had charged in 1951, "the outstanding characteristic of the Truman administration has been its persistent effort to usurp legislative functions." The Republican senator warned that "the constitutional power of Congress to determine American foreign policy is at stake." (It is a major irony that twenty years later Bricker's major objective would be sought by liberal Democratic congressmen against a conservative Republican President; ironic, but understandable historically.)

Discussed since 1951, Bricker's proposal was softened until in 1954 the Senate voted on a version whose key section provided that an international agreement other than a treaty (for example, an executive agreement) could become internal law "only by an act of Congress." Eisenhower fought the measure, warning that foreign leaders would view such restraints upon presidential power as redolent of 1930s' isolationism. The proposal nevertheless was supported by a majority, 60 to 31, although falling just one vote shy of the two-thirds needed for a constitutional amendment. The most fascinating result was that the debate produced the exact opposite of Bricker's intentions. In 1955 and 1958 during international crises,

[8]U.S. Bureau of the Census, *Historical Statistics of the U.S., Colonial Times to 1957* (Washington, 1960), p. 566.

Eisenhower carefully asked Congress to authorize his actions (as Bricker wanted), but he did it so ingeniously that Congress gave the President a virtual blank check. Lyndon Johnson later used Eisenhower's tactics in obtaining congressional support for his intervention in Vietnam.

In 1953–1954 McCarthyism did not stop at the boundaries of politics. Although American scientists were increasingly needed for judgments and weapons in fighting the Cold War, the scientific community was not immune to attack. The anti-intellectualism which imbued McCarthyism, and the lack of ardor for the Cold War shown by some scientists, climaxed in the case of J. Robert Oppenheimer in 1954. Oppenheimer was perhaps the most distinguished physicist in the United States. He had directed the laboratory at Los Alamos, which produced the first atomic bomb in 1945. His downfall began when he questioned the building of the hydrogen bomb in 1949–1950. He was not alone. Many scientists, their political awareness made acute by their participation in the A-bomb project, had moved into Washington after 1946 to lobby long and earnestly for the imposition of strong controls upon the development and use of atomic energy. Probably a majority of American physicists opposed the decision to make the hydrogen bomb because they believed it strategically unsound and politically dangerous.[9]

Oppenheimer shared such sentiments, but unlike most of the other scientists, he had had close relations with Communist party members in the United States and had made personal enemies on the Atomic Energy Commission. A four-foot-six-inch-high FBI folder on Oppenheimer detailed his past but concluded that no evidence indicated that Oppenheimer had worked against the national interest. Eisenhower (who once defined an intellectual as "a man who takes more words than is necessary to say more than he knows") refused to take a public position. A special three-man board unanimously declared Oppenheimer to be "a loyal citizen" but nevertheless voted 2 to 1 against giving him continued access to classified information. This effectively removed Oppenheimer's voice from top governmental councils. The Atomic Energy Commission upheld this judgment 4 to 1 not on the basis of disloyalty but because of "fundamental defects in his 'character.'" No one ever proved that Oppenheimer was disloyal; the one AEC member who

[9]Urs Schwarz, *American Strategy: A New Perspective* (New York, 1966), pp. 77–79.

thought so in 1954, Thomas E. Murray, several years later admitted that his vote had been cast "within the exigencies of the moment." This was a euphemism for the McCarthyite influence, which discriminated against important members of the American scientific and intellectual community.

With the cabinet, the military, Congress, and intellectuals increasingly immobile, Dulles found himself torn between these political restraints on the one hand and, on the other, his recognition of the critical changes in international affairs. He had, for example, stalled off a summit meeting by arguing that the Soviets would have to show their sincerity in wanting negotiations by signing an Austrian peace treaty. As a part of their reorientation of policy, the Russians suddenly signed the treaty in mid-May 1955. As Eisenhower later related, "Well, suddenly the thing was signed one day and [Dulles] came in and he grinned rather ruefully and he said, 'Well, I think we've had it.'"[10] Dulles's interpretation of the breakthrough on the treaty revealed the American dilemma. He initially claimed that "liberation" had borne rich fruit: "an area of Europe is, in a very literal sense, liberated." At the same time, however, Dulles felt compelled to warn Americans that "the new set of dangers comes from the fact that the wolf has put on a new set of sheep's clothing, and while it is better to have a sheep's clothing on than a bear's clothing on, because sheep don't have claws, I think the policy remains the same."[11]

Dulles adopted that latter approach in preparing for the summit. He was concerned that the Soviets would use the conference to gain "moral and social equality" with the United States in order to encourage neutralism. The secretary consequently warned Eisenhower to maintain "an austere countenance on occasions where photographing together [with Russians] is inevitable" and to push hard publicly for "satellite liberation." The secretary then set up American demands that would be quite difficult to realize. His first goal was the unification of Germany "under conditions which will neither 'neutralize' nor 'demilitarize' united Germany, nor subtract

[10]Interview with Dwight D. Eisenhower, Dulles Oral History Project, Dulles Papers, Princeton.

[11]"Press and Radio News Conference . . . , May 15, 1955," Conference Dossiers, Dulles Papers, Princeton.

it from NATO."[12] To this the Russians would never agree. Dulles effectively sealed this policy when West Germany formally regained its sovereignty, commenced rearming, and entered NATO in May, just weeks before the summit conference was to begin. On the eve of the meeting, Republican leader Senator William Knowland proposed the "Captive Nations" resolution; this expressed the Senate's hope that Soviet satellites "subjected to the captivity of alien despotisms shall again enjoy the right of self-determination."

Given this background, the summit could produce little more than a "spirit of Geneva." Eisenhower, Eden (who had succeeded Churchill as prime minister), Bulganin (who fronted for Khrushchev), and Edgar Faure of France opened the meetings on July 18 and immediately ran into a deadlock over Germany. A dead end was reached when Khrushchev overruled a wavering Bulganin by announcing that the Soviets would allow no elections in East Germany until West Germany was disarmed. The United States had successfully armed and tied West Germany to the Western alliance, while at the same time pushing on the Soviets the blame for blocking reunification through free elections.

The only major American initiative at Geneva was Eisenhower's "open skies" plan, proposing the exchange of plans of each nation's military facilities and allowing planes to photograph each nation's territory to insure against surprise attacks. This plan emanated from a panel, headed by Nelson Rockefeller, which was concerned with quieting European fears over the stationing of American nuclear bombs in Europe.[13] The "open skies" proposal would quiet such fears while allowing the bombs to remain. Khrushchev predictably rejected the plan on the grounds that it would infringe on Soviet territorial sovereignty. (This proposal was Eisenhower's second move in the controlled-armaments field. In December 1953 he had proposed before the United Nations a plan to establish an international agency that would control the use of atomic materials for peaceful purposes. Although meeting initial resistance from the Russians and from the American Congress, the speech bore fruit three years later with the creation of the International Atomic Energy Agency.)

---

[12]"Estimate of Prospect of Soviet Union Achieving Its Goals," July 1, 1955, Conference Dossiers, Dulles Papers, Princeton.

[13]Donovan, *Inside Story*, pp. 345–346.

Geneva, and the profitless Foreign Ministers meeting that followed in October, reaffirmed the new Cold War themes. Having failed to gain their coveted European security pact, the Soviets made the best of a disadvantageous situation. They worked out formal diplomatic relations with the Adenauer government in mid-September 1955 and a week later gave East Germany full powers in foreign affairs; the latter move would force Adenauer theoretically to deal with affairs in East Germany directly through the East German communist regime instead of through the Russians. That was most repugnant to the West Germans and consequently reinsured the division of Germany. The split was widened in January 1956, when the East German People's Army entered the Warsaw Pact. Dulles's earlier hopes for reunification on Western terms now lost all foundation.

Dulles and Eisenhower also failed to imagine the extent to which Khrushchev would reorient the Kremlin. At the Twentieth Party Congress in February 1956, Khrushchev surprised his listeners, shocked the satellites, and astonished the West by detailing Stalin's crimes against the Communist party and (the same thing) Russian national interest.[14] But he exorcised the dictator's ghost with a scalpel, not a meat ax. Nothing was said about the particular purges in which Khrushchev himself had controlled the cattle cars slowly moving out of the Ukraine toward Siberia during the late 1930s; instead, he discussed the bloodlettings in which his present enemies on the Presidium had been more closely involved. Khrushchev further emphasized that Stalin and the "cult of the individual" had been at fault, not the communist system. He also carefully defended the party and the army against the Stalinist crimes, but not the masses or the intellectuals whom he himself would soon restrict and attack. Domestically, Khrushchev was trying to increase his own personal power, loosen Stalinist restrictions so that the Soviet economy could boom, and yet keep the society under absolute control without resorting to terrorist methods.

Foreign policy could not be walled off from this internal reorientation. The East European satellites were stunned. Khrushchev destroyed their supposedly unquestioning belief in Stalin and all acts of the Soviet Union. He thereby obliterated the frame of refer-

[14]Nikita S. Khrushchev, *The Crimes of the Stalin Era* . . . . Annotated by Boris I. Nicolaevsky (New York, 1956, 1962).

ence by which the satellites had been told since 1945 to measure their own policies. Khrushchev substituted the idea that several roads led to communism, emphasizing, nevertheless, that communism was the destiny toward which all were heading. The point was made most clearly in the apology for Stalin's tactics toward Tito. Khrushchev recalled Stalin saying that he would shake his little finger and Tito would fall; "we have," Khrushchev concluded, "dearly paid for this shaking of the little finger." In this and other speeches at the congress, the Soviet leadership announced that the two-camp approach, the belief that war was inevitable, and the fear of "capitalist encirclement" were all now unsound doctrines. The new policies were perhaps best illustrated in the destruction of Stalin's "capitalist encirclement" theme, for by questioning this, the "capitalist" and "neutralist" areas surrounding the communist bloc became not objects generating fear in the Soviet peoples but objects to be exploited by Soviet foreign policy. This turn in Russian thinking somewhat resembled the change in American thinking when the United States began to view the surrounding oceans not as barriers insuring isolation, but as highways for internationalism. Within a general policy of détente with the Western world, the Soviets would tear down Stalinist-imposed barriers and move down adjoining highways into the third, uncommitted world. In keeping with this policy, Mikoyan announced the dissolution of the Cominform on April 17, 1956.

After the Geneva conference of 1955, Dulles wondered whether the Soviet "maneuver" of easing tension "may in fact assume the force of an irreversible trend." Such seemed to be the case within weeks after Khrushchev's speech. In March 1956 riots erupted in Soviet Georgia, the home of the now degraded Stalin. In June mobs rioted against Communist party leaders in Poland and Hungary, demanding that more liberal officials assume authority. Khrushchev also came under attack from the other side when such old-line Stalinists as Lazar M. Kaganovich and Molotov demanded that he forcefully quiet the East Europeans before things got completely out of hand.

In a sense, the moment of "liberation" seemed to be approaching. At the crucial point where the prophecy needed a nudge, however, the prophet was looking the other way. Throughout the summer and autumn, Dulles was caught in the maelstrom of Middle Eastern politics. A year and a half before, Israel had dramatically revealed the weakness of the Egyptian Army with a quick, overpowering raid into the disputed Gaza strip. Egyptian leader Gamal Abdel Nasser soon opened negotiations with Western and communist powers for more modern military weapons. Declaring that American prices were not competitive, he discovered the communists anxious to do anything that would weaken the Baghdad Pact. In late September 1955, Nasser signed an agreement to buy arms from the Czechs.

Dulles suddenly became interested in helping Egypt finance the planned Aswan Dam, a huge project which Nasser hoped would harness the vast power of the lower Nile and serve as a symbol of how his regime was triumphantly taking Egypt into the twentieth century. In December 1955 the United States and Great Britain offered to help Nasser. As the United States realized, Egypt would have difficulty in paying for both the arms deal and the dam. To double check this point, World Bank President Eugene Black traveled to Cairo to work out a deal whereby the World Bank, Great Britain, and the United States would supply the immediate funding for the $1.3 billion project. In February 1956 Black and Nasser reached agreement. The Egyptian leader then wrote to Washington regarding discussions on the proposal. Five months later he was still waiting for a reply.

Dulles had become trapped in Washington. Testifying before the Senate Foreign Relations Committee in February, the secretary argued that, although Egypt and Syria might receive communist arms, he should not have to bow before domestic political pressure and send arms to Israel. This could only lead to an all-out arms race in which Arabs would triumph because "thirty-odd million Arabs [have] far greater . . . absorptive capacity" than 1.7 million Israelis. Dulles was forced to admit, however, that the United States was sending tanks to another of Israel's enemies, Saudi Arabia, under terms of a mid-1951 agreement in which the latter country had allowed the United States to occupy Dhahran Airfield. Asked whether the arms buildup might cause Israel to launch a preventive war, Dulles admitted "there is some danger."[15] Having to take a stand on such questions in an election year was bad enough, but Dulles soon found his position worsening.

[15]U.S. Senate, Committee on Foreign Relations, 84th Cong., 2nd Sess., *Hearing . . . on the Situation in the Middle East*, February 24, 1956 (Washington, 1956), pp. 43–46, 68.

In April Egypt, Saudi Arabia, Syria, and Yemen formed a joint military alliance obviously aimed at Israel. These nations, along with Iraq, Lebanon, and Jordan, had refused to recognize the Israeli government. The Czech arms deal with Egypt now assumed a more ominous aspect. In May Nasser withdrew recognition from Chiang Kai-shek and recognized Communist China. This quickly mobilized the many American champions of Chiang to inform Dulles that they staunchly opposed any kind of deal with Nasser. On Capitol Hill this China "Lobby" found an easy alliance with southern congressmen, who demanded to know why the United States was offering to build a dam which would allow huge crops of Egyptian cotton to compete with American cotton. Above all, Egypt had not repudiated the arms deal. Dulles concluded that if he suddenly withdrew the offer, Nasser would suffer a disastrous political blow. The secretary also assumed that Khrushchev would not, in fact could not, replace American aid, an assumption with which Eugene Black concurred because of his belief that Nasser could not afford to become further involved with the communist bloc. Black nevertheless warned Dulles to go through with the deal or "hell might break loose."[16] Both of Dulles's assumptions were tragically wrong. He compounded the mistake by announcing the American decision in a cold, direct announcement on July 19, 1956, at the moment the Egyptian foreign minister was arriving to discuss the project and as Nasser himself sat in a widely publicized meeting with Tito and Nehru.

One week later, Nasser seized the Suez Canal by nationalizing the British-controlled Universal Suez Canal Company. With a single stroke he recovered his lost prestige and gained the $25 million annual profit of the company for use in building the dam. The Egyptian leader also had his thumb on the jugular of the European economy; 67 million tons of oil had moved to Europe through Suez in 1955. As long as he compensated the shareholders of the company, Nasser was legally justified in seizing the canal. He promised, moreover, to keep the waterway open to all former users of the canal. This was not enough for Great Britain and France. Acutely aware of Western shipping interests and the possible disintegration of the Baghdad Pact, perhaps even of NATO, Dulles tried to ameliorate the crisis by establishing a users' association to manage

[16]Interview with Eugene Black, Dulles Oral History Project, Dulles Papers, Princeton.

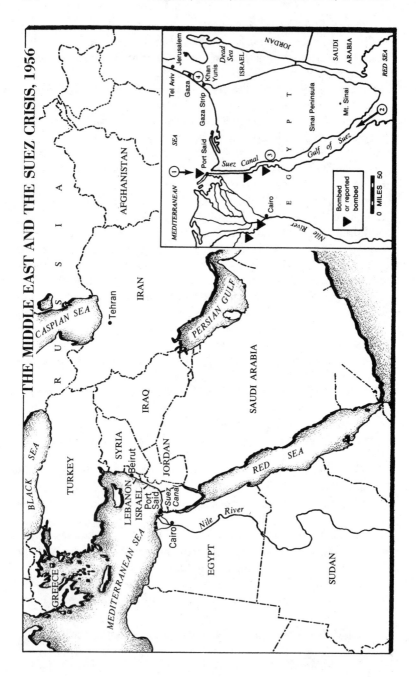

THE MIDDLE EAST AND THE SUEZ CRISIS, 1956

the canal. This proved unacceptable; the British and French had no inclination to put their vital petroleum imports in the hands of Nasser, and the Egyptians refused to share control of the canal. As early as the end of July, British Foreign Secretary Harold Macmillan revealed to Dulles Britain's plans for military action if the problem was not quickly settled.[17] Dulles, however, refused to put excessive pressure on Nasser, did not take the British and French threats seriously, and of course was reluctant to be too closely associated with the former colonial powers.

These policy differences were compounded by the growing personal animosity between Eden and Dulles. Before the 1952 election, Eden had dropped an unsubtle hint to Eisenhower that he preferred a secretary of state other than Dulles. The Eden-Dulles relationship never improved much beyond this point. Yet Anglo-American relations depended upon these two men in the autumn of 1956, for their ambassadors in Washington and London were relatively uninformed; the British ambassador actually left the United States on October 11 just as the crisis began to worsen. During the last two weeks of October, communications between London and Washington almost completely broke down.

This was doubly tragic, for as the Middle Eastern situation deteriorated, rebellion erupted in Eastern Europe. The two events became closely related. Having unleashed unknown forces with his denunciation of Stalin, Khrushchev lost control of Poland's rapid de-Stalinization program headed by Wladyslaw Gomulka. Khrushchev flew to Warsaw, moved Soviet military forces into striking position, and delivered a blistering speech against the Polish changes. Gomulka responded by threatening to call out the Polish people. Khrushchev backed down. The news of Gomulka's success spread to Hungary. On October 23 students moved into the streets to demand that long-time Stalinist Ernö Gerö be replaced with Imre Nagy. When the secret police attempted to put down the protests, workers joined the students. One huge demonstration destroyed a gigantic statue of Stalin in central Budapest. The Soviets agreed to replace Gerö with Nagy, but that was no longer enough. The crowds demanded removal of Russian troops stationed in Hungary and the creation of a political party in opposition to the commun-

[17]Interview with Robert Murphy, Dulles Oral History Project, Dulles Papers, Princeton.

ists. On October 28 the Soviets began withdrawing the tanks that had moved to the outskirts of Budapest.

The next day the Israeli Army made a lightning attack that in hours nearly destroyed the Egyptian Army and conquered much of the Sinai peninsula. In close cooperation with Israel, England and France delivered ultimatums to Israel and Egypt on October 30, warning both nations to keep their forces away from the canal. When Nasser rejected the note, British and French planes began bombing Egyptian military targets. The next day, October 31, the Presidium reversed its policy toward Hungary. Nagy had announced the withdrawal of Hungary from the Warsaw Pact. This was going too far, much farther, for example, than Gomulka was going in Poland.

The confrontation in the Middle East provided Khrushchev with the perfect opportunity for counteraction. As Anglo-French columns moved into the canal area on November 4 and 5, Russian tanks crushed the Hungarian uprising. The Soviets captured Nagy under false pretenses, shipped him off to Russia, and executed him sometime in 1957. The State Department watched all this helplessly. As one high official later remarked, Dulles, "like everybody else in the Department was terribly distressed," but "none of us had whatever imagination it took to discover another solution. We just were boxed."[18] At the height of the crisis on November 3, Dulles underwent emergency surgery on the cancer which would later kill him.

Having smashed the Hungarian rebellion, Khrushchev entered the Middle Eastern scene. He suggested to the State Department that a Russo-American settlement be imposed upon the area and warned Anglo-French forces that, unless they quickly withdrew, the Soviets would use force, perhaps long-range rockets, to squash their armies. On November 6, as Americans went to the polls in a presidential election, Eisenhower responded to Khrushchev's demands by placing American military forces on an emergency alert. He was not, however, primarily afraid of Soviet military action in the Middle East. The greater danger was that Khrushchev might inveigle his way into negotiating a settlement and thereby interject Soviet power in an area which for centuries Western Europe had fought to keep free of Russian influence.

Attempting to short-circuit the Soviet move, the State Department put tremendous pressure on London and Paris by passing a

[18]Interview with Robert Murphy, Dulles Oral History Project, Dulles Papers, Princeton.

resolution through the General Assembly urging a truce, and then cutting off oil supplies from Latin America that England and France needed to replace their oil, which could not get through the clogged canal. Hours before they would have seized the canal area, the British and French agreed to a cease-fire and pullback. Throughout November, Washington carefully rationed the oil flow to Europe. Not until the United Nations resolution was obeyed and the troops withdrawn did the oil flow freely. American officials argued that they could not afford to turn on the oil too quickly, for this would infuriate the Arab nations which held huge reservoirs of oil leased to Americans.[19]

By December 22 the armies had left, and a United Nations emergency force restored the canal area to Egyptian control. The Suez crisis was a graphic study of how the newly emerging peoples were reordering the power balance at the expense of the older and more powerful nations. These lessons were immediately taken to heart in Washington and Moscow.

In the United States the events in Poland and Suez occurred at the climax of the presidential campaign. Beginning at a time of relative quiet in foreign affairs, the early weeks of the campaign were marked by a discussion of farm issues and the possible effects of the heart attack suffered by Eisenhower a year before. Democratic nominee Adlai Stevenson tried to overcome this apathy, but he did so in a curiously paradoxical manner. At times he argued that disarmament must be placed at the heart of American policy, urged a restudy and possible discontinuance of the military draft, suggested the suspension of nuclear weapons tests, and accurately pinpointed "events in Eastern Europe and the Middle East" as "symptoms of a vast new upheaval in the balance of world power." At other times, however, Stevenson reaffirmed the Cold War clichés: half of Indochina had "become a new Communist satellite and . . . America emerged from that debacle looking like a 'paper tiger'"; NATO's decline threatened the entire Western world; and in his last speech, Stevenson detailed how Harry Truman had stood up to the Russians while Eisenhower

[19]Robert Engler, *The Politics of Oil* (New York, 1961), pp. 261–263; "Memorandum of Conference with the President," November 20, 1956, White House Memoranda Series, Box 4, Dulles Papers, Eisenhower Library, Abilene, Kansas.

rejected the "great opportunities to exploit weaknesses in the Communist ranks and advance the cause of peace."[20]

In playing such a political game with Eisenhower, Stevenson
was outmatched. Republican spokesmen could detail the times
Dulles had gotten "tough" with the Russians (or had "gone to the
brink" of war, to use Dulles's phrase), while Eisenhower could pose
as the military man who made peace in Korea and knew just when
to step back from the brink. When the United States and Russia
again approached the brink in the last hours before the election,
most Americans had no doubt whom they would entrust with their
lives and their Middle Eastern interests.

Eisenhower overwhelmed Stevenson partly because of the President's personal popularity; he received 57 percent of the vote, but
the Democrats captured both Houses of Congress, the first time
that such a split had occurred since 1848. Yet in judging the rhetoric
of the campaign and the postelection analyses, the election clearly
demonstrated something more than personal popularity. It marked
a consensus of ideology. Voting analyses later revealed that a small
majority of Americans preferred Democratic domestic policy, but a
larger majority supported Republican foreign policy.[21] Since 1952
Eisenhower had brought nearly all sectors of the Republican party
into the internationalist camp, adding numerous Democrats and independents by combining appeals for peace with the history of
brinksmanship. Henry Wallace, for example, could vote to have
John Foster Dulles as secretary of state because Wallace believed
that "Eisenhower . . . is the man most likely to preserve world
peace." Reinhold Niebuhr, however, supported Stevenson because
Eisenhower's foreign policies were "catastrophic" as a result of being
based too much upon the peaceful "Geneva spirit." The United
States, Niebuhr warned, had lost ground among the neutrals and (a
fascinating if illogical conclusion on Niebuhr's part) had therefore
made "former neutralist nations into virtual allies of Communism."
"We are in greater peril than at any time since our victory over the
Nazis," the theologian gravely concluded.[22]

Niebuhr's explanation revealed a basic agreement with Dulles's
views. Accurately pinpointing the growing dilemma of American

[20] Adlai E. Stevenson, *The New America* (New York, 1957), pp. 27–34, 40–41.
[21] Angus Campbell et al., *The American Voter* (New York, 1960), pp. 198–200,
526–528.
[22] *Life*, May 14, 1956, p. 184; *New Republic*, October 29, 1956, p. 11.

policy in Vietnam a year earlier, Niebuhr had warned against using military power when "it lacks a moral and political base"; but he then applauded the "disinterested" Americans who were replacing the French as the Western power in South Vietnam.[23] Dulles, of course, had initiated this displacement and was trying to build the moral and political base which Niebuhr wanted. In these circumstances, Niebuhr's dislike and mistrust of Dulles became less significant, for both men agreed on a fundamental point: the United States could not keep its hands off politically unstable nations because such instability could turn "former neutralist nations into virtual allies of Communism," to use Niebuhr's phrase.

Eisenhower wove this consensus into policy just a few months after his reelection. The Suez crisis had seriously weakened the Baghdad Pact and had stimulated Nasser to attempt to increase his power in the Middle East. On January 5, 1957, Eisenhower tried to reverse those trends by replaying his performance of 1954–1955 in the Formosa Straits crisis. He asked Congress for authorization to extend economic and military cooperation and, if necessary, to employ American military forces in the Middle East if any nation in that area requested help against communist-instigated armed aggression. The Middle East Resolution, or the "Eisenhower Doctrine" as it came to be known, sailed through the House. The Senate, however, balked.

Senators attacked the resolution as being anti-Israeli, too vague, and injurious to the Western alliance. Dulles did not lessen this last criticism when he remarked that Anglo-French forces should remain in Europe, for "If I were an American boy . . . I'd rather not have a French and British soldier beside me, one on my right and one on my left." Such a remark was hardly tactful, but in a single sentence Dulles had given his view of how collective the security decision making should be in the Middle East.[24] With the help of Majority Leader Lyndon Johnson, the administration finally passed the resolution in March, 72 to 19. It did so despite little public support. Heavy congressional mail, in fact, ran eight to one

---

[23]Reinhold Niebuhr, "The Limits of Military Power." In *The World Crisis* (New York, 1958), pp. 114–121.

[24]U.S. Senate, Committee on Foreign Relations, 85th Cong., 1st Sess., *Hearings . . . to Authorize the President to Undertake Economic and Military Cooperation with Nations in the General Area of the Middle East*, Parts 1 and 2 (Washington, 1957), especially pp. 4–41.

against the proposal in February. The passage of the Eisenhower Doctrine had interesting political overtones. A Democratic Congress formally surrendered some of its power, especially that of controlling the outbreak of war, to a Republican President.

If anyone doubted that Eisenhower would use this gift of power, they learned otherwise within a month after the Senate completed action. In April young King Hussein of Jordan came under attack from pro-Nasser elements within his country. Hussein asked for help because he was under attack from "international Communism and its followers." The Eisenhower Doctrine specifically and the general American ideological view of revolutions now faced a test: Would the United States help Hussein defend the status quo against the Nasserite elements by brandishing the argument that Hussein was being saved from "international Communism"? Eisenhower responded by sending $10 million to Hussein and dispatching the Sixth Fleet to the Mediterranean area near Jordan. The official State Department announcement on the sending of this aid did not directly blame "international Communism"; instead it explained the action as safeguarding "the preservation of the independence and integrity of the nations of the Middle East."[25] With such ease was a resolution giving the President military powers to war against international communism transformed into presidential power to intervene in any Middle Eastern situation which, by American definition, threatened the independence and integrity of any nation in the area. Anticommunism had become a rather strange phenomenon. It had also been integrated into a global Monroe Doctrine. The Eisenhower Doctrine was an extension of the dogmas of 1823 into the Middle East in the same sense that, as Dulles observed, SEATO extended the original doctrine into Southeast Asia.

In the early spring of 1957 the Eisenhower administration could believe that it had emerged from the winter crises with increased powers and prestige. Such was not the case with Nikita Khrushchev. Despite his triumphant proclamation that Dulles's failure to interfere in the Hungarian uprising had proven the hollowness of "liberation," the fiasco of Khrushchev's policies in Eastern Europe and his inability to take advantage of the power vacuum in the Middle East immersed him in deep political trouble in Moscow. He

[25]Department of State, *American Foreign Policy: Current Documents, 1957* (Washington, 1961), p. 1024.

came under vigorous attack for having invited Chinese officials to fly to Warsaw at a critical moment to quiet the Poles. Having the Chinese play the role of mediator in Eastern Europe because of Khrushchev's mistakes at the Twentieth Congress gave Molotov, Malenkov, and Kaganovich their opening. Khrushchev soon counterattacked with his tactics of 1953–1955. "We are all Stalinists," he loudly announced at a New Year's Eve party, and then launched into a denunciation of "capitalist countries" who wanted "a feverish arms race." His talk became increasingly tough. For the first time since 1955 the Soviet press accused the United States of following, in the words of a joint Chinese-Soviet announcement, "a policy of aggression and preparation for war."[26] With these moves, Khrushchev tried to divide Malenkov from the old-line Stalinists, while at the same time consolidating his alliance with Marshal Zhukov and the military.

During the summer of 1957, Khrushchev gained supreme power. His first target was the military. Having helped make him, Zhukov could perhaps help break him. Khrushchev's opportunity arose when the marshal began to issue pronouncements on sensitive political issues as well as on military strategy. Party leaders interpreted this as a direct and dangerous threat to the supremacy of the party over the military. The danger was indeed even greater, for since Beria's execution four years before, the weakening of the secret police had allowed the military to gain a large measure of independence from party control. In late October Zhukov was stripped of his post as defense minister. When he apparently tried to fight back, he was also removed from the Presidium and the Central Committee.[27] Khrushchev next attempted to educate the Soviet intellectuals who had apparently misunderstood the de-Stalinization campaign to mean that more candid criticisms of Soviet society would be tolerated. At a garden party, Khrushchev made such a verbal assault upon the invited intellectuals that one woman fainted. That harangue climaxed with Khrushchev shouting that Hungary would have remained orderly if several writers had been shot at the proper time; if such a threat ever faced the Soviet Union, he added, "My hand would not tremble."[28] The fol-

[26]H. S. Dinerstein, *War and the Soviet Union*, revised edition (New York, 1959, 1962), pp. 154–163.

[27]Raymond L. Garthoff, *Soviet Military Policy* (New York, 1966), p. 52–54.

[28]Edward Crankshaw, *Khrushchev, A Career* (New York, 1966), pp. 253–255.

lowing year when the distinguished Russian author Boris Pasternak expressed some doubts about the results of the 1917 revolution in his novel *Dr. Zhivago,* the book was banned from mass circulation inside Russia, and Pasternak was prohibited from traveling to Stockholm to receive the Nobel Prize in literature. De-Stalinization had its limits, particularly if it threatened the power of the party and Khrushchev.

After a four-year struggle, Khrushchev was supreme. In the United States Eisenhower began his second term in power. The world outside Moscow and Washington had greatly altered between 1953 and 1957. Having created an acceptable status quo in Europe, Washington shifted more and more of its energies to fighting the Cold War in the Third World. In the Soviet Union Khrushchev brought about changes that allowed his government to exploit opportunities within the newly emerging nations. Dwight Eisenhower provided the proper epitaph for the history of those years: "Somehow or other," he wrote Dulles in February 1955, "it seems not at all extraordinary that you should celebrate your birthday in Bangkok."[29]

---

[29]The President to Secretary of State, February 15, 1955, Correspondence, Dulles Papers, Princeton.

9

New Frontiers
and Old Dilemmas
(1957-1962)

On the morning of October 4, 1957, the Soviet Union successfully launched the world's first artificial satellite. Named "Sputnik," Russian for "traveling companion," the 184-pound satellite swirled above the earth at 18,000 miles per hour. More significant than the satellite was the powerful booster rocket that thrust Sputnik into orbit, for it indicated Soviet capability of sending a powerful weapon at very high speeds to targets within a 4000-mile radius. The launching also demonstrated the skill of Soviet missile science. Niebuhr's argument that scientists could be as efficiently exploited by a totalitarian as by a democratic society seemed true—and ominous.

Americans were extremely disturbed. Strategic air force units were dispersed and placed on alert, short-range Jupiter missiles were installed in Turkey and Italy to offset the long-range Soviet weapons, money was poured into missile and bomber programs, and "gaps" were suddenly discovered in everything from missile production to the teaching of arithmetic at the preschool level. Dulles attempted to play down the Soviet feat because he understood the impact it would have on world affairs. The newly emerging nations could view Russia as a people who in 1917 had been generations behind other industrialized nations but who, through harsh regimentation, had assumed first place in the race for control of outer space. They could also interpret the launching as a dramatic swing in the balance of military power toward Moscow. In August 1957 the Soviets had fired the world's first intercontinental ballistic missile (ICBM) and that same month had announced, "Coexistence is not only the absence of war between the two systems, but also peaceful economic competition between them, and concrete cooperation in economic, political and cultural areas."[1] Khrushchev could welcome such competition with the knowledge that the Soviet gross national product (the total amount of goods and services in the economy) had increased on the average of 7.1 percent annually between 1950 and 1958, nearly 50 percent greater than the American rate.

This economic growth was real, but the Soviet lead in ICBMs was not. The Soviets made a basic decision in 1957 not to build an elementary first-generation ICBM complex but to wait for the second- and third-generation models. This meant that for the next few years Russian foreign policy would attempt to exploit an imaginary lead. One interesting way Khrushchev did this was to have Russian radio and newspapers quote back to the West the West's own exaggerated views of Soviet missile capacity, thereby reinforcing the exaggerations.[2]

United States arms experts and politicians warned that Americans faced the grave danger of being on the wrong side of a "missile gap." Such warnings from John F. Kennedy and Lyndon Johnson grew more shrill as these Democrats opened early campaigns for the 1960 presidential election. In late 1957 their warnings received support from the Gaither Report. A top-secret investigation of American military posture, it had been commissioned by Eisenhower's National Security Council. Named after its author, Rowland Gaither, the report updated NSC-68 of seven years before. The report ominously informed Eisenhower that unless United States military spending increased 50 percent in the near future, the "expansionist" Soviet threat "may become critical in early 1959 or early 1960." Along with a massive arms buildup, the paper urged a $25 billion ("simple, even spartan") program of fallout

[1]"The Leninist Course of Peaceful Coexistence," *Kommunist*, No. 11, 1957, p. 5.

[2]Arnold Horelick and Myron Rush, *Strategic Power and Soviet Foreign Policy* (Chicago, 1966), pp. 36–38.

shelters which would not only supposedly protect Americans from Soviet attack but permit "our own air defense to use nuclear warheads with greater freedom." Such vast spending would have few bad effects on the United States economy and could even "help to sustain production and employment."[3]

Eisenhower (correctly, as it turned out) dismissed the Gaither Report as misguided. He ordered it pigeonholed, and it did not become public until 1973. The President knew from his intelligence sources that Soviet missile forces posed little threat to the United States. He blamed much of the post-Sputnik panic (again correctly) on ambitious politicians or on long-time defense specialists—such as Paul Nitze, an author of both the Gaither Report and NSC-68, and later a top Reagan administration official—who could apparently not be satisfied no matter how large United States nuclear forces became.

Eisenhower believed that current programs more than sufficed: between 1958 and 1960 the nation's nuclear stockpile stunningly tripled, from 6000 to 18,000 weapons. These included fourteen virtually untouchable Polaris nuclear submarines (each with sixteen missiles), the first of which went into service in 1960. Allies and new domestic pressure groups—such as SANE, or the National Committee for a Sane Nuclear Policy—meanwhile pushed Eisenhower to stop nuclear testing and to negotiate arms reduction. Testing temporarily stopped in late 1958 after a series of huge Soviet and American explosions released dangerous amounts of radioactive materials in the atmosphere and, ultimately, into rain and even milk. But Eisenhower and Khrushchev never took the second step to arms control, particularly given the pressures of the Gaither Report and Democratic rhetoric on the President, and of Soviet military officials on the premier.[4]

Despite those pressures, Eisenhower refused to panic. He also refused to further skew the economy by dramatically increasing military spending. That refusal required some courage, because in

[3]Text available in Joint Committee on Defense Production, 94th Cong., 2nd Sess., *Deterrence and Survival in the Nuclear Age (The "Gaither Report" of 1957)* (Washington, 1976), especially pp. 12, 22–23, 30–31; on NSC-68, see pp. 96–98 above.

[4]Robert A. Divine, *Blowing on the Wind: The Nuclear Test Ban Debate, 1954–1960* (New York, 1978), especially chapters 9–11; David Alan Rosenberg, "The Origins of Overkill," *International Security,* VII (Spring 1983): 66; David Holloway, *The Soviet Union and the Arms Race* (New Haven, 1983), pp. 38–40.

1957–1958 and again in 1959–1960 the economy suffered its second and third significant downturns of the decade. In retrospect the years between 1957 and 1960 marked a historic turn: in such key areas as Detroit's automobiles and Pittsburgh's steel, the United States economy became less competitive in world markets than Japan's and West Germany's. Not able to maintain large, favorable trade balances and forced to continue paying the costs of acting as a global policeman, Americans had to begin shipping abroad large amounts of gold to pay their bills — $2 billion of gold in 1958 alone. The dollar, the foundation of the West's economic and military system, wobbled. A top government official finally declared in 1960, "This is the first time in my lifetime that the credit of the United States has been questioned. A serious shadow lies over the American business picture."[5]

Eisenhower privately blamed the problem on greed and a lack of discipline in the United States which he believed threatened to undermine the capitalist system. In a cabinet meeting he also singled out the huge sums spent on weapons that were "just negative stuff adding nothing to the earning capability of the country." In 1960 he blasted the "almost hysterical fear among some elements of the country" that prevented slashes in military budgets.[6] This line of thinking climaxed in early 1961 with the President's famous farewell speech, which warned that a military-industrial complex threatened to distort the economy. At the same time, however, Eisenhower's own view of both the Soviet Union and revolutionary dangers in the Third World prevented him from trying to negotiate arms control agreements or even to educate his fellow Americans on the need to rethink foreign policy in the aftermath of the astonishing events of 1956–1959. Eisenhower understood the causes and costs of the Cold War better than most of the post-1945 Presidents. He also reigned when United States military superiority allowed him to negotiate on the causes and reduce the costs. Because of his anti-communism and caution, Eisenhower did neither. But he did

[5]Godfrey Hodgson, *America in Our Time* (New York, 1978), p. 7; Walt Whitman Rostow, *Diffusion of Power, 1958–1972* (New York, 1973), pp. 60–61.

[6]"Minutes of Cabinet Meeting, June 3, 1960," Cabinet Meetings of President Eisenhower, pp. 1–3, Dwight D. Eisenhower Library, Abilene, Kansas. On Eisenhower and capitalism, see Robert Griffith, "Dwight D. Eisenhower and the Corporate Commonwealth," *American Historical Review,* LXXXVII (February 1982): especially 117–122.

manage to scotch (at least until John F. Kennedy moved into the White House) the Gaither Report's recommendations.

Eisenhower could thus afford to ignore Khrushchev's game of missile bluff, but for the rotund Russian leader the game turned out to be most costly. In months it contributed to a widening of the surprising split between the two communist giants. Khrushchev began by being properly cautious; he termed the ICBM the "ultimate weapon" and painted a picture of the horrible destruction that could result from a nuclear exchange. Mao Tse-tung, however, insisted in 1957 that "the international situation has now reached a new turning point. There are two winds in the world today; the East wind and the West wind. . . . I think the characteristic of the situation today is the East wind prevailing over the West wind."[7] Mao assumed, as a Chinese newspaper commented in February 1958, that the Soviet successes had created a "qualitative change in the distribution of world power [which] had . . . torn apart the paper tiger of American imperialism and shattered the tale of the 'position of strength.'"[8] The Chinese urged strong support for "wars of liberation" in the newly emerging nations, wars that could be safely fanned because the American strategic power had been neutralized. Khrushchev refused to cooperate in such recklessness. He knew that his ICBM program was considerably more of a "paper tiger" than the American long-range bombing force.

The break between China and Russia also became evident in other areas. The Soviets strongly disagreed with Mao's "Great Leap Forward" program in 1958, with its emphasis on forced collectivization. This disagreement pinpointed internal communist differences, for the Russians, as they had historically, insisted first upon industrial productivity and only secondarily upon infusing the masses with revolutionary ideology. Mao, however, was trying at best to balance the two and, in fact, actually to reverse the Soviet priorities in order to mobilize his tremendous manpower through mass revolutionary indoctrination. The Chinese became increasingly critical of Khrushchev's emphasis on consumer goods instead of military

[7]William Zimmerman, "Russia and the International Order," *Survey,* 58 (January 1966): 209–213.

[8]Donald Zagoria, *The Sino-Soviet Conflict, 1956–1961* (Princeton, 1962), pp. 160–162.

hardware and of the Soviet insistence on aiding "bourgeois" regimes in the underdeveloped world instead of fomenting revolution.

Dulles precisely and colorfully described the new Soviet attitude in May 1958. He no longer feared that the Soviets would pose a greater threat with their disavowal of force and "this policy of the smile." Dulles found hope in the belief "that a nation tends to become what it pretends to be. . . . I have seen lots of tough guys who have made their pile, who come to New York, wanted to get into society, and who have to behave differently."[9] The secretary of state attempted to readjust American military thinking by placing increased emphasis on small nuclear weapons which could be used in limited wars.

In these last months of his life, Dulles also tried to influence the newly emerging areas by readjusting American economic aid. Nothing could be done through direct trade arrangements. The traditional reciprocal trade agreements program was in fact seriously injured when, in March 1959, Eisenhower imposed quota restrictions on foreign crude oil imports after two large oil companies refused to join in voluntary restraints. The restrictions were a body blow to Venezuelan and Middle Eastern oil producers and affected American foreign policy in those areas. The administration only slightly offset that misfortune by increasing foreign aid assistance. In fiscal 1957 Mutual Security Program funds were raised nearly 40 percent, and much of this went to Burma, Indonesia, and South Vietnam.

This increased emphasis upon Southeast Asia indicated the Eisenhower administration's growing concern over Mao's China. The President's policy became clear in late summer and autumn 1958, when the Chinese began to shell the offshore islands. Mao probably did not plan to invade the islands but hoped that, with the United States immersed in another Middle Eastern crisis, one of two results would occur: either the Quemoy garrison would surrender without being invaded, or the United States would strike back by bombing mainland China and thus bring the Soviets into the affair back of the Chinese. Neither occurred. The American Seventh Fleet escorted Nationalist troops and supplies into the islands, Dulles announced that Quemoy was "increasingly related" to Taiwan's safety, and American Marines moved into Quemoy

[9]"Remarks to U.S. Ambassadors to Europe," Paris, May 9, 1958, NATO ministerial meeting, Conference Dossiers, Dulles Papers, Princeton.

eight-inch howitzers capable of firing atomic shells. Eisenhower's tough stand on the Chinese problem and his emphasis on tactical atomic weapons had merged into a concrete policy position. Khrushchev did little except assure Mao that Russia would help if China was actually attacked.

The Chinese calculations of the probable American response and the Soviet-American balance of power should have been more accurate, for Mao could have drawn the appropriate conclusions from the Middle Eastern crisis of July. In that episode the United States landed marines in Lebanon without any counterstroke from Moscow. Two months before the landings, Dulles had expressed the fear that the growing power of Nasser and the United Arab Republic (formed by Egypt, Syria, and Yemen in early 1958) would endanger Jordan, Iraq, and Lebanon. On July 14 General Abdel Karim Kassim led a nationalist revolt which overthrew the Iraqui government and established a regime friendly to the UAR. The Baghdad Pact suddenly had a gaping hole. Repercussions were felt in Lebanon where pro-Nasser Moslems had been fighting Christians.

The news of the Kassim coup and the turmoil in Lebanon arrived in Washington early on the morning of July 14. Lebanese President Camille Chamoun, a Maronite Christian, urgently requested help from the United States. At 9:45 A.M. Dulles began explaining to congressional leaders "recent Soviet political activities" in the area. He declared that "it was time to bring a halt to the deterioration in our position in the Middle East." The administration wanted to land troops in Lebanon. There would be no military problem. General Nathan Twining of the Joint Chiefs assured Dulles, as General Twining later recalled, that the "Russians aren't going to jump us," and "if they do jump us, if they do come in, they couldn't pick a better time, because we've got them over the whing whang and they know it."[10]

The only problem was again the proper interpretation of the Eisenhower Doctrine. Some congressmen argued that, because any communist threat was only dimly apparent, Dulles was asking them to condone intervention in a Lebanese civil war. Logically, they continued, troops should also be sent into Iraq. But they placed no obstacles before Eisenhower, and at 2:30 P.M. the President issued the order. While British paratroopers landed in Jordan to

[10]Interview with General Nathan Twining, Dulles Oral History Project, Dulles Papers, Princeton.

help King Hussein once again stabilize his government, 14,000 American troops waded ashore around public bathers on Lebanon's beaches to quiet the threat of civil war. The size of the force warned both the new Iraqi government and Nasser that any threat to Western oil resources in the area would not be tolerated.

Kassim assured the West that its Iraqi interests were safe, and his government soon moved away from Nasser's influence. The Egyptian leader, so one top American official believed, received "one of the greatest lessons in world power politics that he ever had."[11] When Nasser flew to Moscow during the crisis to request Soviet help, Khrushchev refused to make any significant response. As for the United States, Dulles informed the cabinet that again the free world had ruined Stalin's and Lenin's prophecies that communism would march through the newly emerging nations to conquer the capitalist West. In 1959 Kassim destroyed the shell of the Baghdad Pact by formally withdrawing Iraq. The United States then immediately signed new bilateral military aid treaties with Pakistan, Turkey, and Iran, while the remaining members of the pact formed the Central Treaty Organization (CENTO).

By the autumn of 1958 Eisenhower had turned Khrushchev's game of missile bluff into a string of real American victories. The Soviet leader suddenly moved to play for much higher stakes: the control of West Germany. Some of the Cold War's most tense moments followed in 1958–1959. Eisenhower had to respond to Khrushchev's challenge, moreover, amidst a bitter debate that threatened to divide the Western alliance.

The debate had been triggered in 1956 when West Germany dragged its feet on building conventional forces. Chancellor Adenauer instead ominously began to request missiles, artillery capable of firing nuclear shells, and fighter bombers that could haul nuclear bombs. The West soon delivered the artillery and bombers. This turn in German affairs set off speeches by European leaders, who proposed the neutralization and reunification of Germany before Central Europe entered a full-fledged arms race. In the United States the debate climaxed in an angry exchange between two architects of postwar policy, George Kennan and Dean

[11]Interview with Robert Murphy, Dulles Oral History Project, Dulles Papers, Princeton.

Acheson. In words strikingly similar to those of Walter Lippmann's proposals of ten years before, Kennan proposed that before Germany received nuclear arms, the threat of such a possibility should be used to negotiate with the Soviets a neutralization of Central and Eastern Europe. Terms would include the withdrawal of both the Soviet and American armies.[12] This plan soon became known as "disengagement."

Acheson's response in January 1958 was acerbic. If the United States withdrew its troops from Germany and Western Europe, he declared, the Soviets would sooner or later exterminate "independent national life in Western Europe." Acheson particularly feared that Communist parties in Europe would gain the initiative. This indicated his belief that NATO shaped the internal political life of European countries as well as the overall military strategies. Withdrawal from and neutralization of Germany would be disastrous, Acheson warned, for, as he had once remarked, without American troops "to monitor the continued integration of Germany into the West, we should be continually haunted by the spectre of a sort of new [Nazi-Soviet] Agreement." As for Kennan, Acheson sarcastically observed that "Mr. X" had tried but had failed to convince any "responsible leader" of these ideas as early as 1949. "Mr. Kennan has never, in my judgment," Acheson commented, "grasped the realities of power relationships, but takes a rather mystical attitude toward them. To Mr. Kennan there is no Soviet military threat in Europe."[13]

This last sentence indicated a fundamental assumption on the part of Acheson and Dulles. During the six months following Acheson's outburst, however, a strange phenomenon occurred in Washington. Dulles apparently began to move away from Acheson and toward Kennan. The first indication of a change came in a little-noted speech by the director of the White House disarmament staff, Robert E. Matteson. He declared in February 1958 that "we may very well be at one of those great historical divides where a boldness in exploration of the relaxation-of-tension concept might pay greater dividends than we now suspect."[14] In May Dulles remarked

---

[12]George F. Kennan, *Russia, the Atom and the West* (New York, 1957).

[13]*U.S. News and World Report,* January 17, 1958, p. 63.

[14]Richard Rovere, "Letter from Washington," *New Yorker,* March 22, 1958, pp. 136–141.

that "disengagement" was such a "naughty word" that it "couldn't even be translated into a good language like French."[15]

On June 30, 1958, however, Dulles wrote a "My dear friend" letter to Adenauer. At the outset the secretary discounted any dismantling of existing military establishments, but he then observed that domestic and satellite demands were making the Soviets more open to negotiation. Dulles wondered if there could not be a "limitation of armament . . . through establishing significant zones of inspection which would greatly minimize the fear of massive surprise attack."[16] He disavowed any talk of paying a high political price, such as cutting the power of the West German government through a reunification of Germany. The implication, however, was clear: negotiations with the Soviets could lead to the first hesitant steps toward a military neutralization of Central Europe.

Within ten months Dulles would be dead. Where the secretary's thoughts of mid-1958 would have led is only speculation, but clearly he was taking into account those new international events that were reorienting East-West relations. The European status quo was further shaken in June 1958 (the month Dulles wrote Adenauer) when Charles de Gaulle returned to power in France. Franco-American relations had not improved since the Suez debacle. Dulles watched de Gaulle with some concern, for he appreciated how the general hoped to regain the *grandeur* of France through the reorientation of French foreign policy.[17] The reorientation would require considerable freedom of action, and that, Dulles believed quite accurately, would result in "neutralist" policies advanced by de Gaulle within the NATO alliance. At the same time that the communist bloc was dividing into Russian, Chinese, and Yugoslav factions, the Western alliance was also splitting apart.

The postwar world, like most thirteen-year olds, was entering a new and uncertain stage. The widening split within NATO became more evident in late 1958 when France, West Germany, Italy, and the Benelux prepared for the formal initiation of the European Economic Community, or Common Market, on January 1, 1959. Following an accord first reached in March 1957, these nations agreed

[15]"Remarks to U.S. Ambassadors to Europe," Paris, May 9, 1958, NATO ministerial meeting, Conference Dossiers, Dulles Papers, Princeton.

[16]Dulles to Adenauer, June 30, 1958, Correspondence, Dulles Papers, Princeton.

[17]Alfred Grosser, *La Politique extérieure de la Ve République* (Paris, 1965), p. 44.

that within fifteen years they would form an economic union by eliminating tariffs and equalizing taxes within the community while creating a common tariff for outside goods. The immediate impact was political as well as economic, for in a stroke "the six" had decreased their economic dependence upon the United States, tied West Germany firmly to the rest of Western Europe, taken their first step toward possible political federation, and created a middle bloc between the United States and the Soviet Union. The importance of this last development became evident during the eighteen months following New Year's 1960 when, much to American dismay, Western Europe, and, particularly, West Germany, France, and Italy shipped approximately $1 billion worth of strategic goods and equipment to the Soviet Union.

In the last months of 1958, Great Britain attempted to enter the Common Market, but it failed after refusing to surrender its economic ties to the Commonwealth and to the United States. The British countered by forming, in November 1959, the Free Trade Association (or "Outer Seven") comprised of themselves, Sweden, Switzerland, Portugal, Austria, Norway, and Denmark. The new grouping, however, failed to keep pace with the booming Common Market, and Washington watched as the British became increasingly isolated from Western Europe's economic upsurge.

Moscow feared these developments even more than did Washington. The success of the Common Market and, above all, West Germany's possession of artillery and aircraft that had nuclear capabilities, raised once again before the Soviets the specter of a militarized and economically aggressive Germany. After several days of publicizing his growing ICBM arsenal, Khrushchev began a series of moves on November 10, 1958. They climaxed in the demand that the United States, Great Britain, and France withdraw their 10,000 troops from West Berlin, make it a "free city," and negotiate with the East German government (which none of the Western powers recognized) for access into Berlin. If agreement was not reached within six months, Khrushchev threatened to turn the access routes over to East German control. With complete Western support, Dulles rejected Khrushchev's demands, refused to contemplate recognition of East Germany, and intimated that, if the East Germans did gain control of the access routes and refused to allow Western vehicles through, NATO would retaliate "if need be by military force." Khrushchev replied that this would mean World War III.

In focusing upon West Berlin, the Soviet leader had pinpointed the fulcrum that could change the balance of power within Europe. For American policy makers feared that, if the United States did evacuate West Berlin, the Adenauer government's confidence in NATO and the Common Market would be shaken and the basis laid for a West German–Russian deal. It soon became evident, nevertheless, that Khrushchev had concluded that the fulcrum was not worth a nuclear exchange. Denying that he had issued an ultimatum, he modified the six-month limit so discussions could be held. Over strong Chinese protests, the Soviet leader visited the United States in September 1959. Just before his arrival, a Soviet "Lunik" (a rocket shot with a scientific payload) hit the moon. Khrushchev reminded the world of his nation's capabilities by presenting a replica of the Soviet pennant aboard the "Lunik" to the President. The visit produced few diplomatic results. Plans were made for a summit conference in Geneva the following spring, after which Eisenhower was to visit Russia.

By the end of April 1960, hopes for a settlement had shriveled before blistering announcements from Moscow and Washington. During trips to Indonesia and France in early spring, the Soviet premier again demanded a German settlement. On April 20, 1960, Under Secretary of State C. Douglas Dillon attacked Khrushchev's statements with the observation that "the so-called German Democratic Republic [East Germany] is one of the outstanding myths in a vast Communist web of prodigious mythology." Requesting Soviet concessions in Eastern Europe, Korea, and the United Nations as well as in Berlin, Dillon gravely announced that in making his recent threats, Khrushchev "is skating on very thin ice." Six days later Khrushchev reiterated the Soviet policy on Berlin, interpreted Dillon's remarks as a change in the American position since the Camp David discussions, and warned "such hotheads that when they start invoking force and not right and justice, it is but natural that this force will be countered with the force of the other side."[18]

On May 5, the eve of the summit conference, Khrushchev suddenly announced that the Soviets had shot down a U-2 American reconnaissance plane which had been violating Russian territorial sovereignty. The United States first denied that the aircraft had

[18]Richard P. Stebbins, ed., *Documents on American Foreign Relations, 1960* (New York, 1961), pp. 106–113.

been on a spying mission but then became trapped when Khrushchev produced the pilot who had parachuted to safety. After some hesitation, Eisenhower accepted full responsibility for the incident. He also finally announced that there would be no future overflights. The damage, however, had been done. This episode at Geneva did not ruin the conference. That had been accomplished by the growing intransigence over Berlin, the Sino-Soviet rift, and the decision (made by high American officials) to send a U-2 plane over Russian territory during highly critical hours in Russian-American diplomacy.

Khrushchev's major concern was not his relationship with Eisenhower; the President would shortly leave office anyway. More important was the embarrassing position in which the U-2 flights, which had been occurring over Russia for at least four years, placed him in his struggle with Mao. There could be little doubt that on previous U-2 flights the United States had discovered the truth about Russian ICBM strength. This thought probably influenced Khrushchev to call off the Berlin crisis temporarily while intensifying his threats of how Russia would destroy any American ally allowing U-2 planes to leave from its territory. He particularly seized upon an issue in the summer of 1960 that somewhat appeased China and at the same time allowed him to wave his strategic power before the United States: Khrushchev welcomed Fidel Castro as a new force in Latin America and threatened to destroy the United States, "figuratively speaking," if it tried to attack Castro. The Monroe Doctrine, Khrushchev announced, was dead.

This turn of events had begun on July 26, 1953, when the young middle-class lawyer, a species which the unbalanced Cuban society turned out in overabundance, led an armed assault on the regime of Fulgencio Batista. Castro was jailed, but he escaped to Mexico, organized a small revolutionary band, and landed in Cuba in 1956. Batista's police were waiting, and Castro struggled into the mountains with only ten other survivors. American officials paid little attention, believing Batista's word that Castro was dead. In 1957 *The New York Times* correspondent Herbert Matthews found the rebel's hideaway and revealed to the world Castro's program and his astonishing success among the Cuban peasants. Matthews's reports had little positive effect on Washington, however.

The American failure to worry about or understand Castro was not the major mistake, for this was symptomatic of a Cuban policy that had left much to be desired ever since the United States had first taken de facto control in the summer of 1898. By 1956 Americans owned 80 percent of Cuba's utilities, 40 percent of its sugar, 90 percent of its mining wealth, and the island's key strategic location of Guantanamo Bay. The Cuban economy could be manipulated simply by changing the amount of Cuban sugar allowed into the American market. The United States had also landed marines three times after 1902 in efforts to stabilize Cuban politics. Washington had not intervened when Batista overthrew a constitutionally elected government in 1952 and began consolidating his power by following such diverse policies as allowing American advisors to train his military forces while inviting Cuban Communist party members to assume governmental positions. The communists were so close to Batista that they almost missed joining Castro's movement before Batista was driven from power. In 1960 the American ambassador to Cuba during Batista's last years, Earl E. T. Smith, summarized past Cuban-American relations and implicitly explained how disastrous the American colonial policy had been in Cuba for sixty-two years: "Senator, let me explain to you that the United States, until the advent of Castro, was so overwhelmingly influential in Cuba that . . . the American Ambassador was the second most important man in Cuba; sometimes even more important than the President. . . . Now, today, his importance is not very great."[19]

His importance declined because, upon grasping power on New Year's Day 1959, Castro determined to balance the Cuban economy and rectify the social injustices within the society. To accomplish this, a thoroughgoing revolution would be required. In the new ruler's mind this meant ending Cuba's dependence on Washington. Castro's trip to the United States in April almost inevitably produced no positive results. The following month he announced an agrarian reform program which met American resistance. By the summer Castro's personal power was unquestioned, but in his need for organized political support to carry out the revolution, he moved closer to the communists within his 26th of July movement. By the end of the year, the anticommunists within the movement were isolated and leaving Cuba. Confiscations of American property intensified, signaling increased anti-Americanism, as well as Castro's

[19]Robert F. Smith, *What Happened in Cuba? A Documentary History* (New York, 1963), p. 273.

need for resources to finance socioeconomic changes. That need, moreover, prohibited him from paying for the confiscated property.

In February 1960 the Russians signed a trade agreement to exchange Cuban sugar for Soviet oil, machinery, and technicians. Ironically, as Cuban-Soviet bloc trade increased from 2 percent of the island's trade in 1960 to 80 percent by the end of 1961, Castro was forced to accept the position as a food and raw material producer which he had so strongly deprecated in past Cuban-American relations. In July 1960 the United States cut the Cuban sugar quota from the American market. In August Washington began to mobilize hemispheric opposition to Cuba, and three months later American naval forces moved to Central American waters to quell a rumored invasion from Cuba. At this time, Eisenhower accepted a Central Intelligence Agency–State Department plan to train an anti-Castro army. Preparations began for an invasion in early 1961. In the first days of January 1961, United States–Cuban diplomatic relations were formally severed.

The attention of Americans now focused on this bearded jungle fighter who made four-hour long speeches to entranced Cuban audiences and who had the gall to defy the world's greatest superpower just ninety miles away. But Castro was only an incredible symbol for a larger danger that confronted United States policy in its own hemisphere. In the late 1950s Latin America began passing through its most important change since it had obtained independence from Spain 140 years earlier.

Latin America is fundamentally different from most of the newly emerging areas in Asia or the Middle East. It is more highly developed and, in some areas, in an intermediate stage of economic growth that presents sophisticated economic and social problems. Large areas of Latin America were controlled by extremely conservative governments (the "oligarchs") that could not be removed from power as Africans and Asians removed European colonial rulers from their continents. In Vietnam, for example, the radical nationalists could fight an anticolonial war to send the "foreigners"—the French—back to Paris. But in El Salvador, Nicaragua, or Bolivia, the radical nationalists had to fight a revolution against oligarchs who were their own flesh and blood. The oligarchs, moreover, received strong support from the military elite and the United States, which had frowned on Latin American revolutions throughout the twentieth century.

CENTRAL AND SOUTH AMERICA, 1954–1984

UNITED STATES

CUBA
Batista overthrown 1959
Attempted anti-Castro invasion 1961
Soviet military aid, U.S. quarantine 1962

MEXICO
Threatened by $80 billion foreign debt 1980s

Miami
Havana

BAHAMAS *(Br.)*

DOMINICAN REP.
U.S. broke diplomatic ties 1960
Trujillo assassinated 1961
Diplomatic ties restored 1962
U.S. and O.A.S. intervention 1965

BELIZE

Mexico City

JAMAICA

HAITI

PUERTO RICO
Pérez Jiménez overthrown 1958
Anti-Nixon riots 1958

GUATEMALA
Arbenz overthrown 1954
Castillo Armas assassinated 1957

HONDURAS
U.S. naval and air bases 1981–

BARBADOS

GRANADA *Invaded by U.S. 1983*

NICARAGUA
Canal Zone

CARIBBEAN SEA

TRINIDAD AND TOBAGO

EL SALVADOR
COSTA RICA

Caracas
VENEZUELA

GUYANA

SURINAM *(Neth.)*
FR. GUIANA

PANAMA
Anti-U.S. riots 1959
U.S. returns canal zone to Panama by treaty 1978

Bogotá

COLOMBIA

Sandinistas overthrow Somoza 1979
U.S. supports anti-Sandinista "contras" 1981–

Quito

ECUADOR

PERU

PACIFIC OCEAN

Anti-Nixon riots 1958
Military coup 1962
Military coup 1968

Lima

BRAZIL
Military seizes power 1964 and rules 1964.
Threatened by $90 billion foreign debt 1980s.

BOLIVIA

La Paz

Brasília

Average annual per capita income 1978–1981

Argentina	$2300
Barbados	3000
Bolivia	510
Brazil	1500
Chile	2000
Colombia	1100
Costa Rica	2200
Cuba	840
Dominican Rep.	1200
Ecuador	1050
El Salvador	640
Grenada	500
Guatemala	1080
Guyana	600
Haiti	260
Honduras	822
Jamaica	1340
Mexico	1800
Nicaragua	800
Panama	1100
Paraguay	1040
Peru	650
Trinidad & Tobago	4800
Uruguay	2800
Venezuela	3600
United States	10,600

Salvador Allende elected 1970 Overthrown by military and died 1973

PARAGUAY

Asunción

Rio de Janeiro

CHILE
Santiago

Buenos Aires

URUGUAY
Montevideo

Punta del Este Conferences 1961, 1962

ARGENTINA
Threatened by $50 billion foreign debt 1980s
Returns to civilian government 1983

ATLANTIC

OCEAN

The southern nations remained quiet between 1948 and 1958 as Latin America's economy grew at an impressive annual rate of 4.3 percent. But this growth occurred in a powder keg: the region's population grew 3 percent annually, an amount greater than that of any area of the world. By the year 2000, some 600 million people would live where 200 million lived in 1960. The economic growth also varied from country to country. Venezuela's oil and Mexico's viable political system gave those nations strong advantages. Elsewhere, poor resources and cementlike political systems contributed to internal pressures that threatened to explode in revolution. Outside of democratic Costa Rica and Mexico, 2 percent of the population owned 75 percent of the agricultural land on a continent whose people had to live on their ability to scratch a living from the soil. Many of the poor moved out of the countryside to exist in some of the world's worst slums on the outskirts of major cities. Then in 1957–1958, economic recession in the United States dragged down an already stumbling Latin American economy. Since 1945 Washington officials had made no major effort to correct inequities in the economies of the southern nations—many of which were dependent for survival on American producers and consumers. Between 1945 and 1960, Washington had given three times more aid to Belgium, Luxembourg, and the Netherlands than to all twenty Latin American nations. Private American capital, meanwhile, had invested $1 billion in oil, $500 million in mining, and $750 million in manufacturing, thus increasing the imbalance of the Latin American economies.

After signing their first trade agreement with Argentina in 1953, the Soviets tried to take advantage of these conditions. By 1957 Soviet trade with Latin America amounted to only $200 million annually. It increased to only $450 million by 1960. Nevertheless, it had doubled within three years (while the United States proportion of that trade had slipped), and it focused on a few select countries, such as Argentina, Brazil, and later Cuba.[20] During these same years, anti-Yankeeism spread. Its intensity was not appreciated in Washington until April 1958 when Vice President Richard Nixon and his wife visited several Latin American nations. The North Americans were spat upon, had eggs and stones hurled at them,

---

[20]Ronald James Clark, "Latin-American Economic Relations with the Soviet Bloc, 1954–1961," unpublished doctoral dissertation, Indiana University, 1963.

and in Caracas had their limousine attacked by mobs. Eisenhower rushed a thousand marines to United States bases in the Caribbean, but Nixon escaped and flew home before further outbreaks occurred.

President Juscelino Kubitschek of Brazil seized this opportunity to push for Eisenhower's acceptance of a proposed "Operation Pan America," in which the United States and Latin America would cooperate to promote long-term development. A pivotal part of the plan was an Inter-American Development Bank that would channel low-interest United States loans into the southern nations. Eisenhower had been cool toward this proposal in 1957 — he wanted only private capitalists to handle development — but after Nixon's encounters and Castro's sudden appearance, Eisenhower's view changed. The bank was established in 1959 with $1 billion in capital. In 1960, with the Act of Bogotá, the hemispheric nations began working out details for a comprehensive program of economic development. These events marked the real beginnings of what John F. Kennedy would later popularize as the Alliance for Progress. But they appeared too late to prevent the rise of Fidel Castro and the stirring of revolutionaries in Central and South America.

Castroism and the rumbling problems in other newly emerging nations dominated the foreign policy debates in the 1960 presidential campaign. The Democratic nominee, John F. Kennedy, charged the Republican nominee, Richard Nixon, with allowing a "missile gap" in the Soviets' favor, but Kennedy started a more significant debate when he suggested American support of "non-Batista democratic anti-Castro forces." Nixon appeared appalled at even the suggestion of American support for such intervention. He later explained that, having access to the invasion plans already under way, he was forced to act surprised publicly at Kennedy's suggestion. Outside of these exchanges, the two nominees differed significantly on few other foreign policy issues. The Eisenhower consensus, forged in 1956, was making its mark, and each candidate simply tried to exploit, not destroy it. In one of the closest presidential elections, Kennedy won by a margin of 114,000 votes out of 68.3 million cast. The electoral college vote went to the Democrats 303 to 219.

John F. Kennedy was a most sensitive and astute politician, and the narrow victory margin affected the development of his foreign policy. Presidential assistant Theodore Sorensen defined the problem:

"President Kennedy is acutely aware of Jefferson's dictum: 'Great innovations should not be forced on slender majorities.'"[21] Kennedy tended to defer to military and intelligence experts and to those in Congress who preferred to fight the Cold War rather than risk negotiating its problems. His experiences abroad while his father, Joseph P. Kennedy, was ambassador to Great Britain in the late 1930s convinced him that democracies moved too slowly in reacting to totalitarian aggression, a view that permeated his widely read book, written while he was a Harvard senior, *Why England Slept*. His sensitivity to the political climate was also demonstrated during 1950–1954, when he was extremely reluctant to oppose Senator McCarthy. As a young senator from Massachusetts, Kennedy nevertheless realized that the growing importance of the newly emerging nations required changes in foreign policy. A 1957 speech was outspoken in support of Algeria's fight against France. In 1954 he warned against any American attempt to prop up the French regime in Indochina, but on this issue Kennedy equivocated, for in June 1956 he lauded Diem as an "offspring" of the American effort to keep Southeast Asia free. Aware of the challenge of the newly emerging peoples and fearful that the United States would not respond quickly or properly, Kennedy emphasized in a special message to Congress on May 25, 1961, "The great battleground for the defense and expansion of freedom today is . . . Asia, Latin America, Africa and the Middle East, the lands of the rising peoples."[22]

In his first annual message on January 30, 1961, the President listed the priorities for waging the conflict between "Freedom and Communism," by noting that "First, we must strengthen our military tools."[23] Upon entering office, the administration had discovered that the "missile gap," which Kennedy had heavily emphasized in the campaign, was only fictional. The Soviets and the Chinese also knew this, and, consequently, Kennedy and his advisors feared that the communists would place more emphasis on conventional, local wars. In 1961 the administration increased the defense budget 15 percent, doubling the number of combat-ready divisions in the army's strategic reserve, expanding the marines,

[21] Theodore C. Sorensen, *Decision-Making in the White House: The Olive Branch or the Arrows* (New York, 1963), pp. 44–48.

[22] U.S. Government Printing Office, *Public Papers of the Presidents, J. F. Kennedy, 1961* (Washington, 1962), p. 397.

[23] *Public Papers of the Presidents, Kennedy*, pp. 23–24.

adding seventy vessels to the active fleet, and giving a dozen more wings to the tactical air forces. General Maxwell Taylor returned to act as the President's military advisor.

Varying little in objective from Eisenhower's approach, this policy was a different kind of attempt to contain communism and revolutionary instability. The policy had been thought through and widely publicized by the reports of the Rockefeller brothers in the late 1950s and was the result of a logical progression of thought on the part of intellectuals such as Henry Kissinger. In this sense particularly, the Kennedy administration seized upon American intellectuals in a manner unmatched since 1933. The scholars responded.

Other parts of the society also responded. In his farewell address in January 1961, Eisenhower had warned the American people against the "conjunction of an immense military establishment and a large arms industry" which was "new in American experience," and whose "total influence . . . is felt in every city, every state house, every office in the federal government. . . . In the councils of government, we must guard against the acquisition of unwarranted influence, whether sought or unsought, by the military-industrial complex." The President declared, "The potential for the disastrous rise of misplaced power exists and will persist." For Eisenhower, this was strong language. The Kennedy administration, however, took little heed of this speech. Determined to help noncommunist nations militarily, and worried over the outflow of American gold caused by an unfavorable balance in the nation's financial and trade exchanges with the rest of the world, the new President established in 1961 a special post in the Defense Department to sell American arms through private corporations to foreign nations. By 1965 American companies exported $1.9 billion worth of arms to Europe, Japan, Iran, Venezuela, and Saudi Arabia, among others. General Dynamics Corporation alone sold more than $1 billion worth of arms overseas between 1962 and 1965. Most of the goods were sophisticated and expensive electronic equipment. As one business periodical observed, in the 1930s such companies were known as "'Merchants of Death.' . . . Times have changed."[24]

The drive for a unified but multimilitary response to foreign policy problems was typified by Secretary of Defense Robert McNamara's management of the Pentagon. No more would indi-

[24]*Forbes*, February 1, 1966, pp. 15–16.

vidual services have wholly independent programs. McNamara instead brought the various services together under "program elements" in which the military units were coordinated for efficient war making on various levels. The professional soldiers lost some of their political power, but they gained greatly in military efficiency. By mobilizing resources in this way, the administration could massively retaliate on many military levels. The change under way since the days of Dulles had matured. Particular emphasis was placed upon preparing the United States for guerrilla wars. The Jungle Warfare School in the Canal Zone and another at Fort Bragg, North Carolina, brought United States Army Special Forces troops together with Latin American units. More than 600 Latin American policemen sharpened their talents in counterintelligence work and the handling of mobs by undergoing training in the Canal Zone school established by the Agency for International Development. At the end of 1966, anti-American guerrillas nevertheless operated in Venezuela, Bolivia, Colombia, Peru, Nicaragua, and Guatemala.

Kennedy picked Latin America for special attention. Besides the training of antiguerrilla forces and the establishment of the Peace Corps (young men and women trained to perform teaching and technical services in newly emerging nations), the President announced, on March 13, 1961, the Alliance for Progress. To the Eisenhower policies of 1959–1960, Kennedy added a ten-year commitment of $20 billion of American money and an appropriate image. The plan was worked out at the Punta del Este, Uruguay, conference in August. The United States aid, including $300 million annually from private capital, would quadruple the annual economic assistance given the area between 1946 and 1960. In return, Latin America pledged $80 billion of investment over the ten-year period and, most important, land, tax, and other socioeconomic reforms. Kennedy hoped these efforts would result in a 5.5 percent increase in Latin America's growth rate, or a modest net increase of 2.5 percent over the population increase.

These ambitious plans quickly encountered major difficulties. The programs were undercut by bureaucratic infighting in Washington; the marked reluctance of such major Latin American nations as Brazil, Argentina, and Mexico to submit their development programs to hemispheric scrutiny; and particularly by the inability or unwillingness of many governments to undertake the promised reforms. In some nations the requisite political stability could not be established; between 1961 and 1966, military forces overthrew nine Latin American governments. The Kennedy administration, trapped between the alternatives of intervening in the affairs of sovereign nations or watching the Alliance grow increasingly weaker, could not work out an effective response. By 1963 Alliance officials could claim that 35 million Latin Americans had benefited from the program, but only at the end of the first five years would the 5.5 percent growth rate be in sight, and not even then would there be evidence of the reforms which could ensure fair distribution of the benefits.

The Alliance was designed to create a stable and orderly Latin America without having the hemisphere endure a series of Castro-like revolutions. The Cuban ruler had become a primary concern of American officials, and they moved to eradicate him on April 17, 1961, when the administration supported an invasion at the Bay of Pigs by a group of Cuban exiles. This force had been trained for months in Guatemala by the Central Intelligence Agency. Although it was supposedly a secret operation, news of the preparations was widespread in American newspapers by April. President Kennedy was assured by the CIA, State, and military officials that the invasion could succeed if, under American-provided air cover, the anti-Castro units could establish a beachhead and then link up with other guerrillas in the mountains. Taking the word of his experts, Kennedy acquiesced, demanding only that no American troops be committed. Fifteen hundred Cubans waded ashore on the morning of April 17, only to find that one key air strike had been canceled because of clouds, that other naval and air supporting units had been immobilized by Castro's small air force, that the beachhead was indefensible, and that they had no hope of reaching the mountains. In the aftermath, American Ambassador to the United Nations Adlai Stevenson was caught lying about United States support of the operation. Kennedy ordered an investigation of the CIA and removed some top officials. In Cuba, Castro was ensconced more securely in power than ever before.

"All my life I've known better than to depend on the experts," the President wondered aloud shortly afterward. "How could I have been so stupid, to let them go ahead?"[25] The problem went deeper than that, however. Certainly the Guatemala operation of

[25]Theodore C. Sorensen, *Kennedy* (New York, 1965), p. 309.

1954 colored the view of both the CIA and the White House when they analyzed the Cuban project. The political-military philosophy of the invasion, moreover, was quite compatible with the new emphasis placed by the administration upon guerrilla-like warfare. The more fundamental problems were revealed by a State Department White Paper, written by White House aide and Harvard historian Arthur Schlesinger, Jr., which attempted to rationalize the invasion just days before the tragedy occurred. The paper condemned the Castro movement as communist and attempted to place the United States on the side of social and economic reform within the hemisphere. It was, however, an unfortunate example of how history was misconstrued to serve political ends. From the first, when the paper claimed that "the hemisphere rejoiced at the overthrow of the Batista tyranny" (a fact not overly obvious in Washington in January 1959), until the conclusion that the "inter-American system was incompatible with any form of totalitarianism" (which failed to show how Trujillo, Duvalier, Somoza, and even Batista, among others, had prospered within that system), the State Department paper was more propaganda than a sober recital of facts.[26] But the paper revealed the dilemma of American policy toward Latin America. The Bay of Pigs was a public confession by the United States that it had failed to understand or deal with the most significant political change in the hemisphere in fifty years. This conclusion would have been tenable whether the invasion had succeeded or failed.

The President publicly accepted complete responsibility for the Bay of Pigs, and it was in the weeks immediately following this debacle that he traveled to Europe to visit West European leaders and Premier Nikita Khrushchev. The meeting in Vienna on June 3 and 4 with the Soviet leader resulted in an agreement to stop the growing conflict in Laos, but otherwise only increased Kennedy's apprehension that the Soviets were determined to create dangerous tensions by supporting what Khrushchev called "wars of liberation," that is, support of nationalist and procommunist elements in the newly emerging countries which were fighting Western political and economic influence. Worst of all, Khrushchev was militant about the necessity of eliminating Western power in West Berlin. The six-month notice was reimposed by the Soviet ruler,

[26]Smith, *What Happened in Cuba?* p. 211.

who became deeply angry at Kennedy's repeated warnings not to miscalculate American intentions. "I will tell you now," the President reported to the American people upon his return, "that it was a very sober two days."

Worried about the effects of the Bay of Pigs upon American credibility and disturbed at public reports that Khrushchev had browbeaten him at Vienna, Kennedy accepted Dean Acheson's argument that the Berlin issue was a "simple conflict of wills" and that no negotiations could be considered until the Soviets lifted their threat of turning over the access routes to East Germany. This argument refused to touch the Soviet premier's real problems: the growing military power of West Germany, its strengthened ties with the West, its attractiveness to technicians and other experts living in East Germany, the very weak position of the East German communist regime, the position of West Berlin as an espionage and propaganda center within the communist bloc, the growing fear of the Soviet peoples over West Germany's power, and, finally, Khrushchev's realization that with his ICBM braggadocio punctured as only myth, he needed a major strategic victory. Kennedy's reaction came in a national broadcast on July 25, 1961. He asked that National Reserve troops be placed on active duty and announced a dramatic increase of nearly 25 percent in American military strength. His premise was simple. The Berlin "outpost is not an isolated problem. The threat is worldwide," endangering Southeast Asia, "our own hemisphere," and "wherever else the freedom of human beings is at stake," as well as Berlin. That city and Saigon were, in this crucial sense, alike. Kennedy, like Eisenhower, defined the communist threat in global terms.[27]

On August 13 the Soviets suddenly built the Berlin Wall. The flow of young and skilled labor from East Germany to the West stopped, and Khrushchev partly sealed the bloc from Western influences. The United States protested, but the wall stood, a final obstacle to hundreds of East Germans who were shot trying to escape to the West. It was mute and bloody testimony to the policy of both East and West which, since 1945, had preferred a divided rather than a neutralized and united Germany.

The wall had solved one of his problems, at least temporarily, but Khrushchev's supposed strategic power continued to come

[27] *Public Papers of the Presidents, Kennedy, 1961*, pp. 533–540.

under attack in the West. In mid-1961 the Defense Department revealed that only a "handful" of Russian ICBMs were operational. Administration officials wondered aloud about Soviet credibility in the military realm. This no doubt made Khrushchev's political situation in Moscow uneasy, a situation already under attack because of the Sino-Soviet split. The division within the communist world had become irreparable by late 1960. Two weeks after the Berlin Wall appeared, Khrushchev broke the three-year Russian-American moratorium on the testing of nuclear bombs by beginning a series of tests which climaxed with the explosion in November of a 58-megaton weapon, 3000 times more powerful than the bomb that had obliterated Hiroshima.

Kennedy responded with underground testing in September 1961, but he remained fully confident that the United States held a wide lead in nuclear weapons capability. The President did attempt to reconvene the Geneva Disarmament Conference, which had been meeting intermittently since 1958. France refused to attend; having exploded his first nuclear device in September 1960, de Gaulle did not want to be bound by any restraints at this early stage of his career as a nuclear power. The Soviets again refused Western demands for inspection and international control. On April 25, 1962, Kennedy ordered the first of some thirty American tests that occurred during the following year.

The President viewed his first eleven months in office as a period of continual international crisis, and it was in this context that he made two of his most fateful decisions. The first involved Laos. That former French colony was a key to Southeast Asia, for it rimmed China, both Vietnams, Cambodia, Thailand, and Burma. In 1958, a gimcrack agreement between center, right, and communist forces collapsed when the center and right attempted to reconstitute the government and cut communist influence. When Pathet Lao communist forces began major guerrilla action, the United States stepped up aid until, by April 1961, over 300 American military advisors were in Laos, and the country received $32 million in economic assistance, three times the annual rate of 1955–1959. An army coup and expanding communist control in eastern Laos worsened the situation until the Eisenhower administration supported a right-wing coup in December 1960. Receiving large amounts of aid from Russia, the Pathet Lao responded by launching a major offensive which, by the Vienna meetings in June, had conquered the eastern half of Laos.

As China began building roads to the Laotian border for its own military power, the Soviets and Americans decided that the war must stop. With the support of Kennedy and Khrushchev, Great Britain and Russia reconvened the Geneva conference members of 1954. The sessions agreed on neutralizing Laos, but the United States–supported government of Boun Oum refused to surrender any of its power. The Pathet Lao revived their attacks. Kennedy responded by channeling in American supplies, mobilizing United States troops in Thailand after signing a sudden military aid treaty with that country, and, most important, causing Boun Oum's downfall simply by stopping American economic aid. This opened the way for a coalition government to be formed under neutralist Souvanna Phouma in June 1962. Nineteen nations, including China, promised to respect Laotian territorial integrity and sovereignty, and the SEATO powers explicitly excluded Laos from their area of control. It was a tenuous agreement, but a Soviet-American decision to enforce neutralization of a key area had moved Laos outside the torrid zones of the Cold War. "Thank God the Bay of Pigs happened when it did," Kennedy remarked privately. "Otherwise we'd be in Laos by now — and that would be a hundred times worse."[28]

The implications of that remark were not quite accurate, for meanwhile the President was making a pivotal commitment of American power to South Vietnam. The regime of Ngo Dinh Diem had become very unpopular by 1958, for it had stopped agrarian reforms begun by Ho in the countryside, canceled elections, arrested political opponents, and concentrated power in the hands of Diem, his brother, and his brother's wife, Madam Ngo Dinh Nhu. Anti-Diem guerrilla attacks stepped up in 1958. Two years later Ho's government in Hanoi acknowledged and encouraged the southern procommunists by establishing the National Liberation Front (NLF). The American-trained South Vietnamese Army could not handle the guerrillas, but it also disliked Diem and tried unsuccessfully in November 1960 to overthrow the president. The Viet Cong guerrillas meanwhile grew in number to nearly 10,000 in

[28]Sorensen, *Kennedy,* p. 644.

1961, receiving support from the peasants and, for the first time, from Communist China.

With this civil war intensifying, President Kennedy sent Vice President Johnson on a fact-finding mission in May 1961 and followed this with a mission in October headed by General Maxwell Taylor and State Department official Walt Whitman Rostow, a fervent disciple of thwarting communism with guerrilla warfare. The Taylor-Rostow team recommended increasing the number of American military advisors and pledging complete support to Diem. Kennedy faced a momentous decision. Restraining him was the inability and unwillingness of the SEATO nations as a whole to make any major commitment, his knowledge that the Vietnamese situation was extremely complex and could not be divided into simple communist versus anticommunist groups, and his own doubts that the "domino theory" had any validity. He apparently believed that whenever Red China exploded a nuclear bomb, its influence would be dominant in Asia, regardless of what the United States did in Vietnam.[29] Military members of the "Never-Again Club" and some State Department officials, particularly those who gave first priority to European affairs, also warned against any large commitment.

Opposing these views were some of the President's highest advisors, including Vice President Johnson, who, during his trip to Vietnam, had called Diem the "Winston Churchill of Asia" (which Diem unfortunately believed). Johnson warned the President that the United States must make a "fundamental decision . . . whether we are to attempt to meet the challenge of Communist expansion now in Southeast Asia . . . or throw in the towel."[30] Others argued that this was the opportunity to contain China and that Vietnam's long coastline and apparently stable government provided optimum conditions. Most important, however, the President began to see Vietnam as part of the global communist menace. If the Viet Cong were not stopped, the whole world balance might be upset.[31] Kennedy soon found himself no longer questioning the Eisenhower-Dulles policies he had inherited, including the "domino theory," but adopting them. Kennedy also had more motivation, since abroad

[29] Arthur Krock, in *The New York Times*, February 14, 1965, p. E9.

[30] Philip Geyelin, *Lyndon B. Johnson and the World* (New York, 1966), pp. 34–40.

[31] Arthur M. Schlesinger, Jr., *A Thousand Days: John F. Kennedy in the White House* (Boston, 1965), p. 548.

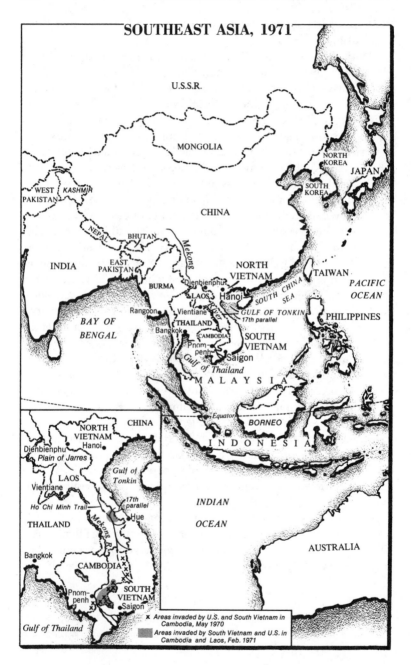

SOUTHEAST ASIA, 1971

x   Areas invaded by U.S. and South Vietnam in Cambodia, May 1970

    Areas invaded by South Vietnam and U.S. in Cambodia and Laos, Feb. 1971 (and also at home), he was determined to blot out the image given his administration by the Bay of Pigs, the Vienna meetings, and the Berlin Wall. For an administration which prided itself on its "realism," its political pragmatism, and its determination to save the newly emerging nations, which were "the great battleground . . . of freedom," these arguments were irrefutable. The force was already present. The United States Pacific Command was a great military power with its 300,000 men, the largest mobile force on the globe (the Seventh Fleet), and logistics problems solved by bases in Okinawa, the Philippines, and Japan.

Within fifteen months following the Taylor-Rostow report, Kennedy expanded the American commitment from 500 to 10,000 men, allowed these "advisors" to engage in combat, ordered United States Air Force units to strike Viet Cong strongholds in South Vietnam, and promised full support to Diem. The Vietnamese president interpreted this promise to mean that he could intensify his authoritarian methods without worrying about any questions, or a possible pullout, from the American side.[32] The American-Diem forces attempted to secure the countryside with a strategic hamlet program which uprooted and then concentrated peasants in fortified villages.

These decisions were signal and symbolic, for they, like many other policies adopted in 1961 to mid-1962, indicated that the Kennedy administration could not lessen but only intensify Cold War tensions. These policies differed in no important essential from the Eisenhower policies after 1954. The new administration was only much less restrained in carrying them out. When a reporter remarked in the autumn of 1961 that he wanted to write a book about the President's first year in office, Kennedy inquired, "Who would want to read a book about disasters?"[33]

[32]David Halberstam, *The Making of a Quagmire* (New York, 1965), pp. 67–69.
[33]Told by Elie Abel, quoted by I. F. Stone in *The New York Review of Books*, April 14, 1966, p. 12.

10

Southeast Asia–and
Elsewhere (1962-1966)

What could have been the greatest of disasters nearly occurred one
year later. The Cuban missile crisis, as President Kennedy remarked
to Premier Khrushchev, at one moment approached the point
"where events could have become unmanageable." This confrontation rechanneled the policies of the United States and the Soviet
Union, affecting many facets of world affairs.

The roots of the crisis ran back to Khrushchev's ICBM-oriented
foreign policies after 1957 and his intense concern with removing
NATO power from West Berlin. By 1962 these policies were related,
for the Soviets needed credible strategic force if they hoped to neutralize Western power in Germany. By the spring of 1962, however,
high American officials had publicly expressed their skepticism of
Soviet missile credibility. President Kennedy further observed in a
widely publicized interview that under some circumstances the
United States would strike first. In June, Defense Secretary
McNamara indicated that American missiles were so potent and
precise that in a nuclear war they could spare cities and hit only
military installations.[1]

[1]Stewart Alsop, "Kennedy's Grand Strategy," *Saturday Evening Post*, March 31,
1962, p. 14; Richard P. Stebbins, ed., *Documents on American Foreign Relations,
1962* (New York, 1963), pp. 232–233.

Khrushchev and Marshal Rodion Malinovsky angrily responded that, contrary to McNamara's beliefs, cities would be the first victims in any nuclear war. The Soviet premier warned Kennedy against engaging "in sinister competition as to who will be the first to start a war." For the first time in five years, however, Khrushchev emphasized Soviet bomber strength instead of missiles. As for West Berlin, the building of the wall and Kennedy's quick military build-up in 1961 had quieted Khrushchev's demands.

In the summer of 1962, Khrushchev moved to regain the initiative in the strategic realm. In late August an American U-2 reconnaissance plane flying fourteen miles above Cuba reported the first Soviet surface-to-air missile site (see map, p. 210). Forty-two Russian medium bombers were next observed on Castro's airstrips. On October 14 high administration officials expressed their disbelief that the Soviets and Cubans would try to install offensive, ground-to-ground missiles, particularly after President Kennedy had expressly warned against any such attempt in mid-September. This disbelief was also based on Khrushchev's repeated assurances that he would not jiggle East-West relations during the American congressional election campaign. On that same day, October 14, however, the first photographs appeared of a launch pad under construction that could fire ballistic missiles with a range of 1000 miles. Several days later a 2000-mile missile site was observed under construction.

The President was in a delicate political situation. Some Republicans for weeks had warned of threatening Soviet moves in Cuba. These warnings, plus the frustrations which Castro was causing so many Americans, created in the early autumn what one acute observer called "a war party" which demanded military action against Cuba.[2] The elections were less than three weeks away. In this pressure tank, a special committee of top administration officials began virtual round-the-clock meetings to consider the response to the Soviets. The alternatives narrowed down to a blockade or an air strike against the missile sites. Dean Acheson, supported by General Maxwell Taylor and the Joint Chiefs of Staff, argued vigorously for the air strike, even though such an attack would probably kill Soviet technicians working on the sites. Other officials changed their minds several times in the course of five days,

[2]Richard H. Rovere, "Letter From Washington," *New Yorker*, October 6, 1962, pp. 148–157.

but Under Secretary of State George Ball slowly won support for a blockade. McNamara supported Ball with the argument that, if the blockade failed, the air strike option could still be used. Attorney General Robert Kennedy, pointedly alluding to the Japanese attack on Pearl Harbor, endorsed Ball's position with the words, "My brother is not going to be the Tojo of the 1960's." Acheson so strongly opposed the final decision that he resigned from the committee.[3]

At 7 P.M. on October 22, the President broke the well-kept secret to the American people. Because the Soviets were building bases in Cuba "to provide a nuclear strike capability against the Western Hemisphere," Kennedy announced, the United States was imposing "a strict quarantine on all offensive military equipment" being shipped into Cuba. American military forces, he added, were on full alert, and the United States would "regard any nuclear missile launched from Cuba against any nation in the Western Hemisphere as an attack by the Soviet Union on the United States, requiring a full retaliatory response upon the Soviet Union." He appealed to Khrushchev to remove the offensive weapons under United Nations supervision.

The premier replied four days later in a long, rambling letter that apparently offered removal of the missiles in return for an American pledge not to invade Cuba. A second letter the next day raised the price to the dismantling of the American Jupiter missiles in Turkey. The special committee, worn down by ten days of the most intense pressures ("I saw first-hand," Theodore Sorensen later remarked, "how brutally physical and mental fatigue can numb the good sense as well as the senses of normally articulate men"[4]), now made the crucial decision to bypass the second letter and accept the first. On Sunday morning, October 28, as American military officials prepared an air strike on the missile sites for Tuesday morning, Khrushchev endorsed the American offer.[5] Sixteen Soviet ships sailing toward Cuba turned around in midocean to return to Russian ports. The crisis was over.

The effects, however, will ripple on at least through the lifetime of the generation that lived through those October days. In a speech of February 27, 1963, Khrushchev explained that in removing the missiles he had saved the world from a possible nuclear disaster.

[3]Elie Abel, *The Missile Crisis* (Philadelphia, 1966), pp. 63–64, 70, 81, 88, 118–119.
[4]Theodore Sorensen, *Decision-Making in the White House* (New York, 1963), p. 76.
[5]*Documents on American Foreign Relations, 1962*, pp. 392–404.

This step back from the brink set the tone for a Soviet policy line which was epitomized in a June 1964 press announcement that "in order to guarantee the final preponderance of the forces of socialism over the forces of capitalism, to win victory in peaceful competition, peace is essential." Even Soviet military support of "wars of liberation" became considerably more conditional.[6] In the summer of 1963 the United States and Russia negotiated and signed their first agreement to limit the arms race by prohibiting aboveground nuclear testing. These policies intensely angered the Chinese, widening the Sino-Russian split to the point of a complete break. The Chinese called Khrushchev foolish for putting the missiles into Cuba and cowardly for removing them. They feared the growing Russian-American cooperation and deprecated the less militant Soviet policy.

This crisis did not enhance Khrushchev's personal power within the Soviet bloc. His decline, combined with the Sino-Soviet breach and the warmer East-West relations, opened new opportunities for the satellites in Eastern Europe to regain more autonomy. Some competent observers believed that the fear of Germany, as much as Russian control, kept the Warsaw Pact nations together. Certainly no generalization could fit the spectrum of intellectual freedom which stretched from Poland's liberalism to Albania's Stalinism, the agricultural collectivization which was almost total in Russia but declining in Poland and Yugoslavia, the use of terror which was manifest in Czechoslovakia but little evidenced in Poland, or the ideological framework which was rigidly dogmatic in Albania but quite loose in Yugoslavia and Poland.[7] By 1963 anyone who talked about a monolithic communist threat was discussing a world that no longer existed.

In contrast to Khrushchev's decline, President Kennedy emerged from the missile crisis with new support and political charisma. His own concepton of this power was exemplified at American University in Washington, D.C., on June 10, 1963. There Kennedy spoke of peace "as the necessary rational end of rational men" and dramatically appealed to the Soviets to seek a relaxation of tensions. This speech sped the negotiations of the nuclear test ban treaty, a pact which Kennedy then drove through the Senate over the strong op-

---

[6]Raymond L. Garthoff, *Soviet Military Policy* (New York, 1966), pp. 200–201, 213.

[7]H. Gordon Skilling, "National Communism in Eastern Europe Since the 22nd Congress," *Canadian Journal of Economics and Political Science*, XXX (August 1964): 313–327.

position of American military officials and a few scientists led by Edward Teller of the University of California.[8]

The new warmth toward Russia did not improve the NATO alliance. De Gaulle and Adenauer had been angered when Kennedy offered to negotiate bilaterally with the Soviets over Berlin in August 1961, and when the United States twice rejected (in August 1961 and January 1962) de Gaulle's pleas for establishing a joint directorate for military strategy. These rejections reaffirmed the French determination to build an independent nuclear power. De Gaulle viewed the British application for admission to the Common Market in 1961–1962 as the stalking horse of American economic and political power. The French pondered Kennedy's July 4, 1962, speech, which urged Europe to join in a "declaration of interdependence," but which pointedly omitted any mention of possible nuclear sharing. This speech, together with American trade legislation that allowed large reciprocal cuts in tariffs, indicated that the United States sought increased economic leverage in Europe. De Gaulle's mistrust intensified during the missile crisis, when Acheson flew to Paris to "inform," not "consult" (the words were de Gaulle's) the French on the confrontation. The French president fully supported Kennedy, but the episode convinced Paris officials that the United States would involve them in a nuclear war without consulting them beforehand.

De Gaulle's views were confirmed at the conference between Kennedy and British Prime Minister Harold Macmillan at Nassau in December. The United States unilaterally cancelled its development of the Skybolt missile on which the British had hoped to base their nuclear striking force. Instead, Kennedy offered nuclear submarine and warhead information to Macmillan. The President pointedly did not make a similar offer to France. In January de Gaulle dramatically announced that he would veto the British entry into the Common Market. He explained that Great Britain had nitpicked for sixteen months of negotiations in an effort to bend the Common Market to British interests but had surrendered control of its own defense to the United States in a mere forty-eight hours at Nassau. De Gaulle, however, had made this decision for a more fundamental reason. He feared that if Great Britain entered the European Economic Community, "the end would be a colossal Atlantic Com-

[8]U.S. Senate, Committee on Foreign Relations, 88th Cong. 1st Sess., *Nuclear Test Ban Treaty* (Washington, 1963), pp. 422–423, 427.

munity dependent on America and directed by America, which would not take long to absorb this European Community." Shortly afterward, a Franco-German friendship treaty was signed, which de Gaulle hoped would be the axis for an independent European diplomacy.

De Gaulle correctly believed that in the wake of the missile crisis East-West tensions would ease; in the long run, a united Europe led by France would be able to influence international diplomacy if that Europe was free of both Russian and American control and if France had its own nuclear power. He also feared unchecked American military and economic power, believing that, because the United States would use the power unilaterally and irresponsibly, the French could suffer annihilation without representation.

The missile crisis did not advance Kennedy's "Grand Design" for Europe, but it tragically accelerated the American rush into Vietnam. Key Washington policy makers assumed that the one result of the October confrontation was a nuclear standoff between the two superpowers. Both had clearly indicated their reluctance to use nuclear force. The United States had won primarily because Khrushchev unwisely challenged Kennedy in the Caribbean, where American conventional naval power was decisive. Within months, both sides were discussing the easing of Cold War tensions. If the assumption was correct that the two great powers mutually feared each other's nuclear arms, then, the Kennedy administration concluded, the leaders of the emerging nations might feel that they had considerable opportunity to play West versus East, or, as in Southeast Asia and Africa, to undertake revolutionary changes without fear that either the United States or Russia would be able to shape these changes. If nationalist leaders acted on these beliefs, the newly emerging world could become increasingly unmanageable, perhaps dangerously radical from Washington's point of view.[9] Such a view meshed perfectly with the other American fear that the communist policy line of support for (but not direct involvement in) "wars of liberation" had been established in 1960–1961 precisely to exploit the emerging nationalisms. The New Frontiersmen dedicated them-

[9]The best analysis is Walt Whitman Rostow, "Domestic Determinants of U.S. Foreign Policy; The Tocqueville Oscillation," *Armed Forces Journal,* June 27, 1970, 16D–16E; see also Rostow's *From the Seventh Floor* (New York, 1964).

selves to shattering "wars of liberation" within such nationalist movements. Vietnam would be used as the example.

The President also focused on Southeast Asia because he hoped to discipline what he believed to be the expansiveness of Communist China. In 1949–1950 Kennedy, then a member of the House of Representatives, had joined Republicans in denouncing the Truman administration for supposedly "losing" China. He softened these views during the 1950s, but in preparing to run for the presidency in 1960 he was reluctant to consider disavowing the use of nuclear weapons: "I wonder if we could expect to check the sweep south of the Chinese with their endless armies with conventional forces?"[10] After the missile crisis, Kennedy summarized his position in a conversation with André Malraux, French cultural affairs minister. Assistant Secretary of State for European Affairs William R. Tyler has described this talk:

> [Kennedy] wanted to get a message to de Gaulle through Malraux . . . that really there was no reason why there should be differences between us and France in Europe, or between us and our European Allies, because there was no longer a likely Soviet military threat against Europe [since the Cuban missile crisis]. . . . But the area where we would have problems in the future . . . was China. He said it was so important that he and de Gaulle and other European leaders should think together about what they will do, what the situation will be when China becomes a nuclear power, what will happen then. . . . This was the great menace in the future to humanity, the free world, and freedom on earth. Relations with the Soviet Union could be contained within the framework of mutual awareness of the impossibility of achieving any gains through war. But in the case of China, this restraint would not be effective because the Chinese would be perfectly prepared, because of the lower value they attach to human life, to sacrifice hundreds of millions of their own lives, if this were necessary in order to carry out their militant and aggressive policies.[11]

The missile crisis and the Berlin confrontation in 1961 also reinforced the administration's belief that it knew how to threaten to

[10]Kennedy to George Kennan, January 21, 1960, Oral History Interview with Mr. Kennan, March 23, 1964, Kennedy Library. Used by permission.

[11]Oral History Interview with William R. Tyler, March 7, 1964, Kennedy Library; and Mr. Tyler to author, December 10, 1971.

apply or, if necessary, actually apply conventional military power to obtain maximum results. White House officials joked that poor John Foster Dulles had never been able to find a suitable war for his "massive retaliation"; these pragmatic Kennedyites, however, had apparently solved the great riddle by perfectly matching power to crisis. One false premise ultimately wrecked this self-satisfaction: in Berlin and Cuba the Russians had backed down (Castro, noticeably, had been willing to fight to keep the missiles); in Vietnam the United States dealt with nationalist Vietnamese who, like Castro, had much to win by continuing to fight against apparently overwhelming American firepower.[12]

This fatal flaw did not clearly appear in 1962–1966. On the contrary, during the autumn of 1962 the President's policies seemed to be proved correct during the brief war between India and China. India provoked the war during a border dispute over territory more important to the Chinese than to the Indians. The Chinese attacked with devastating force, destroying both the myth of Indian power and the American hope that India could serve as a cornerstone in the containment of China. The Chinese carefully occupied only some of the disputed territory, voluntarily withdrawing from other conquered areas. On November 20 Prime Minister Nehru urgently asked Kennedy for aid. An American aircraft carrier moved across the southern Pacific toward India, but before it could become a factor the crisis ended.[13] Some Washington policy makers nevertheless drew the false conclusion that the Chinese had backed down only after receiving warnings from the United States and, independently of the American move, from Russia.

Kennedy's advisors displayed similarly unwarranted confidence in their ability to control power in late 1962 when they decided to turn Laos into a pro-American bastion. They thereby helped destroy the Geneva Agreements which the United States had solemnly signed in midsummer 1962. Under the agreements, all foreign troops were to withdraw from Laos. The communist Pathet Lao were to join neutralist Souvanna Phouma's coalition government. American military advisors, indeed, began to leave, but the Central

---

[12]David Halberstam, "The Programming of Robert McNamara," *Harper's*, February 1971, p. 68.

[13]Allen Whiting's review of Neville Maxwell's *India's China War* in *Washington Post*, May 25, 1971, p. B6.

Intelligence Agency stepped up the supplying of the Meo tribes-men, an effective guerrilla army operating behind Pathet Lao lines.

In April 1964, however, a right-wing coup in Vientiane made Souvanna only a figurehead leader. The Pathet Lao retaliated with an offensive that threatened to conquer the entire Plain of Jarres. The United States then began initially small but systematic bomb-ing raids on Laos, which Washington carefully tried to keep secret. To save a supposedly pivotal domino, the Kennedy-Johnson advis-ors confidently escalated their application of power.[14] The actual result, however, was that at the very time the United States esca-lated its commitment to South Vietnam, the key area of Laos became uncontrollable and formed an open channel for aid to the National Liberation Front in South Vietnam.

In 1962–1963 the assumptions that would govern American pol-icies in Vietnam fell into place. First, Vietnam was vital to Ameri-can interests because, in John F. Kennedy's words of 1956, "Vietnam represents the cornerstone of the Free World in Southeast Asia, the keystone to the arch, the finger in the dike. . . . Her economy is es-sential to the economy of all of Southeast Asia; and her political liberty is an inspiration to those seeking to obtain or maintain their liberty in all parts of Asia — and indeed the world."[15] As Kennedy em-phasized in his May 25, 1961, address to Congress, the battle of "free-dom versus tyranny" was being waged in newly emerging areas such as Vietnam. While belittling the foreign policies of the previous ad-ministration, the Kennedy advisors gulped down whole the Eisen-hower "domino" theory. More precisely, the Dulles and Eisenhower formulation of the 1950s remained valid because, without an open Southeast Asia for its raw materials and markets, Japan, essential to the entire American strategic policy in the western Pacific, would have to turn toward its traditional market of China.

Second, the Kennedy administration assumed that China not only was to be isolated but, as some thought it had been in India, militarily disciplined. Both the Chinese and the Russians were to be taught that "wars of liberation" were not possible in areas the United States considered vital to its own interests. Third, the missile

[14]D. Gareth Porter, "After Geneva: Subverting Laotian Neutrality." In Nina S. Adams and Alfred W. McCoy, eds., *Laos: War and Revolution* (New York, 1970), pp. 179–212.

[15]Quoted in Chester Cooper, *Lost Crusade* (New York, 1970), p. 168.

crisis, the India-China conflict, and the emerging Laotian situation gave the administration confidence in its ability to escalate military power while keeping it under control. Because of McNamara's work, moreover, the military power was available. For the first time in their history, Americans entered war with a great army at the ready, a force created by self-styled "realists" who, in the tradition of Forrestal and Acheson, believed that they could ultimately shape world affairs with American firepower.

These assumptions — the validity of the domino theory (particularly its economic implications for Japan), the century-old American fear of a "Yellow Peril," and the belief held by American liberal spokesmen that, as children of Niebuhr, they knew the secrets of using military force effectively — these governed the Kennedy administration as it moved deeper into Vietnam.

In 1962 Secretary of Defense McNamara had observed, "Every quantitative measurement we have shows we're winning this war."[16] Some factors in Southeast Asia, however, could not be computed. Twelve thousand American military personnel were involved in the conflict, yet the Viet Cong continued to gain ground. The strategic hamlet program, geared to secure the countryside, was failing despite, or perhaps because of, the determination of the Diem regime. The peasants disliked being forced to leave their homes and to be resettled elsewhere, particularly by a government that had condemned any meaningful land reform program. "No wonder the Viet Cong looked like Robin Hoods when they began to hit the hamlets," one civilian American official remarked.[17] Viet Cong successes mounted despite their kidnapping and brutal murdering of village and hamlet officials.

Kennedy's hope of reversing the situation rested on the ability of Diem's government to wage a successful military campaign while stabilizing South Vietnam's political situation. Saigon's military capability was dramatically called into question on January 2, 1963, in the village of Ap Bac, approximately fifty miles from Saigon. A small Viet Cong force was surrounded by a Vietnamese unit that was ten times larger, but despite the demands of American advisors to attack, the South Vietnamese refused. The Viet Cong then methodically shot down five American helicopters, damaged nine more,

[16]Arthur M. Schlesinger, Jr., *A Thousand Days* (Boston, 1965), p. 549.
[17]David Halberstam, *The Making of a Quagmire* (New York, 1964), pp. 186–187.

killed three Americans, and disappeared. Apparently only United States soldiers had the will to fight in Vietnam, but Kennedy carefully pointed out after one fire fight between Viet Cong and American personnel that the United States forces in Vietnam were not "combat troops," and that if the situation changed, "I, of course, would go to Congress."[18] He was not prepared to do this in 1963. Nor was the White House even prepared to inform adequately the Congress and the public.

With an American presidential election little more than a year away, and his own belief that in 1964 his main challenge would come from the right wing of American politics, Kennedy carefully threw the best possible, even if misleading, light on Vietnamese affairs. American newspaper correspondents who candidly reported Diem's failures were rewarded either with Kennedy's unsuccessful attempt to give one critical correspondent a "vacation" from Vietnam, or with rejoinders to their questions like the one given by Admiral Harry Felt, commander of American forces in the Pacific: "Why don't you get on the team?"[19] In 1963 there was a widening abyss between the actual situation in Vietnam and the self-assurance of the Kennedy administration that it could manipulate military power to control nationalist revolutions.[20]

By late summer 1963 the abyss was so wide that it could no longer be covered. Throughout the early part of the year, Diem, with the assistance of his brother Nhu Dinh Diem and Madame Nhu, ruthlessly suppressed domestic opposition. When Washington protested the Nhus' activities, Diem and his brother openly objected to this pressure. The beginning of the end for Diem and Nhu occurred on May 8, when Diem's troops shot into a crowd of Buddhists who were celebrating Buddha's birthday by waving religious flags, thereby violating the regime's rule that forbade the exhibit of any banner but the government's. The firing climaxed years of bitterness between the Roman Catholic regime of Diem and the Buddhists, who comprised more than 80 percent of the country's population. Many Buddhist leaders wanted no part of the war, no part of any foreign intervention in their nation, and no part of the Diem

---

[18]Cooper, *Lost Crusade*, pp. 193–194; also in U.S. Government, *Public Papers of the Presidents . . . Kennedy, 1962* (Washington, 1963), p. 228.

[19]Halberstam, *Making of a Quagmire*, p. 72.

[20]James Aronson, *The Press and the Cold War* (New York, 1970), pp. 182–183.

regime. They represented a new, potentially radical nationalism that neither the Diem regime nor the American officials in Vietnam could understand, let alone cope with. In June Buddhist-led anti-government riots spread through Saigon. Diem retaliated by raiding Buddhist pagodas. Several Buddhists burned themselves to death in public protest, an act that Madame Nhu sarcastically welcomed as a "barbecue show." Students in normally quiet schools and universities joined the Buddhists. Diem confronted a full-scale rebellion.

The Kennedy administration's confusion in dealing with the revolutionary situation became glaringly evident during the crisis.[21] While continuing to announce that the military program was going well, the White House attempted to push Diem into making necessary domestic reforms by cutting off relatively small amounts of military and economic aid. That move, however, was sufficient to encourage anti-Diem elements in the army. On November 1 and 2, with, at least, the knowledge and approval of the White House and the American ambassador in Saigon, Henry Cabot Lodge, a military junta captured Diem and his brother.[22] Within hours the two men were shot and the junta assumed power. Three weeks later President Kennedy was assassinated in Dallas, Texas.

President Lyndon B. Johnson inherited a set of badly decomposed foreign policies. In the last weeks of his life Kennedy had said that the war was for the Vietnamese to win or lose. But the American consent given for Diem's overthrow, and the administration's full commitment to fighting what were intended to be limited wars with the conventional forces that Kennedy had so painstakingly developed, indicated that the United States would, if necessary, become further involved in Southeast Asia. Certainly Kennedy would have

[21] *The Pentagon Papers*, as published by *The New York Times* (New York, 1971), pp. 163-177, 191-196. *The Pentagon Papers* is a condensed version of a massive study of Defense Department documents on the involvement in Vietnam. Commissioned by Secretary McNamara as a secret analysis, the larger study was written and compiled by three dozen experts and finally covered 3000 pages of analyses and 4000 pages of supporting documents. The shorter *Pentagon Papers* is crucial and revealing, but it should be used carefully because it contains little from either State Department or presidential files. See especially, George Kahin, "*The Pentagon Papers:* A Critical Evaluation," *American Political Science Review*, LXIX (June 1975): 675-684.

[22] *The Pentegon Papers*, pp. 158-159, 215-232, especially Lodge to Bundy, October 30, 1963, No. 57, pp. 226-229.

done nothing to change radically the American involvement until after the 1964 elections. By then he might have been unable to throw four years of policy suddenly into reverse. In Europe the administration's "Grand Design" was coming apart piece by piece, allowing de Gaulle to assume the leadership in the Western European community. The Alliance for Progress was crumbling, the victim of the false assumption that enough money and bureaucratic technicians could tinker with and adjust the dynamic nationalisms of an economically unbalanced Latin America to the policy objectives of a prosperous, satisfied, and expanding United States.

As these policies encountered the inevitable obstacles, bitter infighting appeared among Washington officials. The White House staff blamed the State Department for not having sufficient imagination and initiative to solve important diplomatic problems. Two talented biographers of Kennedy who were on the White House staff, Theodore Sorensen and Arthur Schlesinger, Jr., wrote their histories from this point of view. Their interpretation was questionable, for it glossed over several points. Nothing on the record indicated that the White House and State Department ever argued much over whether the United States should become more involved in the newly emerging nations; the argument was usually over how. If the State Department could not always discover the appropriate tactics, the fault lay perhaps in contradictions in the policy, not State Department incompetency.

There was no indication, moreover, that President Kennedy and Secretary of State Dean Rusk differed on fundamental points of policy. This is important, for Kennedy must have appointed and kept this key official in the full knowledge that Rusk, having served under Dean Acheson and Robert Lovett, accepted the military-oriented policies that those two officials had followed. Rusk had also been assistant secretary of state for Far Eastern affairs during the Korean conflict. It did not require Kennedy's acute perception to conclude that Rusk, like the President himself, might have an uncommon commitment to building positions of military strength around the periphery of China. The Kennedy administration bequeathed to Lyndon Johnson deteriorating foreign policies along with the test ban and, much to Johnson's discomfort, the overpowering image and somber rhetoric of the fallen President.

The new Chief Executive's first important diplomatic pronouncement explained that he would continue his predecessor's Vietnam policies.[23] The ensuing policy, as well as the style with which it would be carried out, could be understood in terms of the President's own history and resulting world view.

Lyndon Johnson's administration marked the point at which the historical legacies of Woodrow Wilson, Franklin D. Roosevelt, and the American frontier merged in the 1960s. Wilson believed that the American mission was to extend individual liberties throughout the world, but not out of altruism; it grew out of the belief that American liberties could not long exist at home unless the world was made safe for democracy. The basis of liberty at home was found in the economic system, for, as Wilson once observed, without "freedom of enterprise there can be no freedom whatsoever." Lyndon Johnson's own version was that "the very basis of a great nation is an educated mind, a healthy body, and a free enterprise system." With this established, the President could repeat time after time during the 1964 campaign that "Our cause has been the cause of all mankind." Whether the American system could work as well in the boiler houses of newly emerging nations as it had during its 300-year growth, and several mutations, in the United States, was not discussed by the President. He simply moved to the conclusion: "Woodrow Wilson once said: 'I hope we shall never forget that we created this nation, not to serve ourselves, but to serve mankind.'"[24]

Emerging as a national political figure during the 1930s, and further developing the New Deal's domestic programs in the 1950s as the most powerful Senate leader in history, Johnson understood that even a well-functioning free enterprise system needed frequent governmental injections to provide balance and some economic justice. The New Deal, for example, had developed a poverty-stricken region of the United States through the Tennessee Valley Authority's electrical-power system in the 1930s. "The over-riding rule which I want to affirm," the President remarked in Denver in 1966, "is that our foreign policy must always be an extension of our domestic policy. Our safest guide to what we do abroad is always what we do at home." This concern was easily translated to Vietnam: "I want to leave the footprints of America there. I want them to say, 'This is what the Americans left — schools and hospitals and

[23] *The Pentagon Papers*, pp. 232–233.

[24] The Johnson quotes are cited from *The New York Times*, June 28, 1967, p. 24; and *Public Papers of the Presidents, 1964*, pp. 1242, 1103.

dams. . . .' We can turn the Mekong [River area] into a Tennessee Valley."[25] The role of the government, therefore, both in the United States and Vietnam, was first to clear away the obstacles (the unenlightened American businessman in the 1930s, the Vietnamese communist in the 1960s), build the infrastructure (the Tennessee Valley and the Great Society at home, the Mekong Valley projects in Vietnam), and then let free enterprise develop the resources, and therefore the freedoms, of the areas.

Johnson had an equally simple view of how this was to be accomplished, a view formed when he grew up in the frontierlike region of central Texas. His incredible ambition and energy exploited the opportunities of Texas and Washington, D.C., until he was privately wealthy and politically supreme. He had risen by making sharp distinctions between friends and enemies. "We are not a formal people," he observed in 1965. "We are not a people so much concerned with the way things are done as by the results that we achieve. Since the frontier really opened we have been this way." This remark, perilously close to an end-justifies-the-means point of view, could serve as a rationalization for both the Kennedy and Johnson conduct of the Vietnamese conflict. After all, as the President declared in 1965, "America wins the wars that she undertakes. Make no mistake about it." If the struggle became difficult, Johnson could again use the development of the American frontier as an example to reassure Americans that not they but a more inexorable power put them into Vietnam: "We had the good fortune to grow from a handful of isolated colonies to a position of great responsibility in the world. We did not deliberately seek this position; in a real sense the force of history shaped it for us."[26] History during the 1960s became a political tool to wield rather than a burden requiring understanding and humility.

Given this vision of American history, the President determined he must do nothing less than create a Great Society at home and wage the Cold War abroad. He demanded consensus for these objectives: "We cannot keep what we have and we cannot preserve the brightening flame of hope for others unless we are all — repeat *all* committed; all — repeat *all* willing to sacrifice and to serve wherever we can, whether it be in Vietnam, whether it be at home." John-

[25] *The New York Times*, August 27, 1966, p. 10; Interview with Henry Graff in *The New York Times Magazine*, March 20, 1966, p. 133.

[26] *Public Papers of the Presidents, 1965*, pp. 770, 821; *Public Papers of the Presidents, 1966*, p. 984.

son justified using the widest possible presidential powers in foreign policy to shape this consensus. For there was the other side of the coin if Americans did not "sacrifice": "There are 3 billion people in the world and we have only 200 million of them. We are outnumbered 15 to 1. If might did make right they would sweep over the United States and take what we have. We have what they want."[27] Given such a world view, if discontent appeared at home the dissenters too quickly could be labeled "appeasers" of the "Munich variety"; national press and television could justifiably be manipulated; and policies acquitted by the latest poll, pulled from a coat pocket, which demonstrated through apparently incontrovertible quantitative data that "body count" indicated the war was being won in Vietnam and consensus reigned at home.

Johnson's policies in Vietnam were not aberrations but the culmination of nearly three-quarters of a century of American foreign policy. He only presented those policies — and their consequences — more starkly than had his predecessors. In this sense his continuation of Kennedy's approach to Vietnam was natural, but, like the New Frontier, the Great Society's hope for military-imposed stability in Southeast Asia soon vanished. Saigon politics was in chaos. Seven different governments rose to power in South Vietnam during 1964, three during the weeks of August 16 to September 3 alone. This was the struggle within the civil war.

Nor was the civil war itself abating. State Department Director of Intelligence Thomas Hughes remarked on June 8, 1964, that "by far the greater part of the Vietcong forces in South Vietnam are South Vietnamese, the preponderance of Vietcong weapons come not from Communist countries but from capture, purchase, and local manufacture."[28] In such a civil war, the United States could not find sufficient leverage to roll back the National Liberation Front. When Hanoi offered to negotiate in August 1964, the United States consequently rejected the proposal. U.S. officials argued fifteen months later, when the offer was finally revealed, that Ho Chi Minh was not serious about making an equitable settlement and that the military situation at the time gravely weakened the American negotiating position. The presidential campaign in the United

[27]*Public Papers of the Presidents, 1964*, p. 1640; *Public Papers of the Presidents, 1966*, p. 1287.

[28]Quoted in Philip L. Geyelin, *Lyndon B. Johnson and the World* (New York, 1966), p. 193.

States may also have been a factor. Johnson did not want to be open to the charge of appeasement, particularly when his Republican opponent, former Senator Barry Goldwater of Arizona, urged a "Let's Win" policy of total military victory.

The war entered a new phase on August 2, 1964, when North Vietnamese torpedo boats attacked the American destroyer *Maddox* in the Gulf of Tonkin. Bounded by North Vietnam and China, the gulf was a sensitive strategic area. Despite American warnings and the reinforcement of the fleet, the attack was apparently repeated on August 4. Hanoi claimed that the American ships had been participating in South Vietnamese raids on two North Vietnamese shore areas. *The New York Times* also reported that the destroyers had collaborated with South Vietnamese commando raids.[29] President Johnson, however, interpreted the attack as "open aggression on the high seas," adding in an ironic historical prophecy, "We Americans know, although others appear to forget, the risk of spreading conflict." He insisted that "the attacks were unprovoked."[30] Without consulting NATO or SEATO allies or the United States Congress, the President ordered the first American air attack on North Vietnamese ports in retaliation.

Four years later in congressional hearings, Secretary McNamara admitted that the American warships attacked in the gulf had been cooperating with South Vietnamese forays against North Vietnam. Since February 1964 the United States had developed a program of clandestine attacks on North Vietnam. Termed 34A, these operations included parachuting sabotage teams, commando raids, and the bombardment of coastal installations. As the Saigon political situation deteriorated, these raids were stepped up, although the administration concealed them from Congress. This evidence contradicted McNamara's statement of August 6, 1964: "Our Navy played absolutely no part in, was not associated with, was not aware of, any South Vietnamese actions, if there were any."[31]

The truth, however, appeared much too late to prevent Congress from making one of its worst foreign policy errors. The President requested a resolution supporting "all necessary measures" that

[29] *The New York Times*, August 5, 1964, p. 4; and August 4, 1964, p. 2.

[30] *Public Papers of the Presidents, 1964*, p. 928.

[31] U.S. Senate, Committee on Foreign Relations, 90th Cong., 2nd Sess., *The Gulf of Tonkin, The 1964 Incidents* (Washington, 1968). *The Pentagon Papers*, pp. 234–242, 258–279, also analyze the 34A operations and Gulf of Tonkin attack.

the President may take to "repel any armed attack" against American forces. He demanded and received more, for Congress also gave advance consent that the President could "prevent further aggression" and take "all necessary steps" to protect any nation covered by SEATO which might request aid "in defense of its freedom." This Gulf of Tonkin Resolution sailed through the House of Representatives after forty minutes of debate by a vote of 416 to 0. In the Senate, however, Senator Gaylord Nelson, Democrat of Wisconsin, attempted to amend the resolution so that it would not justify a widening of the conflict. He was stopped by J. William Fulbright, Democrat of Arkansas and chairman of the Foreign Relations Committee, who argued that the President should be trusted and that an amendment would require further consideration by the House at a time when speed and the appearance of national unity were essential. The Senate then voted 88 to 2 (Democratic Senators Wayne Morse of Oregon and Ernest Gruening of Alaska dissenting) to give the President virtually unlimited powers in the Vietnamese conflict.

During the next four years Johnson waged war without an explicit declaration of war from Congress. He argued that the Gulf of Tonkin Resolution and the President's powers as commander in chief of the military gave him sufficient authority to send one-half million Americans into combat in Vietnam. The Senate finally repealed the resolution in 1970.

To examine the Vietnam War in isolation would be a grave historical error. The conflict was not an exception to the world view of American foreign policy makers during the 1960s. Vietnam was only one of a number of revolutions in the newly emerging world with which Johnson had to deal during his first eighteen months in office. Since 1960 Africa had been the most chaotic area. In all of Africa in 1945 only Egypt, Ethiopia, Liberia, and South Africa could lay claim to independence. Otherwise, the continent was under Belgian, British, French, Spanish, or Portuguese control. World War II destroyed the power of European colonialism; the Suez crisis and then the termination of British control of Ghana in 1957 (giving the first black African state its independence in the postwar era) set off a chain reaction. In 1960 sixteen new African states joined the United Nations. By 1970 fifty African nations were independent. Many of these states were national entities only in the sense that colonial authorities had formerly imposed central governments over the areas. Tribal ties often remained stronger, factionalizing the new nations, creating insoluble problems for nationalistic leaders, and thereby allowing army generals to use military force to consolidate their own as well as their nations' power. Nearly all new African nations, moreover, had been poorly prepared by the colonialists for independence. Necessary capital, technical skills, stable governmental institutions, and educated elites were in short supply. Both Washington and Moscow suffered serious reverses in attempting to come to terms with these changes.

The United States held a precarious position among black Africans because it refused to use sanctions to penalize the Republic of South Africa for its policy of apartheid, under which a small white minority of less than 20 percent of the population isolated and ruthlessly suppressed the black majority. That dilemma intensified in November 1965, when Southern Rhodesia, with a white population of 200,000 and a black population of nearly 4 million, broke away from the British Empire to establish another apartheid system. The United States publicized its dislike for these apartheid policies but refused to go further. Vast economic investments, strategic naval ports in South Africa, a reluctance to oppose military allies (such as Portugal) that still controlled colonial African territories, and a fear that such action would be a precedent for other nations to pass judgment on the American domestic racial situation—all of these factors prevented the United States from effectively opposing apartheid.

Washington officials, however, did not hesitate to intervene in the Belgian Congo during the 1960s. This area, tragically unprepared by Belgium for independence, became a sovereign nation on June 30, 1960. Katanga Province, led by Moise Tshombe and bolstered by European and American copper and cobalt interests, attempted to secede from the Congo and become an independent state. In the ensuing two-year struggle the most popular nationalistic Congolese leader, Patrice Lumumba, was murdered by Katanga authorities. Order was restored only after the United Nations, with vast American support, helped the Congolese government capture Tshombe and reunite the country in January 1963. The United States had decided that removing Tshombe was less distasteful than allowing the continuation of a civil war that could become an open invitation to Soviet or Chinese intervention. The Soviets actually supported United Nations intervention, but independently and outside UN channels.

Congolese stability proved short-lived. In the spring of 1964, left-wing nationalists attempted to overthrow the government. By this time the United States had replaced Belgium as the most powerful foreign element and had spent more than $6 million attempting to bolster the central government. As rebellion spread, the Central Intelligence Agency formed a mercenary army and air force, many of whose planes were piloted by exiled Cubans. The multilived Tshombe returned to head this central government. He recruited white mercenaries from southern Africa, Europe, and the United States. The rebels opened contact with Communist China, although communist influence in the movement was extremely small. The antigovernment forces tortured and executed perhaps 20,000 opponents. When they gathered 280 Belgians and 16 Americans as hostages, the United States organized a quick Belgian paratroop strike.[32] On November 24, 1964, the hostages were freed, and the rebels were dispersed. Shortly thereafter, Tshombe was driven from power by a military regime led by General Joseph D. Mobutu. The political structure remained unstable, and Tshombe's use of white mercenaries enraged African nationalists. American influence continued to grow until by 1967 Belgians had to make appointments through the United States embassy to talk with Congolese governmental officials.[33] When rebellion again erupted in the summer of 1967, however, powerful senators, led by Richard Russell, Democrat of Georgia, so strenuously objected to further aid for Mobutu that the State Department acquiesced. Racial tensions at home as well as the rising combat fatalities in Vietnam were beginning to limit American initiatives in other newly emerging nations.

Africa ranked much lower on Washington's priority list than either Vietnam or Latin America. In the latter area, Johnson continued the downgrading of the Alliance for Progress. He placed control of policy under a new assistant secretary of state, Thomas C. Mann. A fellow Texan, Mann's top priorities were the stabilization of Latin American politics, protection of American private investments in the area, and a vigorous struggle against radicalism. He willingly accepted military governments in Latin America, particularly if these regimes replaced liberal reform governments that threatened to pass destabilizing economic measures. United States

[32] Richard J. Barnet, *Intervention and Revolution: The United States in the Third World* (New York, 1968), pp. 248–251.

[33] *The New York Times*, August 3, 1967, p. 2.

encouragement and acceptance of such a military *coup d'état* occurred first in Brazil in 1964. The new Brazilian military regime became one of the most stable — and repressive — governments in the hemisphere.

When President Johnson did attempt to increase investment in social enterprises such as education or health, his policies were attacked by the Treasury Department and its new secretary, Henry Fowler. The secretary's uppermost concern was not Latin American development but the correction of the worsening dollar deficit being incurred by the United States in international trade. Since the late 1950s, Americans had spent more overseas than they had sold. The deficit was made up by shipping gold abroad. By the mid-1960s the United States gold supply had shrunk 40 percent since 1945, and the situation threatened to get out of hand as Vietnam costs spiraled upward in 1965–1966. One of the first victims of America's inability to balance its international budget was the Alliance for Progress.

Fowler and the Treasury insisted that support for American exports (the most important suction for drawing money back into the United States) receive preference over all overseas social investments. The department inserted an "additionality" clause in aid grants. Under this clause, Latin American recipients of American aid promised to spend all of that money on American goods, even though those goods were more expensive than, say, similar British or French goods. "Additionality" drastically drove up the cost of development for the Latin Americans. The president of Colombia observed sardonically in 1968, "Colombia has received two program loans under the Alliance. I don't know if we can survive a third."[34] This intensified attention to securing more exports also made the Johnson administration very sensitive to any unsettling factor that might threaten markets in Latin America. By 1966 the Alliance had failed to achieve its objectives. It had created rising expectations in Latin America, expectations that demanded more than American support for military regimes or the use of Latin America as a mere export market for United States goods. But worse was to come.

In the Dominican Republic on April 24, 1965, a civilian government headed by Donald Reid Cabral was attacked by liberal and

[34]Jerome Levinson and Juan de Onís, *The Alliance That Lost Its Way: A Critical Report on the Alliance for Progress* (Chicago, 1970), is the best analysis; see especially pp. 120–123.

radical followers of Juan Bosch (see map, p. 210). The nation's 3.3 million people were among the poorest in Latin America. Between 1916 and 1940 the government had been controlled by American Marines and customs officers, but the United States had withdrawn by 1940 in favor of Rafael Trujillo. The dictator, whom Franklin D. Roosevelt accurately characterized as "an s.o.b." but "our s.o.b.," brutally ruled and ruthlessly exploited his countrymen until he was gunned down by assassins in May 1961. When the dictator's relatives attempted to claim his power, President Kennedy deployed American naval units to safeguard the provisional government. In December 1962 the reform party led by Juan Bosch obtained 60 percent of the votes in a national election. Ten months later, Bosch fell to an army *coup d'état* that was supported by conservative businessmen, landholders, and church leaders. Neither the White House, whose staff had become dissatisfied with Bosch and viewed him as a mere "literary figure," nor the State Department protected Bosch's popularly elected government. The Reid Cabral junta which assumed power was soon deserted by both conservative and radical forces; it was deserted by everyone, apparently, except the United States. When Reid Cabral insisted on running for president in the June 1965 elections, and when Washington then extended a $5 million loan to his regime, pro-Bosch forces overthrew what was only the shell of a government.

Two days of fighting between the rebels and army forces followed. On Monday, April 26, the rebels began arming thousands of civilians. By April 28 the military seemed to have the upper hand, but Washington officials, acting on conclusions too hastily formed by the American embassy in Santo Domingo, concluded that marines would have to land to prevent a Castro-like revolution. Johnson and Mann had taken a tough line on Castro. Despite approaches from the Cuban government in the autumn of 1963 which hinted at its desire to have normal relations with the United States, Washington had replied very cautiously. When Castro then suggested an agenda for the talks, Johnson was President. Athough he saw the Cuban memorandum, Johnson had refused to make any conciliatory move.[35] By late 1964 the United States, working through the Organization of American States (OAS), had successfully encour-

---

[35]Oral History Statement by William Attwood, November 8, 1965, Kennedy Library, Boston. Used by permission.

aged every Latin American nation except Mexico to break off diplomatic relations with Cuba. Faced with the Dominican revolt, the
administration adopted a view that American policy makers had
amplified from the Truman Doctrine to the Kennedy-Johnson interpretation of Vietnam: the revolt was part of a larger challenge, and
a challenge in any area was thus a challenge to American security
everywhere.

The initial public pretext for landing nearly 23,000 troops was
the protection of Americans in strife-torn Santo Domingo. (This
rationale was probably publicized in part because the United States
action violated Articles 15 and 17 of the OAS Charter, which prohibited intervention "directly or indirectly, for any reason whatever, in the internal or external affairs of any other State.") On
April 30, however, Johnson gave a different reason: "People trained
outside the Dominican Republic are seeking to gain control." When
the American embassy issued a poorly documented list of fifty-
eight (or fifty-three) "identified and prominent Communist and
Castroite leaders" in the rebel forces, American newspapermen on
the scene considered the list propaganda, not fact, and agreed with
Bosch's assessment that "this was a democratic revolution smashed
by the leading democracy of the world."[36] In intervening unilaterally,
the United States maneuvered a very reluctant vote of consent from
the OAS, but Johnson's disdain for the organization's failure to be
enthusiastic about the American Marines was unconcealed. "The
OAS," the President remarked privately, "couldn't pour———out
of a boot if the instructions were written on the heel."[37]

The President went further. On May 2, 1965, he announced that
the "American nations cannot, must not, and will not permit the establishment of another Communist government in the Western
Hemisphere." He warned that change "should come through peaceful process" and pledged that the United States would defend "every
free country of this hemisphere." The importance of this "Johnson
Doctrine," like both the Truman and Eisenhower doctrines, depended
on how broadly the United States would define "communism" and
how easily force would be committed to defend "every free
country." The contradictions inherent in the administration's policies (in both Southeast Asia and Latin America) appeared on May 9

[36]*Newsweek*, May 17, 1965, p. 52.
[37]Geyelin, *Lyndon B. Johnson and the World*, p. 254.

in an interview with Mann. Having just intervened with a large force, the assistant secretary of state said that the United States only wanted every nation to choose its "own government free of outside interference."[38]

In the spring of 1966 a conservative government led by Joaquin Balaguer assumed power through nationwide elections. Four years later Balaguer was reelected, but amidst increasing violence. Although the opposition pulled out of the campaign, more than 200 political murders occurred. During the first six months of 1971, political killings happened at the rate of one every forty-eight hours. Balaguer's police evidently committed most of the crimes. "Even under Trujillo we had nothing like this," said a veteran Dominican reporter.[39] The effect of Johnson's intervention on United States policy toward Latin America and on the Latin Americans themselves was incalculable.

The administration's policy came under severe attack at home, but most critics were concerned with the evolving pattern of American intervention around the globe and the resulting justifications issued by official sources. In this sense Santo Domingo was a microcosm of South Vietnam. During the 1964 presidential campaign, Johnson had answered Goldwater's demands for bombing North Vietnam with the remark on September 25, "We're not going north and drop bombs at this stage of the game" because "I want to think about the consequences of getting American boys into a war with 700 million Chinese." The same day, however, William P. Bundy, assistant secretary of state for Far Eastern affairs, commented, "Expansion of the war outside South Vietnam . . . could be forced upon us by the increased pressures of the Communists." Bundy proved the more accurate prophet. At the time Johnson was campaigning, his closest advisors had decided that North Vietnam would have to be bombed. Target lists were drawn up, bombings were expected to begin at the outset of 1965, and only the President's permission, which his advisors now thought to be "inevitable," remained to be obtained. These counselors further understood that the bombing, once undertaken, would only be a stopgap measure to shore up the

[38] *The New York Times*, May 9, 1965, p. E3.
[39] *Washington Post*, July 15, 1971, p. F7.

revolving South Vietnam regimes until American ground troops could be rushed into action.[40]

On February 8, 1965, the American bombing raids on North Vietnam began. The ostensible reason was a Viet Cong attack on the American camp at Pleiku, killing seven Americans; this was one of a series of attacks against United States bases that had taken place since the autumn. In March the President began "Rolling Thunder," a systematic, long-term bombing program against the North. Curtis LeMay, air force chief of staff, thought it time: "We are swatting flies when we should be going after the manure pile." By April, however, the bombing had only stiffened Hanoi's resistance. Johnson ordered more than 20,000 American troops into Vietnam, and now they were openly instructed to enter into combat. The inescapable logic of the commitment began to become apparent. Over 100,000 United States troops went to Vietnam in approximately four months. The escalation saved the tottering South Vietnamese government, but at an unimagined price.

"Rolling Thunder" aimed to cut off supplies being infiltrated from North Vietnam and to help stabilize South Vietnam politically. It accomplished neither objective. Hanoi, with aid from Russia and China, matched the American escalation step by step, sending 60,000 men into South Vietnam in 1966 (three times the number of 1965) and increasing daily tonnage of supplies by 150 percent. Bombing had little effect on the primitive supply route, which needed to provide only six tons of goods a day (an amount that could be carried by several hundred people) to keep the Viet Cong refueled. Bombings north and south, moreover, probably killed a ratio of two civilians to one Viet Cong, according to one estimate; American-Vietnamese search-and-destroy operations on the ground perhaps killed as many as six civilians for each Viet Cong.[41] Ground fighting increased, with Americans assuming the burden. In April 1966, for the first time, more Americans were killed in action than South Vietnamese.

On the political side, prospects only slightly improved. In June 1965 strongman Air Vice Marshal Nguyen Cao Ky came to power as premier. A North Vietnamese who had fought with the French against Vietnamese independence forces and later made a widely

[40]*Pentagon Papers*, pp. 307–342.
[41]Roger Hilsman, *To Move a Nation* (New York, 1965), p. 530.

publicized remark praising Adolf Hitler, Ky was nevertheless welcomed by American officials because he promised to provide the necessary political stability. But desertions continued to rise dramatically in the South Vietnam Army. Inflation and corruption, appearing almost in proportion to the intensified American effort, decimated the Vietnamese economy. By February 1966 McNamara admitted that even if bombing destroyed all of North Vietnam's power systems, oil, harbors, and dams, "they could still carry on the infiltration of the men and equipment necessary to support some level of operations in the South."[42]

These disasters were visible in 1966 for any American who cared to see them. Too often the scene was blurred by statistics that poured out of Washington, most of them misleading. "Ah, *les statistiques!*" a Vietnamese general explained to an American, "Your Secretary of Defense loves statistics. We Vietnamese can give him all he wants. If you want them to go up, they will go up. If you want them to go down, they will go down."[43] The view was also distorted by various peace initiatives. In an April 7, 1965, speech at Johns Hopkins University, President Johnson offered what he termed "unconditional discussions" and proposed an internationally financed Asian Development Bank for peacetime reconstruction. Actually, peace discussions were impossible from the American view because of the deteriorating military situation. During his first months in office, moreover, President Johnson had ruled out any neutralization of South Vietnam. This undercut totally his professions for "unconditional discussions."[44]

For their part the North Vietnamese would settle for nothing less than a complete withdrawal of American power and the reunification of the country on their terms. They were not about to be betrayed as they felt they had been in the 1954 Geneva Conference. By 1965 the Vietnamese civil war could no more be compromised than the American Civil War could have been a century earlier.

The White House now aimed for military victory, for once a nation fell to "communism" (an elastic term applied to revolutionaries whether in China or Iraq, Cuba or Santo Domingo) or became un-

[42] *The New York Times*, February 16, 1966, p. 1.

[43] Hilsman, *To Move a Nation*, p. 523.

[44] *Pentagon Papers*, pp. 285–286, especially cable from President to Lodge, March 20, 1964, Document No. 65.

steadily "neutralized," American liberty in the world was decreased and communism occupied a springboard for toppling other "dominoes." In this sense, the enemy of the 1960s was China. On the one hand, the Johnson administration believed that because of internal difficulties the Chinese would not intervene in Vietnam as long as the fighting remained away from their borders. On the other hand, "Over this war — and all Asia — is another reality: the deepening shadow of Communist China," as the President told the nation in his Johns Hopkins speech. "The contest in Vietnam is part of a wider pattern of aggressive purposes." During the same month McNamara explained most fully in a private conversation why the United States was in Vietnam.

The alternative to fighting, he observed, was not to negotiate a neutral noncommunist South Vietnam, for this was impossible. The real alternative was a Chinese-dominated Southeast Asia, which would mean a "Red Asia." If the United States withdrew, a complete shift would occur in the world balance of power. Asia would go Red, American allies would be shaken, and at home there would be a "bad effect on [the] economy and a disastrous political fight that could further freeze American political debate and even affect political freedom." Chinese attitudes might soften over the decades, but this would take longer than had the Russian change, for China "started from farther back than [the] Soviet Union in [the] industrializing process. The Soviet Union was contained by a military alliance in an expansionist period. So [it is] possible to contain China in her expansionist phase by similar alliances." To stop China, the United States would not recognize "any sanctuary or any weapons restriction. But we would use nuclear weapons only after fully applying non-nuclear arsenal."[45]

The secretary of defense offered this explanation at a time when the Chinese were suffering a series of devastating foreign policy setbacks that helped to cause a severe internal upheaval within China between 1966 and 1968. A domestically generated coup in Indonesia led by nationalist army elements, and having little to do with the American presence in Vietnam, destroyed pro-Peking communists in a bloodbath. Castro's Cuba, revolutionary Algeria, Egypt's Nasser, and a number of African nations publicly attacked Chinese policies, restricting or severing diplomatic ties. Despite China's ex-

[45]"Memorandum" of Background Session with Robert McNamara, April 22, 1965, Arthur Krock Papers, Princeton University Library.

plosion of an atomic bomb in 1964 and a thermonuclear device in May 1966, that nation's diplomatic leverage dissipated.

These failures influenced Mao to launch a "cultural revolution" within China, transforming foreign policy and enabling him to eliminate personal enemies within Peking. The turning point came in September 1965, when General Lin Piao, second in command to Mao, announced that China would encourage wars of liberation throughout the newly emerging nations. Lin Piao gave no hint that China would become directly involved in any of the revolutions. He warned other revolutionaries to help themselves as the Chinese had done.

In Washington, however, policy makers led by Secretary of State Dean Rusk immediately compared Lin Piao's statement to Hitler's *Mein Kampf*. The President announced that Lin Piao had confirmed that, if the domino of Vietnam fell, others would follow.[46] Chinese experts such as Harvard's John Fairbank deplored this interpretation. Nearly 200 scholars of Asian affairs urged a re-evaluation of the policy toward China, but without success. They observed that, regardless of how the rhetoric was interpreted, Chinese capabilities and power could not and might never be able to achieve Lin Piao's objectives. Developments in Indonesia, Cuba, and Africa confirmed this view.

As usual, the greatest irony could be found in Vietnam. Following the Lin Piao statement, China pleaded with Hanoi to fight a protracted struggle that would tie down and bleed American power. Ho Chi Minh disliked such advice. He saw no logic in an indefinite conflict that would benefit only China's objectives. He wanted to defeat the United States rapidly. A long war would leave a weakened North Vietnam more open to Chinese pressure.[47] Meanwhile, much to the consternation of the Chinese, the Soviet Union replaced China as the most important source of aid and support for Ho's regime. Worse, in early 1966 clashes between Chinese and Russian troops occurred along their long common border. The Chinese were being squeezed from two directions by Russia; they were losing influence in Hanoi as well as other key Third World capitals; and they were undergoing major political upheavals inter-

---

[46] *Public Papers of the Presidents, 1966*, p. 936; see also *The New York Times*, August 31, 1966, p. 9.

[47] David Mozingo, "China's Foreign Policy and the Cultural Revolution," Interim Report: Number 1, International Relations of East Asia Project, Cornell University, Ithaca, New York, 1970.

nally. At this point in 1965–1966, the Johnson administration decided to send 400,000 American soldiers to save Vietnam from China.

The Soviet Union was the primary, perhaps the only, nation that benefited from American intervention. With United States attention and resources tied down in Southeast Asia, Russia made a dramatic recovery in world affairs between 1965 and 1971. After 1958 the Russian economy had grown at a considerably slower rate than previously, thus discouraging hopes of challenging the American economic supremacy. The decline also weakened Khrushchev's power within the Kremlin. Dissenting party leaders and some military officials combined to oust Khrushchev in October 1964. The victors divided his posts between two former protégés of Stalin, Alexei Kosygin, who became premier, and Leonid Brezhnev, the new first party secretary. This change occurred as the United States stepped up its effort in Vietnam. Kosygin was actually visiting Hanoi at that moment in February 1965 when, for reasons best known to the State Department, the United States chose to begin the bombing. As Soviet influence grew in Hanoi, Moscow did nothing to mediate the war, partly because the two sides seemed irreconcilable but also because the conflict — as long as it remained limited — drained the United States and benefited the Soviet Union.

The Russians further gained as the war helped divide the Western alliance. France, the former colonial power in Southeast Asia, now condemned the "foreign intervention" of the United States. (In the spring of 1966, American policies received a further blow when de Gaulle pulled France out of the NATO military organization.) The Western Europeans refused outright to send men for the American buildup in South Vietnam. Of the forty nations linked to the United States through treaties, only four (Australia, New Zealand, South Korea, and Thailand) committed combat troops. Korea and Thailand did so only after the United States promised to pay handsomely for their troops. Japan also grew critical of the escalation in the war.

No matter where he looked, Johnson had difficulty finding support for his policies. Soviet military and diplomatic leverage grew as unstable conditions spread in Africa and Latin America. The trouble with foreigners, the President lamented, "is that they're not like folks you were reared with." By mid-1966, however, the problems with the allies were rapidly becoming less important than the eruptions of the "folks" back home.

11

A New Containment: The Rise and Fall of Détente (1966-1976)

Ironically, as the United States escalated the war in Vietnam to contain communism, the Johnson administration deescalated conflict with the Soviets. The seeds of détente, or lessening of international tension, were sown in 1967–1968, at the moment United States forces suffered setbacks in Vietnam and blossomed in 1971–1972 as American bombers obliterated people and villages in large areas of Southeast Asia. Thus détente did not signal an American retreat from world affairs but was a new — and necessary — tactic for carrying on traditional containment policy. Overall, the power of the United States economy and military (not to mention American culture, especially music, art, and McDonald's) remained dominant on the globe. But that power could no longer influence Soviet policy or the newly emerging areas as it had before the 1960s. A new world had appeared. For a decade (1966–1976), détente became both a safety valve for releasing tension in that world and a tactic for controlling the emergence of the Soviet Union as a global power. The collapse of détente in the mid-1970s tellingly revealed how both the United States and Russia had not yet been able to come to terms with the new world.

Johnson initially pursued détente in the hope that the Soviets, who were the largest suppliers of military goods to North Vietnam, might be able to pressure Ho Chi Minh to make peace. The Americans' hope was badly misplaced. On the battlefields the war dragged on, while at home the inflation rate doubled to 5 percent and antiwar protests intensified. Johnson's beloved Great Society program, created to erase domestic poverty and injustice, became a victim of a war 11,000 miles away. A top White House official caught the President's dilemma with the remark, "What the hell do you say? How do you half-lead a country into war?"[1]

Growing problems thus forced Johnson to approach the Soviets. Brezhnev and Kosygin were willing to talk, but not necessarily about Vietnam. Their influence in Southeast Asia increased each day the war dragged on. Unlike their late mentor, Stalin—whom Khrushchev once sarcastically described as thinking that "foreign policy meant keeping the antiaircraft units around Moscow on a twenty-four-hour alert"[2]—the new Russian leaders pushed their influence into such areas as the Middle East and South and Southeast Asia. Their military power was burgeoning. After the 1956 Suez crisis, the Russians began a rapid buildup of conventional land and sea forces until by the late 1960s their fleet, once a subject of ridicule, began to appear regularly in the Mediterranean, Indian Ocean, and even Caribbean areas.[3] As for their nuclear forces, after the 1962 missile crisis a Soviet official warned an American that "you'll never be able to do that to us again," and by 1968 the Russians approached strategic parity with the once-supreme American arsenal.

The Vietnam morass and the new balance of power therefore also required that Johnson deal with the Soviets. Brezhnev and Kosygin were receptive, for although the Russians' military power had sharply increased, their economic growth rate had dropped drastically in the 1960s. They needed economic relief. The Soviets, moreover, have always delighted in bargaining as an equal with the United States, a nation they simultaneously fear, dislike, and try desperately to emulate. The time was ripe for a deal.

[1]Harry McPherson Oral History Interview, Tape #4, p. 20, Lyndon B. Johnson Library, Austin, Texas. (Hereinafter cited as LBJ Library.)

[2]Nikita Khrushchev, *Khrushchev Remembers*, translated and edited by Strobe Talbott (Boston, 1970), pp. 392–393.

[3]J. M. McConnell and Bradford Dismukes, "Soviet Diplomacy of Force in the Third World," *Problems of Communism*, XXVIII (January–February 1979): 15–20.

But the first deal on Vietnam was never struck. Rusk urged the Soviets to call off their North Vietnam ally because, he warned, if Russia was "backing the north to seize the south, then we [the United States and U.S.S.R.] were in trouble," for the United States would never allow it. The Soviets responded by threatening to give Ho new surface-to-surface missiles and flatly announcing that "since North Vietnam is a part of the Communist community, the Soviet Union must support and will assist it increasingly as the U.S. escalates its efforts."[4] Americans acted, moreover, as if the Soviets could actually force Ho to give up his struggle; that was a highly doubtful assumption.

Johnson was luckier in his attempts to slow the nuclear race. At a summit meeting with Kosygin at Glassboro, New Jersey, an impassioned warning by Defense Secretary McNamara about the suicidal arms race both nations were running helped lead to an announcement that a nonproliferation agreement had been reached. Each power pledged to halt the distribution of nuclear weapons. Ominously, China, France, and India, among others, refused to sign the pact.

Détente seemed to be moving ahead. And then it suffered two stunning setbacks. The first began in February 1968, when the North Vietnamese launched a surprise Tet (New Year) offensive that was not beaten back until they threatened even the grounds of the United States embassy in Saigon. Until that occurred, Johnson could claim that the war was going better and Americans could see "light at the end of the tunnel." Now the light seemed to be an onrushing freight train engineered by Ho. The North Vietnamese suffered heavy casualties during Tet, but they broke the illusion held by many Americans that the war could soon be won.[5]

Johnson consulted a group of elder statesmen, and the most famous "wise man," Dean Acheson, bluntly told the President that his advisors had led him "down the garden path." A month later, Senator Eugene McCarthy, Democrat of Minnesota, ran on an anti-

[4]Memorandum of Conversation between Rusk and Ambassador Anatoly F. Dobrynin, May 26, 1966, White House Confidential File (Asia), Box 7, LBJ Library; Thomas L. Hughes to Rusk, May 4, 1967, National Security File, Country File, U.S.S.R., LBJ Library; Memorandum of Conversation between Zbigniew Brzezinski and Yuri Zhukov, April 13, 1967, National Security File, Country File, U.S.S.R., LBJ Library.

[5]McPherson Oral History, Tape #9, p. 10, LBJ Library.

war platform and nearly defeated Johnson in the New Hampshire presidential primary. On March 31, 1968, the President dramatically announced on national television that he was pulling out of the race so he could devote all his energies to making peace with Ho. Johnson turned down a military request for 206,000 more men to be added to the nearly 500,000 already in Vietnam, but he secretly allowed the numbers to rise to 549,000. He planned to turn up the military pressure as he moved toward negotiations; if Ho refused to talk, then, as the State Department secretly informed United States ambassadors in Asia, it would "give us a clear field for whatever actions" were "required."[6]

At home the United States seemed to be approaching a crisis. Between 1964 and 1968 ghetto riots claimed dozens of lives in Los Angeles, Detroit, and Newark. After Martin Luther King, Jr., was murdered in April 1968, even Washington erupted in flames, as army troops moved into the city and used the Capitol Hill lawn as a bivouac area. Three major political assassinations (John Kennedy in 1963, King and Robert Kennedy in 1968) shocked the world. When the Democratic National Convention met in Chicago during the summer of 1968, massive antiwar riots broke out. Six thousand troops were flown into the city, and Johnson could not attend his own party's meeting because of the danger. Amidst the chaos, Vice President Hubert Humphrey became the party's nominee. Maine's Senator Edmund Muskie (who fought against a proposed peace resolution at the convention) accepted the vice presidential nomination.

When Republicans met in Miami, three blacks died in a ghetto riot, but the media paid scant attention. Instead the nation watched Richard Nixon arise from the political grave. His 1962 defeat in the California gubernatorial race, one liberal columnist wrote at the time, had supposedly sent Nixon "to that small place in history which belongs to national disasters which did not happen." But Nixon refused to go. By 1968 he had become the most important Republican spokesman on foreign policy. With surprising ease, he beat back the challenge of New York Governor Nelson Rockefeller (whose foreign policy speeches were largely drafted by Harvard Professor Henry Kissinger) and won the Republican nomination. Maryland's governor, Spiro Agnew, who admitted his name was not "a

---

[6] *The Pentagon Papers,* as published by *The New York Times* (New York, 1971), pp. 622–623.

household word," became Nixon's running mate. While Nixon pictured himself as a statesman during the campaign, Agnew took a lower road and accused Humphrey of being soft on communism.

These rapid political changes slowed down the détente process, but it was knocked off its tracks in August 1968 by a second event: the Soviet invasion of Czechoslovakia. Since the mid-1960s, the Soviets and their satellites had moved in different directions. Some Eastern Europeans experimented with more liberal economic policies. The Czechs, during their so-called Prague Spring, even discussed a loosening of their one-party political system. The United States encouraged the process by opening up trade channels. As one State Department official said, Western goods have "tended to open up more and more holes, shall we say, or windows, rather, in the Iron Curtain."[7]

The Brezhnev-Kosygin regime, meanwhile, stolidly and unimaginatively tightened its control within Russia. Stalin's image was refurbished, and a centralized planning system (tagged "Stalinism with computers") emphasized military and heavy industry investment. Intellectuals—especially Jews—were arrested, deported, or declared "insane" when they questioned governmental policies. Brezhnev, who survived an assassination attempt and became the most powerful figure in the Politburo, warned that dissent could not be tolerated because "we are living in conditions of an unabating ideological war."[8] Détente meant a lessening of military and political tensions with the West, but ideological coexistence could not be allowed.

The Prague Spring strained this rigid ideological line to the limit. Soviet officials were divided over how to respond. Some Foreign Ministry officials, who did not want to endanger détente, were among those opposing intervention, but they were overbalanced by party leaders who feared ideological and economic contamination from Czech liberalism, and by some military and secret police officials who believed the Czech policies might infect the entire bloc. Brezhnev at first equivocated, but as the prointervention fac-

---

[7] Anthony Solomon Oral History Interview, LBJ Library.

[8] Wolfgang Leonhard, "The Domestic Politics of the New Soviet Foreign Policy," *Foreign Affairs*, LII (October 1973): 59–74; John Dornberg, *Brezhnev, The Masks of Power* (New York, 1974), chapters XV, XVI.

tion gained strength and threatened his own power, he joined it and ordered Soviet troops to smash the Czech regime.[9]

He did so at the moment Johnson prepared to meet the Soviet leaders at a summit conference. The President quickly canceled the meetings. Brezhnev's willingness to sacrifice détente indicated the extent of his fear of disorder and liberalization in the bloc, as well as his keen sense of how to survive cutthroat Politburo politics. He capped the performance by issuing a "Brezhnev Doctrine" that justified Soviet intervention on the ground that a socialist nation had the right to save another from "world imperialism" and thus preserve the "indivisible" socialist system. Johnson did little in response, not only because of the military realities but perhaps also because the Brezhnev Doctrine for Eastern Europe was not unlike the Johnson Doctrine of 1965 for Latin America. Neither superpower would tolerate new ideological challenges in its own sphere.

As détente stalled, Nixon stumbled toward the White House. His 15 percentage point lead in the polls during September dwindled to less than 1 percent in the November election. Nixon was the first newly elected President in the century who failed to give his party control over either house of Congress. Throughout the campaign, he refused to take a clear stand on the war and said only that he had a mysterious "plan" to end it honorably. Privately he told aides, "I've come to the conclusion that there's no way to win the war. But we can't say that, of course." He preferred not to discuss concrete issues at all. ("You still have to put out a folder saying what you're for and against . . . ," he complained privately. "Women particularly like it. They don't have the slightest idea what it means."[10])

As usual, the election results were not a mandate on foreign policy. Despite the antiwar protests on the campuses, the prowar, third-party ticket of Alabama Governor George Wallace received more support from voters under the age of thirty than it did from the population as a whole. (Throughout the 1965 to 1973 years, the war was most firmly opposed by older, not younger, Americans; by blacks who were doing a disproportionate share of the fighting and

---

[9]Jiri Valenta, "The Bureaucratic Politics Paradigm and the Soviet Invasion of Czechoslovakia," *Political Science Quarterly*, XCIV (Spring 1979): 55–76.
[10]Richard J. Whalen, *Catch the Falling Flag* (Boston, 1972), pp. 137, 154.

dying, rather than whites; by females rather than males; and by lower-class rather than middle-class Americans.[11]) As for the winner, Americans knew he stood for "law and order in the streets," but few knew his plans for Vietnam or détente.

Nixon, however, understood what had to be done, and he thought he knew how to do it. His plans became clearer when, surprisingly, he picked Henry Kissinger as national security advisor. Both men believed the 1970s would be shaped by developments that were sapping United States dominance in world affairs: the Soviet military buildup; the rising economic and political power of Western Europe and Japan, which threatened American markets and worked against Washington's policies in such areas as Vietnam and the Middle East; and the apparently bottomless pit of the Vietnam War.

Above all, as Kissinger liked to say, the greatest problem was how to "manage" the Soviets as they emerged as a global, instead of merely a regional, superpower. Containment was as important in the 1970s as the late 1940s, but because of the new Russian strength, and the relative decline of American power, containment now had to be constructed differently than when Acheson or John Kennedy made policy. Nixon and Kissinger believed the Soviets could be contained not by a massive arms race or increased United States global commitments (which neither the American public nor the economy could tolerate) but by making a deal: the Soviets could have sorely needed economic help if they cooperated in Vietnam and agreed to arms limitation.

In the new containment, Nixon also planned to open talks with China. For twenty years Mao had been the Asian villain to Americans, but since the late 1950s he had also become Russia's main concern. The realization that one communist power could be played off against the other allowed Nixon to believe that an "era of confrontation" was ending and an era of negotiations beginning.[12] Once the relationship between the Americans and the Soviets was

---

[11]William L. Lunch and Peter W. Sperlich, "American Public Opinion and the War in Vietnam," *Western Political Quarterly*, XXXII (March 1979): 21–44; Richard M. Scammon and Ben J. Wattenberg, *The Real Majority* (New York, 1970), pp. 38–49, 92–93.

[12]For the new containment policies see especially, Stanley Hoffman, "The Case of Dr. Kissinger," *The New York Review of Books*, December 6, 1979, p. 24; and I. F. Stone, "The Flowering of Henry Kissinger," *The New York Review of Books*, November 2, 1972, p. 26.

properly adjusted, Nixon and Kissinger concluded, the other problems — Vietnam and the Allies — could be resolved.

All this required time, order, and support at home. With various devices, both legal and criminal, Nixon gained time over the next five years. He also created — temporarily — order and support at home. For above all else, he and Kissinger sought order and control, both at home and abroad, with an awesome single-mindedness. When once asked whether he favored a revolution with justice or an orderly state that was unjust, Kissinger quoted Goethe: "If I had to choose between justice and disorder, on the one hand, and injustice and order on the other, I would always choose the latter."[13] At home, this passion for order led Nixon to use criminal means in attempts to squelch antiwar protesters. Kissinger could not understand why college students refused to fight in Vietnam: "Conscientious objection is destructive of a society. The imperatives of the individual are always in conflict with the organization of society. Conscientious objection must be reserved for only the greatest moral issues, and Vietnam is not of this magnitude."[14] At that point, more than a million people had been killed or wounded in Vietnam.

This determination to have order also led Nixon and Kissinger to control policy making with an iron grip. Perhaps the President could have both directed policy and restored the public's shattered faith in government by structuring political coalitions in which his policies were debated and obtained support. In 1969 political analyst Richard Scammon thought such an opportunity existed. As ethnic and trade union voters became middle class and moved away from their loyalty to the Democrats, Scammon remarked, "There is a possibility that by following a centrist line — . . . moderately conservative — [Nixon] could build up a great new party of the center."[15] Other observers proclaimed the advent of an "emerging Republican majority." Nixon might well have been able to resolve one of the great problems in United States foreign policy: how to use American political institutions to gain support from

---

[13]John G. Stoessinger, *Henry Kissinger: The Anguish of Power* (New York, 1976), pp. 12–14.

[14]Quoted by Clayton Fritchey in *The New York Review of Books,* September 25, 1969, p. 26.

[15]William Whitworth, "Profiles," *The New Yorker,* September 20, 1969, p. 52.

Congress and the public, instead of resorting to an Imperial Presidency that acted without public debate and too often created support through lying.

Nixon never tried to create such political institutions. Highly insecure personally, the President was "the most complete loner I've ever known," said Senator Barry Goldwater. "The man operates all by himself." Carrying the scars of too many political wars, the President preferred to circumvent a Democratic Congress. Nixon did not even trust the CIA: "It was staffed by Ivy League liberals" who had always opposed him politically. As for the State Department, he believed that "no Secretary of State is really important. The President makes foreign policy."[16]

Nixon consequently named William Rogers, a New York lawyer and an old political ally in the Eisenhower years, as secretary of state to keep the department quiet while the White House made foreign policy. Kissinger ensured State's impotence by keeping information from Rogers (and other cabinet members), encouraging Nixon to believe that Rogers was not a loyal team player, courting reporters and congressmen who heard only Kissinger's side of a story, and conducting critical negotiations without informing the State Department. Nixon understood all this. He remarked privately, "Henry thinks Bill [Rogers] isn't very deep and Bill thinks that Henry is power crazy. In a sense they are both right."[17] It was the only time in American history that a secretary of state was appointed because of his ignorance of foreign policy. But then Kissinger often did not consult even his own staff. "Henry's chief lieutenants are like mushrooms," went the joke. "They're kept in the dark, get a lot of manure piled on them, and then get canned."[18]

Without assured congressional support, the trust of the State Department, or sometimes the confidence of Kissinger's staff, the President and his closest advisor had only each other. They considered this to be enough. When Kissinger was the ghost writer for Nixon's "State of the World" report in 1970, an observer thought it resembled a message from the Vatican, except that "the Pope quotes

[16] *Washington Post*, October 17, 1976, p. C4; Henry Kissinger, *White House Years* (Boston, 1979), p. 11; Whalen, *Catch the Falling Flag*, pp. 253–256.

[17] Leslie Gelb, "The Kissinger Legacy," *The New York Times Magazine*, October 31, 1976, pp. 78–79; William Shawcross, *Sideshow* (New York, 1979), p. 103.

[18] Bruce Mazlish, *Kissinger* (New York, 1976), p. 231.

Scripture" while "Mr. Nixon quotes himself 31 times directly."[19] Kissinger meanwhile controlled the foreign policy-making process from the White House and, as the President's personal assistant, did not have to be accountable to Congress. Rogers, although knowing little about any policies, had to testify before committees in what one senator frostily called "a rather empty exercise." Instead of building political institutions, Nixon was systematically undermining them.

Despite his firm control over policy, Nixon enjoyed few early successes. He was reluctant to deal with the Soviets in the aftermath of the Czech invasion. The President knew, moreover, that he could not negotiate with Brezhnev from a position of strength until the Vietnam War and the uproar at home were brought under control. He announced in 1969 that United States troops would leave Vietnam in a phased withdrawal. This policy promised to wind down the war and end the antiwar protests. Nixon, however, had no intention of following what he bitterly called "isolationism." The United States must retain its global obligations, but it had to uphold them with different policies than it had during the post-1945 years when it enjoyed overwhelming power.

In Vietnam, Nixon pursued a policy of "Vietnamization," that is, building South Vietnam's Army so it could replace the departing Americans. This approach actually resembled the failed policies of 1954 to 1965. As one United States official said, it simply meant "changing the color of the corpses." Elsewhere the President followed a "Nixon Doctrine." It provided that as the United States pulled back from some of its military commitments, Americans would help certain friends take up the burden of containment. In Asia the friend was to be Japan; in the Middle East, Iran; and in Africa, Zaire (the former Belgian Congo) and the white-dominated, but black majority, countries of Angola (a Portuguese colony) and South Africa.

Nixon and Kissinger sought containment-on-the-cheap. They even planned to make a profit. Overseas sales of American military arms amounted to $1 to $2 billion in the mid-1960s, but they surged toward $10 billion by the time Nixon left office. Iran alone bought $2.5 billion of arms in 1972–1973. Nixon ordered that the shah could have the newest equipment, and all that His Majesty desired.

[19]Hans Morgenthau, "Mr. Nixon's Foreign Policy," *New Republic*, March 21, 1970, p. 23.

The shah responded by ordering planes and other equipment "as if he was going through the Sears, Roebuck catalog," in the words of one official. In all, the Nixon Doctrine encouraged a dangerous military buildup in the Middle East and southern Africa; nearly bankrupted some nations and encouraged others, such as Iran, to raise oil prices rapidly to pay for the inflation-priced United States equipment; made these nations more likely to use force rather than negotiations to settle disputes; helped create dangerously strained relations with Japan when it refused to become an Asian policeman; and caused Nixon to become a political bedfellow of the shah and white supremicist regimes in Africa. The doctrine's only redeeming virtue was that it gave the President a rationale for pulling back from Vietnam.

But even that virtue was not immediately apparent. As Nixon pulled out troops, he secretly escalated the bombing, particularly in Cambodia, which—although a neutral state—was used by the communists to funnel troops into South Vietnam. The bombings turned out to be a catastrophe. *The New York Times* published a story on the "secret" bombing in March 1969. Nixon set up a "Plumbers" unit to stop such leaks "whatever the cost." This decision led to a series of criminal acts by the Plumbers that climaxed in their attempt to break into Democratic party headquarters at Washington's Watergate Hotel in 1972.

The bombings meanwhile only drove the communist forces deeper into Cambodia and destabilized the country. In early 1970 the government of Prince Norodom Sihanouk, who miraculously had kept Cambodia out of the path of the war's destruction, was overthrown by a right-wing military officer, Lon Nol. The United States apparently was not directly involved in the overthrow, although the CIA certainly knew of Lon Nol's plans. But Nixon rushed to take advantage of the coup. On April 30, 1970, he announced in an emotional speech that the United States must not act as a "pitiful, helpless giant." American troops were therefore invading Cambodia to clean out the communist camps. In the name of winding down the war, Nixon expanded it[20] (see map, p. 222).

Both Cambodia and American campuses were soon devastated. Lon Nol proved to be an incompetent partner who watched help-

[20] The standard account is Shawcross, *Sideshow,* especially pp. 102–121; Kissinger and Nixon quotes to be found in *The New York Times,* December 9, 1973, p. 76; *Washington Post,* February 19, 1974, pp. 1, 12–14.

lessly as his own ally's planes, as well as communist armies, savaged his nation. By 1971 the communists controlled half the country. (By 1975 they had all of it. More than 250,000 persons had been killed, massive starvation began, and one of the world's most beautiful countries lay in ruins.) In the United States students at nearly 500 colleges went on strike to protest Nixon's invasion. At Kent State in Ohio and Jackson State in Mississippi protesters were shot and killed. Thousands of antiwar Americans descended on Washington. Troops were stationed in the White House basement to repel a possible assault. Nixon, Kissinger feared, was on the edge of a nervous breakdown. The President would shout, "Let's go blow the hell out of them," as embarrassed aides looked on in stunned silence. But public opinion polls showed that 50 percent of the Americans surveyed supported Nixon's invasion, although 53 percent did not believe his claim that the action would shorten the war. Congress loyally acted as a lightning rod, absorbing the antiwar protesters' fury but doing nothing until they left Washington and Nixon pulled the troops out of Cambodia. Congress followed the President, not the people in the street.[21]

The Cambodian tragedy was one in a series of disasters that marked 1970–1971 as a nadir in recent United States history. In 1971 Nixon authorized South Vietnamese troops to clean out communist sanctuaries in Laos. "Vietnamization" turned out to be a failure as American television showed South Vietnamese troops clinging desperately to departing American helicopters in order to escape communist gunfire. Nixon responded by stepping up the bombing of Laotian supply trails until Laos became the most heavily bombed country in history. By mid-1971 the communists were in a stronger position in Laos than at any time since 1962.

Vietnamization failed despite an enlarged war and the dropping of bombs at the rate of one ton for every minute Nixon was in office. Between 1969 and 1972, 20,000 Americans died in Vietnam, and over 300,000 Asians were killed while the war was supposedly winding down. In frustration, one popular Saigon newspaper ran a daily contest in which readers submitted stories of such atrocities as rape or homicide committed by Americans. North Vietnam, that "raggedy-ass little fourth-rate country," as Lyndon Johnson once

---

[21]Shawcross, *Sideshow*, pp. 152–153; Marie Gottschalk, "Bring Us Together: Congressional Reaction to the Invasion of Cambodia, 1970," unpublished honors thesis, Cornell, 1980, pp. 54, 72–74.

called it, was tormenting the United States. Americans tired of supporting a South Vietnamese regime that was corrupt and incapable. Many were also sickened by the slaughter dramatized during early 1971 when a military court-martial convicted Lieutenant William Calley, Jr., of killing at least twenty-one South Vietnamese civilians in 1968 at the village of Mylai. It was a war in which the enemy and the civilians were indistinguishable. Meanwhile, American soldiers, unwilling to be, perhaps, the last to die in such a war, used drugs in increasing amounts to avoid combat. Over 9000 were arrested for drug use in Vietnam during 1970, and their superior officers estimated that 65,000 United States troops had used drugs.[22]

And as Vietnamization failed, so too did the American economy. The gross national product (the sum of all services and goods produced) rose over the $1 trillion mark, but an apparently uncontrollable inflation accounted for half the increase in 1971. The nation's industries, moreover, were becoming so uncompetitive that, for the first time since 1894, Americans imported more merchandise than they sold abroad. As the economy weakened, so did the dollar — the foundation that had undergirded the remarkable post-1945 global trading system. In 1971 nearly $50 billion was held abroad, and more and more dollars were being printed in Washington, then pumped overseas, to pay for the nation's military expenditures and private investments. Overseas, dollars increased in number as they decreased in value. Europeans, watching helplessly as these dollars bought up their industries, grew angry and began to raise walls against the dollars and United States trade. "The rest of the world," French President Georges Pompidou announced, "cannot be expected to regulate its life by a clock [the dollar] that is always slow." The efficient Japanese economy sent streams of cars, steel, and electronic goods into American ports, and in 1969 had replaced the United States as Asia's leading trade partner. Nixon became furious when Japan refused to stop certain exports voluntarily until the United States regained its economic health. The Nixon Doctrine, indeed the entire alliance system, was in deep trouble.[23]

---

[22]Robert Shaplen, "Letter from Indo-China," *The New Yorker*, May 16, 1970, p. 125. On drug use, see *The New York Times*, January 11, 1971, p. 13.

[23]Lewis Beman, "How to Tell Where the U.S. Is Competitive," *Fortune*, LXXXVI (July 1972): 54–55; Seymour Melman, *The Permanent War Economy* (New York, 1974), pp. 112–114; *Washington Post*, May 27, 1971, p. A27.

In 1970 Nixon promised he would never impose wage and price controls to stop the inflation that was making American goods more expensive than Japanese or West European products. But in midsummer 1971, the balance of payments suddenly showed the possibility of an unbelievable $48 billion annual deficit. The dollar, and hence the Western trading structure, threatened to collapse. In a Kansas City speech, the President discussed the "five great economic superpowers" (the United States, Russia, Japan, Western Europe, China), four of whom "challenge us on every front." "Because economic power will be the key to other kinds of power . . . in the last third of this century," he continued, and since domestic and foreign policies were so interlinked, Americans had to discipline themselves and their economy before they groveled in the "decadence" that had toppled Ancient Greece and Rome.[24]

In August 1971 the President suddenly imposed a wage-price freeze to curb inflation. He also placed a surtax on foreign imports to stop the inflow of goods from Europe and Japan, a nation that — as a State Department briefing paper reportedly warned Nixon — must be viewed as a potential enemy. He and his secretary of the treasury, tough-talking Texan John Connally, put tremendous pressure on the Allies to revalue their currency while the United States devalued the dollar, thus making the dollar cheaper and more competitive in world markets. Finally, Nixon announced the dollar would no longer be redeemable in gold. The French bitterly called this program "a Marshall Plan in reverse." Unfortunately, it was not enough. In 1973 the economy and the dollar again began slipping after Nixon removed the wage-price freeze. The dollar again had to be devalued. As in 1807, 1893, and 1914, a failing economy forced the United States to change its foreign policies. The era of the all-powerful dollar temporarily ended, and with it went much of Washington's political power (and the good times abroad once cheaply enjoyed by American tourists).

A year before the 1972 presidential campaign began, Nixon was plagued with troubles. Then occurred a remarkable turnabout. The wage-price controls temporarily halted inflation. The economic

[24] *Public Papers of the Presidents . . . Richard Nixon . . . 1971* (Washington, 1972), pp. 806–812.

picture brightened, albeit at the expense of the Allies. The military draft was cut back and student antiwar protests disappeared as if by magic. But most dramatically, in July 1971 Nixon seized the diplomatic initiative with the startling announcement that he would be the first President to visit China.

Since 1969 the two nations had sent subtle signals encouraging a new relationship. Nixon and Mao hoped to use the other to check Soviet power. China's fear of the Russians jumped in 1969–1970, when nearly 1 million Soviet soldiers encamped in a broad area along the Sino-Soviet border. Clashes occurred with Chinese troops. Nixon also hoped to develop a China market so American businessmen could find economic relief — and enter China before the Japanese locked up the most promising trading ventures. Mao was receptive.

The President's major problem might have occurred at home, where for thirty years an anticommunist "China Lobby" had worked, often with Nixon's help, to make Americans believe that Chiang Kai-shek's government on Taiwan, not Mao's, was the real China. Opposition did develop, particularly from the American Federation of Labor, but the President enjoyed wide maneuvering room. A mid-1960s poll showed that about 25 percent of Americans were unaware that China even had a communist government.[25] Nixon, moreover, could not be charged with being soft on communism. He had made his political reputation with such remarks as calling the 1952 Democratic presidential nominee, Adlai Stevenson, "the appeaser . . . who got a Ph.D. from Dean Acheson's College of Cowardly Communist Containment." In 1971 Nixon was not threatened by politicians resembling the earlier Nixon.

His 1972 journey to Peking was a huge success. A friendship treaty was signed, trade opened up, the Soviets were made fearful of a possible Sino-American alliance, and within months the Chinese entered the United Nations while Chiang's delegation was expelled. (Chiang died in 1975, the last survivor of World War II's "Big Four." United States officials increasingly considered Taiwan as an internal Chinese problem, and by 1980 China and Taiwan were cooperating on some economic policies.)

The China trip and the slowing down of the Vietnam War placed Nixon in a position to travel to Moscow. He became the first Presi-

---

[25]Barry B. Hughes, *The Domestic Context of American Foreign Policy* (San Francisco, 1978), p. 57.

dent to visit the Soviet capital. Before his scheduled trip was due to begin in mid-1972, however, the North Vietnamese launched surprise attacks that threatened to overturn the South Vietnam government. Nixon, already called the "biggest bomber in world history," responded with intensified air attacks. In a dramatic departure called "Operation Linebacker" (the President was a devoted football fan), American planes bombed and sowed mines in the vital North Vietnam ports. Lyndon Johnson had refused to mine the ports; he feared Russian and Chinese ships would be hit and the war escalated to a big-power crisis.

Nixon, however, believed he had to show American toughness as American troops left Vietnam and the presidential campaign approached. "Look," Kissinger later explained, "it wasn't just a matter of this summit—his political ass was on the line." Kissinger talked tough with the Soviets. Although the war destroyed Johnson, he informed them, "Nixon will not permit three Presidents in a row to leave office under abnormal circumstances."[26] Then he tossed in the bait. Politics and economics had always been closely related in Russian-American relations, Kissinger noted. If the Soviets wanted economic help, they must cooperate politically. This "linkage" was a key to the summit's success.

Nixon calculated correctly. Regardless of events in Vietnam, the Soviets wanted to negotiate. Their readiness had been announced at the Twenty-fourth Party Congress in 1971 when Brezhnev presented a "peace program" that shaped Soviet views, especially détente policy, through the 1970s. Brezhnev's 1971 program rested on four legs, but only one of these was strong.

The strong leg was the military. In his era, Khrushchev had tried to expand Soviet influence primarily through Russian economic successes and taking advantage of revolutionary situations in newly emerging areas. The plodding Brezhnev held no such illusions; the economy was in trouble and most revolutionaries mistrusted heavy-handed Russians. Brezhnev instead placed his faith in a large buildup of military power. He increased defense budgets at a steady 3 percent annually (while the United States cut its post-Vietnam military) and drafted every able male at the age of seventeen for two-year active service and reserve service until the age of fifty. A force of 5 million stood at the ready. Brezhnev planned to wield it

[26]William Safire, *Before the Fall* (Garden City, New York, 1975), pp. 434–436, 452.

as a diplomatic weapon to obtain political dividends, especially in negotiations with the United States. Americans now had to deal with him as an equal superpower. For his part, he badly needed their help to prop up the other three, weaker, legs.[27]

One was Eastern Europe. Despite the Czech tragedy of 1968, the satellite states, particularly Rumania and Poland, slowly evolved national policies that did not fit the Russian model. The area was in a greater state of flux, and being more drawn to the booming Western economies, than Moscow desired. In a crisis the bloc could be controlled by force; that was one reason for the Russian military buildup. But the army could not resolve the deeper problems. In 1971 Brezhnev therefore made a deal in which the West Germans finally recognized the Eastern European boundaries imposed by the Red Army in 1945; in return, he settled the long-festering Berlin question by guaranteeing Western access to the city. He now wanted Nixon to agree to that arrangement and thereby further stabilize the weak leg.

The second wobbly leg was Sino-Soviet relations. This problem was indeed so dangerous that it provided a central reason for the military's expansion. The fear of "encirclement" that had haunted earlier Soviet leaders now reappeared, especially after the Chinese opened talks with Japan and the United States. Brezhnev designed his détente policy in part to ensure that it would remain in Nixon's interest to deal with him instead of moving closer to Mao.

The leg that needed the most support was the Soviet economy. The five-year plan of 1966–1970 had failed to reach its objectives. Despite, or because of, decades of coercion, Russian farm workers were only one-sixth as productive as the Americans. Brezhnev wanted United States technology and agricultural products. A mammoth wheat deal, part of a larger trade agreement worked out at the summit, nearly doubled Soviet-American trade. Unfortunately, the Russian negotiators outfoxed their capitalist counterparts, bought the wheat at bargain-basement prices, and helped create a grain shortage in the United States that worsened inflation. To Nixon and Kissinger, however, the "Great Grain Robbery" was a cheap price to pay. They opened new markets for American farmers while reaping diplomatic benefits.

[27]Helmut Sonnenfeldt and William G. Hyland, *Soviet Perspectives on Security* (London, 1979), pp. 16–18; Robin Edmunds, *Soviet Foreign Policy, 1962–1973* (London, 1975), chapters 8, 9.

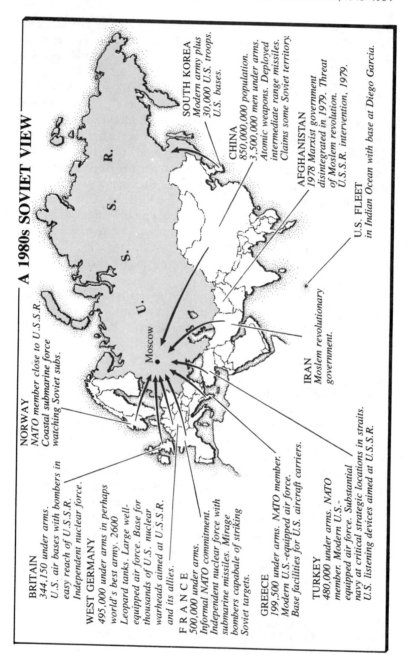

A 1980s SOVIET VIEW

NORWAY
NATO member close to U.S.S.R. Coastal submarine force watching Soviet subs.

BRITAIN
344,150 under arms. U.S. air bases with bombers in easy reach of U.S.S.R. Independent nuclear force.

WEST GERMANY
495,000 under arms in perhaps world's best army. 2600 Leopard tanks. Large well-equipped air force. Base for thousands of U.S. nuclear warheads aimed at U.S.S.R. and its allies.

F R A N C E
500,000 under arms. Informal NATO commitment. Independent nuclear force with submarine missiles. Mirage bombers capable of striking Soviet targets.

GREECE
199,500 under arms. NATO member. Modern U.S.-equipped air force. Base facilities for U.S. aircraft carriers.

TURKEY
480,000 under arms. NATO member. Modern U.S.-equipped air force. Substantial navy at critical strategic locations in straits. U.S. listening devices aimed at U.S.S.R.

SOUTH KOREA
Modern army plus 30,000 U.S. troops. U.S. bases.

CHINA
850,000,000 population. 3,500,000 men under arms. Atomic weapons. Deployed intermediate range missiles. Claims some Soviet territory.

AFGHANISTAN
1978 Marxist government disintegrated in 1979. Threat of Moslem revolution. U.S.S.R. intervention, 1979.

U.S. FLEET
in Indian Ocean with base at Diego Garcia.

IRAN
Moslem revolutionary government.

Moscow

Given, therefore, the economic problems of both nations, and their need to bring spreading military commitments under some control, Brezhnev as well as Nixon designed a détente policy. The two leaders signed a Strategic Arms Limitation Treaty (SALT I). The pact ended the race to develop a defensive antiballistic missile system (ABMs) that promised to be enormously expensive and highly ineffective. SALT I also froze the number of nuclear missiles so the Soviets had no more than 1600 and the United States 1054. Those numbers, however, deceived. For the United States had developed a new monster weapon, the MIRV (multiple independently targeted reentry vehicle) that contained — on one missile — multiple warheads capable of hitting widely separated areas. With the MIRV, Americans enjoyed a 2 to 1 lead in deliverable warheads — another good reason why Brezhnev wanted an agreement that limited the number of missiles. One American submarine possessing MIRVs was capable of inflicting 160 Hiroshima blasts. The United States had over thirty such subs. The Soviets moved rapidly to deploy their first MIRV in the mid-1970s. SALT I therefore only placed a few limits on, but did not stop, the arms race.

The summit was a triumph for both Brezhnev and Nixon. The Russian leader successfully carried out his détente program announced at the Party Congress. In Vietnam the communist offensive ground to a halt; the Chinese and Russians did little publicly to retaliate for the United States bombing and mining. Nixon's policy had worked.

During the 1972 campaign, the Democratic nominee, Senator George McGovern of South Dakota, never had a chance. His left-of-center politics alienated many Americans and left him open to the unfair Republican charge that McGovern was the champion of "amnesty [for men who had illegally avoided the draft], acid, and abortion." He presented a carefully prepared foreign policy program that urged an immediate withdrawal from Vietnam and a sharply reduced defense budget. But McGovern could not stir up a debate. As Nixon isolated himself in the White House, Republicans accused McGovern of following an "isolationist" foreign policy. When the Democratic nominee pointed to the Watergate break-in and claimed the Nixon administration was the most politically corrupt regime in American history, the voters were unmoved. Playwright Arthur Miller observed that Americans tend to respond to calls for righteousness when they think it is also a call for lunch.

The President won reelection by the second largest electoral vote margin in twentieth-century American history.

Kissinger enhanced the margin by announcing just days before the voting that "peace is at hand" in Vietnam. The celebration, however, proved premature. Kissinger had reached agreement with the communists, but he could not convince South Vietnam's President Nguyen Van Thieu to accept terms that allowed large numbers of communist troops to remain in South Vietnam. The deal collapsed. After the election Nixon began the most devastating bombing attack yet launched on North Vietnam. Parts of the country were carpet bombed. Congress watched, nearly 60 percent of Americans polled supported this "Christmas bombing," and no one stopped the President. As one journalist recorded Nixon's private conversation, he "did not care if the whole world thought he was crazy for resuming the bombing," for "the Russians and Chinese might think they were dealing with a madman and so better force North Vietnam into a settlement before the world was consumed in a larger war."[28]

Tragically, however, it was South Vietnam that held up a peace treaty. Nixon finally won Thieu's agreement with huge amounts of supplies and a secret letter assuring Thieu that if he would "go with us, you have my assurance of continued assistance in the post-settlement period and that we will respond with full force should the settlement be violated by North Vietnam."[29] So assured, Thieu agreed. The treaty was signed in February 1973. American prisoners of war returned home. The United States had terminated its longest conflict.

Nixon stood unchallenged at the peak of his power. Free of the Vietnam quicksands, and with the Russians apparently better "managed" by détente and linkage, the President turned to other foreign policy problems. Kissinger grandly announced that 1973 was to be the "year of Europe"—that is, the United States would now deal with the increasingly bitter Western European Allies to whom it had paid little attention while making momentous deals with China and Russia. Critics, who believed the Western alliance was beyond repair, remarked that Kissinger's phrase resembled the words of a long unfaithful husband who grandly announced this was to be the "year of the wife."

[28]Thomas L. Hughes, "Foreign Policy: Men or Measures?" *Atlantic Monthly*, CCXXXIV (October 1974): 56; Seymour Hersh, *The Price of Power* (New York, 1983), ch. 39.
[29]*The New York Times*, May 1, 1975, p. 16.

In the Western Hemisphere, Nixon dealt with the Chilean government of Salvador Allende, a devoted nationalist and sometime Marxist who, since his election to the presidency in 1970, had moved to break Chile free from its dependence on large landowners and American multinational corporations (see map, p. 210). Allende nationalized nearly $1 billion of American investment. At least one multinational, International Telephone and Telegraph (ITT), urged Nixon to get tough. The President did so, but not primarily because of ITT. He and Kissinger viewed Allende's Chile as a potential Soviet satellite, a second Cuba, whose infection could spread through the hemisphere and demonstrate that Nixon was too weak to secure his own backyard. With the help of the CIA and close ties between the United States and Chilean military, Kissinger systematically undermined the Chilean government. Allende lost control of his nation's economy. "We set the limits of diversity," Kissinger bragged, and in September 1973 Allende died as Chile's army seized power. The military established a brutally repressive regime. When the United States ambassador protested the torture methods, Kissinger ordered him "to cut out the political science lectures."[30]

Nixon also moved to control, or intimidate, key parts of the federal government. He gained some of this power through illegal wiretapping, breaking and entering, and misusing campaign funds. Kissinger passed all this off with the joking comment, "The illegal we do immediately; the unconstitutional takes a little longer." But a fundamental question remained: Could American foreign policy be drastically changed, and a public consensus built to support new policies, without an Imperial Presidency that distorted the truth and manipulated the people? The Nixon presidency did not provide a happy answer to that fundamental question. Even Kissinger was apparently not safe. The daring diplomat, winner of a Nobel Peace Prize for his role in ending the Vietnam War, the man with the German accent and gravylike voice — "Superkraut" as he was happy to be called — was popular and powerful. Rumors spread in Washington that a jealous President was prepared to fire Kissinger. Then in mid-1973 Congress began hearings on the Watergate break-in of 1972. Nixon's political career and American foreign policy suddenly changed. A new era was about to begin.

[30]Roger Morris, *Uncertain Greatness* (New York, 1977), p. 241; *The New York Times*, March 6, 1975. p. C37.

The most dramatic event in this new era occurred when Richard Nixon became the first American President to resign from office. That historic turn had begun when he tried to cover up the break-in by his Plumbers unit at the Watergate hotel complex in 1972. But his foreign policy also hastened his exit. In 1973 Congress and public opinion so turned against his brutal bombing of Southeast Asia that the House and Senate finally ordered an end to the attacks.[31] Resembling other Presidents, before and after, who found themselves becoming mired in political trouble at home, Nixon tried to save himself with foreign policy spectaculars. Instead of firing the popular Kissinger as he had planned, the President named him secretary of state in the autumn of 1973. The two men then flew to Moscow for another highly publicized summit meeting. But it was too late; the House prepared impeachment articles, Nixon grew increasingly unstable and, since his finger remained on the nuclear button, increasingly dangerous. In August 1974 his aides and several Republican leaders convinced him to resign.

The Imperial Presidency had collapsed. In its place arose what some worried observers called an Imperial Congress. The legislature had repealed the Gulf of Tonkin Resolution in 1971, and by 1974 it had passed measures preventing American troops from reentering Vietnam. The House and Senate similarly outlawed military involvement in parts of Africa without their explicit consent. In 1974-1975 the Senate struck at the heart of Kissinger's détente policy by attaching conditions to the Soviet-American trade treaty that made the pact unacceptable to the Soviets. (These conditions included the widely discussed Jackson-Vanik amendment demanding that Moscow allow more Jewish dissidents to leave Russia if they wished, and — more important from the Soviet view — a Stevenson amendment sharply limiting the amount of money the stumbling Russian economy could borrow from the United States.[32])

Apart from these riflelike limitations, Congress used a political shotgun in its attack on presidential powers. The War Powers Act of 1973 required that "in every possible instance" the President must consult with Congress before sending troops into hostilities; when

[31] McGeorge Bundy, "Vietnam, Watergate and Presidential Powers," *Foreign Affairs*, LXVIII (Winter 1979-1980): 397-404.

[32] *Congressional Record*, July 26, 1978, p. S11874; Robert Bernstein, "Human Rights and the U.S.-U.S.S.R. Trade Crisis of 1972-1974: Another View," unpublished paper, 1978.

the President commits the forces, he must send a full explanation to Congress within two days and he must withdraw the forces within sixty days unless Congress expressly gives him permission to keep them in battle. The act, in reality, gives the President the power to wage war for sixty days without congressional approval, a power that the founders wisely did not give the chief executive in 1787. Congress hoped, however, that the law could prevent future Vietnams.

Kissinger was furious. He warned that perhaps Congress could deal with domestic issues but, because of its supersensitivity to public opinion and interest groups, it was not designed to carry out long-term foreign policies. When his plans for Vietnam and Africa failed during 1975–1976, the secretary of state blamed Congress and the effects of Watergate. He apparently did not understand that his and Nixon's foreign policies in Southeast Asia between 1969 and 1973 had caused congressional anger and the Watergate scandal (see p. 263). He also failed to understand that by the mid-1970s congressional authority grew precisely because of legislative power in domestic affairs, for domestic and foreign policies were becoming one.

That intimate relationship became dramatically clear in 1973–1974 when Americans found themselves short of gasoline at home because of a war in the Middle East. An Arab-Israeli clash was, as usual, the eye of the conflict. After the Suez crisis of 1956, the Soviets had rebuilt the Egyptian Army while the United States helped make Israel the most powerful military force in the area. In 1967 the Egyptians threatened the Gulf of Aqaba, the entranceway to Israel's key southern port of Elath. On June 5 Israel suddenly struck. In a six-day war the Israelis drove the Egyptians back across the Suez, the Jordanian Army across the Jordan River, and the Syrians away from the strategic Golan Heights. Israel seized the old city of Jerusalem.

The United States and Russia did not intervene, but within months each helped replace its ally's stores. As the Soviets established port bases in Egypt, a confrontation loomed between the two superpowers. The new Egyptian president, Anwar el-Sadat, proposed negotiations, but only after Israel withdrew from lands taken in 1967. The Israelis, after having paid a heavy toll for their withdrawal from the Sinai peninsula following the 1956 war, refused Sadat's conditions and rejected United States pressure to withdraw from all occupied territories. In October 1973, on Yom Kippur, the holiest day in the Jewish calendar, the Egyptians and Syrians launched

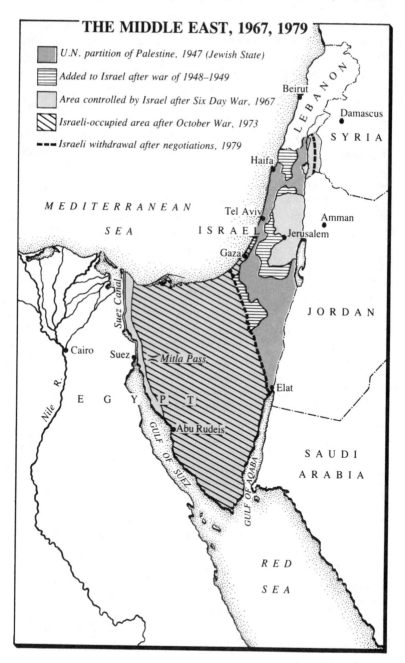

THE MIDDLE EAST, 1967, 1979

U.N. partition of Palestine, 1947 (Jewish State)

Added to Israel after war of 1948–1949

Area controlled by Israel after Six Day War, 1967

Israeli-occupied area after October War, 1973

Israeli withdrawal after negotiations, 1979

a sudden attack that drove the Israeli Army back in a surprising show of strength. The shocked Israelis counterattacked, surrounded the Egyptian Army in the Sinai, and threatened to open all of Egypt to invasion. Sadat appealed to Brezhnev. The Soviets mobilized troops for an airlift into the Middle East.

Kissinger and Nixon warned Brezhnev to stay out of the area. They emphasized their warning by putting the nation's nuclear strike forces on alert. But the Americans also offered the olive branch. They demanded an Israeli cease-fire and the supplying of the surrounded Egyptian forces. Kissinger held back military supplies needed by Israel until it agreed with his demands. With fresh support from Sadat, who had expelled all Soviet military advisors from Egypt when they seemed to threaten his own power, Kissinger began a series of trips among Middle East capitals to work out a settlement. Despite two years of exhaustive efforts (his plane was tabbed the "Yo-Yo express" because it went up and down so often), the secretary of state worked out a cease-fire but could not find the key to a full settlement.

His diplomacy focused on two objectives. He wanted peace, but without Soviet participation. Resembling the nineteenth-century British statesmen he had studied as a historian, and also resembling Acheson and Dulles, Kissinger determined not to allow Russian strength to shape affairs in the Middle East. He also sought to end the danger that the Arabs might try to blackmail the West. This nearly occurred in 1973. When the United States supplied weapons to Israel, using NATO bases in Western Europe as transport points, the Arab-dominated Organization of Petroleum Exporting Countries (OPEC) imposed an oil embargo that threatened to strangle the Western and Japanese economies.

OPEC consisted of thirteen nations, including seven Arab countries, Iran, and Venezuela. It had been formed in 1960 to protest attempts of major oil companies (mostly owned by Americans, British, and Dutch) to reduce oil prices and payments to the producers. By the early 1970s the great international companies suddenly faced a unified bloc of producers. OPEC forced the companies to increase payments drastically, quadrupled the price of oil by 1974 to nearly $12 for a forty-two-gallon barrel, threatened nationalization of the companies' properties, and firmly believed that "we are the Masters."[33] Amidst a sudden energy crisis, New York Stock Exchange shares lost $97 billion in value in six weeks.

[33]Gurney Breckenfeld, "How the Arabs Changed the Oil Business," *Fortune* LXXXV (August 1971): 113–117.

Japan and Western Europe began switching from pro-Israeli to pro-Arab policies. This change further strained the alliance system, for the United States, which imported only 12 percent of its oil from the Middle East (compared with 80 percent for the Europeans and over 90 percent for Japan), remained staunchly committed to Israel. As the Allies changed, Kissinger bitterly commented that they were "craven" and "contemptible."[34] Not only had hopes for the "year of Europe" turned to ashes, but he believed that Western Europe had become his "deepest problem."

The energy crisis would have occurred in the not distant future regardless of the Arab-Israeli conflict. Between 1945 and the late 1970s, the West and Japan consumed more oil and minerals than had been used in all previous recorded history. With 6 percent of the world's population, the United States used nearly 40 percent of that wealth.[35] The West could not continue to increase its energy use 5 percent annually, pay low oil prices, yet sell inflation-priced goods to the petroleum producers. This was emphasized by the shah of Iran, whose nation was the world's second-largest oil exporter, and who was Washington's most trusted Middle East friend, according to the Nixon Doctrine. "Of course [the price of oil] is going to rise," the shah declared. "Certainly! and how! . . . You [Westerners] increased the price of wheat you sell us by 300%, and the same for sugar and cement. . . . You buy our crude oil and sell it back to us, refined as petrochemicals, at a hundred times the price you've paid to us. . . . It's only fair that, from now on, you should pay more for oil. Let's say . . . 10 times more."[36]

The Nixon-Kissinger policies were falling apart. They had focused on Russia and China, but the challenge now came from the Third World. American power was even under attack in Latin America, an area Kissinger had supposedly once dismissed as "a dagger pointed at the heart of — Antarctica." The Republicans devised no alternative to the moribund Alliance for Progress. As terrorism and guerrilla activities increased, Nixon's only major response was to propose doubling the amount of military arms sold

[34] *Washington Post*, March 17, 1974, p. A12.

[35] Richard Barnet, "The World's Resources," *The New Yorker*, April 23, 1980, pp. 45, 47; *Washington Post*, February 24, 1975, p. 1.

[36] *The New York Times*, December 12, 1973, p. 64; for the background, James E. Akins, "The Oil Crisis: This Time the Wolf Is Here," *Foreign Affairs*, LI (April 1973): 470–472.

by the United States and, in Chile, helping a military regime replace Allende. But Allende's overthrow did not remove a more fundamental danger. In 1975 the secretary of state worried that Latin Americans and other newly emerging nations were "tending to form a rigid bloc of their own," a development "particularly inappropriate for the Western Hemisphere."[37] Again his big-power diplomacy was being undercut by the Third World. Again the energy crisis made the challenge possible, for the Latin American bloc was organized and financed in large part by Venezuela and its oil revenues, which quintupled between 1970 and 1975. A similar danger appeared to the north. Canada's television, periodicals, banks, and half its industry were dominated by the United States. Canadians began playing their own balance-of-power game. Trade was opened with China. Pierre Trudeau became the first Canadian prime minister to travel in the Soviet Union, signing consultation and trade pacts with the Russians. In 1973 strict controls were placed on foreign investments for the first time. During the 1970s exports of Canadian oil and natural gas, upon which large sectors of the United States depended, rose dramatically in price, and then exports were cut back so Canadians themselves could be assured of long-term cheap energy. While Kissinger searched for new relations with the four major blocs, hemispheric unity, which Americans tended to take for granted, fragmented.

In the Western Hemisphere and Middle East, United States officials could at least be relieved that the Soviets were not directly involved in the new developments and did not immediately profit from the American troubles. In Africa, however, the superpowers nearly confronted each other in a crisis that typified the new Cold War that was developing in the 1970s.

Since 1970, Kissinger had assumed that the Portuguese, through their colony in Angola, would help maintain stability in Africa.[38] In 1974, however, the forty-year dictatorship in Portugal fell. Angola became independent and black revolutionaries vied for power. The Americans and Chinese supplied one faction, while the Soviets backed the group that ultimately won, the Popular Movement for the Liberation of Angola (MPLA). Most startling of all, the

[37]*Department of State Bulletin,* March 24, 1975, pp. 365–366.
[38]The best background and the key document are in Mohamed A. El-Khawas and Barry Cohen, eds., *NSSM 39: The Kissinger Study of Southern Africa* (Westport, Connecticut, 1976).

Russians flew thousands of Cuban troops into Angola in a move that Kissinger condemned as a dangerous escalation of the Cold War. He asked Congress for massive aid to stop this Soviet aggression "by proxy," but the legislators flatly refused to become immersed in a possible Vietnam-like conflict in Africa. The MPLA triumphed and then, in a wondrous turn of events, used the Cuban troops to protect the American-owned Gulf Oil refinery (one of the nation's most important facilities) and turned increasingly to Washington for technological help. Both superpowers were learning how little Africans cared about a Cold War that seemed to obsess some Americans and Russians.

But Kissinger did not draw that lesson. He believed that Americans, especially the young who "have been traumatized by Vietnam as we were by Munich," lacked the will to stand up to the Soviets.[39] His concern increased in 1974–1975, when the United States sunk into its worst economic recession since the 1930s. He had hoped to use the nation's economic power to "manage" the Russians. Congress, however, had already undercut the 1972 trade treaty, and in 1975, when Kissinger tried to use an embargo on wheat exports as a weapon to make the Soviets behave in Africa, a tremendous uproar of protest from American farm communities forced him to back down. He reflected on how difficult it was for policy makers to protect what they considered to be the national interest, when that job had to be done in a private enterprise economy.[40]

American foreign policy improved little after Gerald Ford replaced Nixon in August 1974. Appointed by Nixon to be Vice President after Spiro Agnew had to resign for taking illegal payments, Ford had been a leader in the House of Representatives. But he had little personal prestige and no background in foreign policy. When he made a serious error while discussing the Middle East, one journalist passed it off: "What the hell, it was just Jerry talking about things he doesn't understand."[41]

---

[39]Speech of April 17, 1975, *Department of State Bulletin*, May 5, 1975, p. 560.

[40]Remarks in Los Angeles, February 2, 1976, *Department of State Bulletin*, March 1, 1976, p. 272.

[41]Richard Reeves, *A Ford Not a Lincoln* (New York, 1975), pp. 174, 181, 200.

Ford became President as Vietnam was finally falling to the communists. The agreement that Kissinger negotiated in 1973 with North and South Vietnam had never worked. President Thieu attacked the communists emplaced in South Vietnam, and in late 1973 they began retaliating. Thieu's forces lost more soldiers in 1974 than during the height of the fighting in 1967. At the same time a recession-ridden United States cut its aid from $1 billion to $700 million. In early 1975 the South Vietnamese Army began to disintegrate. Thieu called for President Ford to provide the American "full force" promised by Nixon in 1973. But Nixon's 1973 promise was of no effect. He and Kissinger had not made the letter public (indeed, Kissinger publicly denied in 1973 that any secret understandings existed), and Congress had prohibited the reintroduction of American forces in Vietnam. In April 1975 South Vietnam fell into communist hands. The thirty-year war was over.

Kissinger asked Americans to put Vietnam behind them — a strange request coming from a former history professor, for the lessons to be learned were many and critical. The war demonstrated that militarily the United States could not single-handedly defeat nationalist movements in Asia. Nor did it have the economic and social resources to fight such a long, inconclusive war. The United States bore great responsibility for the downfall of South Vietnam. The involvement was not comparable to American responsibility for China in the 1940s. The governments of both South Vietnam and Cambodia were Washington's creations. Both depended upon the United States for their existence. Both collapsed after the American forces withdrew. In this sense, the "domino theory" actually worked. (Dominoes is a game in which the pieces are laid flat. It requires special effort outside the rules to set them upright so they can collapse.) American Presidents, supported in the early years by Congress and public opinion, made a mighty effort to prop up the dominoes in Southeast Asia, and the collapse duly occurred.

Ford and Kissinger tried to reinvigorate foreign policy (and Ford's hopes for the 1976 presidential race) with two dramatic acts. They traveled to Russia in late 1974 and agreed with Brezhnev on the outline for a SALT II agreement that set new limits on nuclear arms. The other drama occurred in May 1975, when Cambodian naval units seized an American cargo ship, the *Mayaguez*. The seizure occurred just after Vietnam fell, OPEC had quadrupled oil prices without an American response, and Kissinger had been unable to stop the MPLA in Angola. In this political climate, Ford, with Kissinger's strong encouragement, did what Presidents have often done in similar situations: he used military force to show that he was decisive and not afraid to get tough with communists. Unknown to Ford, however, the Cambodian government had released the thirty-eight crew members. Forty American troops were killed in a needless raid on Cambodian territory. Public opinion polls nevertheless showed strong support for the President's use of military force.

The *Mayaguez* "rescue" and the arms agreement were not enough to save Ford's campaign in 1976. Indeed, Kissinger's foreign policy became an issue. Right-wing Republicans attacked détente until Ford outlawed using the word in his speeches. Kissinger remarked that détente "is a word I would like to forget."[42] Soviet activities in Angola and Cuba, and continued repression of dissidents within Russia, had soured many Americans on the idea that détente could work. Meanwhile, the Democratic nominee, Jimmy Carter, hit Kissinger from the liberal side for being too secretive, supporting dictatorial regimes, and arguing for higher defense budgets. In a style that was typical of Carter, he then blasted the administration from the other direction for giving away too much in the arms talks, and especially for Kissinger's work in the 1975 Helsinki agreements. At Helsinki, Finland, thirty-five countries, including the Western nations, accepted the East European boundaries as permanent; in return, the Soviets pledged to follow a more liberal human rights policy. Carter condemned the deal for not doing enough to protect individual liberties inside Russia.[43]

The Democratic candidate took different sides on so many issues that unfriendly critics charged that Carter's image could never be carved in stone on Mount Rushmore because there was room on the monument for only one face. But his tactics worked. He lost most of his 30 percent lead over Ford in polls taken during late summer but held on to win by a slim popular vote.

Carter's triumph brought a remarkable decade to an end. Between 1966 and 1976 Americans had roller-coasted from heights to depths: from near victory in Vietnam to embarrassing defeat; from

---

[42] *Department of State Bulletin,* December 1, 1975, p. 767.

[43] Henry A. Plotkin, "Issues in the 1976 Campaign." In Gerald Pomper, ed., *The Election of 1976* (New York, 1977), pp. 50–52.

a powerhouse economy to a thieflike inflation; from an Imperial Presidency to the presidential humiliation of Watergate and the War Powers Act; from cheap gasoline to bending before demands of OPEC oil producers; from condemning Chinese communism to cooperation with it; and, most important, from détente to increasing confrontation with the Soviet Union. United States power to deal with the new post-1960s world had dwindled, but frustrated Americans decided that "managing" the Soviets through détente had been a failure. The question now became whether a better approach could be devised. Jimmy Carter and Ronald Reagan were to give quite different answers to that question.

12

Carter, Reagan, and a New Cold War (1977-1984)

In the late 1970s Americans finally emerged from the crises of Vietnam and Watergate only to confront a new Cold War. It was a conflict more dangerous and unmanageable than anything they had faced before. In the old Cold War Americans had enjoyed superior nuclear force, an unchallenged economy, strong alliances, and a trusted Imperial President to direct this incredible power against the Soviets. In the new Cold War, however, Russian forces achieved nuclear equality. Each side could only plan to destroy the other many times; the plan involved a military doctrine known as Mutual Assured Destruction, or MAD. The United States economy reigned supreme, but in such key areas as steel, automobiles, and textiles it no longer could compete in world markets. It certainly could no longer bear the crushing burden of satisfying Americans' demands to be both the globe's greatest consumers and its unquestioned policeman. Meanwhile, the alliance system further cracked and the Imperial Presidency was overthrown. In the 1980s, Ronald Reagan would move to solve these challenges by trying to roll back time to recapture the happier days of the old Cold War. But first, Jimmy Carter, after much indecision and confusion, launched policies that prepared the way for Reagan.

As a little-known Georgia governor in 1973, Carter appeared on the television show "What's My Line?" and none of the panelists could guess who he was or what he did. Three years later Carter turned this anonymity into a political weapon. He ran against the Washington scandals by emphasizing he had never been associated with the capital's politics. Carter instead stressed his decency and religious beliefs, and promised, "I'll never tell you a lie." He was also a tough politician. The two sides of his character, the realistic politico and the caring Christian, combined in his appraisal of Nixon: "I despise the bastard, but I pray that he will find peace."[1]

The 1976 election produced no clear foreign policy mandate. Carter often refused to take clear positions. Working both sides of the political street, he evoked the name of a famous Southern conservative when he described himself as "a Populist in the tradition of Richard Russell." (One observer commented that made as much sense as saying he was "a socialist in the tradition of Herbert Hoover."[2]) With such wordplay, Carter received strong support from independents as well as regular Democrats, who applauded his fight against the Washington "establishment." Independents could recall the words of Carter's top aide, Hamilton Jordan: "If, after the inauguration, you find a Cy Vance as Secretary of State and Zbigniew Brzezinski as head of National Security [Council], then I would say we failed. And I'd quit. . . . You're going to see new faces, new ideas." Vance and Brzezinski, deeply rooted in the "establishment," became secretary of state and national security advisor respectively. Jordan did not resign.

Carter's foreign policy quickly became confused as Brzezinski and Vance clashed. Brzezinski saw the world more in bipolar terms and believed the Soviets posed immediate global dangers. An immigrant and the son of a Polish diplomat, Brzezinski had taught at Columbia University, where he wrote many books on communist systems. A fellow White House official only half-joked that Brzezinski enjoyed being "the first Pole in 300 years in a position to really stick it to the Russians." He had condemned the détente policies of Kissinger, a person with whom he had competed professionally since the early 1950s. Brzezinski both urged the "independence" of

---

[1] James Wooten, *Dasher* (New York, 1978), pp. 33–37.

[2] C. Vann Woodward, "The Best?" *The New York Review of Books,* April 3, 1980, pp. 10–11.

such bloc states as Rumania and criticized the SALT deals, especially if the Russians did not then behave in Africa or the Middle East. He refused, moreover, to believe "that the use of nuclear weapons would be the end of the human race. . . . That's egocentric."[3] (His view had its counterpart in official Soviet military doctrine that Russia could survive a nuclear exchange and, therefore, that blueprints for such an exchange be part of overall military planning.[4]) A close friend since 1972, Carter called Brzezinski "my teacher" in foreign policy. Brzezinski explained the closeness by referring to a passage in *Sophie's Choice*, in which the author, William Styron, "describes a surprising affinity between Poland and the South, two peoples bred on a history that overcame defeat, on a code of chivalry and honor that proudly compensated for backwardness."[5]

Vance, on the other hand, accepted the views of Marshall Shulman, his chief advisor on Soviet affairs and also a former Columbia professor who had been debating Brzezinski for a quarter-century. Vance and Shulman believed that peace rested on negotiations and economic ties between the superpowers—not, as Brzezinski argued, by viewing any crisis anywhere in the world as a Soviet challenge. Unlike Brzezinski, Vance and Shulman saw SALT II as the central diplomatic issue and believed that no problem, even Russian aggressiveness in the Middle East, should be allowed to endanger arms talks. Shulman hoped to influence Soviet behavior through "soft linkage," saying quietly to Moscow officials that they had a greater chance of receiving badly needed American economic help if they better observed human rights within their country and peace elsewhere. Shulman's hope rested on those Russians he called "within-the-system modernizers," that is, young and middle-aged technicians and professionals who would work with the West to improve Soviet society. He saw the modernizers as a check on the older, neo-Stalinist factions, but Shulman understood that time and not a few funerals were required first. Vance and Shulman would never be given that time.

[3] Elizabeth Drew, "Brzezinski," *The New Yorker*, May 1, 1978, p. 126; *Washington Post*, February 18, 1979, p. C4; *Washington Post*, February 5, 1977, p. A10.

[4] Harriett Fast Scott and William F. Scott, *The Armed Forces of the U.S.S.R.* (Boulder, Colorado, 1979), pp. 44–45, 52–62.

[5] Zbigniew Brzezinski, *Power and Principle: Memoirs of the National Security Adviser, 1977–1981* (New York, 1983), pp. 20–21.

If trouble developed in the newly emerging nations, Vance and Shulman, unlike Brzezinski, believed it could usually be handled as a problem of new nationalisms, not a superpower confrontation. Their view received strong support from Andrew Young, the United States ambassador to the United Nations. Young believed profitable political and economic cooperation would develop between the United States and the newly emerging peoples, if they could be kept clear of great power conflicts. He later proved his point with major diplomatic successes in Zimbabwe and Nigeria. Finally, Vance and Shulman differed from Brzezinski in believing that Eastern European changes had to occur slowly. They believed that any rapid development of independent policies could produce a rerun of the 1968 Czech tragedy.

Between these two different views stood the final decision maker. President Carter clearly wanted to hear conflicting advice, but he had to choose among these complex alternatives without having any significant personal foreign policy background. Between 1973 and 1976 he had been the token Southern politician on the Trilateral Commission, a private group of Americans, Western Europeans, and Japanese that Brzezinski and banker David Rockefeller organized to discuss the mushrooming problems of industrial nations. A number of Trilateralists (including Vance and Young) joined the Carter team, but the commission seldom agreed on common policy. One member dismissed his colleagues as mere "boosters," "a bunch of very sophisticated Rotarians."[6] Even Brzezinski, a founder, grew disillusioned. By 1975 he had concluded that resolving the industrial world's problems was less important (and obviously more difficult) than facing up to the Soviets.

Carter learned no useful framework for a consistent foreign policy from the Trilateralists, and he was unable to devise such a framework himself. A trained engineer, he studied problems case by case, "like an engineering student thinking you can cram for the exam and get an A," as one official remarked. He had little historical knowledge and hence little sense of how to construct a comprehensive strategy. Carter admitted in 1979 that he had read more history since entering the White House than in all the rest of his life.[7] Sometimes he simply split the difference. When Vance and Brzezinski

[6]*Washington Post*, January 16, 1977, p. A4.
[7]Interview by Don Oberdorfer, *Washington Post*, February 18, 1979, p. C4.

sent him quite different policy memoranda for an address on Soviet policy, Carter solved the problem by stapling the two memos together as the basis for his speech.[8]

Such an approach had worked with American voters, but it quickly failed in the world of United States foreign policy. Carter, for example, declared that his commitment to human rights was "absolute." In 1977 he openly encouraged Russian dissidents, who demanded more political freedoms. The gesture infuriated Brezhnev. The dissidents suffered under new crackdowns. Because Carter was simultaneously trying to negotiate arms reductions with them, the Russians speculated that his human rights policy was a mere "bargaining chip" to trade. In reality, as Andrew Young admitted, the policy was never "thought out and planned," so it remained ineffective.[9] Carter's tough line, which included sharply reducing aid, did cause military regimes such as those in Brazil, Chile, and Argentina to act more decently. The oppressive South Korean government was more important to United States security, however, so it received fewer public lectures and more arms. When Carter urged China to ease its dictatorial immigration rules in the interest of human rights, Vice Premier Teng Hsiao-ping (Deng Xiaoping) smilingly responded that he would be glad to do so and "send you 10 million immigrants right away." Carter dropped the issue.[10] Soviets soon noted that he said little about the thousands of political prisoners in China, even as he condemned holding such prisoners in Russia. The most glaring and costly inconsistency occurred in Iran. SAVAK, the shah's secret police, tortured and imprisoned upward of 50,000 Iranians. But on New Year's Eve 1977, Carter visited Iran, a vital link in United States defense plans. He toasted the shah for making Iran "an island of stability" and for deserving "the respect and the admiration and love which your people give to you."[11] A year later a revolution drove the shah from power.

[8]James Fallows, "Zbig Without Cy," *New Republic*, May 10, 1980, p. 19.

[9]See especially Stephen F. Cohen's comments in *Détente or Debacle*, edited by Fred Warner Neal (New York, 1979); and Stephen F. Cohen, "Why Détente Can Work," *Inquiry*, December 19, 1977, p. 16; author's interview in Moscow, November 14, 1980.

[10]*Washington Post*, February 4, 1979, p. A10.

[11]*Public Papers of the Presidents . . . Jimmy Carter, 1977* (Washington, 1978), p. 2221.

Not all of the confusion was Carter's fault. At home he inherited a political structure that had historically depended on a strong party system. He had not helped by running against party leaders and the "establishment," but in any case the system was in an advanced stage of disintegration before he appeared on the national scene. Into the vacuum rushed hundreds of private groups, many representing a single interest (for example, doctors, used-car dealers, educators, pro- or anti-abortion advocates), whose members lobbied hard in Washington. No national consensus could be shaped out of these narrowly focused groups.[12] Special economic interests became ever more active as inflation skyrocketed to an annual rate of 13 percent in 1979–1980. In addition, OPEC nations tripled oil prices to nearly $35 a barrel, draining the United States of $100 billion each year without any effective response by the President or a fragmented Congress. Severe economic recession set in. Allied leaders grew disenchanted with such disarray in the nation that supposedly led the noncommunist world.

Despite these problems and a lack of conceptual planning, Carter did score diplomatic victories. He did so most notably when he followed the Vance-Shulman-Young approach. In 1978 the Senate ratified the President's treaty that returned the Canal Zone to Panama over the next twenty-two years while protecting the American right to use and defend the waterway (see map, p. 210). Since 1947 the Panamanians had frequently rioted against the American zone that divided their country. When both sides lost lives in a 1964 outbreak, Lyndon Johnson began a new relationship that would recognize Panama's sovereignty in the Canal Zone. It took fourteen years to complete the arduous process. The decisive Senate figures were the leaders, Democrat Robert Byrd of West Virginia and Republican Howard Baker of Tennessee, who amended the two treaties submitted by Carter to make them acceptable to Republicans. Byrd and Baker took high political risks in fighting such opponents as Republican Senator S. I. Hayakawa of California, who proudly noted how the United States had seized the canal region in 1903 and then claimed, "It's ours. We stole it fair and square." Carter and the Senate scored the most important advance in United States–Latin American relations since the 1930s.

[12]Theodore Lowi, *The End of Liberalism* (New York, 1979), pp. 50–61; Joel Silbey, "The End of American Politics, 1980–1984?" unpublished paper, 1980, pp. 8–10.

The President also followed Vance's suggestions about Africa, despite Soviet intervention and Brzezinski's opposition. When warfare erupted on a border between Zaire (a United States associate) and Angola (where Soviet advisors and 19,000 Cuban troops remained), Brzezinski urged direct involvement to teach the communists a lesson. Andrew Young urged instead that the United States help find "African solutions for African problems." Carter accepted Young's advice and the warfare subsided. The Soviets, however, did not show similar restraint. They intervened in the strategic Horn of Africa to aid Somalia, Sudan, and Ethiopia. But Somalia and Sudan soon threw out the Russians. Brezhnev and 15,000 Cuban troops then found themselves immersed in a costly, uncontrollable military campaign on behalf of Ethiopia. Until Young finally resigned as United Nations ambassador in 1979, his "cool" approach was effective in navigating the whirlpools of African nationalism.

A final Carter triumph occurred in the Middle East during September 1978. A year earlier Egyptian President Sadat had taken the historic step of personally flying to Israel to begin a peace process with Prime Minister Menachem Begin. Carter then invited the two leaders to his private retreat at Camp David, Maryland, where for thirteen nerve-wracking days he helped them hammer out an agreement that ended the thirty-year war between Israel and Egypt. The pact provided for Israeli withdrawal from the strategic Sinai peninsula, which had been Egypt's until the 1967 war. Carter helped ease Begin's acceptance with $3 billion of military aid. It was the Georgian's proudest moment as President.

From that point in September 1978, the Carter presidency began a long decline, pulled downward by internal divisions and uncontrollable external events. Soviet-American relations became the most important victim of the confusion. Even the Camp David agreement worsened relations, for in 1977 Carter and Brezhnev had issued a joint statement on the Middle East. The Russians made significant concessions in return for the President's assurance that they could help construct a Middle East peace. The Egyptians, Israelis, and powerful pro-Israeli lobbying groups in Washington loudly protested reintroducing Brezhnev's unsubtle hand in the region. Awestruck by the reaction, Carter simply "walked away from the statement," to use Brzezinski's words.[13] Infuriated Soviet leaders rushed more arms to friends in the region, including Syria, Israel's archenemy.

Perhaps the crucial turn in the superpowers' relationship, however, occurred in May 1978, when Brzezinski, over Vance's objections, flew to China and began the process that climaxed in the opening of formal diplomatic relations with China on New Year's Day in 1979. Brzezinski hoped to play this "China card" to trump Soviet policies in Africa and the Middle East, and on arms control. In Peking he enthusiastically engaged in a game with Chinese leaders to see who was most anti-Soviet. Brzezinski was "so overwhelmed with the Chinese," Carter recorded later, that "I told him he had been seduced."[14] It is not seduction, however, when one travels halfway around the world to propose. Brzezinski's courtship produced immediate results. United States exports to China nearly doubled in 1979; thus Americans scored against their Japanese rivals in the game to see which would develop the long-fabled China market. Coca-Cola (a Georgia-based firm close to Carter) later opened its first plant in China, with guests drinking "Ke Kou Ke Le" (translated as "Tasty Happiness") as Beethoven's "Ode to Joy" played in the background.[15] (Pepsi-Cola, whose officials were close to Nixon, had earlier obtained a monopoly on the Soviet soft-drink market.)

In reality, China played an "American card" even more effectively against the Russians. Peking leaders shrewdly timed the announcement of formal diplomatic ties with the United States so that it poisoned a meeting between Vance and the Soviets to discuss SALT II. The SALT process consequently was fatally delayed. Then China's powerful leader, Vice Premier Teng Hsiao-ping, visited the United States in early 1979. After his return home, he launched an invasion of Vietnam, Russia's ally in Southeast Asia. By his timing, Teng made it appear as if the United States was a silent partner in the invasion. Moscow, at least, must have thought of it as collusion by Russia's two leading enemies. In Washington, however, Carter had no firm idea of where he was heading. "All sweaty in his tennis

---

[13]Brzezinski, *Power and Principle*, p. 175.

[14]Jimmy Carter, *Keeping Faith: Memoirs of a President* (New York, 1982), p. 196.

[15]*The New York Times*, April 16, 1981, p. A3; U.S. Department of State, *Gist*, November 1979, p. 1.

outfit," the President's top aide, Hamilton Jordan, stopped in Brzezinski's office in mid-1978 to observe that Carter's new toughness against the Soviets was "all a big accident, and who the hell knows whether the President will not veer in some direction tomorrow."[16] In retrospect, mid-1978 marked a sharp turn in Soviet-American relations. Brzezinski's influence rose as Vance's fell, especially on Chinese affairs. The Soviets were locked out of the Camp David arrangements. Months later a high Chinese official captured the moment when, in splendid White House ceremonies, he praised Carter and Brzezinski, then turned to his translator and said publicly in Chinese, "I suppose I should also mention the Secretary of State; what's his name?"[17]

Brzezinski was amused by the incident; Brezhnev, no doubt, less so. Soviet leaders were still stunned by Nixon's resignation and the Senate's emasculation of the 1972 trade treaty that had undergirded détente. Carter was becoming a political bedfellow of the hated Chinese. Evictions from Egypt, Somalia, and Sudan were sharp setbacks for the Russians. Brezhnev nevertheless moved cautiously.[18] Scuttling détente could involve paying a high price, especially in the economic and military realms.

The Soviet economic system became less efficient as official communist ideology (that "fig-leaf" of the system, as Kennan had called it in 1947) withered. Few people still shared the old hope that other revolutions would follow the Soviet model. Nor did anyone believe that a utopian communist community was just over the horizon — unless, as a Russian joke put it, "you understand that an horizon is an imaginary line that recedes as you approach it." But the ideology could not be disavowed because, bankrupt or not, it legitimized the Communist party's monopoly on power. After 1971 Brezhnev had attempted to solve these complex problems with a dual approach: increasing trade with the West to invigorate the Soviet economy, but brutally treating dissidents (while allowing more Jews to emigrate to Israel) to ensure the party's control. By

---

[16]Brzezinski, *Power and Principle*, p. 222.

[17]Brzezinski, *Power and Principle*, p. 418.

[18]Paul Marantz, "Foreign Policy." In Alexander Dallin, ed., *The Twenty-Fifth Congress of the CPSU* (Stanford, California, 1977), pp. 89–90.

the late 1970s this policy had failed. The expected economic payoffs from détente never appeared.

The Soviet Union actually outpaced the United States in coal, steel, and cement production, and was the world's largest oil producer, but a disproportionate share of the wealth went to nonproductive military budgets or disappeared in the floundering Cuban or devastated Vietnam economies. With the world's largest area of tillable land, Russia could not feed its own population. Equally embarrassing to the communists, under 3 percent of the farm area was privately owned, but it contributed as much as 40 percent of the meat, dairy goods, and vegetables. As computers, electronic items, and other high-technology goods became crucial for highly industrialized societies, a system run by narrow party officials and fearful bureaucrats gave little encouragement to innovation. Projections indicated that Russia might even have to import oil by the mid-1980s unless it could buy massive American or Japanese technology to exploit new fields.

The outlook was bleak. Since 1945 the Soviets had tended to increase their gross national product not through innovation but simply by employing more laborers. In the 1970s, however, Soviet growth rates declined from 5 percent annually during Brezhnev's first years in power to 0.8 percent in 1979. A sharp drop in the birth rate during the 1950s and 1960s meant fewer laborers after 1975. Astonishingly, death rates and infant mortality rose rapidly in the 1970s, the first time such increases had ever been noted in such a developed nation. Poor medical care, alcoholism, bad safety facilities, and the tendency of Soviet women to have several abortions before finally bearing children relatively late in life contributed to these embarrassing figures. Population increases occurred almost wholly in Central Asia among Moslem groups. But historic hatreds divided these peoples from the Great Russians who ruled the land. Soviet leaders feared giving the ethnic peoples extensive economic power.[19] Brezhnev and his closest associates meanwhile grew older, slower, and more enfeebled. Brzezinski remarked to Carter that "under Lenin the Soviet Union was like a religious revival, under

[19]Michael Binyon, *Life in Russia* (New York, 1983), pp. 39–40, 58–65; John P. Hardt, "Highlight: Problems and Prospects," in U.S. Congress, Joint Economic Committee, 97th Cong., 2nd Sess., *Soviet Economy in the 1980s: Selected Papers* (Washington, 1983), pp. vii–xiii; Marshall I. Goldman, *U.S.S.R. in Crisis: The Failure of an Economic System* (New York, 1983), especially pp. 100–102.

Stalin like a prison, under Khrushchev like a circus, and under Brezhnev like the U.S. Post Office."[20]

In foreign affairs the Russians began to shiver from their old Stalinist fear of "capitalist encirclement" — only now it was communist as well as capitalist. Parts of the long Chinese-Russian border continued to be armed camps. A possible American-Chinese-Japanese partnership loomed on the Soviets' western flank. In Eastern Europe, economic crises and the energy crunch made the satellite states restless. Yugoslavia became unpredictable as Tito (who had cooperated with, as well as fought, the Soviets) became less active and then died in 1980.[21]

The most startling crisis suddenly appeared on Russia's own southern border. The shah of Iran's dynasty suddenly collapsed. Iran had been enduring terrible strains: half the population was younger than sixteen; the urban population was expected to quadruple to 20 million in just twenty-five years; an oil-dependent economy produced few jobs for an expanding population; 70,000 Iranians educated each year abroad (35,000 alone in the United States) returned with liberal, often anti-shah ideas; and — of special importance — modernization threatened the country's ancient religious ties, especially the Moslem leaders (the mullahs), who were becoming implacable foes of the shah. The shah meanwhile squandered the nation's wealth by importing more arms from the United States in the 1974–1978 era than Iran had bought in its entire history. The shah used SAVAK, his secret police that had close ties to the CIA, to remove enemies. By 1978 he was nevertheless losing control to the religious leaders and political fanatics (moderate leaders were dead or in prison), and he was suffering from cancer.[22]

American, and probably Soviet, officials understood few of these developments. At the "King of King's" demand, United States intelligence had virtually no contacts with opposition parties. As the revolution gathered force, Brzezinski and Vance split over a response. Brzezinski urged helping the shah establish a military regime to drown the revolt in bloodshed or, if that failed, mobilizing

---

[20]Carter, *Keeping Faith*, p. 223.

[21]Paul Marantz, "Probing Moscow's Outlook," *Problems of Communism*, XXVIII (March–April 1979): 49–50; Ernest Kux, "Growing Tensions in Eastern Europe," *Problems of Communism*, XXIX (March–April 1980): 21–37.

[22]Abul Kasim Mansur [a pen name], "Why the U.S. Ignored a Quarter-Century of Warning," *Armed Forces Journal International*, January 1979, pp. 27–33.

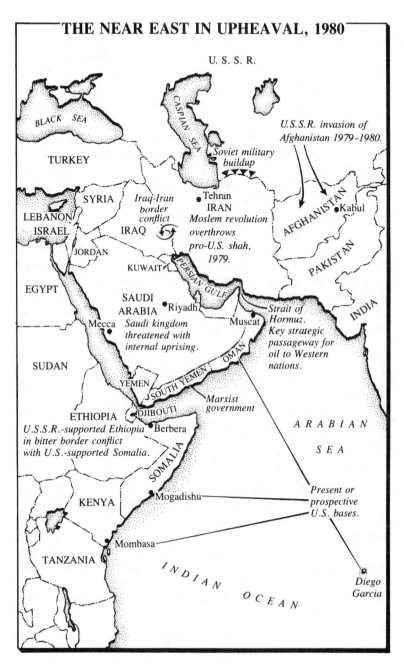

THE NEAR EAST IN UPHEAVAL, 1980

U. S. S. R.

U.S.S.R. invasion of Afghanistan 1979–1980.

BLACK SEA

CASPIAN SEA

TURKEY

Soviet military buildup

SYRIA

Iraq-Iran border conflict

Tehran
IRAN
Moslem revolution overthrows pro-U.S. shah, 1979.

AFGHANISTAN   Kabul

LEBANON
ISRAEL
IRAQ

JORDAN

PAKISTAN

KUWAIT

PERSIAN GULF

EGYPT

SAUDI ARABIA   Riyadh

Mecca

Saudi kingdom threatened with internal uprising.

Muscat

Strait of Hormuz. Key strategic passageway for oil to Western nations.

INDIA

SUDAN

OMAN

SOUTH YEMEN

YEMEN

Marxist government

ETHIOPIA   DJIBOUTI
Berbera

U.S.S.R.-supported Ethiopia in bitter border conflict with U.S.-supported Somalia.

A R A B I A N

S E A

SOMALIA

KENYA   Mogadishu

Present or prospective U.S. bases.

Mombasa

TANZANIA

I N D I A N   O C E A N

Diego Garcia

United States parachute troops for actual intervention. Vance urged
Carter to contact the revolutionary leaders, distance himself from
the shah, and assume that any military move could lead to the disintegration of the weakened Iranian Army. Carter again could not
make a clear choice. On February 20, 1979, the leading religious
figure, Ayatollah Ruhollah Khomeini, led forces that drove the
shah from power.[23]

United States foreign policy had suffered a major defeat. The
Soviets publicly applauded this setback, but they could not take too
much pleasure because Khomeini led a violently anticommunist
Moslem group whose fanaticism could easily spread to the large and
expanding Moslem population in Russia. As these revolutionary fires
burned in the autumn of 1979, David Rockefeller, Henry Kissinger,
and Brzezinski, all with close ties to the shah, convinced Carter to
allow the fatally ill monarch into an American hospital.[24] Enraged
mobs invaded the United States embassy in Tehran and seized sixty-
nine hostages. Khomeini released sixteen women and blacks but
would not free the remaining fifty-three, who, with their defiant cap-
tors, began to dominate American television screens as the American
presidential campaign got underway.

Carter's foreign policies began to unravel ever more rapidly. At
a summit conference in Vienna during mid-1979, Carter and Brezhnev finally agreed on a SALT II pact that limited the number of
nuclear arms launchers on each side to 2400 (with no more than
1320 to have MIRVs, the multiple warhead rockets). Each side retained its high card. For the United States the card was its small
cruise missile, which could fly too low for Soviet detection; for the
Russians it was their 300 huge land-based missiles. As Carter sent
the treaty to the Senate, however, a group called the Committee on
the Present Danger attacked the treaty. Established in 1976, the
committee was headed by Paul Nitze and Eugene Rostow, both
with long Washington experience, and both driven by the fear that
Americans were losing their will to oppose communism. The
seventy-two-year-old Nitze resurrected his old rhetoric from
NSC-68 of thirty years before and lobbied the Senate incessantly

[23]Brzezinski, *Power and Principle*, pp. 355, 388–393.
[24]Carter, *Keeping Faith*, pp. 452–453.

until he and other opponents finally stalled the treaty. Nitze's highly theoretical arguments were picked apart by some arms experts, but Carter's relations with Congress were so poor, and the Cold War atmosphere in the country so tense, that Nitze and others against détente gained the upper hand. They did so even after Brezhnev suddenly allowed more than 50,000 Jews — the highest number in history — to emigrate from Russia in 1979. He thus met a key demand of the antidétente forces, but neither they nor Carter now reciprocated.[25]

The President was under attack from all sides. The Iranian debacle triggered a jump in oil prices. Western European Allies blamed the United States for the jump, and they also criticized Carter's indecisiveness in planning a weapons program to defend Western Europe. After a summit meeting with West European leaders in 1979, Carter recorded in his diary, "We then had a luncheon that was very bitter and unpleasant. [West German Chancellor Helmut] Schmidt got personally abusive toward me."[26] The President and his advisors also grew angry over attempts by Schmidt and other West Europeans to profit from moving closer to Moscow. Secretary of Defense Harold Brown remarked caustically that the Allies seemed to say, "'Yes, there should be a division of task — we'll sell stuff to the Russians and you defend us.'" Brown added, "That's not what I mean by a division of task." Brzezinski glibly rationalized these failures by writing that the "world had entered a new post-Eurocentric era."[27] To paraphrase, this meant that his Trilateral approach was dead. The United States had few, if any, friends in the industrialized Western world who would fully cooperate in containing Soviet power or disciplining Third World revolutionaries.

Even the "American backyard" seemed unsafe. In July 1979 the revolutionary Sandinista forces overthrew the dictatorial Somoza dynasty that, with strong United States support, had been ruling Nicaragua since the mid-1930s. Named after the peasant fighter Augusto Sandino, who had successfully fought United States Marines in his country between 1927 and 1933, the Sandinistas had

[25]Fred Kaplan, *The Wizards of Armageddon* (New York, 1983), pp. 378–384; Adam Ulam, *Dangerous Relations: The Soviet Union in World Politics, 1970–1982* (New York, 1983), p. 250.

[26]Carter, *Keeping Faith*, p. 112.

[27]Brzezinski, *Power and Principle*, p. 515; the Brown quote is from *The New York Times*, December 7, 1980, p. 44.

been battling Somoza's brutal national guard for nearly twenty years. By the late 1970s the dictator's greed (he personally owned 25 percent of Nicaraguan land) and the guard's terrorism had turned most Nicaraguans, including leading business figures, to the Sandinistas' side. As Anastasio Somoza was about to fall, however, Jimmy Carter tried to mobilize the Organization of American States to intervene so the revolutionaries could not gain power. The President could not find a single significant Latin American supporter. He then tried to make the best of a bad situation by asking Congress for $75 million in aid to draw the Sandinista government closer to Washington. The new regime, however, did not want to move closer to the nation that had helped kill its supporters for two decades. The Sandinistas determined to follow a nonaligned foreign policy, but then drew close to Cuba, which had supported them in the final months of the war and now sent thousands of teachers, health experts, and military advisors.

Relations with Nicaragua approached the breaking point in 1980 as the Sandinistas supplied revolutionaries fighting to overthrow the military government in El Salvador. With one of the most inequitable societies and brutal militaries in the hemisphere, El Salvador was ripe for revolution. Carter actually cut off aid to the government after four American Roman Catholic churchwomen were murdered (three also had been sexually assaulted) in late 1980, and Salvadoran officials did nothing. Their military forces, after all, had committed the crime. But the revolutionaries launched a major offensive in January 1981, and Carter quickly reopened aid channels. His Latin American policy, resembling his policy with the Allies and the Soviets, lay in fragments.

Unable to devise coherent policies, in mid-1979 Carter seized the only alternative. He embarked on a major military buildup that, in retrospect, was the first chapter of the massive military spending program undertaken by the Reagan administration in the 1980s. The Defense Department budget began to grow as Carter built bases in the Persian Gulf region and authorized a so-called Rapid Deployment Force that (at least on paper) could strike quickly into Third World regions, especially in the oil-rich Middle East. Brzezinski later admitted that by this time, "There was neither dialogue nor deterrence in our relationship" with Moscow.[28] The rela-

[28] Two fine analyses are Melvyn P. Leffler, "From the Truman Doctrine to the Carter Doctrine," *Diplomatic History*, VII (Fall 1983): 245–266; and Stanley Hoffman, "In Search of a Foreign Policy," *The New York Review of Books*, September 29, 1983, p. 54.

tionship had been reduced to SALT II, and the pact was nearly dead because arms control proved too fragile, too politically exposed, to carry the entire burden of Soviet-American relations. It needed the kind of supporting political and economic structure that Nixon and Brezhnev had tried to create and that had now been dismantled.

As Carter turned to the military, so did Brezhnev. On Russia's border, the Moslem state of Afghanistan began to move away from the control that the Soviets had wielded through puppet governments. In the nineteenth century British colonialists had talked about "the great game of empire" in the Near East, a game in which Afghanistan, because of its pivotal location, was a critical pawn. Now, to Soviet eyes, a hostile China and Iran run by Moslem fanatics threatened the country. In 1979 the Soviets decided the stakes were worth reopening the game. On December 27 the Red Army invaded Afghanistan, executed the ineffective Marxist leader, and soon committed nearly 100,000 troops to a long, costly struggle with Moslem guerrillas. American experts speculated it would be the Soviets' Vietnam. To avoid such a disaster, the Russians used brutal force, including the killing of college students who demonstrated against the occupation. Brezhnev also ordered new arrests of Russian dissidents, including Nobel Prize-winning physicist Andrei Sakharov, the leader of the Soviet human rights movement. A high State Department official believed that the invasion and arrests resulted in part from a "domestic crisis within the Soviet system. . . . It may be that the thermodynamic law of entropy has finally and fully caught up with the Soviet system, which now seems to expend more energy on simply maintaining its equilibrium than on improving itself. We could," he concluded, "be seeing a period of foreign movement at a time of internal decay."[29]

A beleaguered Carter, naively complaining that the Soviets had "lied" to him about their peaceful intentions, accelerated his military buildup, which had begun before the Afghanistan invasion. He withdrew SALT II from the Senate (where it was nearly dead anyway), began registering young men for the draft, embargoed United States wheat and technology exports to Russia, and ordered Americans to withdraw from the 1980 Olympic Games in Moscow. He promised to increase defense spending by 5 percent in real terms.

[29]Charles W. Maynes, "The World in 1980," U.S. Department of State, *Current Policy,* April 1980, pp. 1–2.

Finally, the President dramatically announced a "Carter Doctrine" that pledged American intervention—unilaterally if necessary—if the Soviets threatened Western interests in the Persian Gulf region. Brzezinski persuaded Carter to announce the doctrine by directly comparing the crisis to Truman's in 1947. The Georgian, who revered the earlier President, now saw himself once again propping up the dominoes of Western civilization.[30]

Cyrus Vance refused to join the crusade. He believed the Soviets had invaded Afghanistan because they had a "dangerous problem" on their border and, moreover, had little more "to lose in [their] relationship with the United States."[31] In April 1980 Vance finally resigned when, over his protests, Carter ordered a secret military mission to rescue the fifty-three American hostages in Iran. The complex mission failed as a collision between two of the helicopters and a transport plane killed eight American soldiers.

The President entered the 1980 presidential campaign with one of the lowest approval ratings in recent history (77 percent negative, with 82 percent negative for his handling of foreign policy). Spirits sank so low that when Carter stood up to Senator Edward Kennedy's challenge for the Democratic party nomination by replying "I'll whip his ass," Carter's staff told the President that it had done more for their morale than anything "since the Willie Nelson concert" of months before.[32] Carter tried to regain the initiative with his arms buildup. He secretly signed Presidential Directive 59 (PD-59), which ordered massive new forces built to fight a prolonged, limited nuclear war. Critics quickly compared PD-59 with NSC-68 of three decades earlier when Soviet military power had been exaggerated, American policy became shaped by a rigid military strategy, a rapid and expensive American arms buildup started, tension mounted, escalation provoked escalation, and a right-wing reaction swept through American politics.[33]

The nation's policy was taking a turn back to 1950. Unfortunately for Carter, his political fortunes turned not at all. In his foreign policy he tried to outflank the Republican nominee, Ronald

[30] Brzezinski, *Power and Principle*, p. 30.

[31] Cyrus Vance, *Hard Choices* (New York, 1983), pp. 388–389.

[32] Carter, *Keeping Faith*, p. 464; polls in *Washington Post*, July 30, 1980, p. A12.

[33] Fred M. Kaplan, "Our Cold-War Policy, Circa '50," *The New York Times Magazine*, May 18, 1980, p. 94; and Milton Leitenberg, "Presidential Directive (P.D.) 59," *Journal of Peace Research*, XVIII (1981): 309–317.

Reagan, from the right—an act that resembled an attempt to be more Roman Catholic than the Pope. After several years of inconsistency and indecision, Carter had finally chosen a policy: a quest to recapture those simpler days of the Truman Doctrine and NSC-68. He again proved to be no match for Reagan in convincing Americans to embark on such quixotic quests for the Holy Grails of America's Cold War.

A former Hollywood actor and governor of California, Ronald Reagan won the presidency in a landslide with 489 electoral votes to Carter's 49, and 51 percent of the popular vote to Carter's 42 percent. The winner's view of world affairs was simple: "Let's not delude ourselves," he declared in June 1980. "The Soviet Union underlies all the unrest that is going on. If they weren't engaged in this game of dominoes, there wouldn't be any hot spots in the world."[34] Many of Reagan's strongest supporters, especially religious fundamentalists, blue-collar workers, and the Committee on the Present Danger, agreed with that assessment. Reagan captured in beautifully modulated tones (perfect for television and radio) the frustration, anger, and hatred—all the aggressive American nationalism that had emerged from bitter experiences in Vietnam (which Reagan now called a "noble cause"), Central America, and the Middle East.[35] Reagan had exploited this nationalism in 1978 by opposing the Panama Canal treaties, although then he had been outgunned by another right-wing actor, John Wayne, and conservative columnist William Buckley, who favored the pacts. Upon entering the White House he removed Harry Truman's picture and hung a portrait of Calvin Coolidge, the Republican of the 1920s who reduced taxes and sent the marines to occupy parts of the Caribbean and Central America. But Reagan built on, not destroyed, Truman's foreign policies. Reagan became as predictable as Carter had been indecisive. "Ronald Reagan has been more consistent than anyone else before him," a high State Department official observed in late 1983, adding, "Of course you may not like what he is consistent about."[36]

[34] *The Wall Street Journal,* June 3, 1980, p. 1.

[35] Robert Dallek, *Ronald Reagan: The Politics of Symbolism* (Cambridge, Massachusetts, 1984), p. 133.

[36] *Washington Post,* November 21, 1983, p. A13.

The consistency included hatred for the Soviets (that "evil empire" he called them) and a massive military buildup. Hatred and nuclear weapons, however, were not a global strategy. There was not a single top Reagan official by 1983 who had extensive experience in Soviet affairs. The most qualified at the beginning of Reagan's term had been Secretary of State Alexander Haig. Haig ran afoul of a powerful White House staff that disliked his political ambitions, his earlier work for Nixon's détente policies, and his warnings about being insensitive to Allies in Europe and the Middle East. The staff cared almost entirely about domestic policies and Reagan's public image. In mid-1982 Reagan fired Haig. He was replaced by George Shultz — former Nixon associate, corporate executive, low-keyed, ex-United States Marine — who, it turned out, more willingly deployed the nation's military power than did the military itself. Reagan's other close foreign policy advisor was William P. Clark, first Haig's deputy then the President's national security advisor. Clark had no qualifications except his close friendship with Reagan. After he served more than two years as the President's closest foreign policy aide, one official who dealt with Clark said, "I'd be afraid to ask him what he thinks because I'm not sure he'd be able to answer."[37]

The President could not compensate for such deficiencies. He knew little about the details, nuances, or often the substance of foreign policy. While building up the strategic forces, for example, he deflected criticism by pledging his commitment to arms reduction talks with the Soviets. His knowledge about those talks was questionable, however. For two years he blasted the Russians for not accepting his arms proposals (which, among other items, asked for across-the-board percentage cuts of Soviet and American land-based missiles) and then, in late 1983, told astonished congressmen that he had just discovered that 70 percent of Russia's missiles were land based, while only 20 percent of America's were. He had never before understood why the Russians thought his proposal unfair. The figures, however, were easily found even in newspapers.[38] For a brief period in early 1981, the Soviets apparently wanted to explore

[37]Alexander M. Haig, Jr., *Caveat: Realism, Reagan, and Foreign Policy* (New York, 1984), especially pp. 80–86; Steven R. Weisman, "The Influence of William Clark," *The New York Times Magazine*, August 14, 1983, pp. 17–20.

[38]Steven R. Weisman, "Can the Magic Prevail?" *The New York Times Magazine*, April 29, 1984, p. 48.

ways of reducing tensions. Given their problems in Afghanistan, Poland, and China, Reagan could hold a strong negotiating position. He refused, arguing the need to build more arms before parleying.[39] He also seemed to have little real interest in, or knowledge of, issues that could reduce tensions with the "evil empire."

In the early 1980s the President's foreign policy was his arms budget. Instead of Carter's projected spending of $1.2 trillion, Reagan proposed $1.6 trillion over five years. That amount nevertheless appeared insufficient because he had no strategy in which to use the power — except his belief that the United States should have the power to act unilaterally, over long periods of time, virtually anywhere. Given power realities of the 1980s and distances, however, that belief was a wish, not strategy. He emphasized the need to build forces that could fight nuclear war against Russia "over a protracted period." At the same time he wanted to build the capacity to fight conventional wars globally, and without the two-and-one-half war limit that the Kennedy administration set for itself. Examining these open-ended plans, the Joint Chiefs of Staff concluded that $1.6 trillion was insufficient. Another $750 billion would be required.[40] The President's foreign policy resembled less a strategy than an adding machine.

The massive buildup rested on assumptions that merit close attention. First, Reagan argued that for fifteen years the United States had disarmed while Russia armed, so that huge sums were needed to make up for lost time. Critics, however, noted that during the 1970s Americans deployed 550 land-based MIRV missiles that remained the world's most advanced; put about 600 invulnerable submarine-based missiles into service; deployed a new strategic bomber more advanced than any Russian bomber in service; and, of special importance, added the cruise missile, which made the Soviet air defense system obsolete. In the nuclear submarine and the cruise missile, the United States held two invulnerable strategic forces.[41] (Americans,

[39]Ulam, *Dangerous Relations*, pp. 289–290.

[40]Jeffrey Record, "Jousting with Unreality: Reagan's Military Strategy," *International Security*, VIII (Winter 1983–1984): 3–18; Barry R. Posen and Stephen Van Evera, "Defense Policy and the Reagan Administration," *International Security*, VIII (Summer 1983): 30–32; *Washington Post*, March 8, 1982, p. A1; *The New York Times*, May 30, 1982, p. A1.

[41]Congressman Thomas J. Downey, "We Never Dropped Out of the Arms Race," *Washington Post*, November 29, 1983, p. A17; Hans Bethe, "The Inferiority Complex," *The New York Review of Books*, June 10, 1982, p. 3.

moreover, had used their military power as a political threat on some 215 occasions in the postwar world and were involved in hostilities, without a declaration of war, some 80 times.[42]) Meanwhile, the CIA estimated that since 1976 Soviet defense spending increases actually dropped from 5 percent annually to about 2 percent. Moreover, the Russians must target at least 20 percent of their strategic forces on their "second front"—China. The United States could focus on the Soviet Union.[43]

Second, Reagan's military buildup assumed that a "protracted" nuclear war could be fought and won. A high Pentagon official, T. K. Jones, said Americans could be protected in that conflict if they would "dig a hole, cover it with a couple of doors, and then throw three feet of dirt on top." One newspaper wondered whether Jones was really "a character in 'Doonesbury,'" a comic strip, but he was actually the technician who performed the statistical work for Nitze's fight against SALT II. Another Reagan official also reassured Congress: after a nuclear war, mail would be delivered "even if the survivors ran out of stamps." He refused to change his mind even after a congressman noted difficulties in delivering mail when "there will be no addresses, no streets, no blocks, no houses."[44] A scientific study demonstrated, moreover, that the use of just one-third the 50,000 nuclear weapons available world-wide would produce lethal radioactive fallout and a cloud that, by darkening the earth for about one year, could fatally affect the food chain feeding humans.[45] Another study showed that 200 severe burn cases could saturate all existing facilities for treatment in the nation; a nuclear war could result in 25 million such cases.[46]

Third, the administration believed America had the resources for a buildup; it needed only determination. The Committee on the Pres-

[42]Milton Leitenberg, "The Impact of the Worldwide Confrontation of the Great Powers," unpublished manuscript, October 1982, pp. 8–10.

[43]*The Wall Street Journal*, November 21, 1983, p. 5; Franklyn Holzman, "Administration Misrepresentations of Soviet Military Spending." In Congressman Ronald V. Dellums, *Defense Sense*, with R. H. Miller and R. Lee Halterman (Cambridge, Massachusetts, 1983), pp. 96–105.

[44]This account draws heavily on Robert Scheer, *With Enough Shovels: Reagan, Bush, and Nuclear War* (New York, 1982); see also Kaplan, *The Wizards of Armageddon*, p. 388; and Dallek, *Ronald Reagan*, pp. 146–157.

[45]Carl Sagan, "Nuclear War and Climatic Catastrophe: Some Policy Implications," *Foreign Affairs*, LXII (Winter 1983–1984): 257–292.

[46]*Washington Post*, November 21, 1980, p. A3.

ent Danger had also emphasized the need for determination. It was thus ironic that the committee's two founders, Nitze and Rostow, joined the government, examined the military line-up, and concluded negotiations were necessary with Russia. Rostow became so insistent on negotiations that Reagan fired him.[47] The President, who had hotly criticized SALT II, now quietly observed the pact's provisions because he discovered they were in the national interest. Nor were resources inexhaustible. Although Reagan demanded a 7 to 10 percent real increase annually in military spending, he had to accept half that amount. Larger sums inflated an already incredible $200 billion budget deficit that threatened to undermine the American economy by driving up interest rates and making American factories less competitive.

Fourth, Reagan believed he could expand military spending while taking government "off the backs of the people." Within two years, however, he increased the government's share of the gross national product from 23 percent to 25.2 percent, the highest since World War II. (In addition, the money was not spent wisely. At the end of fiscal 1983, the military spent $4.2 billion in just one day so it would not have to return the money to the Treasury.[48]) Other forms of government involvement were more ominous. After the White House stated that the CIA would never spy on Americans at home, Reagan signed an executive order that allowed the CIA to infiltrate domestic groups and conduct covert operations inside the United States.[49] After the White House declared it favored releasing more information to Americans, Reagan signed an executive order raising censorship and the withholding of information to new levels.[50] After the White House promised to lessen governmental controls, Reagan signed National Security Decision Directive 84 allowing bureaucrats to call in the FBI to give lie detector tests to employees suspected of being merely insubordinate or leaking information to reporters. Conservative columnist William Safire wrote that "the so-called lie detector is a civil-liberties abomination; NSDD-84 is a disgrace to conservative principle." Another observer explained

[47]Kaplan, *The Wizards of Armageddon*, pp. 378–384.

[48]*The New York Times*, October 9, 1983, p. 31; *Washington Post*, January 30, 1983, p. A5; Dr. Gordon Adams, "The 'Iron Triangle' and the American Economy," in Dellums, *Defense Sense*, pp. 171–173.

[49]*Washington Post*, November 13, 1981, p. A19.

[50]*Washington Post*, September 10, 1983, p. A3.

such acts by half-jokingly suggesting that the President had come down with "an acute case of Moscow envy."[51]

Fifth, the arms buildup implied that the military would willingly use its new power. The top Pentagon armed service officers, however, objected to deploying their forces in Lebanon during 1982–1983 and fought plans for United States intervention in Central America.[52] The uniformed officers, having learned from the Vietnam War, were reluctant to engage in conflicts unless the American people solidly supported them and the civilian officials gave them virtually a blank check for fighting the war. The military was even reluctant to invade the small island of Grenada in October 1983. Reagan ordered the invasion supposedly to rescue American students threatened by civil war on the island and to overthrow a government that was moving closer to Cuba. The campaign turned out to be Reagan's major foreign policy success, but even though troops met little resistance, 18 Americans were killed and 116 wounded. No other Grenadas existed for such a relatively easy application of American military power. The military consequently retained its skepticism about involvement elsewhere.

That other world trouble spots little resembled Grenada provided insight into the sixth assumption of Reagan's military policies. He was building forces to fight in Third World areas. The forces proved ineffective, however, in the two crucial areas of Lebanon and Central America. In 1982 an Israeli invasion of Lebanon nearly destroyed Israel's hated enemy, the Palestinian Liberation Organization. Lebanese Moslem forces, however, fought back against the Israelis and were helped by Syria, newly resupplied by the Soviet Union. After Reagan's diplomacy failed, he accepted Secretary of State Shultz's strong recommendation that American troops be sent as part of a multinational force to keep peace. The Israelis drew back, but the multinational force became trapped in bitter warfare between Christian and Moslem groups. American troops were soon perceived by the Lebanese as supporting the Christians, so Moslem guerrillas began sniping at a virtually defenseless American garrison. In October 1983 a Moslem suicide mission blew up the United States military barracks and killed 239 American soldiers.

[51] *The New York Times*, November 24, 1983, p. A23; *The New York Times*, October 22, 1983, p. 23.

[52] *The New York Times*, November 16, 1983, p. A22

Reagan announced that vital interests were involved, the Soviet-supported Syrians had to be checked, and United States forces would not leave. But 1600 marines were pinned down while the President could devise no diplomatic solution. He also faced the 1984 election. Reagan finally pulled out American troops in early 1984. Syria and its Moscow supporters won an important victory. After the American withdrawal, various Lebanese factions and Syria began to lower the level of fighting and arrange peace terms.

Central America offered a similar lesson: military power is central, but to be effective it has to be supported by workable political plans. A military buildup without a diplomatic plan resembles a powerful motor without a car frame. In Nicaragua the Sandinistas had built the region's most powerful military but had also begun reforming their society by increasing literacy, health facilities, and food production (see map, p. 210). Reagan immediately cut off aid to the Sandinistas in 1981 and began a military confrontation. The President argued that the Nicaraguans were too close to Cuba and the Soviet bloc and, moreover, supplied the growing revolution in neighboring El Salvador. Direct use of United States military power ran into strong opposition from both Pentagon military officers and vocal American civilian groups — especially churches led by Roman Catholics whose missionaries knew Central America intimately. Nicaragua was not Grenada. The Sandinistas were tough former guerrillas who trusted their people to the extent of arming masses of civilians to fight any Yankee invasion. The last time the marines intervened they had to remain in Nicaragua twenty years (1912–1933) before providing stability in the form of the Somozas' dictatorship. The next intervention could be as long and more costly. Reagan therefore ordered the CIA to train "Contra" groups, whose officers included former Somozans. Between 1981 and 1984 the CIA invested at least $70 million in the Contras' efforts, but they scored few victories. The Sandinistas meanwhile increased their own military power despite economic hardship caused by the CIA's illegal mining of Nicaraguan harbors.

Reagan enjoyed limited success in El Salvador. The revolutionaries grew until, by 1983, they claimed control of about one-third of the country. Government-associated death squads responded by killing anyone suspected of liberal views; about 40,000 civilians were slaughtered between 1979 and 1984. The United States moved into the country in force to oppose both extremes. It supervised several elections, and in the second, which was held in May 1984, the American-sponsored candidate, José Napoleon Duarte, won. Reagan propped up the regime with large aid programs that retrained the corrupt Salvadoran Army and tried (largely without success) to install a land reform program to win the peasants' favor. By 1984 the overpowering United States presence produced scattered military victories. The question became whether any native centrist groups remained to govern on their own, or whether American policy was instead leading to a larger war. A group of regional, democratic nations feared the larger war. This "Contadora group" — Venezuela, Colombia, Panama, and Mexico — was a friend of the United States but condemned its military approach and worked instead for negotiated settlements in Nicaragua and El Salvador. Reagan nevertheless continued his military escalation by turning El Salvador and neighboring Honduras into virtual American bases (the U.S.S. Honduras, one observer termed the small country). Here, as elsewhere, the President exhibited little diplomatic strategy but a dependence on military power.[53]

Conditions had changed, however, since the CIA had overthrown Guatemala's government in 1954 (see p. 159). In Guatemala the government and the military had divided. Cubans, Nicaraguans, and Salvadorans learned the lesson: revolutionary governments and armies had to be one. To overthrow Castro or the Sandinistas now required fighting the army. In the new revolutions, moreover, the rebels successfully mobilized masses of people. American officials confronted not an isolated elite (which they had controlled with ease in Central America through most of this century), but a mass, Vietnam-style opposition.

Reagan, however, saw the revolutions only as part of a Soviet plot. Secretary of State Haig had advocated taming them by "going to the source," that is, eliminating Castro. Few experts agreed. The revolutions finally depended on Central Americans, not Russians or Cubans.[54]

In dealing with the Soviets in the global arena, Reagan was most proud of his work in Western Europe and China. In 1977 the

[53]Raymond Bonner, *Weakness and Deceit: U.S. Policy and El Salvador* (New York, 1984), especially pp. 62–63, 344–369.

[54]Robert S. Leiken, ed., *Central America, Anatomy of Conflict* (New York, 1984), pp. 175–176.

Russians had begun deploying medium-range missiles targeted on Western Europe. The Allies asked Carter to provide security, and the United States responded by planning to put 572 Pershing II and cruise missiles in Europe, while also promising to try to restrict all arms buildups with SALT II. Carter and Reagan accomplished the first objective but not the second. In 1983, over vocal opposition from European and American peace groups, the President began deploying the weapons. He argued the missiles were "bargaining chips" to force the Soviets to scale down their missile system. Moscow officials replied their missiles necessarily countered French, British, and American weapons trained on them. When Reagan began emplacing the Pershings, which would take less than ten minutes from launch to hit Soviet targets, the Russians broke off arms talks. "Bargaining chips" had, as usual, become just another part of the arms race.

His European policies were unswerving, but Reagan's views on China turned 180 degrees. As a candidate he had worked closely with the remnants of the old China Lobby (see p. 86) and condemned Nixon's and Carter's breakthroughs on China as triggering "a chain of events that could be disastrous" for the United States.[55] But after he entered the White House, his hatred of communism gave way to his hatred of the Soviet Union. By 1984 he had even moved beyond Brzezinski's policies by selling China sensitive high technology that had military uses. The Soviets were furious, Reagan pleased, but the Chinese were the real winners. Given the President's rigid anti-Russian feelings, China's leaders no longer worried about a possible Soviet-American détente that could harm Chinese interests. They thus not only could afford to embarrass Reagan during a 1984 state visit to the Middle Kingdom by censoring his anti-Soviet statements taped for Chinese television, but they could then approach an increasingly isolated Russia to seek trade and political favors.[56] Reagan's anti-Soviet policies ironically allowed the two communist giants to move closer together.

Surprisingly, in 1980 the Soviets had favored Reagan's candidacy over Carter's. They believed that as a Republican he would

[55]Lou Cannon, *Reagan* (New York, 1982), p. 272.

[56]Joel B. Harris, Bruce H. Turnbull, and Jeffrey P. Bialos, *Compliance with U.S. Export Control Laws and Regulations* (Washington, 1984), pp. 39–41; *Washington Post*, May 3, 1984, p. A36.

ultimately act as Nixon had acted.[57] But Reaganism turned out to be a new phenomenon. The Soviets found themselves locked into an ideological war and an arms race. They fought these battles with a stumbling, hidebound system that drowned in 800 billion documents a year—an average of 7000 produced by each Russian factory and office worker. Soviet foreign policy meanwhile suffered setbacks in such newly emerging areas as Africa. Angola and Mozambique, former Russian friends, turned westward for the capital and technology only the United States and the Allies could provide. Moslem guerrillas in Afghanistan fought on despite more than 110,000 Soviet troops. Those troops suffered nearly 20,000 casualties and, to the horror of Moscow officials, turned increasingly to drugs, alcohol, and black-market sales of weapons to the Afghans.[58]

Amidst these problems, the Soviets faced not one but two succession crises. Brezhnev died in 1982. His successor was Yuri Andropov, who had risen to power in the 1970s as head of the secret police (the KGB). Supported by the secret police and military, Andropov tried to spur Russian workers by jailing those who tried to escape from the daily rigors of the socialist utopia through alcoholism and absenteeism. Andropov tried no major reforms. Decentralizing the economy—not to mention the possibilities of personal computers and electronic mail—terrified the KGB. Andropov had no more time to try new policies at home or abroad. In February 1984 he died after a lingering illness and was succeeded by Konstantin Chernenko.

Another leader in his seventies, and also plagued with illness, Chernenko had risen as "Brezhnev's valet," in the words of one Soviet official. His main claims to power seemed to be his age (thus he prevented a younger generation from displacing the old that clung to control of the Politburo) and his long, dependable performance as a Communist party hack. His rise meant that the party's rigid predictability would replace the less predictable KGB approach. In his first major speech as leader, Chernenko admitted that Khrushchev's 1961 claim that by 1980 communism would triumph over capitalism had been a bit premature. "Capitalism is doomed

---

[57]Ulam, *Dangerous Relations*, pp. 287–290; author's interviews in Moscow, November 13–14, 1980.

[58]U.S. Department of State, *Special Report No. 112: Afghanistan. Four Years of Occupation* (Washington, 1983), pp. 1–8.

by history," Chernenko declared, but he reckoned "it still possesses quite substantial and far from exhausted reserves for development."[59]

That belief combined with his personality (London's magazine *The Economist* described him as a "dull, heavy, decent fellow, running out of puff; the sort who in a pluralist society should be pottering around in a house of lords"[60]) directly affected Americans. Chernenko and his colleagues had little imagination in dealing with the new Cold War other than pulling the Soviet team out of the 1984 Olympics in Los Angeles and breaking off arms negotiations — at least until they were certain who would win the 1984 American elections. Internally they were ruthless. Dissident (especially Jewish) emigration dropped from 51,000 in 1979 to 1300 in 1983; direct-dial international phone calls and other forms of communication were cut off; and Chernenko personally attacked authors who produced "loose and whining" characters in ideologically deficient works.[61] In 1983 Soviet fighter planes shot down a South Korean civilian airliner (killing 269 people, including a United States congressman) after it strayed over highly sensitive Russian military bases. Moscow officials refused to apologize. They instead accused the United States of a provocative act.

The question was not whether the Soviets were good or bad, but how the United States and the Soviet Union could improve relations so tension would drop and explosive confrontations would be avoided. Such improvement could also allow Americans to study the new generation that in the near future would replace Chernenko. One leading candidate, Mikhail Gorbachov, was in his early fifties, was associated with economic reforms and détente policies (although he also strongly supported the Afghanistan invasion), and had some experience in the West and with foreign affairs. The other leading candidate, Grigori Romanov, was a decade older, more ideologically rigid, and a tough party man who had shown less understanding of the West.

In both Moscow and Washington there were those who paraded patriotic purity, but then had to accept unpleasant compromises. An example occurred with the crisis in Poland. It began in the early 1970s when the communist regime in Warsaw borrowed huge sums

[59] *The New York Times*, April 26, 1984, p. A15.
[60] *The Economist*, May 19, 1984, p. 12.
[61] *Washington Post*, January 16, 1984, p. A11.

from Western banks to build heavy industry and new technology. The experiment failed and by 1980 the Poles owed the banks over $20 billion. When officials tried to install tough austerity programs, a workers' movement, Solidarity, appeared to demand the right to strike and then—to the communist officials' horror—the right to vote in open, democratic elections. Solidarity received support from the powerful Roman Catholic Church. Angry Soviet officials had invaded Czechoslovakia for less, but the Polish Army was unpredictable (it had already once refused to fire on strikers), and both Carter and Reagan warned against any invasion. In February 1981 the Soviets installed Polish General Wojciech Jaruzelski in power. The economic crisis nevertheless worsened. The Reagan administration refused to make any move to help what it called a "failing Communist regime."[62] Jaruzelski then moved to solve the problem by declaring martial law and jailing thousands of dissidents. Poland entered that empty gray twilight that Russians had long wished upon their upstart neighbors.

Furious, Reagan could do nothing but embargo American exports to Poland. This trapped him. Honoring a campaign pledge to farmers, he had earlier removed Carter's wheat embargo against Russia. He now found himself feeding the despised Soviets and starving the beleaguered Poles. Some trade later opened, even as martial law continued. Conservative columnist George Will acidly wrote that the Reagan administration "evidently loves commerce more than it loathes communism. . . . It is the West that is immobilized by the centrality and banality of its commercial values."[63] Reagan was never able to develop a consistent economic policy. If he controlled trade, he interfered in the hallowed marketplace; if he did not, he helped build communist economic and perhaps military power. If he tried to regulate the trade, as he did during 1982–1983, his closest allies—Japan and the West Europeans—refused to cooperate, undercut American companies, and loudly objected to this country's pressures.

This economic problem was only part of a larger crisis within the capitalist world. During the 1970s Third World nations sought—

[62] See *Washington Post*, January 2, 1982, p. A12 for the quote and a good overview.
[63] George Will, "Reagan's Dim Candle," *Newsweek*, January 18, 1982, p. 100.

and Western bankers happily supplied—loans that by 1984 amounted to $700 billion in outstanding debt. The debt resembled a ticking time bomb. The amount grew so huge that if it had to be paid off the Third World regimes could do so only by going bankrupt or ruthlessly exploiting their own people. If the amount was not paid, major Western banks faced bankruptcy. At first the Reagan administration refused to interfere. Then Mexico and Argentina threatened to stop paying their immense debts. When the Dominican Republic tried to impose an austerity program to pay off its debt, riots killed sixty people in the bloodiest outbreak since the 1965 intervention by the United States. At that point, the federal government finally provided support funds to help prop up both the strife-torn countries and the faltering banking system.

Reagan could provide less help, however, when other nations begged him to reduce the incredible $200 billion United States government deficit. They argued that it raised American interest rates (by forcing the government to compete with business for limited funds) and thus drove up world prices and costs. Reagan denied links between the deficit and interest rates, and refused to reduce military spending to cut the deficit. A global economic slump cut $1 trillion from world production in the early 1980s and raised unemployment in just the developed world to 32 million. When Reagan once pledged to put "the mob" of organized crime "out of business," a Republican jokester responded, "Good. Why should they be an exception?"

By the mid-1980s United States policies had helped arm the time bomb. Two scholars placed the problem in a 400-year context and concluded that the United States might be following the course of such former empires as the British. The authors demonstrated that a nation becomes a great world power through military victories that must be paid with indebtedness (as the United States paid for its victory in World War II). The debt becomes so expensive and draining that the nation loses its competitive advantage in world commerce. It can then have problems paying for its military eminence. Trying to regain his nation's superiority in the globe's military arena, Reagan had immensely increased the debt. A number of economists claimed that he had also severely weakened the nation's economic foundations.[64]

[64]Karen A. Rasler and William R. Thompson, "Global Wars, Public Debts, and the Long Cycle," *World Politics*, XXXV (July 1983): 489–516; Emma Rothschild, "The Philosophy of Reaganism," *The New York Review of Books*, April 15, 1982, pp. 19–26.

Few Americans noted these shifts in United States strength or seemed concerned about the reasons for them. They instead focused on the President, who became highly popular. He scored remarkable political victories at home, especially over Congress, because of his appealing personality and his talent in using television and radio. "You'd be surprised how much being a good actor pays off," he observed to a group of students when he visited China. He also had the ability to touch the historic fear Americans have felt about Russia and Third World revolutions, while assuring those Americans that all would be well. Reagan's political victories resulted from both those traits and his luck that Congress was divided and rudderless.[65] His foreign policy failures (to mid-1984 only the invasion of tiny Grenada and his implementation of Carter's 1979 pledge to place missiles in Western Europe ranked as successes) resulted from several factors: an ideological inflexibility that prevented his (and his advisors') understanding the new power relationships; a failure to perceive the changing role of the United States in the long cycle of history; and a belief that in a world of 50,000 nuclear weapons, higher military spending could somehow replace the lessons of history and the need to reconceptualize American diplomacy. In foreign policy he attempted to succeed with a smile, anticommunism, arms, and utterances. As he neared the end of nearly four years in the White House one consequence was, as a close military advisor of the President worried, that the American-Soviet relationship had turned "as bad as it's been in my memory."[66]

Reinhold Niebuhr had worried years earlier that Americans would try to escape complex political and economic dilemmas by placing their faith in military power. Some Reaganites considered themselves Niebuhrites as well, but the theologian would probably have questioned any connection.[67] He once warned that "a frantic anti-communism can become so similar in its temper of hatefulness to communism itself." In one of the last essays he wrote before his

[65] A fine analysis is I. M. Destler and Eric Alterman, "Congress and Reagan's Foreign Policy," *The Washington Quarterly,* VII (Winter 1984): 91–101.

[66] The quote, by General Brent Scowcroft, is in *The New York Times,* April 18, 1984, p. A26.

[67] Tracy Early, "Lefever vs. Niebuhr," *Christianity and Crisis,* April 27, 1981, pp. 125–126.

death in 1971, Niebuhr seemed to anticipate the 1980s by warning against the "realist" belief in power:

> It is one of the mysteries of human nature that while most of us are unconscious of an inevitable mixture in our motives, we try to atone for this error by too constant emphasis on "the law in our members which wars against the law that is in our minds."[68]

With the limits placed on American power by the new conditions of the Cold War, it seemed imperative that "the law that is in our minds" be applied to solve the central domestic and diplomatic problems. Otherwise the "law in our members" could again be used too easily, and perhaps tragically.

[68]Reinhold Niebuhr, "Toward New Intra-Christian Endeavors," *Christian Century*, December 31, 1969, pp. 1662–1667.

BIBLIOGRAPHY FOR ADDITIONAL READING
(See also the footnote citations in relevant chapters because most of those references are not repeated here.)

General Bibliographic Tools and Reference Works

The most helpful and complete work—the compilation all students must first consult—is Richard Dean Burns, editor, *Guide to American Foreign Relations Since 1700* (1983). The bibliography that follows does not repeat many relevant references listed in Burns's *Guide* but tries to update those references, as well as to provide some of the standard works. For periodical literature, see *Social Sciences and Humanities Index*. Soviet references for the earlier years are in Thomas Taylor Hammond, *Soviet Foreign Relations and World Communism: A Selected Annotated Bibliography of 7000 Books* (1965). United States government publications are listed in U.S. Superintendent of Documents, *Monthly Catalog of U.S. Government Publications* (since 1895). Important reference works include Alexander DeConde, editor, *Encyclopedia of American Foreign Policy*, 3 volumes (1978), which has detailed bibliographies; John E. Findling, *Dictionary of American Diplomatic History* (1980), and for the Russian and bloc events, the Hoover Institution's *Yearbook on International Communist Affairs*.

Journals

Among the many available journals, perhaps the most influential are *Foreign Affairs* and *Foreign Policy*. For the government's view, consult *Department of State Bulletin* and the State Department's *Current Policy*, along with the Department of Commerce's *Commerce Today*.

Journals containing good historical analyses include *Diplomatic History, International Security, Political Science Quarterly, World Politics, International Organization,* and *International History Review,* as well as the *Journal of American History, American Historical Review,* and *American Political Science Review.* For the Russian side, see *Current Digest of the Soviet Press, Problems of Communism, International Affairs* (Moscow), and *Slavic Review.*

General Works: United States and American-Soviet Relations

The Department of State, *Foreign Relations of the United States* (now available from 1861 to 1954) is indispensable. This is the primary documentary source for American foreign policy. See also the New York Council on Foreign Relations, *The United States in World Affairs,* an annual survey, and its companion volume, *Documents on American Foreign Relations.* The Department of State, *American Foreign Policy: Current Documents* published two volumes on 1950–1955, single annual volumes from 1956 through 1966, and recommenced publication in 1979. Especially valuable is the series, *Public Papers of the Presidents,* annual volumes published by the Government Printing Office with nearly all public utterances by Presidents since 1945.

Good general surveys include Robert D. Schulzinger, *American Diplomacy in the 20th Century* (1984); Raymond Aron, *The Imperial Republic, 1945–1973* (1974), a distinguished French authority; Ernest R. May, *"Lessons" of the Past* (1973); Alexander L. George and Richard Smoke, *Deterrence in American Foreign Policy* (1974); and Robert A. Packenham's stimulating overview, *Liberal America and the Third World* (1973). Important interpretive studies include William Appleman Williams, *The Tragedy of American Diplomacy* (1971), a pathbreaking study; as is Lloyd Gardner's *A Covenant with Power: America and World Order from Wilson to Reagan* (1984). Also see Richard Barnet's two works, *Intervention and Revolution* (1968), and *Roots of War* (1972), which stresses bureaucratic policy making; Ronald Steel, *Pax Americana* (1967); Gabriel Kolko, *Roots of American Foreign Policy* (1969); and for a provocative British view, D. C. Watt, *Succeeding John Bull: America in Britain's Place, 1900–1975* (1983).

For surveys of the American-Soviet relationship, see John Lewis Gaddis, *Strategies of Containment* (1982); N. V. Sivachev and N. N. Yakoviev, *Russia and the United States* (1978), which gives the Soviet point of view; Paul Hollander, *Soviet and American Society, a Comparison* (1978); Fred Holliday, *The Making of the Second Cold War* (1983); Morton Schwartz, *Soviet Perceptions of the United States* (1978); U.S. House of Representatives, Committee on Foreign Affairs, *Soviet Diplomacy and Negotiating Behavior* (1979), which is nicely detailed. For economic issues, the following are useful: Marshall Goldman, *Détente and Dollars* (1975); Philip Hanson, *Trade and Technology in Soviet-Western Relations* (1981); and Gordon B. Smith, editor, *The Politics of East-West Trade* (1984). Alexander I. George et al., *Managing U.S.-Soviet Rivalry* (1982) contains superb case studies on a range of issues and geographic areas.

Specific Topics in United States Policy Since 1945

For domestic politics and opinion, a good survey and bibliography are in Barry B. Hughes, *The Domestic Context of American Foreign Policy* (1978). See also Ralph B. Levering, *The Public and American Foreign Policy* (1978); Bernard C. Cohen's invaluable *The Public's Impact on Foreign Policy* (1973); Robert Divine's two-volume study, *Foreign Policy and Presidential Elections, 1940–1960* (1974); Bernard C. Cohen's *The Press and Foreign Policy* (1965); Jeremy Tunstall, *The Media Are American* (1977); Ronald Radosh, *American Labor and U.S. Foreign Policy* (1969); Alfred O. Hero, Jr., *The Southerner and World Affairs* (1965); Robert W. Tucker, *The Radical Left and American Foreign Policy* (1972); and Thomas Franck and Edward Weisband, *Foreign Policy by Congress* (1979), which is a key resource.

For individuals and elite groups, in addition to those books listed below under specific presidential administrations, see George Kennan's two-volume *Memoirs* (1967, 1972); Charles D. Bohlen, *Witness to History* (1973); Robert Murphy, *Diplomat Among Warriors* (1964); Vernon Walters, *Silent Missions* (1978), by an ex-CIA officer and United States Army general with close ties to right-wing governments world-wide; Ronald Steel's magisterial biography,

Walter Lippmann and the American Century (1980); John C. Donovan, *The Cold Warriors* (1974). For dissenters (in addition to Lippmann), see Thomas G. Paterson, editor, *Cold War Critics* (1971); Ronald Radosh's stimulating essays in *Prophets on the Right;* and Justus Doenecke, *Not to the Swift* (1979), which is especially valuable on the late 1940s. For a pioneering study, see Robert D. Schulzinger, *The Wise Men of Foreign Affairs: The History of the Council on Foreign Relations* (1984).

On cultural impact and the role of cultural influence, see Morrell Heald and Lawrence Kaplan, *Culture and Diplomacy* (1977); Robert Dallek's provocative account of post-1890s diplomacy, *The American Style of Foreign Policy* (1983); Edward H. Herman, *The Influence of the Carnegie, Ford, and Rockefeller Foundations on American Foreign Policy* (1983); Sig Mickelson, *America's Other Voice: The Story of Radio Free Europe and Radio Liberty* (1983), an insider's account of these crucial institutions.

On the Western alliance system two splendid recent accounts on the entire post-1945 era are Richard Barnet, *The Alliance* (1983); and Alfred Grosser, *The Western Alliance* (1982), written by a leading West European analyst.

For defense policies the historical background is in Raymond G. O'Connor, editor, *American Defense Policy in Perspective* (1965); and Russell F. Weigley's authoritative, *The American Way of War* (1973). Three superb recent accounts that analyze the post-1945 era are Lawrence Freedman, *The Evolution of Nuclear Strategy* (1983); Fred Kaplan, *The Wizards of Armageddon* (1983); and Barry M. Blechman and Stephen S. Kaplan, *Force Without War: U.S. Armed Forces as a Political Instrument* (1978). See also Duncan L. Clarke, *Politics of Arms Control* (1979). On the economic aspects two standard works are Jacques Gansler, *The Defense Industry* (1981); and James L. Clayton, editor, *The Economic Impact of the Cold War* (1970). Two monumental volumes on atomic and nuclear development are R. G. Hewlett and O. E. Anderson, *The New World, 1939–1946* (1962); and R. G. Hewlett and Francis Duncan, *Atomic Shield 1947–1952* (1970).

Recent studies on the CIA include Thomas Powers, *The Man Who Kept the Secrets: Richard Helms and the CIA* (1979); William R. Corson, *The Armies of Ignorance* (1977); Victor Marchetti and J. D. Marks, *The CIA and the Cult of Intelligence* (1974); and the Snepp and Stockwell books listed below in the Nixon section.

For economic developments, see especially these four excellent surveys: Joan Edelman Spero, *The Politics of International Economic Relations* (1981); Fred L. Block, *The Origins of International Economic Disorder* (1977); Alfred E. Eckes, *The U.S. and the Global Struggle for Minerals* (1979); and for a provocative view of the internal U.S. influences, Alan Wolfe, *America's Impasse: The Rise and Fall of the Politics of Growth* (1981). On multinational corporations, starting points are Mira Wilkins, *The Maturing of Multinational Enterprise* (1974), covering 1914 to 1970; Lewis D. Solomon, *Multinational Corporations and the Emerging World Order* (1978); Richard J. Barnet and R. E. Müller, *Global Reach* (1974); and studies by Raymond Vernon and Charles P. Kindelberger, especially the latter's *American Business Abroad* (1969). A striking analysis of the American decline is by the Business Week Team, *The Decline of U.S. Power* (1980).

For United States relations with the United Nations, see Toby Trister Gati, editor, *The United States, the United Nations and the Management of Global Change* (1982). For the newly emerging nations, see Robert L. Rothstein, *The Third World and U.S. Foreign Policy* (1981).

On the cause of the Cold War's eruption, see Thomas Paterson's two fine books, *On Every Front* (1979) and *Soviet-American Confrontation* (1974); Gaddis Smith, *American Diplomacy During the Second World War* (1965); Robert Dallek, *Franklin D. Roosevelt* (1979); Lloyd Gardner's two pioneering volumes, *Economic Aspects of New Deal Diplomacy* (1964) and *Architects of Illusion* (1970); Michael Sherry's pathbreaking *Preparing for the Next War* (1977); Martin Sherwin's prize-winning *World Destroyed* (1975), on atomic diplomacy; and Robert Divine's *Second Chance* (1967). On China relations, see Kenneth Chern, *Dilemma in China* (1980); and Michael Schaller, *U.S. Crusade in China* (1979). David Green, *The Containment of Latin America* (1971) remains standard on the 1940s. Hugh DeSantis, *The Diplomacy of Silence* (1981) superbly interweaves personalities and policy to 1947. For the British perspective, see Graham Ross, editor, *The Foreign Office and the Kremlin: British Documents on Anglo-Soviet Relations, 1941–1945* (1983).

For the Truman years most of the above are essential, but start with Richard Dean Burns, editor, *Harry S. Truman: A Bibliography of His Times and Presidency* (1984); Barton J. Bernstein and Allen Matusow, *The Truman Administration* (1966); Robert J. Donovan's two-volume biography, *Conflict and Crisis* (1977), on 1945–1948, and *Tumultuous Years* (1983), on 1949–1953; and, of course, Truman's two-volume *Memoirs* (1955, 1956), to be used carefully. A fine perspective is in Gregg Herkin, *The Winning Weapon: The Atomic Bomb in the Cold War, 1945–1950* (1981). The crucial books on Byrnes in 1945–1946 are Robert L. Messer, *The End of an Alliance* (1982); and Patricia Dawson Ward, *The Threat of Peace* (1979). For Acheson, see his own *Present at the Creation* (1969); and two fine biographies, Gaddis Smith, *Dean Acheson* (1972), and David S. McLellan, *Dean Acheson* (1976). On Greece and the Truman Doctrine the standard is now Lawrence Wittner, *American Intervention in Greece, 1943–1949* (1982); but see also Richard Freeland, *The Truman Doctrine and the Origins of McCarthyism* (1971). A fine recent account is Imanuel Wexler, *The Marshall Plan Revisited* (1983). McCarthyism is well-discussed in Athan Theoharis and Robert Griffiths, editors, *The Specter* (1974); and Thomas C. Reeves, *The Life and Times of Joe McCarthy* (1982). On Israel a good recent account is Dan Tschirgi, *The Politics of Indecision* (1983).

On Asia and Korea, see Dorothy Borg and Waldo Heinrichs, editors, *Uncertain Years: Chinese-American Relations, 1947–1950*; William P. Head, *America's China Sojourn* (1983), on the 1942–1948 years; Nancy Bernkopf Tucker, *Patterns in the Dust* (1983), outstanding on the Chinese recognition debate; Ronald Pruessen, *John Foster Dulles* (1982), covering Dulles from his birth to 1952, with fine analysis of the 1949–1950 Asian crises; and William W. Stueck, Jr., *The Road to Confrontation* (1981), on the 1947–1950 events in Asia. A key volume, which is changing our perspective on the Korean War, is Bruce Cumings, editor, *Child of Conflict: The Korean-American Relationship, 1943–1953* (1983). Allen Whiting's *China Crosses the Yalu* (1974) remains indispensable; Ronald J. Caridi, *The Korean War and American Politics* (1969), and Robert Griffith's prize-winning *Politics of Fear* (1970) are standards on the politics. Francis H. Heller, editor, *The Korean War* (1977) gives good perspectives. For a superb overview from the British side, see Alan Bullock, *Ernest Bevin* (1984), on the 1945–1951 years. Robert Blum, *Drawing the Line* (1982) is key for 1949–1950.

There has been an explosion of new scholarship on the Eisenhower years. Start with R. D. Bohanan, *Dwight D. Eisenhower: A Selected Bibliography of Periodical and Dissertation Literature*

(1981); Robert Divine, *Eisenhower and the Cold War* (1981); and David Carlton's most important *Anthony Eden: A Biography* (1981). Eisenhower himself is seen in his two-volume memoir, *The White House Years* (1963, 1964); Peter Lyon, *Eisenhower* (1974); Herbert Parmet, *Eisenhower and the American Crusade* (1972); Blanche Wiessen Cook, *The Declassified Eisenhower* (1981), important for the President's involvement in covert operations; and Robert A. Divine, *Blowing on the Wind* (1978), on the nuclear test-ban debate. Burton I. Kaufman has analyzed a key topic in *Trade and Aid: Eisenhower's Foreign Economic Policy, 1953–1961* (1982). The Guatemala intervention is superbly described in Richard H. Immerman, *The CIA in Guatemala* (1982); Stephen Schlesinger and Steven Kinzer, *Bitter Fruit* (1981); and the Cook volume listed above. For the 1956 Suez crisis, see Donald Neff, *Warriors at Suez* (1981); and Chester L. Cooper, *The Lion's Last Roar* (1978), which is too often overlooked. African policy is dissected in Madeleine Kalb, *The Congo Cables: The Cold War in Africa—from Eisenhower to Kennedy* (1982). For Dulles (besides the Pruessen volume listed above), see Townsend Hoopes, *The Devil and John Foster Dulles* (1973); and especially Bennett Kovrig, *Myth of Liberation* (1973).

The Kennedy policies can be found in Arthur Schlesinger, Jr., *A Thousand Days* (1965), the standard favorable biography; Herbert S. Parmet, *JFK* (1981), a balanced view; Garry Wills, *Nixon Agonistes* (1971), a critical analysis; as is Richard Walton, *Cold War and Counterrevolution* (1972); Warren Cohen, *Dean Rusk* (1980), a sensitive biography; Montague Kern et al., *The Kennedy Crises: The Press, the Presidency, and Foreign Policy* (1983); Desmond Ball, *Politics and Force Levels* (1981), which is superb on the 1960s military buildup; Elie Abel, *The Missile Crisis* (1966), still a standard account; Ronald Pope, *Soviet Views of the Cuban Missile Crisis* (1982); and Richard D. Mahoney, *JFK: Ordeal in Africa* (1983).

For the Johnson years, the starting point is the essays and bibliographical references in Robert Divine, editor, *Exploring the Johnson Years* (1981), and note especially the essay on Vietnam by George Herring. Besides Cohen's biography of Rusk noted above, other personal accounts include Johnson's own *Vantage Point* (1971); to be used with Ronnie Dugger, *The Politician: The Life and Times of Lyndon Johnson* (1982). Piero Gleijesis has written a superb account of *The Dominican Crisis* (1978). Material on Vietnam is overwhelming, but along with references below in the "Vietnam" section, see especially Larry Berman, *Planning a Tragedy* (1982), on LBJ's fateful 1965 decisions; George Herring, *The Longest War* (1979); and Irwin Unger, *The Movement* (1974), on the antiwar groups.

On Nixon four books are indispensable: Nixon's own memoirs, *RN* (1978); Henry Kissinger's *The White House Years* (1979), on 1969–1972; Kissinger's *Years of Upheaval* (1982), on 1973–1974; and Seymour Hersh, *The Price of Power* (1983), an extensively researched journalistic account that undermines the Nixon and Kissinger accounts in key places. Covert operations are detailed in James Petras and Morris Morley, *The U.S. and Chile* (1975); Paul E. Sigmund, *The Overthrow of Allende* (1977); John Stockwell, *In Search of Enemies* (1978), on the CIA in Angola; and Frank Snepp, *Decent Interval* (1977), on the CIA in Vietnam. On Africa, see Anthony Lake, *The 'Tar Baby' Option* (1976), about Rhodesia; and Mohamed A. El-Khawas and Barry Cohen, editors, *NSSM 39* (1976) on southern Africa. Stanley Hoffman puts all of this in context in his fine *Primacy or World Order* (1978).

The Carter presidency is analyzed from the inside in Carter's own *Keeping Faith* (1982); Zbigniew Brzezinski, *Power and Principle* (1983), by far the most revealing of the "insider" accounts; and Cyrus Vance, *Hard Choices* (1983). Good insights are in William Lee Miller, *Yankee from Georgia* (1978), and Betty Glad, *Carter* (1980). Two volumes are standard on human rights: Sandy Vogelgesang, *American Dream, Global Nightmare* (1980), and Lars Schoultz, *Human Rights and U.S. Policy Towards Latin America* (1981). Thomas W. Wolfe, *The SALT Experience* (1979) is good on both sides. For the Iranian tragedy, begin with Barry Rubin, *Paved with Good Intentions* (1980), and see "Middle East" section below. Robert G. Sutter, *The China Quandry* (1983) is good on domestic sources of United States policy.

For the early 1980s there are already three useful biographies: Lou Cannon, *Reagan* (1982); Laurence I. Barrett, *Gambling with History: Reagan in the White House* (1983); and Robert Dallek, *Ronald Reagan: The Politics of Symbolism* (1984). See Thomas Ferguson and Joel Rogers, editors, *The Hidden Election* (1981), especially Bruce Cumings's essay on foreign policy and the 1980 election. Alexander M. Haig, Jr., *Caveat* (1984) is the former secretary of state's bittersweet account of 1981–1982; Robert Scheer,

With Enough Shovels (1982) is indispensable for insight into the administration's thinking on military matters; Ronald V. Dellums (with R. H. Miller and H. Lee Halterman), *Defense Sense* (1983) critiques Reagan's defense plans and offers alternatives; Itamar Rabinovich, *The War for Lebanon, 1970–1983* (1984) is the best account; Joseph S. Nye, editor, *The Making of America's Soviet Policy* (1984) is analytical and critical.

Important area studies cover several or all of the areas noted above.

Latin America (except Central America, *see below*)

Good overviews are Samuel L. Baily, *The U.S. and the Development of South America, 1945–1975* (1976); Dick Steward, *Money, Marines, and Mission* (1980), on recent United States–Latin American relations; Joseph S. Tulchin, editor, *Hemispheric Perspectives on the United States* (1978); Cole Blasier, *Hovering Giant* (1974); Robert Smith, *The U.S. and Cuba* (1961); Carla Anne Robbins, *The Cuban Threat* (1983); Lester L. Langley, *The U.S. and the Caribbean, 1900–1970* (1980), readable and standard; David N. Farnsworth and James W. McKenney, *U.S.-Panama Relations, 1903–1978* (1983).

Central America

The material is profuse. The Reagan perspective is found in most of *The Report of the President's National Bipartisan Commission on Central America* (1984), which has a foreword by Chairman Henry Kissinger, but this must be read with the following: Robert S. Leiken, editor, *Central America: Anatomy of Conflict* (1984), especially the Vaky and Leiken essays; Policy Alternatives for the Caribbean and Central America [or PACCA], *Changing Course* (1984), a good, short overview with alternatives; Martin Siskin, editor, *Trouble in Our Backyard* (1984), especially the Womack and Montgomery sections; Marvin Gittleman et al., *El Salvador* (1982), a series of readings; Tommie Sue Montgomery, *Revolution in El Salvador* (1982), a fine historical perspective; and several works by Thomas A. Walker, especially *Nicaragua in Revolution* (1982), which Walker edited. John A. Booth, *The End and the Beginning* (1982) is superb on the Nicaraguan revolution. Walter

LaFeber, *Inevitable Revolutions* (1983, 1984) attempts to provide historical framework for United States policy.

The Middle East

Good overviews are Robert Stookey, *America and the Arab States* (1975); William Quandt, *Decade of Decisions* (1977); Nadav Safran's many works, especially *From War to War* (1969); Seth P. Tillman's provocative *The United States and the Middle East* (1982); Robert O. Freedman, editor, *The Middle East Since Camp David* (1984); Itamar Rabinovich, *The War For Lebanon, 1970–1983* (1984). For one root of the United States involvement, see Irvine Anderson, *Aramco, the United States, and Saudi Arabia* (1981), on the 1933–1950 years; and Aaron Miller, *Search for Security* (1980) on American-Saudi relations, 1939–1949. On the Iranian revolution, begin with Marvin Zonis, "Iran: A Theory of Revolution from Accounts of the Revolution," *World Politics*, XXXV (July 1983): 586–606; and R. K. Ramazani, *The U.S. and Iran* (1982); along with Rubin's account noted in the Carter section.

Vietnam

The standard volume is George Herring, *America's Longest War* (1979), which includes an excellent bibliography. Other recent volumes of importance are Ronald H. Spector, *U.S. Army in Vietnam. Volume I: Advice and Support. The Early Years, 1941–1960* (1983), an indispensable account; Gareth Porter, *A Peace Denied* (1975), superb on peace discussions; Joseph Buttinger, *Vietnam* (1970), a good source for the country itself; Harry G. Summers, Jr., *On Strategy* (1981), a seminal volume from the military point of view; Dave R. Palmer, *Summons of the Trumpet* (1978), good on the military side; Guenter Lewy, *America in Vietnam* (1978), a detailed defense of United States policies; William Appleman Williams, Thomas McCormick, Lloyd Gardner, and Walter LaFeber, *America in Vietnam* (1985), newly available documents with commentaries that are critical of United States policies.

Asia Outside Vietnam

John K. Fairbank, *U.S. and China* (1971) is better on China than on the United States. See also Joseph Camilleri, *Chinese Foreign Policy*

(1980), a first-rate account; I. M. Destler et al., *Managing an Alliance* (1976), on relations with Japan; and Akira Iriye's stimulating overview of 1941 to 1951, *The Cold War in Asia* (1974).

Europe

The most recent and readable on the post-1945 years is Richard Barnet, *The Alliance* (1983); see also John H. Backer, *Decision to Divide Germany* (1978); Roger Morgan, *U.S. and West Germany* (1975); Stanley Hoffman's excellent *Decline or Renewal?* (1974), on France; and Max Beloff, *U.S. and the Unity of Europe (1963)*.

Africa

In addition to the Kalb and Mahoney accounts listed, respectively, in the Eisenhower and Kennedy sections above, see Richard Leonard, *South Africa at War* (1983); Alfred O. Hero, Jr., and John Barratt, editors, *The American People and South Africa* (1981), especially the Crocker essay; and case studies in Alexander L. George, *Managing U.S.-Soviet Rivalry* (1983).

The Soviet Union and Eastern Bloc Since 1945

Useful surveys, containing additional bibliography as well, include Adam B. Ulam, *Expansion and Coexistence* (1973), now updated for the 1970–1982 years in his *Dangerous Relations* (1983); Jan F. Triska and David Finley, *Soviet Foreign Policy* (1968); the excellent essays in Stephen F. Cohen et al., *The Soviet Union Since Stalin* (1980); Paul Marantz's fine *Soviet Doctrine and East-West Relations, 1917–1978* (1980); Severyn Bailer, editor, *The Domestic Context of Soviet Foreign Policy* (1980), of special importance; Michael Binyon, *Life in Russia* (1983), highly readable; Marshall I. Goldman, *U.S.S.R. in Crisis: The Failure of an Economic System* (1983); Bruce Parrott, *Politics and Technology in the Soviet Union* (1983), the standard work; and John Barron, *KGB* (1976).

Important specialized works are Myron Rush's books, *How Communist States Change Their Rulers* (1974) and *The International Situation and Soviet Foreign Policy* (1970). Kevin Klose,

Russia and the Russians (1984) is a superb first-hand view of the dissident movement. On the Soviet military the key volume is now David Holloway, *The Soviet Union and the Arms Race* (1983); but see also Stephen S. Kaplan et al., *Diplomacy of Power: Soviet Armed Forces as a Political Instrument* (1981). For the top Soviet academic expert on the United States, see Georgi Arbatov's *The War of Ideas* (1973).

A series of fine recent monographs carry Soviet foreign policy from the early 1940s to the mid-1980s: Vojtech Mastny's standard, *Russia's Road to the Cold War* (1979), on 1941–1945; Werner G. Hahn, *Postwar Soviet Policies: The Fall of Zhdanov and the Defeat of Moderation, 1946–1953* (1984); Roy Medvedev, *Khrushchev, A Biography* (1983); Harry Gelman, *The Brezhnev Politburo and the Decline of Détente* (1984); Jonathan Steele, *Soviet Power* (1983), tracing foreign policy from Brezhnev to Andropov; Martin Ebon, *The Andropov File* (1983); Strobe Talbott, *The Russians and Reagan* (1984).

For area studies, see Edwina Moreton and Gerald Segal, editors, *Soviet Strategy Towards Western Europe* (1984), especially the Freedman and Sharp essays; Elizabeth Kridl Valkenier, *The Soviet Union and the Third World* (1984); Cole Blasier, *The Giant's Rival: The U.S.S.R. and Latin America* (1983); Gerald Segal, editor, *The Soviet Union in East Asia* (1983). On Afghanistan two key studies are Alexandre Bennigsen and Marie Broxup, *The Islamic Threat to the Soviet State* (1983), and Anthony Arnold, *Afghanistan* (1981). On Eastern Europe important recent accounts are Sarah Meikeljohn Terry, editor, *Soviet Policy in Eastern Europe* (1984); Robert L. Hutchings, *Soviet-East European Relations* (1984), on the 1968–1980 years; Jiri Valenta, *Soviet Intervention in Czechoslovakia, 1968* (1979), a superb study of policy making; and Abraham Brumberg, editor, *Poland: Genesis of a Revolution* (1983).

INDEX

Acheson, Dean: view of postwar world, 9; Turkey, 37; 1946 atomic plans, 41–42; Truman Doctrine, 50–58; Marshall Plan, 59–60; background and views, 80–82; and Kennan 1949, 86; China, 86–89; 1950 speeches and policies, 91–93; Hiss, 93–94; NSC-68, 96–98; Korean War views, 98–103; public opinion, 105–106; crossing of 38th parallel, 113–116; MacArthur debate, 122–123; 1951 military aid, 127; German rearmament, 128–130; 1958 debate on Germany, 202–203; Berlin 1961, 218; 1962 missile crisis, 225, 228; Vietnam, 233, 255; Rusk, 236; Nixon condemnation, 267

Acheson-Lilienthal proposal, 41–42

Act of Bogotá (1960), 212

Adams, John, 134

Adams, John Quincy, 152–153

Adenauer, Konrad, 85, 152, 168–169, 182, 202–204; Acheson 1951–1952, 128–129

Advisory Defense Committee, 67

Afghanistan, 299, 303, 310

Africa, 153, 209, 299; Truman Doctrine, 53, 55; UN, 107; changed by 1960, 241; Nixon, 263; Kissinger, 279–280; Carter, 290

Agnew, Spiro, 256, 280

Agriculture, US, and détente, 269

Alaska, 1

Albania, 227

Aleutians, 92

Algeria, 213, 250

Allende, Salvador, 273, 279

Alliance for Progress: origins, 212, 215–217; Johnson, 243–244; Nixon, 278

American Legion, 5

Americans for Democratic Action, 46, 79, 112

American University (Kennedy's speech), 227

Andropov, Yuri, 310

Angola, 262, 279–280, 282

Antiballistic missile (ABM), 271

ANZUS Treaty (1951), 120

Apartheid, 242

Ap Bac, 233

Arbenz Guzmán, Jacobo, 159–161

Arévalo, Juan José, 159

Argentina, 159, 211, 288, 313

Armas, Castillo, 160–161

Asia: 19th and early 20th centuries, 1–6; 1941–1943, 9; 1945, 25–26; turn in 1949–1950, 86–90; Acheson view 1950, 91–93; MacArthur debates, 122–123; 125; 1951–1952 debates, 130–137; Eisenhower view, 149. *See also individual nations.*

Aswan Dam, 184–189

Atlantic Charter (1941), 28

Atlantic Conference (1941), 10–13

Atomic Development Authority, 42

Atomic Energy Commission, 42, 179–180

Atomic weapons: Hiroshima, 25–26; US debates, 26–27; USSR in 1945, 28; Churchill view

ABOUT THE AUTHOR

Walter LaFeber is the Marie Underhill Noll Professor of History at Cornell University. His publications include *The New Empire: An Interpretation of American Expansion, 1865–1898* (1963), for which he received the Beveridge Prize of the American Historical Association; *Inevitable Revolutions: The United States and Central America* (1983, 1984); *The Panama Canal: The Crisis in Historical Perspective* (1978, 1979); *The American Century: The United States Since 1890* (1985), which he coauthored; and *America in Vietnam: A History with Documents* (1985), also a coauthored work. In addition, Professor LaFeber won the first Clark Award for undergraduate teaching at Cornell.

A NOTE ON THE TYPE

The text of this work was set on the Editwriter 7500 in Palacio, a variation of the Palatino typeface designed by the noted German typographer Hermann Zapf. Named after Giovanbattista Palatino, a writing master of Renaissance Italy, Palatino was the first of Zapf's typefaces to be introduced to America. The first designs for the face were made in 1948, and the fonts for the complete face were issued between 1950 and 1952. Like all Zapf-designed typefaces, Palatino is beautifully balanced and exceedingly readable.

Composed by Dianne Rooney Enterprises, Inc., Staten Island, New York. Printed and bound by Haddon Craftsmen, Inc., Scranton, Pennsylvania.